THE IRISH LITERARY TRADITION

THE IRISH
LITERARY
TRADITION

J. E. Caerwyn Williams
Patrick K. Ford

University of Wales Press, Cardiff
Ford & Bailie, Belmont, Massachusetts
1992

Revised English-language edition of *Traddodiad Llenyddol Iwerddon*, by
J. E. Caerwyn Williams, published by University of Wales Press, Cardiff, 1958.

© Welsh text, J. E. Caerwyn Williams
© English translation, Patrick K. Ford, 1992

This edition first published in 1992
Reprinted, 1997
Reprinted, 2007

British Library Cataloguing-in-Publication Data
A catalogue record for this book is available from the British Library

ISBN   978-0-7083-1165-3 hardback
        978-0-7083-1094-6 paperback

Library of Congress Cataloguing-in-Publication Data
Williams, J. E. Caerwyn (John Ellis Caerwyn)
[Traddodiad llenyddol Iwerddon. English]
The Irish literary tradition/by J. E. Caerwyn Williams and Patrick K. Ford.
        p. cm.

Translation of: Traddodiad llenyddol Iwerddon.
Includes bibliographical references and index.
ISBN 0-926689-03-7 (Ford & Bailie)
1. Irish literature-History and criticism. I. Ford, Patrick K.
II. Title
PB1306.T7313   1992
891.6 209–dc20

                                            92–12263
                                                 CIP

Every effort has been made to contact the copyright holders of material used
in this book. In the event of a query, please contact the publishers.

Typeset in the UK by Megaron, Cardiff, Wales
Printed in Malta by Gutenberg Press, Tarxien

To Gwen and Chadine

CONTENTS

ILLUSTRATIONS

Between pp. 180 and 181

PREFACE

The Irish Literary Tradition is based on *Traddodiad Llenyddol Iwerddon* by J. E. Caerwyn Williams (University of Wales Press, Cardiff, 1958) which was written for Welsh readers but was welcomed in Ireland as well as in Wales. Indeed, several Irish scholars including the late Professors Máirtín Ó Cadhain and David Greene suggested that it should be translated into Irish and eventually it was published in that language with additional material by the author and Mrs Máirín Ní Mhuiríosa under the title *Traidisiún Liteartha na nGael*. Other scholars were kind enough to suggest that it should be translated into English and Dr Patrick Ford undertook to produce an English version. Dr Ford was then embarking on the academic career which took him to Stanford University and the University of California Los Angeles; he is currently Margaret Brooks Robinson Professor of Celtic Languages and Literatures, Harvard University, the University which awarded him his doctorate in Celtic.

Much new material has been incorporated in this English version which is intended to cover the history of the Irish literary tradition down to 1970. It would not have been published at all were it not for the perseverance of the translator and it is right and proper that his name should appear with the author's on the title page and that the long-tried patience of both their wives should be acknowledged in the dedication. The delay in publication has made it possible for the contents to reflect the remarkable surge in literary and scholarly activity witnessed in Ireland after the Second World War. That they could have reflected it more adequately both translator and author are acutely aware and they hope that their deficiencies will prompt some native scholar or scholars to undertake a history more worthy of the literary tradition of which Irish people whether Irish- or English-speaking can be proud.

The author remains indebted to those scholars who helped him to write *Traddodiad Llenyddol Iwerddon* and who patiently and generously answered his many questions then and since. Some of them are no longer with us: Professor Gerard Murphy, Dr Seán Mac Airt, Professor Máirtín Ó Cadhain, Professor T. S. Ó Máille, Mrs Máirín Ní Mhuiríosa. Others are still with us: Professor Tomás de Bhaldraithe and Professor Proinsias Mac Cana. Professor Mac Cana's readiness to answer questions and to discuss difficulties will be appreciated only by those who, like myself, have benefited so much from his great learning and generosity.

A book on Irish literary tradition that did not contain quotations either in the original or in translation would have been severely handicapped. Permission to quote from the Irish of Máirtín Ó Direáin, Seán Ó Ríordáin, and Máire Mhac an tSaoi has been given by Sáirséal and Ó Marcaigh and by Clóchomhar and permission to quote from the work of their translators has been given except by one whom we have failed to locate. No scholarly work on Irish literature could be undertaken without acknowledgement of debt to the scholars, past and present, in the School of Celtic Studies of the Dublin Institute of Advanced Studies, now directed by Professor Máirtín Ó Murchú. For permission to quote the translations of T. Kinsella, Robin Flower, Frank O'Connor, P. C. Power and Donal O'Sullivan we are indebted to Oxford University Press, Ford & Bailie, The Viking Press, New York, and to the Educational Company of Ireland acting as far as it can for the former Browne and Nolan Ltd.

The illustrations have been reproduced with the kind permission of the Curator of Cambridge University Technical Services Ltd., The Board of Trinity College, Dublin, *Comhar*, and the *Irish Times*.

In conclusion thanks are due to Mr and Mrs Iestyn Hughes for undertaking the onerous task of compiling the index, to Ms Liz Powell for her meticulous work on the script on behalf of the University of Wales Press, and to the Press itself and Ford & Bailie for jointly undertaking its publication.

J. E. Caerwyn Williams
March 1992

ABBREVIATIONS

AC	*The Annals of Clonmacnoise*
ACL	*Archiv für celtische Lexicographie*
Add.	Additional MSS, British Museum/British Library
AI	*The Annals of Inisfallen*
AU	*The Annals of Ulster*
BB	*The Book of Ballymote*
BBCS	*The Bulletin of the Board of Celtic Studies*
BM	British Museum/British Library
BN	Bibliothèque nationale, Paris
CLlH	Ifor Williams (ed.), *Canu Llywarch Hen*
DIL	Royal Irish Academy, *Dictionary of the Irish Language*
DNB	*The Dictionary of National Biography*
ÉC	*Études Celtiques*
Eg.	Egerton MSS, British Museum/British Library
EIHM	O'Rahilly, *Early Irish History and Mythology*
EIL	Dillon, *Early Irish Literature*
EILs	Murphy, *Early Irish Lyrics*
FM	*The Annals of the Four Masters*
GL	*The Growth of Literature*
GOI	Thurneysen, *A Grammar of Old Irish*
GPO	*Geiriadur Prifysgol Cymru. A Dictionary of the Welsh Language*
IBP	Bergin (ed.), *Irish Bardic Poetry*
ITS	Irish Texts Society
JCS	*Journal of Celtic Studies*
LB	*Leabhar Breac*
LL	*The Book of Leinster (An Leabhar Laighneach)*
LU	*Lebor na h-Uidre*
MS Materials	O'Curry, *Lectures on the Manuscript Materials of Ancient Irish History*
OIR	Thurneysen, *Old Irish Reader*
PBA	*Proceedings of the British Academy*
PLlH	Ford (ed.), *The Poems of Llywarch Hen*
PMLA	*Publications of the Modern Language Association*
PRIA	*Proceedings of the Royal Irish Academy*
RC	*Revue Celtique*

SC	*Studia Celtica*
SH	*Studia Hibernica*
TBC	*Táin Bó Cúailnge*
TCD	Trinity College Dublin
TPS	*Transactions of the Philological Society*
Trans. Oss. Soc.	*Transactions of the Ossianic Society*
YBL	*The Yellow Book of Lecan*
ZCP	*Zeitschrift für celtische Philologie*
Zu ir. Handschriften	Thurneysen, *Zu ir(ischen) Handschriften und Literatur-Denkmäler*

INTRODUCTION

THE ancient fort of Dún Aonghusa sits at the edge of Inis Mór (Inishmore), the largest of the Aran Islands, which are situated at the mouth of Galway Bay in the west of Ireland. As you stand upon those massive old ruins and look westwards out over the Atlantic toward America, it is not difficult to remember that there was a time when that great continent was entirely unknown. Indeed, it is easy to realize that the people who built the fort thought they were constructing it at the farthest edge of the known world. To them, and to the hosts that followed them in Ireland, it was perfectly natural to look upon the land as a part of the western border of the civilized world. It is quite certain that the earliest immigrants came to Ireland from an easterly direction. Some had arrived by the third millennium BC, but many groups followed, each one coming to the end of its journey at some point in this westerly extremity of the earth. It is interesting to look for traces of them in the monuments they have left behind in the Irish countryside, and it would be even more interesting to know something of the struggles that took place between them and between the languages which they spoke.

Sometime before the beginning of the Christian era—authorities do not agree on the time, and have advanced such widely divergent dates as the first half of the second millenium BC[1] and the first century BC[2]—groups of people speaking a Celtic or different dialects of a Celtic language came to the island. Some seem to have come from Britain, others directly from the Continent; some to live side by side with their predecessors, others to achieve dominance over them. Among the latter there were a group who came to be known at a much later date as *Goidil*, and it appears that their language, called after them *Goidelg* (Goidelic), was not altogether different from the Brittonic spoken in Britain, but it developed and changed as all languages do. The descendants of Goidelic are Irish-Gaelic in Ireland,[3] Scottish-Gaelic in Scotland, and, until fairly recently, Manx in the Isle of Man. Needless to say, these are very different from the descendants of Brittonic (the other branch of Celtic), namely, Welsh, Cornish and Breton.

Unfortunately, we know very little about the *Goidil* of that period, but we know that they eventually dominated the other inhabitants of the island, and that slowly but surely they imposed their language on them and forged a single people from them. To be sure, the modern

Irishman's sense of national consciousness is a far cry from that of his ancient counterpart. But once those early Irish began to be conscious of themselves as a people and to sense their unity, they became a society that took steps to ensure that their past would be a treasured inheritance of the present and that their memories of it would endure.

As we consider their history, it is extremely important to remember that the Irish, as a people, have lived on the same land and have spoken the same language for a very long time. It is no small thing to realize that the same land not only produced food to sustain the population and material to clothe them, but also provided the landscape, the smells, and all the other things that feed the senses of men and thus penetrate their minds and shape their souls. There is probably no other people in north-west Europe that has been longer resident in its land than the Irish. But even more important than the land which a people inhabits is the language which it speaks, for language is the means by which we impose order upon the world about us and one of the ways in which we become fully conscious of ourselves and of the life which is in us. This consciousness, in turn, is most vividly expressed in the literature of a language.

When a people has been resident in the same place as long as the Irish, it is only natural that its literature should be full of references to the land. The names of the mountains, hills and valleys where its history has been enacted are all preserved in its literature; even the names of forests, bogs and lakes seemingly devoid of history are preserved as the scenes of legends and of dreams. And when a nation has run such a long course, its literature cannot help but abound with references to its history as well as its legends, for in the beginning it was very difficult to distinguish between the two. In the early stages, history becomes legend and legend is turned into history. If it is correct to define a sense of tradition as an awareness of history, and to observe that the past exists not only in the past but in the present as well, then it is difficult to conceive of any people possessing such a sense more universally than the Irish, for history has always been a strong element in their life and their culture.[4]

One of the most remarkable things about Irish culture is that it rests firmly on relatively uniform traditions that stretch back across two thousand years and more. The differences between it and that of Wales, the remnant of Brittonic Britain, are striking. Consider: the Roman Empire did not directly affect Ireland at all, but its effect on Wales was very great. It influenced the Welsh way of life and way of thinking, Welsh language and Welsh culture. And that is one reason why Welsh has developed so differently from Irish, and why Welsh literature has depicted from the beginning a world considerably different from the world that is seen in Irish literature. Furthermore, Christianity came to Britain in the wake of the Roman Conquest, sheltered by the conqueror's arms and as part of his civilization. Whatever native Brittonic culture there was in the land could only remain vigorous outside the boundaries of the Empire; within, it became necessarily fragmentary and disintegrated.

The advent of Christianity in Ireland was completely different. It came neither in the wake of any conqueror nor on the heels of any foreign civilization. Indeed, by the time it came the heyday of the Roman Empire was past. Besides, the native culture in Ireland must have been as well developed as any, both vigorous and flourishing. Whatever role the druids played in the work of maintaining it, the efficient system of education with which they were associated in Gaul, probably formed the backbone of the native culture in Ireland as well.

St Patrick, the great apostle of Christianity in Ireland, had come under the influence of the new monasticism, which had developed originally in Egypt, but was spreading in the West from Lérins, and he was eager to see it take roots in this new missionary field. But Irish monasticism did not succeed in doing that very well until its influence returned once more, by way of the monasteries of south Wales early in the sixth century. By the end of that century it had achieved pre-eminence throughout Ireland.[5] As in Lérins, there were two special characteristics of this monasticism in Ireland: it practised a harsh and severe discipline, taking its ideal from that of the anchorite, and it fostered theological and exegetical learning based on a close study of the works of classical authors, both pagan and Christian.[6]

To the Irish the one was as attractive as the other, but it was probably the latter that made it so easy for the monks to compete with native authorities in traditional learning. Be that as it may, the attitude of the Church toward pagan culture in Ireland seems to have been quite different from its usual attitude. Instead of being its implacable enemy, it was extraordinarily tolerant toward it; instead of setting out to destroy the tales which were the backbone of that culture, it assisted in preserving and recording them. In this way, it made it possible for the Irish to listen to the sounds of Tara's harp as well as to the intonations of the Gospel. The traditional native schools and the implanted ecclesiastical schools must have been in keen competition with each other from the beginning, and the one must have spurred the other into greater and greater activity. That is probably why they succeeded between them in making Ireland, for a while, the seat of Christian and classical learning and the object of admiration of the rest of Western Europe. The period from the sixth to the ninth century was the Golden Age of Ireland. There was a remarkable renaissance in culture and civilization in the seventh century, and the arts of peace prospered; missionaries and clerics flourished.

Alas, the arts of peace can offer but little resistance to the arts of war. Fortunately, the Irish were not compelled to learn this in the face of the Anglo-Saxon invasions, as the Britons were, but they were put to a sore test between AD 800 and 1014, when the Scandinavians attacked them mercilessly, killing, burning and plundering wherever they went. The havoc wrought by these raiders may have been exaggerated, for the Irish were capable of making war among themselves without any external incitement.[7] But the damage done was compounded by the actions of the Scandinavian invaders, and Irish civilization was greatly impoverished. The prosperous schools of the Church vanished, as well as the old secular schools, but fortunately, literary families sprung up to preserve national tradition, and they developed a new kind of school, the bardic school. These new schools were the dominant power in Irish literature for many centuries. They themselves handed on the tradition and educated the custodians of it. It can be said that the essential character of Irish literature was determined in and by the bardic schools, as was the case in Wales. In Ireland as in Wales poetry was a discipline and a profession, a discipline taught in schools by masters whose profession was poetry.

Traces of this discipline may be seen clearly, for example, in the uniformity of the poetry. If we take two poems, one written in 1250 and one written in 1650, there is hardly anything in the language or the art which would enable us to determine which poem belonged to the beginning of the period and which to the end. Another way of demonstrating this extraordinary uniformity would be to take a poem written in Connacht and one written in Scotland in this period, and attempt to discover in them any indications of a difference in dialect or discipline of the poets; hardly any would be found.

Of course, such uniformity would not have been possible but for the obstinate conservatism of the tradition. The only metres that were cultivated seriously were the metres recognized by the schools—and poetry was hardly considered possible in any other metres. Even when new themes, such as *amour courtois*, were borrowed from the

Continent, it was necessary to dress them in traditional metres. This conservatism resulted in a lack of variety, but we must remember that uniformity, not variety, was the ideal. Remember too that the poetic tradition of Ireland ran the greatest part of its course in the Middle Ages, and that it was influenced by the poetic theories of that period, even though it remained obdurately faithful to its own traditional practices. That is why the great bulk of the poetry is impersonal in the sense that there is little or no place in it for the poet's personality as part of the poetic process. It is also more 'prosaic' than later poetry, not only because of the prosaic nature of the subject matter (judged by modern standards) but also because there is much less use of the technique of metaphorical and other indirect expression.

It is a testimony to the strength of the schools of poetry as institutions that they were able to survive the Norman invasion (1169–72) in their early years, and managed to endure in their maturity and old age, even through the Tudor Conquest (1540–1603) and until the time of the Cromwellian oppression (1649–58). They did not vanish completely until the Irish—rich and poor alike—were crushed and disenfranchised. By then, it was inevitable that a change should come over the shape and character of the native tradition; instead of parading grandly in the palaces of noblemen, it had to crouch in the closeness of labourers' cottages. But if its dimensions were reduced and restricted, it became the property of the populace in a way it never had before; if adversity was its lot, it was inspired with a patriotism the like of which has been found but rarely in the history of nations. The Protestant Reformation and Puritanism came as different forms of the English Conquest. It is characteristic of the Irish culture and its ties to Catholicism that it resisted the one as it did the other, and that its resources were used to promote the Counter-Reformation.

Of course, the native culture could not help but continue to suffer, because all the instruments of government and education were in the hands of partisans of a foreign culture. One might have expected that the invention of the printing press would have had a great influence on Irish literature, as it did on other literatures. But in Ireland printing presses were found only in the towns and in the hands of the English, and the Irish had to depend almost entirely upon the tradition of copying manuscripts. (It is worth noting that more Irish books were printed on the Continent than in Ireland itself for quite a long time.) That is why the literature of Ireland continued for the most part as a manuscript literature until about the middle of the last century, and therefore longer, probably, than any other European literature. What this meant is strikingly illustrated in the history of *Foras Feasa ar Éirinn* ('The History of Ireland') by Dr Geoffrey Keating (Séathrún Céitinn): it was written in the first half of the seventeenth century, and became immediately popular. There are said to be hundreds of copies of it in manuscripts, but it was not printed fully until 1901 (it fills four volumes in the Irish Texts Society publications). How much Irish literature perished with the manuscripts in which it was written will never be known, but the evidence that it was considerable is overwhelming; consider the following account by Douglas Hyde:

> A friend of mine travelling in the County Clare sent me three Irish MSS. the other day, which he found the children tearing to pieces on the floor. One of these, about one hundred years old, contained a saga called 'the Love of Dubhlacha for Mongan', which M. d'Arbois de Jubainville had searched the libraries of Europe for in vain. It is true that another copy of it has since been discovered, and printed and annotated with all the learning and critical acumen of two such world-renowned scholars as Professor Kuno Meyer and Mr. Alfred Nutt, both of whom considered it of the highest value as elucidating the psychology of the ancient Irish. The copy thus recovered and sent to me is twice as long as that printed by Kuno Meyer, and had the copy from which he printed it been lost it would be unique.[8]

Hyde concludes his remarks thus: 'These things are happening every day.' It would be a mistake, however, to suppose that literature in Ireland had no existence apart from the manuscripts, for it remained very much alive where every literature ought to live—in the minds of the people. It is doubtless true that 'a book's memory is the best memory', and it is difficult for us who are so accustomed to rely upon books to comprehend the feats of which human memory is capable. It is significant that the special circumstances of the Gaeltacht (the Irish-speaking districts) in Ireland permitted it to remain a bastion of human memory longer than almost any other place in Europe; until fairly recently there was many a storyteller there (even today some can be found) who knew orally between fifty and two hundred long tales.[9] When we consider that there are others there who are equally skilled in remembering poetry, we get a glimpse of the importance of the oral tradition in Ireland. The remarks of Thomas MacDonagh bear witness to the fact:

> Some years ago in West Cork I spent a day with such a one, an old man who knew more poems, more hero-tales, more biographical tales of the

Munster Bards than he ever had a chance of saying or telling. When I brought him a copy of the works of Eoghan Ruadh Ó Súilleábháin, he was able to explain passage after passage, reference after reference, in terms of this tradition of his. He was able to detect the passages and poems wrongly attributed to the poet. 'That's not by Eoghan Ruadh. That was written by Mary O'Shea, from Carriganimy beyond. I learned it for a wedding forty years ago. This is it, isn't it?' He sang the poem, many verses of it, to a monotonous tune, marking the emphatic points by slapping my knee.[10]

We are occasionally reminded of the feats of memory of which the 'medieval mind' was capable. It is not without reason that James Delargy, the renowned authority on Irish folklore, said more than once that the Middle Ages persisted longer in Ireland than anywhere else in Europe.[11]

It is well to remember that the numerous invasions and the deliberate policies of the English conquerors prevented Ireland from becoming wealthy. When you add to this the fact that the Irish language survived in the country and not in the towns, you can see why Irish-speaking Ireland, after its golden age, had no success in those arts that require wealth for their cultivation—architecture, painting, and drawing—or in those that require a large population—instrumental music and drama. The creative spirit of the people, therefore, went entirely to the other arts: literature, oratory, and song. Undoubtedly, the success of these was even greater because they fulfilled a special need in the society for amusement and entertainment, and because they could be cultivated equally by the poorest labourer and his richest neighbour. Whatever the explanation may be, there is probably no other people in Western Europe who showed more interest in their literature or more love toward it than did the Irish-speaking people of Ireland. Indeed, until fairly recently, there was not a village in the Gaeltacht that could not boast of its own storyteller, nor a neighbourhood that could not point to its bards, and listening to verses and songs was a recognized form of entertainment for the whole population.

Despite the fact that it was never really the language of Ireland's chief city, nor hardly even the language of the smaller towns, Irish kept a firm grip on most of the rest of the land until the beginning of the nineteenth century. No doubt the conservatism of the small farmer, his democratic spirit, and his poverty accounted to a certain degree for his adherence to the language, despite every attempt to detach him from it. But there was more than that behind his loyalty.

After all, it was his key—and his only key—to a world of treasures, the world of his history, his dreams, his beliefs, indeed, his self-esteem; into that world the foreigner could not follow him.

Strangely enough, not every nationalist or freedom-fighter saw the value of the language and its culture. The most famous example of an Irish leader who cared nothing or very little for the language is Daniel O'Connell. He once said that he could witness the slow death of Irish without uttering a single sigh. But as early as 1787, we find a man by the name of Daniel Thomas stating emphatically that 'to destroy the vernacular is an attempt to annihilate the nation,'[12] and in the following century Thomas Davis stressed the fact that a people ought to be prepared to defend its language even more than its lands, because language is a more sure barrier and a more important boundary than a fort or a river, and he proclaimed that a people without its language is but half a nation.

This doctrine was embraced by Patrick Pearse, one of the leaders of the 1916 rebellion. For him and for many of his generation, the ideal was a free Ireland and an Irish-speaking Ireland. The free Ireland was achieved in Éire, the Republic of Ireland; but in today's world, securing an Irish-speaking Ireland is an extremely difficult task. However the story may end, it is difficult to disagree with the judgement of the historian, Alice Stopford Green:

> If we turn to Ireland . . . we find a country where for some 1,500 years, as far back as historic knowledge can reach, one national force has overshadowed and dominated all others. It has been the power of a great literary tradition. Political power was not centralized, and no single man was in a position to determine what the people should think, believe or do. But in the learned tradition of the race there was a determined order. In their intellectual and spiritual inheritance was the very essence of national life, the substance of its existence, the warrant of its value, the assurance of its continuity.[13]

Notes

1 Myles Dillon and Nora Chadwick, *The Celtic Realms* (London, 1967), p. 214.
2 T. F. O'Rahilly, *Early Irish History and Mythology* (Dublin, 1946), henceforth EIHM, p. 208. For a view radically opposed to that of

O'Rahilly, see J. Raftery, 'Some Archaeological Aspects of the Goidelic Problem', in Séamus Pender, ed., *Féilscríbhinn Torna* (Cork, 1947), pp. 101–7, also J. Raftery, *The Celts* (Dublin, 1967). S. Piggott, *Ancient Europe* (London, 1965), p. 222, suggests the possibility of linking the arrival of Q-Celts, i.e., the ancestors of the Goídil, in Ireland with the appearance of bronze Hallstatt-derived swords in the island from the seventh century BC onwards. The Urnfield peoples probably spoke an early form of Celtic, but the first stage of Celtic culture is identified with that of the Iron Age Hallstatt, so called after a village in Salzkammergut in Austria, where a cemetery and the nearby salt mines preserved goods typical of the early flowering of that culture in the early years of the first millennium. In the seventh century BC the Hallstatt culture began to influence parts of Britain, whether as the result of real invasion or as a result of the establishment of a series of coastal stations is not clear. The flowering of a later stage in Celtic culture is called La Tène after a type-site on Lake Neuchâtel in Switzerland. Settlers with a La Tène culture appear to have been established in the region of present-day Yorkshire around the fourth century BC, and Irish La Tène has connections with northern England and Scotland. A site at Lisnacrogher, Co. Antrim, has yielded very rich finds belonging to La Tène culture. See Etienne Rynne, 'The Introduction of La Tène into Ireland', *Bericht über den 5. internationalen Kongress für Vor- und Frühgeschichte, Hamburg . . . 1958* (Berlin, 1961), 705–9. See also T. G. E. Powell, *The Celts* (London, 1967); the introductory chapter by J. X. W. P. Corcoran in N. K. Chadwick, *The Celts* (London, 1970); M. Herity and E. Eogan, *Ireland in Prehistory* (London, 1977); Lloyd Laing, *Celtic Britain* (London, 1961). See now J. P. Mallory, *In Search of the Indo-Europeans* (London, 1989), pp. 96, 106–7, 166, 266, especially for its bibliographical references. It is worth remembering that the words *Goidel* and *Goidelg* are borrowings from the Welsh. See J. Mac Neill, 'Ancient Irish Law: The Law of Status or Franchise', PRIA 36, sect. C (1923), 265–316. J. Loth, 'Feni et Goídil', RC 41 (1924), 350–53, thought that the Welsh words were borrowed from the Irish.

3 Classical Old Irish, *c.* AD 700–950; Middle Irish, *c.* 950–1350; Early Modern Irish, *c.* 1350–1650; Modern Irish, *c.* 1650–; R. Thurneysen, *A Grammar of Old Irish*, trans. by D. Binchy and Osborn Bergin (Dublin, 1946), p. 2: 'The language of the earliest sources is called Old Irish, that from about 900 AD. Middle Irish, and that from the beginning of the seventeenth century, Modern Irish.' But see the translators' note on p. 673: 'the date suggested for the beginning of Modern Irish is too late.' Some would date Classical Old Irish *c.* 700–850, and Middle Irish from *c.* 900 AD. Naturally, all dates concerning language changes cannot be other than approximate.

4 Frank O'Connor in his book on Irish literature, *The Backward Look* (London, 1967), p. 2, writes of the obsession of the Irish with their past and suggests that the secret of Irish literature, as 'the backward look', is probably the existence at its very origin of an immense mass of oral tradition, the sheer mystery of which overwhelmed the simple imagination of uneducated people in early Christian times.

5   J. Ryan, *Irish Monasticism* (Dublin, Cork, 1931), p. 406f.
6   See Ludwig Bieler, *Ireland, Harbinger of the Middle Ages* (London, 1963).
7   See A. T. Lucas, 'Irish–Norse Relations: Time for a Reappraisal?', *Journal of the Cork Hist. and Arch. Soc.*, 71 (1966), 62–75.
8   D. Hyde, *A Literary History of Ireland* (London, 1901), p. 634, n.2, and see John O'Donovan's poignant chronicle of 'The Lost and Missing Irish Manuscripts', *Ulster Journal of Archaeology*, 9 (1861), 16–28.
9   Without a true appreciation of its oral background one cannot understand some of the basic features of Irish literature. This point is well made in O'Connor's important statement in *The Backward Look*, p. 13: 'A thousand years after the introduction of *writing Irish* [the italics are ours], professional poets composed as though it had not been introduced at all.' In other words, they composed and delivered their poetry for the most part *orally*; for such a delivery, features such as rhyme, alliteration and consonance were necessary as mnemonic devices as well as artistic embellishments. One should, however, distinguish this type of oral composition from the extempore type described by A. B. Lord in *The Singer of Tales* (New York, 1965).
10 Thomas MacDonagh, *Literature in Ireland* (Dublin, n.d.), p. 164.
11 See *Béaloideas*, 3 (1932), 103, and cf. the claim of J. Szöverffy, *Irisches Erzählgut im Abendland* (Berlin, 1957), 'Da das Mittelalter in Irland nie zu einem Ende kam . . . .'
12 D. Thomas, *Observations on the Pamphlets published by the Bishop of Cloyne, Mr. Trant and Theophilus on one side; and on those by Mr. O'Leary, Mr. Barbar and Doctor Campbell on the other* (Dublin, 1787), p. 28. D. Thomas describes himself as 'a person of Welsh origin'.
13 Alice Stopford Green, 'Irish National Tradition', *History: The Quarterly Journal of the Historical Association*, new series, 2 (1918), 67–86; the quotation is found on pp. 68–9.

CHAPTER 1

THE BEGINNINGS

§1

IT is a generally accepted concept that the connection between literature and society is a strong one, that in the history of the one can be traced developments that reflect, among other things, some of the changes that are seen in the evolution of the other. Now there exists in many cultures a special kind of literature called heroic.[1] It did not take the same shape in every language; in fact, it differs considerably in its forms, but in subject matter and content it varies hardly at all. As a rule, heroic literature presents a picture of a society that has reached a stage in its development wherein the rulers come from the military class, and, in fact, they are described as a body of chieftains or princes who are warriors by profession. They give their services to a leader, who is a kind of overlord to them, although ultimately there is nothing but their loyalty and their faithfulness binding them to him.

The only important group in the society apart from the leaders is the class of 'learned men', an order represented by the prophets of the Jews, the brahmans of the Hindus, and the *druides* and *uātes* of the Continental Celts. These and the entertainers of the court, the storytellers and musicians, produce the literature of the society. At times it is possible to distinguish between the literary contributions of these two classes; at other times it is difficult, if not impossible, to do so.

As one might expect, the ideals and values of the warrior class are those reflected in the heroic literature. The chief interest centres on the heroes, who come almost exclusively from among the chieftains. Despite the fact that they are cast in an ideal form in the tales, they do not cease to be creatures of flesh and blood; their success or failure depends more on character than on chance or divine intervention, even though fate has an undeniable (if incomprehensible) place in their lives. The chief virtues are valour on the battlefield, unfailing allegiance, and the ability to fulfil a promise. Boasting is not considered a fault, since the deed is likely to be as good as the word. The overlord, or pre-eminent chieftain, is usually pictured as a man of middle age. Among his followers we regularly find an old man renowned for his wisdom and good sense, and a very young hero who surpasses everyone in bravery and daring.

In some literatures it is possible to distinguish between a primitive heroic literature and a more developed one. In the former we find the following characteristics: heroic and non-heroic elements are mixed; there is some attention given to matters relevant to the society; the hero can come from a class other than the warrior-aristocracy; his actions are detailed, but his character and personality are ignored; women play no part in the tales about him. In the latter, non-heroic elements are rare, and very little attention is paid to social matters. The hero comes consistently from the nobility, and the chief interest is in his character rather than in his actions. In the tales about him, women can play nearly as important a part as men.[2]

In Irish, as in Greek, there is a heroic literature that represents a special period in the history of the people. For the sake of convenience we can call this period in Ireland the Age of the Táin—it is only right, after all, that the period that provided the historical background and traditional spirit for the Irish heroic tales should be named after them, and especially after the greatest of them all, the *Táin Bó Cúailnge* ('The Cattle Raid of Cooley').[3] The tale is so pre-eminent among the class of Irish cattle raid stories, that it is usually referred to simply as 'The Táin'.

We cannot be certain as to what dates to assign to the Age of the Táin.[4] Tradition places the heroes in the first century before Christ, and the period could reach back as far as that. However, it is quite possible that the age begins a good deal later. Indeed, Professor Kenneth Jackson, who compares the social customs and material culture of the society depicted in the *Táin Bó Cúailnge* and related tales with those of the Celts in Gaul as they are described by classical authors, cannot date the formulation of that epic on the available evidence earlier than about the fourth century AD.[5] It may be, too, that in such a continuity of oral tradition as that assumed for early Irish literature, the question posed and answered by Professor Jackson may not be strictly relevant.[6] But whatever temporal limits are assigned to it, there is no doubt that the age was a barbaric one (the *Táin* itself is consistently pagan), for the Irishman is depicted living in a society not altogether unlike that of the Greeks 900 years before Christ, a time when such an honoured leader as Achilles, exulting in his victory, could drag the naked body of Hector around Troy before the eyes of the dead hero's aged father; a time when warriors began their battles by hurling reproaches at each other and by boasting to one another;

and a time when military might was a thing to strive for as life's
highest good, rather than as a means to secure the fruits of peace.
The general tenor of the Age of the Táin can be sensed in Conall
Cernach's boast: 'I swear', he said, 'that which my people swear, that
from the time I took spear in hand, I have not failed to kill one of the
men of Connacht every single day, nor to destroy by fire every single
night, and that I have never slept without the head of a Connacht man
under my knee.'[7] This boast is found in *Scéla Mucce Meic Dathó*
('The Tale of Mac Dathó's Pig'). It is believed to date in its written
form from about AD 800, but it is quite evident that the literary
conservatism so characteristic of the Irish and the Welsh has
preserved some very old elements in it, such as giving the best joint of
meat to the warrior whose battle prowess is greatest, the boasting
contest that this entails, and the interruption of the debate when one
of the heroes produces a head which has just been cut off:

> 'True,' said Cet, 'you are a greater hero than I. But if my brother
> Anluan were in the house he would offer argument to dispute every
> contention of yours.'

> 'But he is in the house,' said Conall, and then he drew the head of
> Anluan out of his girdle and flung it across the breast of Cet, so that a
> gush of blood spilled over his mouth.[8]

That is the characteristic barbaric response. Achilles and his
companions could have understood it and imitated it easily in that
society whose traditions are so splendidly portrayed in the Homeric
poems.

Scéla Mucce Meic Dathó had its source in the history of enmity
between the men of Ulster and the Connachtmen, an enmity which
found its fullest expression in the *Táin Bó Cúailnge*.[9] The Ulstermen
were the people who constituted the paramount society depicted in
the tales of the Táin Age. Their Ulster was very much larger than the
Ulster we know, and it is a constant feature of the period depicted that
the men of Ulster are on one side and the 'men of Ireland', i.e., the rest
of the Irish, are on the other. Such a division is not inconsistent with
the theory that the latter regarded the former as men who had come
from abroad and as 'outsiders'.[10] It is not insignificant that these
people, whose traditions are reflected so clearly, had completely lost
their supremacy long before history could shed any light on events in
Ireland, and long before the tales had taken the form in which they are
known to us. Not less impressive is the fact that many of the customs
associated with the Ulstermen and their stories have vanished from

Ireland so completely that nothing can be found to compare with them without going back to the descriptions of the Continental Celts by classical writers. Two customs referred to in *Scéla Mucce Meic Dathó* will serve as examples: fighting from chariots and taking the heads of men as the spoil of war.[11] On the other hand, in emphasizing these customs we should not lose sight of the fact that the stories also provide us with examples of institutions which persisted in Irish society well into the historical period: the practice of clientship, the obligation to provide unstinted hospitality, the need to seek and to give protection. It was the violation of the protection given by three of the Ulster heroes to the sons of Uisliu that caused them to attack Emain Macha and afterwards to go over to the forces of Medb and Ailill. They had no compunction about doing this, for to contravene protection was a matter of the greatest gravity.[12]

We do not know when the Age of the Táin came to an end, but there is reason to believe that a way of life not unlike that generally portrayed in it persisted in Ireland until late in the sixth century. It is a well-known fact that tales were woven about some of the historical kings of early Ireland, and the one told about those that took part in the battle of Dún Bolg[13]—as late as AD 594—suggests that they could be as barbaric in spirit and as bloody in purpose as Cet and Conall Cernach in *Scéla Mucce Meic Dathó*. The last tale to be added to the cycle of the kings of Ireland, it seems, is that of the Battle of Allen (*Cath Almaine*) in AD 722.[14] The battle may have been a decisive event in the fight for supremacy between Cathal, king of Ulster, and Fergal, overlord of the Uí Néill. The saga tells us that it was fought in an attempt by Fergal to impose submission on Leinster, but that is almost all that it tells us of politics. The hero of the tale is Donn Bó, Fergal's *fili*. Two reasons have been offered to explain why there were no tales about historical kings after that.[15] For one thing, by the eighth century, the annalists who recorded the kings' activities had developed a spirit too rationally critical to allow tales of the old sort to take shape. Furthermore, it is likely that the kings themselves had conformed more and more to the conventions of Christian conduct, and that as a result they had ceased to be subjects of such interest as to engage the attention of the storyteller and his audience. These reasons are not inconsistent with the belief that the old paganism was uprooted gradually and not suddenly. Without belittling at all the success of St Patrick in the land,[16] it is difficult to believe that the new faith was accepted any more rapidly in Ireland than in the other countries of Europe.

Whenever the Age of the Táin ended, there is no doubt that it lasted a long time, and the tales connected with it most certainly belong to different generations. Among these tales there is one group—the Ulster cycle[17]—that appears to have been more popular than the others at the time when men began to write them down. It is so called because the characters in the stories either belong to Ulster, or are otherwise connected with those people that inhabited the north eastern part of Ireland.[18] It seems fairly certain that these tales belonged at first to a specific people and region, but finally achieved a notable, if not pre-eminent position in the literary inheritance of the nation. At one time the *Ulaid* (Ulstermen) must have been one of the most important and most prominent peoples of Ireland, but they had ceased to be so before they entered on the stage of historical records. When that happened, those who succeeded them in pre-eminence must have cultivated their stories—perhaps because they themselves had no similar stories, or perhaps—and this is more likely—because their stories could not compete with those of the Ulstermen in interest or excitement. The literary excellence of the Ulster tales was certainly one of the reasons why they achieved extraordinary popularity at such an early date and retained it over such a long period; another reason, no doubt, was the antiquity claimed for them.[19]

The king of the Ulstermen in the principal tales of this cycle was Conchobar. His palace is said to have been in Emain Macha, near the present city of Armagh, on the spot where the ruins known now by the name 'Navan Fort' are found, about two miles to the west of that city. He betrayed the sons of Uisliu—that is, Naoise and his brothers— and caused the death of the matchless Deirdre. Because of that betrayal, he lost some of the heroes of his court, who went in self-imposed exile to the court of Ailill and Medb in Connacht, and joined that royal pair in the attack which they launched aginst him.

The immediate cause of the battle celebrated in the *Táin Bó Cúailnge* was a conversation that took place between Ailill and Medb one night as they lay in bed.

> Once when their royal bed had been made ready for Ailill and Medb, they conversed as they lay on the pillows.
>
> 'It is a true saying, girl,' said Ailill, 'that the wife of a good man is well off.'
>
> 'It is true,' said the girl. 'Why do you say so?'
>
> 'Because,' said Ailill, 'you are better off today than the day I married you.'
>
> 'I was well off without you,' said Medb.

'I did not hear or know it, except that you were an heiress and that
your nearest neighbours were robbing and plundering you.'
    'That was not so,' said Medb, 'for my father, Eochu Feidlech son of
Finn, was high king of Ireland.'[20]

And she went on to boast of her riches, and he of his, until, to her
acute embarrassment, she discovered that her husband owned a
splendid bull (*Findbennech*), whose equal could not be found among
her own herds. In fact, there was but one like it anywhere, and it
(*Dond Cúailnge*) was in the possession of a man who owed homage to
Conchobar. Medb attempted to get the bull by fair means, but when
those failed she decided to carry it off by force of arms. When the
attack came, all the Ulstermen were disabled by a strange malady[21]—
all of them, that is, except the youth Cú Chulainn, and for a long time
he alone was able to fight against the men of Connacht and to defend
the land. After he had accomplished incredible feats of bravery, the
Ulstermen recovered from their ailment and were ultimately
victorious over their enemies, but the two bulls that were the cause of
all the fighting killed each other. That is the bare outline of the *Táin
Bó Cúailnge*, the most famous story in the literature of Ireland, but
only one among many that deal with King Conchobar, the youth Cú
Chulainn, and the two that sometimes rival him in valour—Conall
Cernach and Loegaire Buadach—and others such as Bricriu
Nemthenga, Fergus, King Ailill and Queen Medb, and their daughter
Findabair.
    Of course, there are heroic tales that belong to other cycles, such as
the Historical Cycle, which contains tales about the early kings of
Ireland, and especially about the most famous of them all, Cormac
mac Airt.[22] Similarly, there are non-heroic tales that deal with the
heroic period.[23] That category includes tales about the early Christian
saints, their miracles and their prophecies, such as those found in
Adamnán's Life of St Columba,[24] as well as tales about soothsayers,
magicians, and others to whom unusual and supernatural powers
were ascribed (though none of them was a saint), such as the story
about Néde and Ferchertne.[25] In the latter group we should include
such stories as *Echtra Cormaic i Tír Tairngiri* ('The Adventure of
Cormac in the Land of Promise').[26]
    But the Ulster Cycle is the heroic cycle *par excellence* in the
literature of Ireland, and although we can scarcely believe that its
original form has been preserved in the long process of transmission it
must have undergone, we may take the following to be a general
description of the most characteristic features of the stories in that

cycle. The social class that is pre-eminent in the tales is the warrior aristocracy, including its womenfolk. Sometimes their attendants and even their bondservants are mentioned, and there are many references to the *filid* and to druids, but the other people who made up the society (e.g., food producers and purveyors) are ignored almost completely. On the other hand, there is enough evidence to support the view that the Irish society reflected in these tales had some of the features of the tripartite divisions or functions that Georges Dumézil has shown to have existed in ancient India and other Indo-European societies. Beside the warrior class, there was a learned and priestly class, and below these two, the class made up of farmers and artisans (makers of material goods).[27]

There is considerable variation in the settings that are presented. In the *Táin Bó Cúailnge* the events take place either in the camp of Ailill and Medb or in the various places where Cú Chulainn meets his opponents. Events in other stories are set in the court of Conchobar or of Ailill and Medb, in Cú Chulainn's residence, and elsewhere. Not infrequently the action takes place in the home of a nobleman where the king has gone either on circuit or by invitation. In later tales, the most common setting is the court of a king or a battlefield.[28]

There is a predilection for describing the appearance and dress of the aristocracy, both men and women, but no originality is shown in the descriptions. They are conventional for the most part, and sometimes the same details occur with hardly any variation in different stories. On the other hand, there are few details which describe for us the scenes of everyday life.

Life in the courts of Irish kings was perhaps simple and to be distinguished more by the number of people thronging them than by their regal appurtenances:

> Hounds, ale, horses and teams,
> Women, well-bred fosterlings,
> A harvest of honey, wheat for the first reaping,
> Mast for feeding goodly swine
> Shall be in thy populous household,
> Many women and pet animals,
> Musicians for ale-feasts.[29]

But the stories give us the impression that it was also elaborately formal and that some of the ceremonies held were quite barbaric. For example, we hear of the 'marriage feast' of Tara, whereby the king in the fifth and sixth centuries was wedded to the land,[30] and in the twelfth century Giraldus Cambrensis describes an inauguration rite in Tyrconnell in which the king actually mates with sovereignty, there represented by a white mare (although one may doubt whether the rite was practised as described as late as the twelfth century.)[31] But it is not the ceremonies that concerned the storytellers, rather those occasions when they were abruptly set aside. And apparently that happened often enough, for it is a youthful society that is described, one full of passion and vigour, and it took very little to cause the most honourable warriors to forget momentarily their dignity and take part in a skirmish in the midst of a ceremonial occasion.[32] Nor is that any wonder, for making war in some form or another was the essence of the life of the society, and war was its principal interest. As might be expected, a conspicuous place in the tales is given to the heroes' horses, and frequent reference is made to weapons that were an inseparable part of the warrior's gear—to the *gae bulga* of Cú Chulainn and the *caladbolc* of Fergus.

The standard form of the stories is prose narration, not epic poetry as in the heroic literature of Greece and the Germanic countries.[33] Very rarely are the tales cast in metrical form, although there is room for poetry in the prose narration when it becomes necessary to express emotions that are of unusual intensity, those that arise as a rule from dramatic situations. Windisch drew attention to the same literary convention in the kind of epic found in early Sanskrit sources,[34] and Sir Ifor Williams showed that many of the old stanzas found in Welsh manuscripts appear to have been at one time part of prose tales of which the prose sections have been lost.[35] There is reason to believe that similar instances of verses surviving the loss of their prose framework are to be found in Irish literature. For example, nothing has survived of the story *Comracc Liadhaine ocus Cuirithir*[36] ('The Meeting of Liadhan and Cuirithir') apart from the poetry and a few scattered lines of prose. *Comracc Liadhaine ocus Cuirithir*, as it has been transmitted to us, is the moving lament of Líadhan the nun for the poet Cuirithir whom she had rejected as a lover. The first and last stanzas will give some indication of the intensity of the emotion expressed and will at the same time serve as a reminder that early Irish literature provides us with examples of love poems rarely found in other western literatures before the twelfth century.

> Joyless is the thing that I have done. I have angered the one I loved. It would be madness not to do what pleased him were it not for the fear of the King of Heaven . . .
>
> Do not hide it! He was my heart's love, though I had loved every one else beside.

A blast of flame has pierced my heart. Most certainly it will not endure without him.[37]

It may have been from the Irish that this prose interspersed with verse form of narration was borrowed by the Scandinavians, to be handed on later to the saga writers of Iceland.[38]

As a rule, and indeed almost without exception, the heroic literature of Ireland deals with adventures, or, as already suggested, with the dramatic situations arising from them. Most of it was composed for the sake of entertainment, as anyone can easily see, but there is also a good deal of didactic prose and poetry. Except for the authors of a few poems composed on special occasions, the works are anonymous.

The poetry which is found in Irish heroic literature was composed in a number of metres which are represented in their various stages of development, ranging from the earliest, which seems to be devoid of every ornamentation except alliteration, to the comparatively well developed with a specific number of syllables, rhyme and stanzaic form. Professor Calvert Watkins has made out a case for accepting the view that the metres of archaic Old Irish poetry are Indo-European in form and in function.[39] One of the terms applied to some of the oldest verses is *roscad*, but it is an ambiguous term and in early times it seems to have been applied 'to three fairly distinct types of composition, speeches in short-lined rhymeless verse, speeches in long-lined rhymeless verse, and speeches in artificially obscure diction (as yet not analysed from the point of view of metrical structure).'[40] The Greeting of Cet to Conall Cernach in *Scéla Mucce Meic Dathó* is described as a *roscad*:

Fo-chen Conall,	guss flann ferge
cride licce,	fo chích curad
lindbruth loga,	créchtaig cathbúadaig
luchair ega	At-comsa mac Finchoime frim[41]

'Welcome, Conall, heart of stone, fierce boldness of a lynx, glitter of ice, red-strength of anger under the breast of a scarred, battle-victorious warrior. Let the son of Findchoim encounter me.'

The Irish word *retoiric* is derived from Latin *(ars) rhetorica*, but there is nothing to suggest that *retoiric* was ever used as a term denoting a particular form or genre in Irish literature before the eleventh century. Professor Mac Cana has shown that the abbreviation .r. has been mistakenly understood as an abbreviation for *retoiric*, whereas in fact it must be for *roscad* or *rosc*. Setting aside the question of the origin of rhymeless verses properly described as *roscad* rather than as *retoiric*, one can easily believe that they are earlier than the metrical verses that have stanzaic form, rhyme and a set number of syllables. As might be expected, many of the speeches, which constitute such a large part of the narration, are set in metrical form, although the majority of them are in prose. The usual practice is to give a poetic form to speeches that contain prophecy, vaticination, elegy, or eulogy.

The events of the tales are treated as events in the past, and very rarely—if at all—are we told how much time has passed since then. The audience probably did not expect any chronological details. Besides, one must always remember that many of the heroes of the tales had found a place in the genealogies of the chief families and that some of the audience were members of those same families.

This raises the question of how much historical truth one can believe is contained in the heroic tales, or rather in the only two classes of stories worth considering in this respect, the Ulster Cycle and the Historical Cycle. Concerning the latter, the general consensus now seems to be that they contain a fair amount of history. For example, Professor Myles Dillon, who has given us the fullest study yet of the cycle, says that reading the tales and comparing them chronologically with the genealogies, the annals, and the historical documents has deepened his conviction that there is considerable truth in them.[42] But Professor T. F. O'Rahilly would have us believe that they contained no historical truth: to him Cormac mac Airt was a totally unhistorical person.[43] In favour of the belief that the Ulster Cycle has a basis in historical fact, one can cite the opinions of such scholars as E. O'Curry, H. Zimmer, K. Meyer, E. Hogan, E. Windisch, J. Mac Neill, and H. M. and N. K. Chadwick. Against their views are those of A. Nutt, Sir John Rhŷs, and O'Rahilly.[44] According to the last of these scholars, there is not the least connection between the stories of the Ulster Cycle and anything that can be called history either, apart from the fact that the tradition about the war between the Ulstermen and the men of Connacht was introduced by accident into some of them and especially into the greatest and most famous of all, the *Táin Bó Cúailnge*. His own view was that one could demonstrate that Cú Chulainn was originally none other than the god *Lug* or *Lugaid*, and that the other principal characters such as Cú Roí, Fergus, Bricriu, and Medb were nothing but gods who had been reduced to human stature.

Tomás Ó Cathasaigh's very fine study of the Cormac Mac Airt Cycle illustrates the complex nature of the Old Irish sagas.[45]

He shows that the historical Cormac, if there ever was one, is but a shadow: the substance, the 'real' Cormac, is a creature of myth. Yet Cormac has been treated by the genealogists as an ancestor of the Dál Cuinn and his legendary achievements used to enhance the prestige of the Uí Néill kins of the northern half of Ireland. In some of the texts his 'life' is founded on the basic pattern of the international heroic biography, albeit adapted to the Irish ideology of kingship with the king as centre of the cosmos. But his various roles as ideal king are not uniformly nor consistently emphasized in all the tales. It is interesting to note that Ó Cathasaigh thinks that with certain qualifications the Cormac Mac Airt Cycle fits in with O'Rahilly's theory of the Irish hero, and that Dumézil's theory of the tripartite functions, although it does not provide an adequate model for the analysis of Irish legends as a whole, does illuminate the Cormac Mac Airt legend.

§2

Reference has already been made to the two classes that produced literature in the typical heroic period, the one producing it for the sake of entertainment, the other for the sake of instruction, and we noted that it is often difficult to distinguish between their compositions. Such a distinction cannot be clearly made in the heroic literature of Ireland; it is even more difficult, in fact, to draw a line between the two classes of literary men, for there was but one figure of importance who appeared on the literary scene in the last part of the heroic period and that was the *fili*. The word is usually translated into English as 'poet' or 'bard', but the *fili* had many functions that do not belong to a poet according to our conception of him, and since the word 'bard', in the form *bard*, pl. *baird* (cf. Welsh *bardd*, pl. *beirdd*) exists in Irish and denotes an inferior grade of *fili*, it is perhaps best to keep the word *fili* and its plural *filid* here, as in Irish, to denote the early poets who governed the literary life of the land during the final period of the heroic age in Ireland.

The word *fili*, it appears, comes from the same root as the Welsh *gweled* 'see', and this suggests that in the beginning it was a name for a kind of seer. It is possible that an early feminine form containing the same root has been preserved, as H. M. and N. K. Chadwick suggested, in *Veleda*, the name of a prophetess among the Bructeri whom Tacitus mentioned (Hist. iv, 61, etc.), and that the Romans took a common name for prophetess as a proper noun.[46]

In the text of *Immacallam in dá thuarad* ('Colloquy of the Two Sages')[47] the *fili* is called a *fáith*, that is, a prophet (cf. OI *fáth* 'prophecy'), and the name *banfhili* (*ban*, 'woman') is sometimes used for the *banfháith*, the prophetess, who is encountered in the *Táin Bó Cúailnge*.[48] Consistent with this, *fáithsine*, 'prophecy', that is, the function of the *fáith*, is attributed to the *fili* in an old law tract.[49] All of this suggests that the *filid* and the *fátha* originally formed a single class,[50] and that they represented in Ireland the learned and mantic class that existed in Gaul, and which was known to the Romans as *uātes* and to the Greeks as οὐάτεις or μάντεις, because etymologically *uātes* and οὐάτεις correspond to *fátha* (singular *fáith*) in Irish.

If the *filid* in Ireland correspond to the *uātes* in Gaul, as is commonly supposed, then one could expect that the Irish druids, a class consistently portrayed as enemies of Christianity, correspond to the sacerdotal druids of Gaul, the *druides* of Caesar, Lucan's *druidae*.[51]

The classical accounts agree in attributing religious and sacrificial duties to the *druides*, but they are not so unanimous in linking the *uātes* to the sacrifices.[52] Since the word *uātes* and its cognates in the Celtic languages[53] and in other languages implies seeing, inspiration, prophecy, and poetry (the Welsh cognate of *uātes* is *gwawd*, a word which meant 'song' before it came to mean 'satire, scorn'), there is reason to believe that the *uātes* were present as 'seers' when there was sacrifice to the gods, but that the *druides* served as priests at the sacrifice.[54] This is consistent with Caesar's statement about the *druides*, and is one way of explaining the inconsistency and ambiguity concerning the offices of *uātes* and *druides* in the other commentaries, which are evidently not independent of one another.

Be that as it may, there is no doubt that when the light of history first dawns on Irish society, the *filid* have a higher status than the druids. Indeed, in the law tract *Uraicecht Becc* the *filid* are classified with the lords (*flatha*) and the bishops as *soirnemid*,[55] while the druids are listed with the smiths and other craftsmen as *doirnemid*.[56]

It could be that the druid (*drui*)[57] had at one time as lofty a position in Irish society as his counterpart on the Continent; indeed, that seems likely, and it is difficult not to believe that the coming of Christianity did not have something to do with his loss of status. We know that his ultimate fate was to vanish from the land, but that probably did not happen before the *fili* had acquired some of the functions and not a little of the aura attached to his office. Among those functions may have been that of preserving and transmitting the traditional native lore. One can believe this without going as far as Mac Neill, who insisted that *druí* and *fili* were but two titles for the same office.[58] Both classes versified their lore,[59] no doubt, but we must remember that in early times there was no knowledge that could not be cast in verse,[60] and that Ireland exemplifies this better than most countries. Some of the oldest Irish law tracts are in verse.[61]

Just as the *filid*'s status was higher than that of the druids, so it was higher than that of the *baird*,[62] a lesser order of poets whose name is linked directly with that of the Continental Celtic poets whom the Greeks called βάρδοι and the Romans *bardi*. Possibly, the original meaning of the word *bardos* was 'one who sings praises',[63] and the *baird* of Ireland were like the *bardi* of the Continent to the extent that singing praises was their exclusive activity. But in Ireland the *baird* were not held in much respect. Could it be that some of the superiority of the *filid* was won at their expense?

According to one tradition,[64] the *eneclann* ('honour-price') of a *bard* was but half that of the *fili*. The middle Irish text *Leabhar na gCeart*[65] says that knowledge concerning kings and their privileges belonged by right to the *fili*—not to the *bard*—and a lawyer of the same period says that a *bard* could claim nothing for being a learned man, but must be content with whatever his innate talent can win for him (*bard, dano, cin dliged fogluime acht indleacht fadeisin*).[66]

When Patrick came to Ireland, so we are told, he permitted the right of public speaking to only three: to the historian for narrating events and telling stories, to the *fili* for praise and satire, and to the *brithem* (English *brehon*) for passing judgment according to tradition and custom.[67] This suggests there had been a clear differentiation between the duties of *fili*, *senchaid* (that is, 'narrator' or 'historian')[68] and *brithem*, but the evidence of tradition does not confirm it. As we shall see, it is difficult to separate the work of the *senchaid* from that of the *fili*. And while the *Immacallam in dá thuarad* suggests that the function of the *brithem* had been separated from that of the *fili* before the advent of Christianity to Ireland,[69] that separation had apparently been neither effective nor final, for the work of the *brithem* as well as the work of the *senchaid* was attributed to the *fili* thereafter. Professor Myles Dillon probably put his finger on the correct explanation of all this when he suggested that the *fili*, the *brithem*, the *senchaid*, and the *drui* all belonged originally to the same privileged class, a class that corresponded to that of the Hindu *brahman*.[70] He adduced support for this in the fact, attested by a series of linguistic correspondences that J. Vendryes discovered long ago, that India, Rome, and Celtic Gaul had in common the tradition of acknowledging and maintaining a privileged class of priests: the *brahman*, the high-priest (*pontifex*), and the druid.[71]

There is no doubt about the dignified and honourable position accorded the *filid* in Irish society. It is possible, and in fact quite probable, that the traditional way in which that position is depicted is not historically accurate in its details; nevertheless, it is sufficiently valuable to deserve our attention. We are told that each *fili* had a retinue that varied in size according to his rank and position. For example, according to one account, there were thirty men in the retinue of the chief *fili* (*ollam*), fifteen in the retinue of the *fili* ranked just below him (*ánrud, ánruth*), and a smaller number according to the rank of each of the others.[72] The *ollam*, like the Welsh *pencerdd* ('chief poet') had a chair reserved especially for him (*cathair ollaman*) in the court.[73] There is also the hint that he wore a garment made partly or completely from feathers.[74] He was the highest of the seven grades of *filid* and according to one law tract his honour price was equal to that of a bishop and a petty king.[75] The Annals distinguish between three kinds of *ollam*: *ollam re filidecht, ollam re brethemnas, ollam re senchas*, i.e., between chief poet, chief judge, and chief historian.

It appears that some of the *filid* restricted their service to a single king; for example, Ferchertne is depicted as *fili* in the service of Cú Roí mac Dairi. But it is evident that a *fili* was not obliged to bind himself to a single lord: he could sojourn with a number of kings and avoid being dependent on any one. The poet Aithirne is a case in point. He was one of the Ulstermen, but despite that, he was able to act quite independently of their king, Conchobar. In fact, the inference is that the *filid* formed an order which embraced the entire land, and that there existed an *ard-fhili* 'high-fili' or *ard-ollam*, who claimed to rule over them, just as an *ard-rí* claimed to rule over the other kings. However, it is quite possible that such a system would be more valid in theory than in practice, and more so in some times than in others. Needless to say, there is no basis in the Irish law tracts for assuming that there was a king whose authority extended over all Ireland, although some of the kings of Munster and of Tara were to claim complete overlordship over other kings.[76]

There was a tendency for the profession of *fili* and even the office of *ollam* to be hereditary. In *Immacallam in dá thuarad* it is said the Néde, son of the *ollam* Adna, came to claim his father's chair when he heard the news of the latter's death.[77] Apparently, the same thing was true of the *bard*'s profession. In the first treatise on metrics in *The Book of Ballymote*, we hear of a *bard áne*, that is, a *bard* who was not practising his art, even though he had inherited the profession from his father.[78] But notwithstanding this tendency, we must not believe that the ranks of the *filid* were completely closed to outsiders, for there are examples of princes in the legendary period who bore the titles *fili* and *ollam*: Finn Fili comes to mind, the man from whom the kings of Leinster claimed descent, and Ollam Fódla, a renowned but probably legendary law-giver in the royal line of Ulster.[79]

The sources agree that the training of the *filid* was long and thorough, though they differ in stating the number of years it took.[80] There is a suggestion that the first part was common to the *bard* and the *fili*, but that the former finished his education at the end of seven years while the latter went on to study further. One may assume that the *fili* was required to complete a course of study lasting at least seven years before he could obtain the qualification necessary to become an *ollam* or chief poet. The course must have provided instruction in the tales and antiquities, in the poetry and the several metres in which the *fili* were expected to be fluent. In this connection it is interesting to observe that, theoretically, there were special metres for the *fili* distinct from those of the *bard*, but normally the *fili* employed the bardic metres (*bairdne*) quite freely. During the last years of his schooling, probably, the *fili* received instruction in the metres proper to his rank, and during the same period, no doubt, he learned divination and the magical arts.[81]

This kind of course would require special educational preparation, and it is likely that *filid* served as teachers for the young men that wished to follow their profession as well as for other youths. It is generally believed that Gemmán, the teacher at whose feet Colum Cille studied, was a *fili*.[82] The instruction was given orally, no doubt, despite the fact that the *fili* was expected, according to one tract, to learn fifty ogams each year during the early years of his schooling—a requirement we would like to know more about, for ogam is an unwieldy system of writing at best.[83] It consists of notches cut on a central line for vowels and of three sets of one to five strokes on either side (i.e., to the left and to the right), and across the central line for consonants; sufficient for short inscriptions on a tombstone and the like, but if a modern novel were to be written in it, it would require a surface over a mile in length.[84]

The *filid* could claim many privileges by virtue of their office and education. For every song they composed, they could claim a payment, and the payment seems to have varied according to the metre: the more difficult the metre, the greater the payment.[85] The tracts on versification in the *Book of Ballymote* show that there was at least a tendency to look down upon *bairdne* metres as *núa-chrutha* ('new-forms') or *óig-recta* ('young', i.e., 'new-systems'). When a *bard* sang in one of those, there was no set price he could claim. On the other hand, when the same metre was used 'according to the rule of science' (*iar f irdligud na h-écsi*), that is, by the *fili*, the price was fixed.[86]

When we remember that the *filid* were instructed in magic and divination, and that they were capable, according to popular belief, of causing sickness and even death, we can imagine how dangerous it was to oppose any request of theirs. Evidently they were aware of the strength of their position, and were ready to take advantage of it. An example of an exceptionally impudent request can be seen in the case of Aithirne, who asked the one-eyed king Eochaid for his eye—and who was not denied it![87] (It is comforting to know that, according to the tale, God rewarded the king's generosity by restoring both his eyes to him.)

The arrogance of the *filid* became proverbial and was lampooned in the text called *Tromdámh Guaire* ('The Great Visitation to Guaire'), or *Imtheacht na Tromdháimhe* ('The Proceedings of the Great Bardic Institution').[88] The tale describes a host of them accompanying the chief *fili* Senchán Torpéist to the court of Guaire, king of Connacht. Their coming caused fear and commotion in the entire neighbourhood, for they were all equally arrogant in their demands. 'They did not go to bed any night', says the story, 'without requesting something, and they did not rise any morning without some of them desiring things which were unusual, strange, rare, and difficult to get.' If they did not get their most unreasonable wishes at the end of twenty-four hours, they would threaten satires and curses. The king's heart was filled with terror. At the end, he is on his knees praying to God to be stricken dead before he is satirized by such a rapacious host.

It is no wonder that the *filid* were not always on good terms with the kings, and we are told that they were exiled three times. It is quite likely, too, that the coming of Christianity did little to enhance their popularity, and the kings probably sought to take advantage of that fact. However, it appears that the enmity between them became so intense as to make co-existence seem impossible. Whether it reached its climax in the assembly (*mordál*) of Druim Cetta,[89] said to have been held in County Derry in AD 575, is another matter.[90] According to tradition,[91] the royal party there was led by Aed (Aidus) mac Ainmire; the leader of the *filid* was Eochaid Dallán Forgaill.[92] Dallán seems to have been a personage of influence by virtue of his family connections as well as his ability, but the man who saved the day for the *filid*, it is said, was Colum Cille. The high king strove to abolish and destroy the order; the saint argued for its reform and reorganization, and he was able to persuade the assembly that that was the best course.[93] If this was the case, it is easy to see why Ireland should honour Colum Cille so, for it is he who would have been mainly responsible for saving the old native culture from obliteration by the foreign Latin culture that came in the wake of the new faith.

Apparently, Dallán Forgaill was entrusted with the work of reforming the order. On the authority of a source now lost, Keating says that he appointed four *filid*, one for each district, to preside over the schools of the *filid*. He is also said to have reduced the number of *filid*. According to the new system, the 'high king' was to maintain an *ard-ollam*, and each regional king and lord to maintain an *ollam*.[94]

The history of Dallán Forgaill demonstrates too the reconciliation that took place between the *filid* and Christianity. To him is attributed the encomium (*amra*) that was sung to Colum Cille,[95] a song in a metre and language archaic enough to confirm the authenticity of the date if not of the authorship; he is said to have composed poems to other clerics of that period, too.[96] Naturally, the accommodation achieved between the *filid* and the new faith implies that they severed every connection with the old religion and erased every trace of it from the native literature, but, as a matter of fact, it appears that they did no more than cease referring to the pagan gods as supernatural beings and began treating them as men of exceptional powers.

Professor and Mrs Chadwick suggested that the order of *filid* was not unanimously in favour of the arrangement agreed upon at Druim Cetta,[97] and there is more than a little evidence to support them. There is a story about a certain Eochu Rígéices[98]—claimed by one historian to be identical with Eochaid Dallán Forgaill[99]—who was invited by the king of Ulster, Fiachna mac Báetain, to come to his court as *fili*. Eochu was reluctant to go, apparently because Mongán, the king's son, surpassed everyone in knowledge, and the *fili* said, 'if I come to your court, some will surely set him to compete with me, I will curse him, and that will be the cause of a quarrel between me and thee.' Nevertheless, Eochu was persuaded to go, and what he had feared came to pass.

The anecdote is especially interesting for us because it represents hostility between a particular poet and Mongán, the principal figure of a group of stories that are pagan in aura and meaning. This is not the place to discuss those stories, but it is worth making reference to a poem that occurs in the *Immram Brain maic Febail* ('The Voyage of Bran mac Febail') to illustrate Mongán's supernatural character.[100]

There are three parts to the poem. The first describes *Mag Mell*, that is, 'the Plain of Pleasure', based on the doctrine of an earthly paradise and dwelling place of the gods. It has been suggested that this teaching was evolved, though not specifically fashioned, for the purpose of counteracting the influence of the Christian belief about eternal life, and that perhaps it has not itself entirely escaped that influence. In the second part there is a treatise on Christian doctrine, which has been added, apparently, to counteract the influence of the first part, although this section is completely separate from the first and last sections. The third part contains a prophecy about the birth, life and death of Mongán who is portrayed here as son to Manannán. In a section that calls to mind part of the Welsh tale of Taliesin, it says, 'he will be (*biaid, bid*) in the shape of every wild beast . . . wolf . . . stag . . . speckled salmon . . . swan.'

There was a version of the *Immram Brain* in the Book of Druim Snechta(i). That manuscript has long since been lost, but fortunately a good deal of its contents is known to us. We know that it contained 'Four Stories of Mongán' and other tales in which visions and prophecies were conspicuous elements, as well as the *Immram Brain*. Thurneysen thought that the material was assembled and the manuscript written by a *fili*, but despite this, the internal evidence identifies it as a product of a monastic scriptorium and its very title says as much, referring as it does to the monastery of Druim Snechta, situated a few miles to the south west of the present town of Monaghan. That most of the material was extant before it was written into the manuscript is a safe assumption.[101] For example, it was believed that the *Immram Brain* was composed toward the end of the seventh or beginning of the eighth century, but a recent study has cast doubt on such a very early dating.[102]

Since Mongán died in AD 624, according to the Annals, the stories about him must have developed within a century of his death. However, in this connection we must remember that there is some evidence that there were two persons named Mongán, and that the old tales which were woven about an earlier mythological character were adapted to the historical entity.[103]

Granted this premise, it is easy to believe, as do H. M. and N. K.

Chadwick, that in the seventh century a group of *filid* set about exalting Mongán as a hero dear to their hearts; and that these could quite possibly be the most conservative *filid*—those that were hostile to the new faith.[104] In that case, it would not be surprising if they produced those stories in the Book of Druim Snechta which give so much prominence to visions, prophecies, and shape-shifting. But even if there was reaction against the policy of reconciliation with the new religion, and even if Mongán was adopted as a hero by the reactionaries as the Chadwicks assumed, it lasted but a short time. Professor Carney has argued that the '*Immram Brain* is, from beginning to end, a thoroughly Christian poem. It seems, in fact, to be an allegory showing Man setting out on the voyage to Paradise ... the Christian nature of the poem is quite clear. It is pervaded by thoughts of the Fall, the Incarnation, and the Redemption.'[105] Professor Mac Cana, on the other hand, has argued no less cogently that 'despite the consciously drawn parallels with Christian belief ... it is not easy to indicate specific instances in which *Immram Brain*'s account of the otherworld is necessarily, or even probably, dependent on sources external to Irish tradition.'[106] Building on the obvious fact that it is only by reference to *Compert Mongáin* that the allusions in *Immram Brain* become completely intelligible and that the poet-author of *Immram Brain* patently used the *Compert* as one of his sources, Mac Cana goes on to show that Mongán was the focus of a wide spread tradition which told of the birth of a wonder-boy, both sage and hero, who proved more than a match for his seniors. It is true that the tale incorporating the Mongán wonder-child appears to be lost. 'Enough remains, however, to suggest that the central motif of the birth of the wonder child had given rise to a whole web of related narratives which were current in the oral tradition of the seventh century.'[107]

The Chadwicks may have been mistaken in their view of the origin of Mongán tales and of the role assigned to Mongán, but they were right in their perception that the *filid* soon overcame any feeling of inferiority they may have had when they first came into contact with ecclesiastical scholars and their way of recording their learning. This is well illustrated in the preface to Fiacc's Hymn, where the young man trained as a *fili* resists taking the tonsure, indeed has to be tricked into doing so, for it is only to save his master Dubthach from the tonsure that he submits himself to it:

'What is attempted?' said Fiacc.
'The tonsuring of Dubthach,' said they.
'That is foolish', said he, 'for there is not in Ireland a poet his equal.'

'You would be taken in his place,' said Patrick.
'My loss to Ireland is less than that of Dubthach,' said Fiacc.[108]

§3

Irrespective of any reaction to reconciliation with the new faith,
divination was undoubtedly an integral part of the craft of a *fili* at one
time. One of the ways in which divination, or acquiring special
knowledge for some particular purpose, was practised is described in
a well-known entry in Cormac's *Glossary*.[109] The practice is explained
under the heading *imbas forosnai* 'manifestation that enlightens'.

> The *fili* gnaws a piece of the raw flesh of a pig or a dog or a cat, and then
> puts it on a flagstone behind the door, and chants an incantation over
> it, and offers it to idol gods, and calls them to him, and leaves them not
> on the next day, and then chants over his two palms on his two cheeks
> and sleeps. And men are watching him so that he may not turn over
> and so that no one may disturb him. And then is revealed to him that
> which is before him until the end of a *nómad* (a nine-day period) or two
> or three *nómad* according to the long or short time that he may arrange
> for the offering. Patrick banished that and the *teinm laída*, 'enlighten-
> ment through singing', and declared that no one who practises those
> belongs to heaven nor to earth, for it is a denial of baptism. However,
> *díchetal do chennaib* 'impromptu incantation' (lit., 'incantation from
> heads, ends'; less usually, *díchetal do chollaib cenn*) was allowed by
> virtue of craft, for it is science that causes it, and offering to devils is not
> necessary but declaring from the ends of bones at once.[110]

Elsewhere, a *tairbfheis* 'bull-feast' or 'bull-sleep',[111] is described, a rite
practised in order to find out who would be the next king of Tara. A
bull would be killed and from it flesh and broth would be prepared for
a man to eat. Then the man would sleep, and in that sleep he would see
the next king. One could compare that rite with the one Keating says
the druids practised in ancient Ireland.[112] Apparently, it included the
killing of bulls, sacrificing them, flaying them, and then having the
diviner lie down upon the skin.

Reference has already been made to the prophetess Fedelm in the
Táin Bó Cúailnge. In the latest version of the tale, we are told that she
was a Connacht woman, and that she had been studying *filidecht*,
that is, the craft of the *fili*, in Britain. She encounters Medb before the
queen sets out with her hosts for the battle against the Ulstermen, and
in response to the queen's query says that she sees a vision of blood.
When Medb refuses to believe the vision, the prophetess rehearses—
in verse—the feats that Cú Chulainn will accomplish.

In the *Immacallam in dá thuarad* 'The Colloquy of the Two Sages', Ferchertne utters prophecy of a more general kind. After Néde has described the good that prevails at the time, Ferchertne answers with a prophecy about the evil things to come—hunger, poverty, destruction, etc. Néde acknowledges his opponent's superiority to him and calls him a great *fili* and *fáith* 'prophet' (RC 26, p. 50, §272).

The gift of prophecy seems to have belonged to the druids as well as to the *filid*, and it is also sometimes attributed to supernatural beings. But the gift is a faculty which the prophet possesses in himself—rarely, if at all, is it traced to inspiration by some god or other supernatural being.

The succession of the kings of Ireland is the subject of two prophetic texts. In *Baile Chuind Chétchathaig* ('The Vision of Conn of the Hundred Battles')[113] Conn prophesies; in *Baile in Scáil* ('Vision of the Phantom')[114] it is the phantom who prophesies. Thurneysen says that a version of the former text was contained in the Book of Druim Snechta, and it is probable that the latter also has been based on ancient material, although in its present form it is not older than the eleventh century.[115]

It is not always easy to distinguish between the *fili*'s curse and his satire in the early literature. A curse would be coupled quite naturally with a satire, and the one would be feared fully as much as the other.[116] It is said that the *fili* Laidcenn took it into his head to curse the men of Leinster for a whole year because they killed his son.[117] The result was that they lost many men, and we are asked to believe that neither corn nor grass nor leaves grew in Leinster that year. In the tale *Oidheadh Chloinne Lir* ('The Tragic Death of the Children of Lir') the story is told of Cathbad cursing Emain Macha because of the murder of Naoise and his brothers.[118]

An example of a curse is found in Cormac's *Glossary* under the heading *gaire, gair-re*, which is explained as 'short-space'.[119] The story is told of the *fili* Néde mac Adnai cursing Caíar, king of Connacht. The words of the curse are 'Evil, death, short life to Caíar;/Spears of battle will have killed Caíar,/May Caíar die, may Caíar depart—Caíar!/Caíar under earth, under embankments, under stones!' and they seem to presage Caíar's imminent death by violence. What actually happens is that three blemishes appear on his face, and he flees in shame out of the land. Later, Néde repents and goes to seek the fugitive, who has gone into hiding in the cleft of a rock. But when the *fili* approaches, the king dies of remorse. Not surprisingly, the *fili*'s ability to inflict injury by his satires or curses was enlisted in the waging of wars: 'And thou, O Cairpre, son of Etain,' says Lug to his poet, 'what power can you wield in battle?' 'Not hard to say,' quoth Cairpre, 'I will make a *glám dicend* on them, and I will satirize them so that through the spell of my head they will not resist warriors.'[120]

As already suggested, charms were a regular part of the instruction of *filid*. Examples of them are found in the *Book of Ballymote*, and they are quite difficult to understand.[121] It appears that one charm was used to recover stolen cattle. It was recited over the trail of the animals, or, if that was not possible, through the right fist of the person by whom it was used. The thief would then be revealed to him in a dream. One of the most interesting of charms is that used to secure a long life. It is called the *Cétnad n-áise* or 'Song of Long Life.' It invokes first of all the 'seven daughters of the sea', then the '*senach* of the seven periods of time', and then there is a series of sentences beginning with *am* 'I am'. Each time this verbal form is repeated, the speaker declares that he is, in succession, a fortress (*dún*) that cannot be destroyed, an immovable rock, a valuable gem, etc.[122] This verbal form is also repeated in the song attributed to Amhairgin on the occasion when he first set foot on the soil of Ireland, according to the Book of Invasions (*Lebor Gabhála Érenn*):

> I am an estuary into the sea,
> I am a wave of the ocean,
> I am the sound of the sea,
> I am a powerful ox,
> I am a hawk on a cliff,
> I am a dewdrop in the sun,
> I am a plant of beauty,
> I am a boar of valour,
> I am a salmon in a pool,
> I am a lake in a plain,
> I am the strength of art.

The text is not very old, but if Amhairgin, like Krishna in the *Bhagavad Gītā* is identifying himself with the whole of creation, the substance is certainly shamanistic and would take its place well in a primitive context. Some annalists claim that this is the first Irish poem to be composed in Ireland,[123] and even a modern scholar like Mac Cana describes the author thus: 'Individual and universal, he epitomizes the emergence of Gaelic literature and the whole Gaelic order as conceived by the medieval transmitters and redactors of tradition: new beginnings in a new terrain, but only as an extension of an already ancient tradition.'[124]

The *fili*, as we have already noted, was at one time capable of filling the office of *brithem*.[125] There is plenty of evidence for this. In the introduction to the *Senchas Mór*—the introduction which Professor D. A. Binchy believes to be historically authentic[126]—Patrick is said to have requested a conference under the aegis of the high king Lóegaire in order to bring the laws of Ireland into harmony with Christianity. It appears that the *fili* Dubthach was entrusted with the task of explaining the old laws and customs of the land to the assembly. According to a later account the laws were systematized first by a body of nine persons: three kings (including Lóegaire), three bishops (including Patrick), and three *filid* or *ollamain*.[127]

Before we leave these matters that oscillate between the fabulous and the factual, we might mention the tradition that the reason the *filid* were deprived of their legal activities was the obscurity of the sort of language that Néde and Ferchertne used.[128] Those two were certainly not exceptional in their fondness for difficult language; we have, for example, the testimony of that king in *Tromdámh Guaire* who, upon hearing a particular poem, is reported to have said, 'That is a good poem for whomsoever can understand it'.[129] In fact, there was a special rhetorical style, which was known by the name *bélre na filed* ('language of the poets'); its most prominent feature was intentional obscurity of speech.[130] In *Tochmarc Emire* ('The Wooing of Emer') it is said that the conversation between Cú Chulainn and Emer was unintelligible to everyone else present.[131] In all likelihood, the metrical passages in the laws to which Mac Neill drew attention were the work of *filid* in the seventh century.[132]

The *filid* must have taken part in the development of the *Leabhar na gCeart* also.[133] It is no longer believed that the book describes conditions in the land any earlier than the eleventh century, but it still remains of considerable interest. Its general form is a series of poems in pairs: one enumerates the tributes which the king can claim from his chieftains and lords, the other enumerates the gifts he gives as a sign that he accepts their homage and loyalty. In the section on Tara it is claimed that the king's rights have been memorized by a Latin scholar, St Benén, but we are also told that these rights are not a subject for 'every prattling bard', only for the *fili*. The tract at the beginning of the present version, *Geasa agus Buadha Riogh nÉireann*, is attributed to Cúán Ó Lothcháin, chief *fili* of Mael Seachlainn, and a man of whom it was believed (incorrectly, as it turned out) that he ruled the land jointly with a monk of Liss-mór after the king's death.[134]

The versifying of proverbs is not less common than the versifying of laws, and in the literature of early Ireland we find plenty of examples of what is generally called gnomic poetry. Of the two principal collections ascribed to judges, the one that bears the name of the legendary judge Morann is believed to be the work of a *brithem* who was also a *fili*.[135] There are two versions, of which the oldest is believed to date from the eighth century. If that is correct, it is the earliest of the Irish gnomic texts. The collection known by the name *Briathra Flainn Fina maic Ossu* is interesting for another reason: it has been attributed, rightly or wrongly, to Aldfrith son of Oswy and king of Northumbria (AD 685–705).[136]

There are two other kinds of didactic verse that can be attributed to the *filid*. First are the genealogical poems, which are nothing more than versified tracts recording the lineage and pedigree of kings and lords.[137] There are some extant that trace the royal ancestral lines of Leinster and Munster, and it is believed that a number of them were composed in the seventh century.[138] Although in form they are more like catalogues, they agree on the whole with the genealogies. It is worth noting that the genealogical lists in the Book of Genesis were connected to the native ones even as early as these poems, and that classical names and others from Latin sources were included.

The number of genealogical collections is exceedingly large, and some of them are very old. The Laud collection comes from an eighth-century text, although there are additions in it that are later, and no doubt many of the genealogies were extant orally long before then.[139] The Irish chronological schemes that were composed in the seventh century were probably based on them. but be that as it may, the preservation of such genealogies was certainly a part of the work of the *filid*.

The second kind of didactic verse is not unlike the first, in that they are poems dealing with the names of places.[140] It is well known that Ireland is remarkably wealthy in ancient remains, cromlechs, forts, castles, and the like, and they are almost all connected in name with heroes—some fictional, some historical.[141] The *fili* was expected to know the meaning and historical origin of every place name, and there exists in the *Book of Leinster* a collection of poems that are merely versified presentations of that traditional knowledge.[142] There are over a hundred of them, some attributed to known poets of the ninth, tenth, and eleventh centuries, but the great majority of them are anonymous.[143] The name *dindshenchas*, that is, history or lore of prominent places, is given to the collection as well as to the individual stories in prose or poetry. There are two later collections, drawn from the *Book of Leinster* for the most part, but in these prose is the most common form of the stories.[144] Both prose and verse versions are invaluable to the historian, for along with the (often fanciful) explanations of the names, a great deal of real information is given concerning what went on at these places—especially at those places where the great *oenaigh* or 'fairs' were held, such as promulgation of law and judgment, recitation of genealogies and stories, horse-racing, and entertainment of all kinds.

The process that underlies many of these onomastic stories is, of course, well enough known. Sometimes the names of famous heroes provide the place names, at other times the process is reversed and the hero is named after the place—and this may have occurred more frequently than is usually supposed. However, a hero must have been quite renowned before his name could be linked with any locale. The explanation offered for the place name Ráith Chruachan (chief residence of Medb) in one of the two collections mentioned above provides a good example of the interest in place names and the attempt to explain them.[145] We are told that Étaín, wife of Eochaid Airem, took her maidservant Crochen or Cruachu with her when she herself was carried off by the god Midir. When the three arrived at a fairy mound (a *síodh-bhruidhean*), Crochen asked Midir whether that place was his residence. He replied that it was not, and then Crochen asked him if she could give it her own name. Midir granted her request, and presented the place to her as a reward for undertaking the journey.

A related genre wherein the names of heroes and places are linked is represented by the poem *Fianna bátar i nEmain*, which is attributed to Cináed Ua hArtacáin, who died in AD 975.[146] It describes the deaths and occasionally the graves of various heroes from the time of Fergus mac Léite to the Battle of Allen (*Cath Almaine*) or later. This interest in names gave rise to the tract which is known as *Cóir Anmann* 'Fitness (Correct Explanation) of Names'.[147] It contains speculations on the meanings of many personal names, some historical, others fictional. There is considerable disagreement over its date.

Obviously, those who wished to be skilled in the lore of place names had to be learned in the tales, and the *filid* were the chief authorities in both fields. In one sense, we should not have expected them to have much to do with the tales, because if one can divide the literature of the Heroic Age into three periods as H. M. and N. K. Chadwick do,[148] according to the purpose and intent of the learned men, namely:

entertainment (Homeric period), instruction (Hesiodic), and personal expression (Archilochic), then the *fili* belongs to the second period, the period of producing literature for the sake of instruction. He probably assumed the role of *scélaige*, that is, a story-teller who performs to give pleasure, only secondarily. However that may be, there is no doubt that the *fili*'s connection with the tales goes back to a very early period.[149]

According to *Cath Almaine*, Fergal, a king of the North, used to go to war accompanied by a youth named Donn Bó.[150] His task was to entertain the king and his warriors with poetry and royal tales. It seems that he could also play the pipes. The night before the Battle of Allen, Fergal called upon Donn Bó to entertain him with stories, poetry, and music. But the youth could offer nothing to divert him, so at his suggestion a certain Ua Maiglinni, the chief jester of Ireland, was summoned to narrate the history of battles and bold deeds of Leth Chuinn (northern Ireland) and Leinster. On the following day, Fergal, Donn Bó, and all the king's *filid* were slain in the battle, but that night Donn Bó and the *filid* were heard entertaining Fergal, in spite of the fact that they all were dead! The head of Donn Bó was taken to entertain the men of Leinster, just as Bendigeidfran's head was brought away by the seven survivors in the Welsh tale of *Branwen Ferch Lŷr*. The head turned its face to the wall so that none could see it, and then sang aloud so sweetly that the entire company wept at the sadness of the music they heard. This tale demonstrates the special background of the tales as well as anything can; it is not very important to decide whether Donn Bó was an official *fili* or not— clearly, the same man could be both story-teller and poet.[151]

In the tale *Longes Mac nUislenn* we are told that Feidlimid mac Daill, the father of Deirdre (Deirdriu), was story-teller (*scélaige*) to Conchobar.[152] If he is a fair representative of the class, then it is clear that the position of *scélaige* in society was as dignified and honourable as that of the *fili*.[153] In one of the stories about Mongán of which there were versions in the old lost book of Druim Snechta, it is said that the king had a *fili* named Forgall, who would tell a different story every night from the beginning of Winter (1 November) to the first of May.[154]

The *fili* as story-teller is the chief character in the tale of *Airec Menman Uraird maic Coise* 'The Stratagem of Urard Mac Coise'.[155] The gist of the story is that Cinél Eogain mac Néill despoiled the dwelling and carried off the cattle and horses of the *fili* Urard (Airard) mac Coise, and as he himself could not exact compensation, he determined to go to the king of Tara, Domnall mac Muirchertaig (d. 980)[156] to seek redress by means of a stratagem (*airec menman*). On his arrival, the *fili* is welcomed by the king and is asked for his tidings. Taking advantage of the two meanings of *scéla*, 'tidings, news' on the one hand and 'stories' on the other, he replies that he has many stories and will recite to the king whichever story he might choose. The king asks to hear the *fili*'s repertory of stories and the *fili* lists them, ending with the title of a hitherto unheard-of story called *Orgain Cathrach Mail Milscothach* 'The Destruction of Mael Milscothach's Fort'. As the *fili* expected, the king chose to hear the story which he had never heard before, and was told how the men of a certain king had despoiled a *fili* named Mael Milscothach (i.e., Mael Honey-words) of his possessions and how the *fili* had sought and been promised redress by the king. And this paved the way for Urard mac Coise to explain that he himself was the *fili* who had been despoiled and that the men who were guilty of that outrage were Domnall's. As a result, Domnall mac Muirchertaig arrested the wrongdoers and convoked the nobles of Cinél Eogain mac Néill to consider the case. They decided that they would make good the *fili*'s losses, that every petty king and royal mercenary among them would give him a cow. The *filid* and the *brethemain* (brehons) were then assembled and asked to determine the compensation and the honour-price to be paid to Urard mac Coise. They consulted Fland, *fer léginn* of Clonmacnoise. In the end, the *fili* received full restitution for his losses and an honour-price equal to that of the king of Tara, for it was decided by this assembly that henceforth every *ollam* or chief poet should have an honour-price equal to that of the king of Tara so long as he is an expert in the three arts of *iomas forasna* (*imbas forosnai*), *dichetal do chollaib cenn* and *teinm laida*.

There is every reason to believe that Urard mac Coise was a historical person. His obit is given as 990 in the Annals of Ulster and the other annals, except those of the Four Masters, which give it as 1023. Poems attributed to him have survived, and it may be that poems wrongly ascribed to him are indirectly responsible for the Four Masters' later obit, for some of them refer to events such as the Battle of Clontarf. Furthermore, there is no internal evidence (linguistic or otherwise) in the tale itself that is inconsistent with Urard mac Coise's authorship. But whether we accept his authorship as genuine or not, the *Airec Menman* is an important composition in the tradition of Irish literature, for its statement of the position to be accorded to the *filid* in Irish society was taken to be authoritative and definitive

throughout the Middle Ages. Urard mac Coise became 'the exemplar
or archetype of the *fili* in his role of eulogist, confidant of kings and
princes, and paragon of learning.'

> The evidence suggests that it was Urard mac Coise himself who
> delivered himself of this essay in vocational propaganda. He was
> acting as the defender and spokesman of his own order in thus
> vindicating its traditional dignity and privileges in the face of certain
> tides of change that threatened to erode the basis of social usage and
> ideology on which they had been erected through the passing of endless
> centuries.[157]

The list of tales given as Urard mac Coise's repertoire is perhaps of
more importance to modern scholars of Irish literature than it was to
the generations of *filid* who succeeded him. It is one of the two major
lists which have survived; they are usually designated as the *A* list and
the *B* list.[158] The former stands independent of any context, although
it has a preface and a colophon and has survived in two copies, the
earlier of which (LL 189b)[159] is found in a manuscript of the twelfth
century. There are also two minor lists which have a common source,
although neither is derived from the other. According to its preface,
list *A* should contain either 250 or perhaps rather 350 titles, but in
point of fact the earliest copy contains only 187 titles, the later 182.
Professor Mac Cana, who has published an excellent edition of these
lists, provides us with a sketch of the history of their development. To
begin with, there was a basic list of uncertain antiquity (list *O*):

> To this were added, probably in the tenth century, the several
> categories which were 'reckoned as *prímscéla*'. The resulting list, list *X*,
> may have received additional titles until such time as it was
> incorporated in *Airec Menman Uraird Maic Coise*. At that time it
> underwent certain changes to conform with its new context and
> thenceforth it pursued an independent course, perhaps acquiring
> further titles before the archetype of the extant manuscripts were
> written . . . Meanwhile, the parent list, list *X*, was preserved separately
> and in the course of time received many expansions . . . Its final form is
> our list A.[160]

Mac Cana argues convincingly that the *prímscéla*, i.e., the most
important tales, originally included all the tales in the list and that this
is the reason why additional tales had to be introduced with a brief
statement to the effect that 'these tales are (also) reckoned as
prímscéla'. Later, *prímscéla* was taken to mean 'principal tales', with
the result that the redactor of list *A* introduced the category of *fo-scéla*
'subsidiary tales', but as some of the tales in the category were not

subsidiary in any sense, he had to explain in what circumstances these *fo-scéla* were 'reckoned as *prímscéla*, and thereby originated the idea that they were reckoned so only for the four highest grades of *filid'*.[161] Urard mac Coise's list (list *B*) is introduced with a category called *gnáthscéla*, 'a miscellaneous collection of titles which quite obviously has been assembled by the compiler (or redactor) of *B*.'[162] These have been culled from two main sources. One of these is *Táin Bó Cúailnge*, which is included in the list along with some eleven of its episodes given under separate titles. The other is a list of the *remscéla* to the *Táin*, i.e., the subsidiary tales which were written around its main theme and which dealt in particular with the events leading up to the attack by Medb and Ailill of Connacht on Conchobar and Ulster.

After the pseudo-category of *gnáthscéla* in list *B* come the more easily recognizable categories: *tánai* ('cattle raids, drivings off'), *echtrai* ('expeditions, journeys, adventures'), *comperta* ('conceptions, begettings, procreations'), *catha* ('battles'), *togla* ('attacks, destructions'), *fessa* ('feasts, feastings'), *buili* or *baili* ('visions, frenzies'), *tochmarca* ('wooings, courtships'), *aithid* ('elopements'), *tomadmann* ('inundations'), *físi* ('visions'), *serca* ('love stories'), *slúaigid* or *slógid* ('hostings, military expeditions'), *tochomlada* ('settings forth, advancings, ?origins'), *oircne* (plunderings, murders').

The list in *A* is not unlike that in *B*. It has twelve categories: *togla*, *tána*, *tochmarca*, *catha*, *uatha* ('terrors, horrors'), *im(m)rama* ('sea voyages'), *aitte* ('violent deaths'), *fessa*, *forbaisi* or *forfess* ('beleaguerings, sieges'), *echtrai*, *aithid*, *airgne* or *oircne*.[163]

It should be emphasized that these lists are not to be taken as indexes, even incomplete ones, of the living repertoire of the *filid* at any particular time, but they do serve a very useful purpose in that the inclusion of the title of any tale is clear proof that the tale was known at the time the list was compiled.

The *ollam*, we are told, was expected to know 350 of these tales— 250 principal tales (*prímscéla*) and 100 secondary tales (*fo-scéla*)— and the *ánruth* (*ánrud*) was expected to know half that number; after them came the *clíi* with eighty, the *cana* with sixty, *doss* with fifty, *mac fuirmid* with forty, *fochlocon* with thirty, *drisac* with twenty, *taman* with ten, *oblairi* with seven. But one should not give too much weight to these figures.[164]

It is difficult to imagine what position was accorded these stories in the old native culture, but we sometimes catch a glimpse of the reverence accorded them, as when we read that among the three virtues accruing to anyone who listens to the *Táin Bó Cúailnge* is protection for a whole year.[165] This interesting fact becomes more significant when we remember that in India similar blessings and rewards were promised to those who heard the old tales of that culture.[166]

The *fili* who narrated these tales viewed them, no doubt, as true history; along with the genealogies and the lore of place-names they formed his historical inheritance, for he, like the Indian poet, was a historian by virtue of his office.[167] This fact illuminates the note found at the end of the list of tales in the Book of Leinster, a note translated by O'Curry as follows: 'He is no poet (i.e., *fili*) who does not synchronize and harmonize all the stories.'[168] Professor Mac Neill thought that it was little enough to ask an *ollam* to know 350 tales.[169] Until fairly recently, there were unlettered folk in the Gaeltacht who could duplicate that feat. It was therefore fair, according to Mac Neill, to believe that much more was expected of the *ollam*, and that probably included the ability to bring the stories into chronological harmony with one another. 'The essential qualification,' according to Mac Neill, 'was the capacity to "synchronize and harmonize all the stories," to give them a chronology and a correlation in other words, to weave them together into a web of ostensible history.' Unfortunately, there is little in the statement to warrant the O'Curry–Mac Neill interpretation, as Seán Mac Airt pointed out in his study. He suggested an emendation and the translation, 'he is no *fili* who does not preserve *coimgne* or all the stories,' adding that the phrase 'or all the stories' may not have been part of the original.[170] Unfortunately, the precise meaning of *coimgne* eludes us. Mac Airt would seem to favour in this context a legal meaning and suggested that 'the *fili*'s duty in preserving *coimgne* (and *scéla*) had perhaps its origin in his early legal functioning, knowledge of *coimgne* being essential for cases with an historical bearing.' For him,

> the *fili*'s main business was not the recital of tales, but first the exposition of them, for example from the genealogical point of view, to the noble classes . . . just as he might have been required to do at an earlier date in a law-suit. Secondly, he was expected to use them for the purpose of illustration . . . The kind of illustration meant is exactly that exemplified by the later bardic poets in their use of incidents from heroic tales.[171]

Mac Cana is not persuaded by Mac Airt's explanation of *coimgne*:

> Assuming that Meyer's derivation of the word *coimcne comgne*, from *com-* and *ecne* is the correct one (*Contribb.* 416, 443), the original meaning may have been something like 'knowledge held in common'

or 'comprehensive knowledge'. At all events, it seems probable that initially it had general reference to learned knowledge of the past, as narrated by those persons whose proper function it was to preserve it intact by the power of memory, and that only secondarily was it applied to the particular types of professional composition reflected in such knowledge.[172]

Up until now, there has been no mention of any activity practised by the *filid* that would remind us of the work of the learned poets in later times.[173] And apart from satires, no reference has been made to anything that would connect the *filid* with the *bardoi*, with whom the Greeks and Romans came into contact in Gaul.[174] But these two classes resembled one another in at least one other activity, namely, praise poetry. 'Among the Gauls,' says Diodorus Siculus (v, 31), writing about the middle of the first century before Christ, 'there are lyrical poets called *bardoi*.[175] They compose songs of praise to some and satires for others, and in their songs they are accompanied on a kind of harp.' The testimony of Posidonius is similar, and it is to him that we are indebted for this anecdote concerning the first *bardos* mentioned in history, a *bardos* of the second century before Christ. Louernios, a king of the Arverni in Gaul, once gave a great feast. One of the poets was unfortunate enough to arrive too late. Seeing the king departing in his war chariot, he ran alongside the vehicle and proclaimed a song of praise. The king liked the poem, and threw his purse to the poet. The latter 'picked it up and sang another song, saying that the very tracks made by his chariot on the earth gave gold and largesse to men.'[176]

This anecdote could have been related of a bard and his patron in either Ireland or Wales even as late as the Middle Ages, and there can be no doubt that it could have been related of them in both countries throughout the preceding centuries. It has been suggested that praise poetry was not one of the primary concerns of the *fili* and that he left it mostly to the *bard*, who, as we have seen, was only a minor figure in the Irish poetic hierarchy. Later, however, according to this view, the *fili* took upon himself the duties of the *bard* and relinquished his other duties with the result that most of the poems composed between 1250 and 1650 are eulogies.[177] Professor Gerard Murphy sums up at the end of his important article on 'Bards and Filidh':

> Under the stress of circumstances the filidh of the end of the twelfth century seem to have turned what had hitherto been a secondary function into a primary function, so that the once neglected praise-poems (originally doubtless considered typical only of bards, or of filidh assuming bardic functions) began to be preserved and held in honour.[178]

We should like to suggest that scholars have been too ready to assume that because the praise poet was called *bardos* among the Continental Celts he must have been the so-called *bard* in Ireland, and that because the *bard* was overshadowed by the *fili*, the essential function of the court poet, eulogy, must have been a minor one in early Ireland. We should remember that our knowledge of the continental *bardos* is at best fragmentary—the possibility must not be overlooked that originally he may have been the reciter, not the composer, of court poetry—and it must be noted that even in Wales it looked at one time as if the court poet would abandon the title *bardd* in favour of *pencerdd*. It is not impossible either that the learning and knowledge on which the early *filid* prided themselves, may have been given greater prominence than they had originally, partly because the *filid* inherited the functions of the druids, and partly because they had to compete with the ecclesiastical scholars, the *sapientes* mentioned in the Annals. Even Professor Gerard Murphy did not deny the evidence that some *filid* composed 'bardic poetry' in the early period, but their 'bardic poems' appeared to him to be too simple, too devoid of learning to be considered characteristic of their work. However, there can be no doubt that much of the early poetry produced in Ireland has been lost and much of the early court poetry may have been lost precisely because it was too learned, too recondite.

One name for a eulogy in Old Irish was *amra*. A poem called an *amra* and composed on Cú Roí has been preserved,[179] and the fact that the latter was a legendary figure does not deprive the composition of its value as an example of the genre. Another is the famous *Amra Choluim(b) Chille*,[180] probably the oldest poem to which a precise date can be given in the Irish language. Its language is difficult, perhaps intentionally so, and if the poem is typical of the work of the *filid* in this genre, it is no wonder if many an *amra* has been lost, and it would occasion no surprise to learn that there had been a powerful reaction against their obscurity.

Some fragments of early praise poems have been preserved in the grammatical tracts composed in the Middle Ages. In his collection of fragments of Old Irish poetry, *Bruchstücke der älteren Lyrik Irlands*,[181] Kuno Meyer lists 1–58 as praise poems (*Loblieder*), 59–88 as satires (*Spott und Schmählieder*), 89–131 as elegies (*Totenklagen*). Even if we disregard some of these as spurious or late productions, it is extremely unlikely that most of them fall into that category. And Meyer's division of these fragments is itself significant. The eulogy and the elegy are obviously two aspects of the same poetic function, and, although this is less obvious to modern eyes, the satire is yet another aspect. Professor Renou has shown that the Vedic root *śams* can denote an action designed to exercise a baneful effect, a fact reflected in the meaning of the Latin *cens-or, cens-us*,[182] and Professor Dumézil has made brilliant use of the story of Bres in the *Second Battle of Moytura* to show how the king who does not provide subsistence for his people ('Never did man or woman go from him drunk or happy') is constrasted with the king who provides abundance, and how the former is satirized and the latter eulogized.[183] After Cairpre Mac Etaine, the *fili* of the Túatha Dé Danann, had come to Bres, seeking hospitality, he was taken to a small dark room where there was no fire nor bath nor bed, and later he was sent three small dry cakes on a little dish. Naturally, when he got up the following morning the *fili* was not very pleased with Bres, already well-known for his niggardliness, and he uttered a satire:

> Without food speedily on a platter,
> Without a cow's milk whereon a calf thrives,
> Without a man's habitation after the staying of darkness
> Be that the luck of Bres mac Eladain.

And after that, 'there was nought but decay on Bres from that hour'.[184] This satire, traditionally the first to be uttered in Ireland, is obviously an incantation, a spell wrought to bring destruction on its victim.

The *fili* most famous (or infamous) in Irish literature for his satires and inordinate demands was Aithirne the Importunate. He is the central figure in 'The Siege of Howth' or, as it is called in Irish, *Forbais Etair*. After Aithirne had made a circuit of Leinster, the land of his enemies, he departed with thrice fifty wives whom he had extorted from the nobility by threatening to satirize them. But the Leinstermen pursued him. The Ulstermen who came to rescue him were routed in a great battle, and they and the *fili* had to retreat to the fortress of Howth.

> Nine watches were they in Howth without drink, without food, unless they drank the brine of the sea, or unless they devoured the clay, but seven hundred kine, in sooth, had Aithirne in the middle of the fort; and there was not a boy or man of Ulster who tasted their milk, but the milking was cast down the cliff, so that of the Ulstermen none might find out Aithirne's food to taste it. And the wounded men were brought to him, and he would not let a drop go into their mouths, so that they used to bleed to death alone. And the chiefs of Ulster used to

come to him entreating a drink for Conor [King Conchobar], and nought they got from him.[185]

We are left with the question, why should Aithirne throw the milk of 700 cattle over the cliff rather than let his comrades, dying or living, drink? Even allowing that he had a reputation for stinginess and inhospitality, and for the tendency of the storytellers to exaggerate, Aithirne's behaviour seems inexplicable. It becomes comprehensible at least in part, however, if we interpret his act of destroying the milk as some sort of ritualistic act to promote fertility and assume that his part in it was dictated by his role as a *fili*.[186]

It is interesting to note that the effects of satire could be wiped out by eulogy. Once, Aithirne the Importunate satirized the river Modarn, and she retaliated in anger by bursting her banks, thus forcing him to pronounce a eulogy, whereupon she receded to within her customary banks. 'That', we are told, 'is the praise which washes out satire'.[187]

Obviously, satire is the obverse of eulogy and both have their roots in the belief that words are magical agents, that they can hypostasize in the sense of creating a self-existent substance or person. Every primitive poet was to some extent a shaman or magician; in other words, he claimed the ability to exercise power over things by means of his poetry. In the beginning we are told God created heaven and earth, and He did so by means of His Word. Explaining the meaning of the Greek word κραίνων in the Homeric Hymn to Hermes, Benveniste writes, 'The god is singing of the origin of things and by his song the gods "are brought into existence". A bold metaphor, but one which is consistent with the role of poet who himself is a god. A poet causes to exist; things come to birth in his song.'[188]

The early court poet practised his art to instill into men those qualities which they and their society esteemed and desired above all else, the qualities which made them heroes and won for them abiding fame, courage, uprightness, effectiveness, the ability to make good one's word. Of course, these qualities were the gifts of the gods, but the poet in declaring that his patron had them was in a way forcing the hands of the gods: he made these qualities exist, or if they already existed, he made them stronger. In a sense, then, by affirming the courage and honour of his patron, he gave and confirmed that courage and honour, and in so doing he ensured his fame. The Welsh court poet Phylip Brydydd, who flourished in the thirteenth century and who told his patron 'I made fame for thee',[189] could have been translating the words of an Indo-European court poet. But whereas the Welsh poet was thinking primarily of the effect of his songs to his patron on his present and future audience, the Indo-European poet would have been thinking of the immediate effect of his songs on the patron he was eulogizing: they were creating or strengthening in him those qualities of mind and body which would produce those actions of which everyone would soon be talking.

There is reason to believe that some Indo-European peoples distinguished between the singers of praise to gods and the singers of praise to men. If the word for a priest among the Celts, *gutuater*, is correctly derived from a compound meaning 'father, i.e., master, of the invocation (to god)', the Celts would seem to have made that distinction. It may be that both the singer of praise to gods and the singer of praise to men could be designated originally by the name *bardos*, and that as *bardos* came increasingly to be used to describe the singer of praise to men, the singer of praise to gods, the *gutuater*, came increasingly to be designated by the word *drui*, with whom the *gutuater* had closer affinity.[190]

Be that as it may, the singing of praise to men probably originated in the singing of praise to gods. On the basis of parallels taken from the literatures of the Hindus and the Persians in the East and of the Romans and Scandinavians in the West, Professor F. R. Schröder has argued that two kinds of hymns were composed in Indo-European societies: one praising and glorifying a single mighty act of a god, the other celebrating a number of such acts. The first kind, according to Schröder, was sung to those remote deities who were far removed from men and their affairs, the second to those hero-deities who had taken an active part as saviours, dragon-slayers, etc. in those affairs.[191] To the second type of hymn he gives the name *Aufreihlied*, and one of his examples is the Virgilian praise song to Hercules (*Aeneid*, viii.287–303), which was based, apparently, on an earlier hymn. In the *Aufreihlied*, he finds with good reason the origin of the *Fürstenpreislied*.

In this connection, it is perhaps important to observe that poetry took over from religion not only this type of song but also, among other things, some of the most primitive stylistic characteristics of this and other types. Professor Jan Gonda[192] has seen an Indo-European, if not *the* Indo-European poetic *Stilform* in the carmen-alliteration style, so called because it is characteristic of the Latin *carmen*[193] or incantation, and so of the formulae of religious rites in Rome. Examples of it are not confined to Latin: they are also found in Greek, Vedic, Germanic, and Celtic.[194] Indeed, if we take its main characteristics to be on the one hand the recurrence or repetition of the same sound, and on the other a symmetry of expression in two or more member parallelisms, it has been the fundamental basis of Welsh and Irish poetics down to modern times.

To return to the *Fürstenpreislied*, the descendant of the *Aufreihlied*, Professor Dumézil has shown us in what circumstances the earliest songs of this type may have been sung.[195] Proceeding from the fact that among the ancient Hindus there were three modes of promotion to kingship, Dumézil analyses the one illustrated in the case of the primeval king Prthu into three acts, first designation by the gods, second, recognition by the wise men, third, acceptance by the people. In the consecration of the king, the essential part was his eulogy by the bards, the *sūtas*, and it is significant that as soon as Prthu is consecrated, he proceeds to shower gifts on the bards and the people, thus giving proof that the local earth-goddess is once again fertile and that he himself is truly *vrdidâtr* 'a giver of the means of subsistence'. As the title of this book, *Servius et la Fortune*, suggests, Dumézil has examined Roman as well as Hindu sources for this type of promotion to kingship and has found traces of it in the legend of Servius who, it will be remembered, was made king by the acclamation of the people and was honoured as the institutor of the census.[196]

The eulogy of the *sūtas* and the *Fürstenpreislied* cannot fail to call to mind the inauguration odes, i.e., the praise songs sung by Irish poets on the occasion of the inauguration of Irish kings and petty kings, although they contain genealogical and historical matter as well as eulogy. It seems that the inauguration rite was also the original *Sitz im Leben* of the composition of the Irish examples of the genre best known under the German name *Fürstenspiegel* or the Latin *Speculum Principum*, the genre which consists of advice or instruction to a ruler, prince or king.[197] Indeed, there is reason to believe that this genre first appeared in Ireland. A. D. Hellmann has edited a tract entitled *De duodecim abusivis saeculi*, which contains a section dealing with the *rex iniquus*, the antithesis of the Irish *firflaith* 'true ruler', and has expressed the belief that it was written in Ireland between 650 and 700 AD, because of some Irish features in the language and the content.[198]

That the genre existed in Irish there can be no doubt, for there are several examples of *teagasg riogh* under different names. The earliest example, dating from c. 700 AD, is *Audacht* (or *Auraiccept*) *Morainn* (*Audacht* = 'Testament', *Auraiccept* = *Airaiccecht* 'first instruction, primer' of Morann). The following quotation indicates the way adopted to advise the ruler and the character of the advice given:

> Tell him, it is through the justice of the ruler that plagues (and) great lightnings are kept from the people.
>
> It is through the justice of the ruler that he judges great tribes (and) great riches.
>
> It is through the justice of the ruler that he secures peace, tranquility, joy, ease, (and) comfort.
>
> It is through the justice of the ruler that he dispatches (great) battalions to the borders of hostile neighbours.
>
> It is through the justice of the ruler that every heir plants his house-post in his fair inheritance.
>
> It is through the justice of the ruler that abundances of great tree-fruit of the great wood are tasted.
>
> It is through the justice of the ruler that milk-yields of great cattle are maintained(?).
>
> It is through the justice of the ruler that there is abundance of every high, tall corn.
>
> It is through the justice of the ruler that abundance of fish swim in streams.[199]

Fergus Kelly, whose translation we have quoted, reminds us that Keating in his *History of Ireland*, iii, 10 (ITS IX) says that a *Teagasg Riogh* was read out at the inauguration ceremony of the king 'from the coming of Patrick . . . to the Norman invasion'. No direct evidence of this has been produced from Old Irish sources, but in a description of the inauguration of Alexander III of Scotland in the thirteenth century, we are informed that 'The ceremony was performed by the bishop of St Andrews, who girded the king with a military belt. He then explained in Latin, and afterwards in Gaelic, the laws and oaths relating to the king'.[200] It should be noted that it is a bishop who gives instructions to the prince in this case, and in her study of the prose tract on 'The Inauguration of O'Conor' Katharine Simms shows that it was Torna Ó Maoil Chonaire, the official *senchaidh* or historian of Ó Conor (Ó Conchobhair), who claims the authorship of the inauguration ode contained in the text; that he was not a trained *fili* is borne out by his curious choice of the loose rhyming system of *óglachas* and the *ae freislighe* metre for such an elaborate ceremonial ode.[201] However, as we have shown, the court historians were an offshoot of the *filid* order, and we should not be surprised that occasionally the historians performed the same function as a *fili* at an inauguration.

At the inauguration of the Ó Dubhda, the poet Mac Firbis had an important part to play:

> The privilege of the first drink (at all assemblies) was given to *O'Caomhain* by O'Dowda, and *O'Caomhain* was not to drink until he first presented it (the drink) to the poet, that is, to Mac Firbis; also the arms and battle steed of O'Dowda, after his proclamation, were given to *O'Caomhain*, and the arms and dress of *O'Caomhain* to Mac Firbis, and it is not competent ever to call him the O'Dowda, until *O'Caomhain* and Mac Firbis have first called the name, and until Mac Firbis carries the body of the wand over O'Dowda; and every clergyman, and every representative of the church, and every bishop, and every chief of a territory present, all are to pronounce the name after *O'Caomhain* and Mac Firbis.[202]

The wand referred to is the white rod of sovereignty given in token of sovereignty in the usual form of inauguration. Mac Firbis was obviously *ollamh* to Ó Dubhda. However, we are not to assume that Mac Firbis was the only *fili* present. Inauguration was the occasion on which other *filid* would wish to press their claims for attention on the new chieftain, the occasion for the writing of an inauguration ode.

The original importance of the *teagasg riogh* or *speculum principum* lay in two beliefs: namely, that there was a correlation between the prosperity of a country and the goodness or righteousness of its king, and in the 'Act of Truth' found in Irish as well as in Hindu tradition and defined by the Hindus as the belief that the 'truth was the highest power, the ultimate cause of all being'.[203] If we take it 'that in many instances the basis of the Act of Truth is the fulfilment of one's station in life,' that the statement of a king's performance of his duty is a way and more than a way to the actual performance, we can easily understand why the recital of such a composition as *Audacht Morainn* was as important as the recital of eulogy to the success of a new king in his office and to the prosperity of his newly acquired kingdom.

It is in the Archilogic period that the Chadwicks would place praise poetry and elegies,[204] but it seems probable that both genres are much older than they thought. Be that as it may, apart from these there is very little to represent that period in the early literature of Ireland. Personal poetry like that found in the corresponding period of Greek literature does not occur in Ireland until the influence of Christianity began to affect the popular temperament.

One of the most famous Irish panegyrics is the poem to the sword of Cerball, king of Leinster (*c*. AD 885–909),[205] where the victories of the king and his ancestors are celebrated. The tone of the poem is established in the first stanza:

> O swinging sword of Carroll hail!
> Often the shuttle of the war,
> Often sustaining fight,
> Splitting the necks of kings.

Apparently it was composed shortly after the death of Cerball, and is attributed to his chief *fili*, Dallán mac Móire. The composition of panegyrics like this was certainly part of the work of the *fili*, and one of the ways in which he was expected to serve his king or lord. It is obvious that his work served a social function.

The same thing may be said about the 'inciting' poems, an example of which can be found in the story of Cellachán,[206] in the poem that urges the warriors of Munster to attack Limerick, which was in possession of the Vikings:

> Come to Limerick of the ships, children of Eogan, men of great feats.
> About the gentle Cellachán come to Limerick of the buttressed rocks.

Professor Dillon has drawn attention to the similarity between the poetic compositions of the *filid* and those of the royal bards of the Hindus: 'In form and temper, in purpose, in authorship these Irish encomiums resemble those in the Gupta inscriptions, and it is safe to say that they echo the songs of the Gaulish bards described by Posidonius and Diodorus Siculus.'[207] If the custom of the Irish and Indian kings of maintaining poets to record their activities and sing their praise in poetry is an old custom stemming from Indo-European times, then the *fili* represents not only the oldest literary traditions of Ireland but those of Europe as well.

Notes

1 H. M. Chadwick, *The Heroic Age* (Cambridge, 1926); H. M. and N. K. Chadwick, *The Growth of Literature*, I (Cambridge, 1932), II (1936), III (1940), henceforth GL; G. Murphy, *Saga and Myth in Ancient Ireland* (Dublin, 1955).
2 GL, III, 748.

3 Cúailnge, i.e., Cooley, in Co. Louth. There is a parish of Cooley, at the east end of which is Cooley Point.

4 See GL I, 16f.; G. Murphy, 'St Patrick and the Civilising of Ireland', *Irish Ecclesiastical Record*, v Series, 79 (1953), 194–204; Proinsias Mac Cana, 'Christianisme et Paganisme dans l'Irland ancienne', in Proinsias Mac Cana and Michel Meslin, edd., *Rencontres de Religions* (Paris, 1986), pp. 57–74; and on St Patrick and his influence, see Ludwig Bieler, *St Patrick and the Coming of Christianity* (A History of Irish Catholicism, ed. P. J. Corish, vol. 1) (Dublin and Melbourne, 1967); D. A. Binchy, 'Patrick and His Biographers', SH, 2 (1962), 7–173; R. P. C. Hanson, *Saint Patrick. His Origins and Career* (Oxford, 1968), and the bibliography there.

5 *The Oldest Irish Tradition: A Window on the Iron Age* (Cambridge, 1964).

6 See the remarks by Proinsias Mac Cana in 'Conservation and Innovation in Early Celtic Literature', ÉC 13 (1972), 61–118, esp. 89.

7 R. Thurneysen, *Scéla Mucce Meic Dathó* (Dublin, 1935), pp. 15–16.

8 Op. cit., p. 16. Dr Kim R. McKone gives a fine analysis of the structure of SMMD in P. Ó Fiannachta, ed., *Ár Scéalaíocht, Léachtaí Cholm Cille* 14 (1983), 5–37.

9 E. Windisch, *Die altirische Heldensage Táin Bó Cúalnge* (Leipzig, 1905); J. Strachan and J. G. O'Keeffe, *The Táin Bó Cúailnge from the Yellow Book of Lecan* (Suppl. to Ériu, 1–3, 6 1904–12); C. O'Rahilly, *The Táin Bó Cúalnge from the Book of Leinster* (ITS XLIX) (Dublin, 1967, rpr. 1970); *The Stowe Version of the TBC* (Dublin, 1961); and *TBC Recension I* (Dublin, 1976). O'Rahilly's translations are accurate and eminently readable, but for the general reader perhaps the best translation is that of Thomas Kinsella, *The Tain* (Oxford U. P., 1970, rpr. 1972, 1974).

10 Kathleen Hughes, *Early Christian Ireland* (London, 1972), p. 177.

11 The use of the war chariot, taking of heads, and challenging to single combat were all customary among the Gauls. See J. J. Tierney, 'The Celtic Ethnography of Posidonius', PRIA, 60 (1960), 189ff.; K. H. Jackson, *The Oldest Irish Tradition*, pp. 17, 19, 33, *et passim*; G. Dottin, *Manuel pour servir l'étude de l'antiquité celtique* (Paris, 1915), pp. 262, 270, 275. For Irish society in general, see K. H. Jackson, op. cit., the introduction to Windisch's edition of TBC, and W. Ridgeway, 'The Date of the First Shaping of the Cuchulainn Saga', PBA, 2 (1905), 135–68. M. E. Dobbs, *Sidelights on the Táin Age and Other Studies* (Dundalk, 1917) is still valuable. There may be a reference to the taking of heads in the series of Welsh stanzas *Pen Urien* ('The Head of Urien') in *Canu Llywarch Hen*, where a kinsman, we are led to believe, has cut off the head of a corpse before the enemy could get to it; see CLIH, III, 7–19; PLIH, pp. 100–5.

12 M. Dillon, *Early Irish Society* (Dublin, 1954, 1959), esp. D. A. Binchy, 'Secular Institutions', pp. 52–65, and the legal glossary in D. A. Binchy, ed., *Crith Gablach* (Dublin, 1941), also E. Mac Neill, *Early Irish Laws and Institutions* (Dublin, 1933.)

13 O'Donovan, *The Annals of Ireland . . . The Four Masters* (Dublin, 1848–51; henceforth FM), I, 218, ad ann. 594, n.*h*; W. M. Hennessy, *Annals of Ulster* (Dublin, 1887), I, 77, ad ann. 597; C. Plummer, *Lives of Irish*

Saints (Dublin, 1922), II, 223, §§139–41 = *Vitae Sanctorum Hiberniae* (Dublin, 1910), II, 161, lv; A. Maniet, 'Cath Belaig Dúin Bolc', *Éigse*, 7 (1953), 95–111.

14 See Myles Dillon, *The Cycles of the Kings* (Oxford, 1946), pp. 99–102, and the footnote on p. 99 for the date of the battle. P. Ó Riain, ed., *Cath Almaine* (Dublin, 1978), p. xxxvi, argues 'that we have to do in *Cath Almaine* with two recensions; *B*, which was composed in the tenth century in an annalistic milieu, perhaps that of Clonmacnoise—and *DF*, a modified version of *B*, redacted in the early twelfth century, again in an annalistic milieu, and very probably at the monastery of Lismore.' Cf. Brian Ó Cuív, 'Literary Creation and Historical Tradition', PBA 49 (1963) 243.

15 The latest historical saga is said to be *Airec Menman Uraird maic Coise* ('The Stratagem of Urard mac Coise'). Domnall mac Muirchertaigh (d. 980) plays a part in it, but the tale does not really belong to the cycles of the kings of Ireland. Although Brian Bórumha (d. 1014) is mentioned in one tale, there is no cycle of tales connected with his name. See Dillon, op. cit., pp. 115, 117.

16 On the argument as to the existence of one or two Patricks who were missionaries to Ireland, see T. F. O'Rahilly, *The Two Patricks* (Dublin, 1942); James Carney, *Studies in Irish Literature and History* (Dublin, 1955), ch. 9; idem, *The Problem of St Patrick* (Dublin, 1961); K. Mulchrone, *Comhar* (Márta, 1950), 16–18; and the magisterial contribution of D. A. Binchy, 'Patrick and His Biographers: Ancient and Modern', SH, 2 (1962), 7–173.

17 Ancient Ireland was divided into five provinces (Ir. *coiced* 'fifth'). Three of them were named from the people who inhabited them: *Ulaid* (Ulster, but the territory of modern Ulster is greater than that of the early historical district and less than that of the sagas), *Laigin* (Leinster), *Connachta* (Connacht). The two other provinces were *Mumu* (Munster) and *Mide* (Meath), but in the Christian era, *Mide* disappears from the list and *Mumu* is counted as two provinces, namely *Urmumu* (East Munster, i.e., Ormond) and *Desmumu* (South Munster, i.e., Desmond). See R. Thurneysen, *Die irische Helden- und Königsage* I (Halle, 1921), 75–76; E. Mac Neill, *Phases of Irish History* (Dublin, 1937), 102–13; T. F. O'Rahilly, EIHM, 171–83.

18 The principal stories of the Ulster Cycle are *Táin Bó Cúailnge* ('The Cattle Raid of Cooley'; *táin bó* = 'a cattle-reaving raid'; D. Greene, in M. Dillon, ed., *Irish Sagas*, Dublin, 1959, raises the question of why the *Táin* is not called *Táin Bó gCúailnge*—that is, where *bó* is genitive plural—and suggests that *bó* should be given the meaning 'bull' here and that the title originally meant 'The Driving of the Bull of Cooley'); *Longes mac n-Uislenn* ('The Exile of the Sons of Uisliu'); *Aided Oenfir Aife* ('The Tragic Death of the Only Son of Aife'); *Fled Bricrenn* ('Bricriu's Feast'); *Tochmarc Emire* ('The Wooing of Emer') among others. For a discussion of these, see M. Dillon, *Early Irish Literature* (Chicago, 1948), henceforth EIL, pp. 1–31.

19 Eoin Mac Neill, *Celtic Ireland* (Dublin, 1921), p. 13f.

20 From LL version, ed., C. O'Rahilly, ll. 1–11. But this scene is not in the

LU version.
21 On this disability, see V. Hull, 'Noinden Ulad: The Debility of the Ulstermen', *Celtica*, 8 (1968), 1–42; 'Ces Ulad: The Affliction of the Ulstermen', ZCP, 29 (1962–4), 304–14; Tomás Ó Broin, 'What is the Debility of the Ulstermen?', *Éigse*, 10 (1961–3), 286–99; 'The Word *Noinden*', *Éigse*, 13 (1969–70), 165–76; C. O'Rahilly, 'Cess Naíden', *Éigse* 15 (1973–74), 252; J. F. Killeen, 'The Debility of the Ulstermen—a Suggestion', ZCP, 33 (1974), 81–86.
22 Ed. and transl. Tomás Ó Cathasaigh, *The Heroic Biography of Cormac Mac Airt* (Dublin, 1977). The other important tales belonging to the Historical Cycle are *Orgain Denna Ríg* ('The Destruction of Dind Ríg'; see T. Ó Concheanainn, *Celtica*, 18 (1986), 12–33), *Cath Maige Mucrama* ('The Battle of Mag Mucrama'; see M. O'Daly, *Cath Maige Mucrama. The Battle of Mucrama*, Dublin, 1975), *Esnada Tige Buchet* ('The Melodies of the House of Buchet'), *Scél Baili Binnbérlaig* ('The Tale of Baile of the Clear Melodious Voice'), *Aided Maele Fothartaig Maic Rónáin* ('The Tragic Death of Mael Fothartaig son of Rónán'), *Buile Shuibne* ('The Frenzy of Suibne'). As to the last of these, P. Ó Riain argues that the text was constructed in the twelfth century in a monastic milieu, using poems of different dates and a list of saints' genealogies; see 'The Materials and Provenance of "Buile Shuibhne" ', *Éigse*, 15 (1973–4), 173–88. Myles Dillon discusses these tales in EIL, pp. 73–100 and *The Cycles of the Kings*.
23 GL, I, 96f. The most important text in the so-called 'Mythological Cycle' which deserves more attention than we have been able to give, is *Cath Maige Tured. The Second Battle of Mag Tuired*, ed. Elizabeth A. Gray (ITS London, 1982 [1983]). For analysis, see Gray's articles in *Éigse*, 18 (1980–81), 183–209; 19 (1982–83), 1–35, 230–62; cf. G. Murphy's notes in *Éigse* 7 (1953–5), 191–8, 204. For a study of its mythology, see G. Lehmacher, 'Die zweite Schlacht von Mag Tured und die keltische Götterlehre', *Anthropos* 26 (1931), 435–59.
24 W. Reeves, ed., *The Life of St Columba . . . by Adamnan* (Dublin, 1857); J. T. Fowler, ed., *Adamnani Vita S. Columbae* (Dublin, 1894); both in large part superseded by A. O. and M. O. Anderson, edd., *Adomnan's Life of Columba* (London, 1961). For the background to the Life, see Máire Herbert, *Iona, Kells and Derry* (Oxford, 1988).
25 W. Stokes, *The Colloquy of the Two Sages (Immacallam in dá thuarad)*, RC, 26 (1905), 4–64; rprt., Paris, 1905.
26 Ed. Stokes, *Irische Texte*, 3 (Leipzig, 1891), 183–229, 283.
27 See especially, B. K. Martin, 'Old Irish Literature and European Antiquity', in B. K. Martin and S. T. Knight, *Aspects of Celtic Literature* (Sydney U.P., 1970).
28 GL, I, 69f.
29 M. Dillon, *Lebor na Cert* (Dublin, 1962 [= ITS XLVI]), p. 158.
30 D. A. Binchy, *Celtic and Anglo-Saxon Kingship* (Oxford, 1970), p. 40; 'The Fair of Tailtiu and the Feast of Tara', *Ériu*, 18 (1958), 113–38.
31 *Topographia Hibernica*, ed. J. Dimock (Rolls Series, London, 1867), p. 169.
32 GL, I, 70.
33 It appears that *Immram Snédgusa ocus Maic Riagla* ('The Voyage of

Snédgus and Mac Riagla') is the only extant example of a tale which was originally all in verse being later retold in prose. See Thurneysen, *Zwei Versionen d. mittelirischen Legende von Snedgus u. Mac Riagla* (Halle, 1904), Corrigenda, ZCP, 5 (1904–5), 418, 6 (1907–8), 234; van Hamel, *Immrama* (Dublin, 1941), 78; RC, 9 (1888), 14; 26 (1905), 132; Bergin, Marstrander, *Miscellany Presented to Kuno Meyer* (Halle, 1912), p. 307.

34 E. Windisch, TBC, xlviii-xlix; also *Geschichte der Sanskritphilologie* (Strassburg, 1920), II, 404, and E. Oldenberg, *Die Literatur des alten Indien* (Stuttgart, 1903), 45; J. Vendryes, 'Sur un caractère traditionnel de la poésie celtique', *Choix d'études linguistiques et celtiques* (Paris, 1952), pp. 225–32. Some scholars believe that heroic prose narrative is always preceded by narrative in verse. See Jan de Vries, *Heroic Song and Heroic Legend* (London, 1963), 92; C. M. Bowra, *Heroic Poetry* (London, 1964), pp. 15–16; H. M. Chadwick, *Heroic Age*, pp. 94–6; GL, III, 716. Felix Genzmer, 'Vorzeitsaga und Heldenlied' in Karl Hauck, ed., *Zur germanisch-deutschen Heldensage* (Bad Homburg vor der Hohe, 1961), pp. 102–37, argues that a saga form of prose and verse must have existed at a very early date in the Germanic literary tradition.

35 I. Williams, 'The Poems of Llywarch Hen', PBA (Rhŷs Memorial Lecture), 18 (1932); CLlH, xxxvii ff.; *Lectures on Early Welsh Poetry* (Dublin, 1944), p. 35ff. An alternative view is advanced in PLlH.

36 K. Meyer, *Liadain and Cuirithir: An Irish Love-Story of the Ninth Century* (London, 1902).

37 D. Greene, and F. O'Connor, *A Golden Treasury of Irish Poetry 600–1200* (London, 1967), p. 74.

38 For 'The Irish Hypothesis', see T. M. Andersson, *The Problem of Icelandic Saga Origins* (New Haven, London, 1964), pp. 56–61.

39 'Indo-European Metrics and Archaic Irish Verse', *Celtica*, 6 (1963), 194–249, and see p. 79, below. For recent work on Welsh metrics, see Kathryn Klar, Brendan O Hehir, and Eve Sweetser, 'Welsh Poetics in the Indo-European Tradition', SC, 18/19 (1983–4), 30–51, and the articles by Sweetser and Marged Haycock in Brynley F. Roberts, ed., *Early Welsh Poetry* (Aberystwyth, 1988), pp. 139–77.

40 P. Mac Cana, 'On the Use of the Term *Retoiric*', *Celtica*, 7 (1966), 65–90.

41 R. Thurneysen, *Scéla Mucce Meic Dathó*, p. 14.

42 *Cycles of the Kings*, p. 118; cf. GL, I, 179.

43 EIHM, pp. 283–85.

44 Ibid., pp. 269–71; the author cites the opinions of other scholars and discusses them. K. H. Jackson, *The Oldest Irish Tradition*, makes no claim that the characters are historical but argues that the Ulster Cycle depicts a real, not a mythical, society. In *The Celtic Realms* (London, 1967), Dillon disagreed with his co-author, N. K. Chadwick, who regarded Medb as the reflection of a queen who once ruled Cruachan.

45 *The Heroic Biography of Cormac Mac Airt* (Dublin, 1977).

46 GL, I, 606. The form *Veleda*, as it stands, cannot be linked to the Irish and Welsh forms. Cf. Thurneysen on *fili*, gen. *filed*, and the old gen. *Velitas* which occurs in an Ogam inscription, *Heldensage*, I, 66, n.4, and GOI, p. 479.

47 RC, 26 (1905), 50, §272.

48 GL, I, 613. In the oldest version she is a Connacht woman, and she is said to have studied *filidecht* in Britain, but in the *Book of Leinster* she is said to be a resident of the *sid* of Cruachain, i.e., she is one of the Túatha Dé Danann.

49 *Laws* (= *Ancient Laws of Ireland, I–VI, Dublin, 1865–1901*), III, 30. cf. Mac Neill, PRIA, 36 (1922), sec. c, 173, n.2. There is a new and far superior edition of the Laws, D.A. Binchy, *Corpus Iuris Hibernici*;i–vi (Dublin 1978), but as there is no translation perhaps reference to the first edition will be more useful to the general reader. To find the old text in the new edition, see 'Concordance of Published Texts', xxiii–xxviii, 'The Introductory Matter.'

50 Cf. GL, I, 613.

51 For a discussion of the druids and their activities, see GL, I, 607ff.; T. D. Kendrick, *The Druids* (London, 1927); J. Zwicker, *Fontes Historiae Religionis Celticae* in *Fontes Historiae Religionum ex Autoribus Graecis et Latinis Collectos*, v, I (Berlin, 1934), II–III (Bonn 1935–6); N.K. Chadwick, *The Druids* (Cardiff, 1966); S. Piggott, *The Druids* (London, 1968); J. J. Tierney, art. cit., n. 11 and 52.

52 The relevant Greek and Roman texts have been ed. and trans. in J. J. Tierney's exellent study of 'The Celtic Ethnography of Posidonius', PRIA, 60 (1960), Sec. C, No. 5, 189–275.

53 H. Pedersen, *Vergleichende Grammatik der keltischen Sprachen* (Göttingen, 1909), I, 408.

54 Cf. GL, I, 610. In *Celtic Realms*, N. K. Chadwick would have us believe that the druids were not priests: see preface.

55 *Laws*, V, 90 (the meaning of *nemid*, sg. *neimed*, here is 'persons or class of persons possessing legal status or privileges.' See DIL, s.v. *neimed*).

56 *Laws*, V, 14.

57 Cf. Welsh *dryw*, J. Lloyd-Jones, *Geirfa Barddoniaeth Gynnar Gymraeg*, 394a, and *derwydd*, 313b, and GPC, s.v.

58 E. Mac Neill, *Early Irish Laws and Institutions* (London, 1935), p. 82.

59 Caesar says of the *druides*, 'magnum ibi numerum versuum ediscere dicuntur', *De Bello Gallico*, vi, 14.

60 Cf. Mac Neill, op. cit., 104.

61 See the Introduction to Dillon, *Lebor na Cert*. On the archaism of the Irish Law Tracts see D. A. Binchy, 'The Linguistic and Historical Value of the Irish Law Tracts', PBA, 29 (1943), 195–227; idem, 'Ancient Irish Law', *The Irish Jurist* , 1 N.S., pt. 1 (1966); idem, 'Linguistic and Legal Archaisms in the Celtic Law-Books', *Transactions of the Philological Society* (1959), 14–44. On early Irish law see Fergus Kelly, *A Guide to Early Irish Law* (Dublin, 1988).

62 O'Donovan, *Leabhar na gCeart* (Dublin, 1847), 183.

63 BBCS, 11 (1944), 138–40 (note on the etymology of the word by Professor D. M. Jones). Professor E. Hamp does not accept the etymology proposed: see SC, 10/11 (1975–6), 154, n.4. Wolfgang Meid, *Dichter und Dichtkunst in indogermanischer Zeit* (Innsbruck, 1978), 18, 24 n.55, derives Celt. *bardos* from *g^wrdhos*: IE root *g^wer(ə)* : *g^wrdhos*, 'das vielleicht eine Hypostase von *g^wr-dh*, lobsetzen ist.'

64 *The Book of Ballymote*, 296, 16; Thurneysen, *Mittelirische Verslehren*

(*Irische Texte*, 3), 107.
65 O'Donovan, op. cit., 183.
66 *Laws*, IV, 360.
67 Ibid., I, 18.
68 In the introduction to Dubhaltach Mac Firbisigh's *Genealogical Tracts*, I, ed., J. Ó Raithbheartaigh, (Dublin, 1932), 18, p. 10, it is expressly stated that one cannot be an exponent of the law without being a historian.
69 Cf. below on *The Colloquy of the Two Sages*, and James F. Kenney, *Sources for the Early History of Ireland: I, Ecclesiastical* (NY, 1929), 2.
70 Dillon, 'The Archaism of Irish Tradition', PBA (Rhŷs Memorial Lecture), 33 (1947), 18.
71 'Les Correspondances de vocabulaire entre l'indo-iranien et l'italoceltique', *Mémoires de la Société de Linguistique de Paris*, 20 (1918), 165–85, esp. 275. Vendryes was following in the footsteps of other philologists, notably P. Kretschmer, *Einleitung in die Geschichte der griechischen Sprache* (Göttingen, 1896), 125ff.
72 'Amra Choluimb Chille', RC, 20 (1899), 38f; LU 11. But cf. *The Book of Ballymote*, 332, where it is said that 24 is the number in the retinue of an *ollam*. For the latest discussion of the grades of bards, see *Uraicecht na Ríar. The Poetic Grades in Early Irish Law*, ed. by Liam Breatnach (Dublin, 1987); it includes texts on the grades of *filid* and bards other than *Uraicecht na Ríar* as well as new information about them and their contents, about patronage and appointment and about bardic families.
73 RC, 26 (1905), 12f.; ('The Colloquy of the Two Sages' §8). There are other points of correspondence between the Irish *ollam* and the Welsh *pencerdd*.
74 See DIL s.v. *tuigen*.
75 Binchy, in M. Dillon, *Early Irish Society*, p. 61.
76 Ibid.
77 RC, 26, 2, 3. Cf. E. O'Curry, MS. Materials (Dublin, 1861), p. 383.
78 Thurneysen, *Mittelirische Verslehren*, 24 (cf. 4), 108.
79 O'Curry, *Manners and Customs of the Ancient Irish* (London, New York, Dublin, 1873), II, 8.
80 Cf. Thurneysen, op. cit., 29ff., 110ff.
81 Ibid., 117, 119, and the discussion by N. K. Chadwick, *Scottish Gaelic Studies*, 4 (1935), 103–4. Cf. also E. Hull, *A Textbook of Irish Literature* I (Dublin, 1906), 190ff.
82 Reeves, *The Life of St. Columba*, p. 137.
83 Cf. Thurneysen, op. cit., 115, 116.
84 Tomás Ó Fiaich in T. W. Moody and F. X. Martin, *The Course of Irish History* (Cork, 1967), p. 61.
85 E.g., the payment for a *dechnad* and a *sétnad* was five milch cows, for an *oll* (*bairdne*), two milch cows and a two-year-old cow; Thurneysen, op. cit., p. 109.
86 Ibid., pp. 107, 109.
87 'The Battle of Howth', ed. Stokes, RC, 8 (1887), 47ff. Cf. O'Curry, *MS. Materials*, 267. For an explanation of this incident, see Dillon, 'The Archaism of Irish Tradition', 4.
88 M. Joynt, *Tromdámh Guaire* (Dublin, 1941). There is an earlier edition

by Owen Connellan, *Imtheacht na Tromdháimhe, Trans. Oss. Soc.*, 5 (1860).

89 Now The Mullagh or Daisy Hill, adjacent to Newtownlimavaddy, Co. Derry. On the historicity of the Convention of Druim Cetta see John Bannerman, *Studies on the History of Dalriada* (Edinburgh, London, 1974), pp. 157ff; P. Mac Cana, 'Regnum and Sacerdotium', PBA, 65 (1979), 444–79, esp. 460ff. For the fullest account of the convention, that in MS. Rawlinson B 502, see W. Stokes, 'The Bodleian Amra Choluimb Chille', RC 20 (1899), 31–55, 132–83, 248–89; RC 21 (1900), 133–6.

90 This is the date generally accepted, although AU gives 573, and AC 587. See Reeves, *The Life of St. Columba*, p. 37, n. b.

91 Thurneysen was in favour of accepting this tradition (ZCP, 20 [1936], 373). Cf. W. D. Simpson, *The Historical Saint Columba* (Aberdeen, 1927), pp. 43, 44.

92 Colgan, *Acta Sanctorum Hiberniae* (Photographic Reprod., D, 1948), XXIX Januarii. See also O'Connell, *The Schools and Scholars of Breiffne* (Dublin, 1942), pp. 1–13.

93 Adamnán refers to Druim Cetta (Dorsum Cette) three times, but he does not mention this convention: Reeves, *The Life of St Columba*, pp. 37, 91, 113.

94 Keating, *The History of Ireland* (ITS IV, VIII–IX, XV, London, 1902, 1908, 1914), III, 94. Cf. O'Curry, *Manners and Customs*, II, 77ff.

95 W. Stokes, 'The Bodleian Amra Choluimb Chille', RC, 20 (1899), 31–5, 132–83, 248–89, 400–37; 21 (1900), 133–6; O'Beirne Crowe, *The Amra Choluim Chilli of Dallan Forgaill* (Dublin, 1871). K. Meyer, 'Miscellanea Hibernica', *University of Illinois Studies*, 2 (1916), 25, is inclined to agree with Zimmer and accept the traditional date, 'pending a minute linguistic investigation'. Cf. D. Binchy, 'The Background of Early Irish Literature', SH, 1 (1961), 18, who quotes Thurneysen that the *amra* 'can with certainty be ascribed to the time it says it was composed, namely the death of St. Columcille in the year 597', and V. Hull, 'On Amra Choluim Chille', ZCP, 28 (1961), 242–51. The *Amra* is not the only genuinely old poem addressed to Colum Cille. Professor Fergus Kelly has edited a poem probably composed within a hundred years of the saint's death and probably by Bec(c)án mac Luigdech; see *Ériu*, 24 (1973), 1–34.

96 Colgan, loc. cit., J. Travis, 'Elegies Attributed to Dallan Forgaill', *Speculum*, 19 (1944), 89–103, an article which, although partly outmoded, deserves to be read.

97 GL, I, 469–70.

98 E. Knott, 'Why Mongán was deprived of Noble Issue', *Ériu*, 8 (1916), 155ff. See also O'Curry, *Manners and Customs*, II, 85. Cf. the story about Forgoll and Mongán in Meyer and Nutt, *The Voyage of Bran* (London, 1897), I, 45ff. See also D. Hyde, *A Literary History of Ireland* (London, 1901), pp. 410–411.

99 M. Joynt, *Tromdámh Guaire*, i. They are different persons in the introduction to 'Amra Choluimb Chille' (RC 20, 42, 18), but Keating (*History of Ireland*, III, 95) says that Eochaidh Éigeas and Dallán Forgaill are one and the same. For *Eochu/Eochaid*, see *Ériu*, 11 (1932), 140ff.

100 Meyer and Nutt, op. cit., I, 17–29.
101 Thurneysen, *Heldensage*, I, 15ff; *Zu irischen Handschriften und Literaturdenkmälern* (Berlin, 1912), I, 23ff.
102 Cf. K. Meyer, *Selections from Ancient Irish Poetry* (London, 1911), p. 111. But see now Séamus Mac Mathúna, *Immram Brain: Bran's Journey to the Land of Women* (Tübingen, 1985), on the date to be ascribed to the text.
103 Meyer and Nutt, op. cit., I, 45ff.
104 GL I, 469f. Cf. the remarks made by J. Carney, *Studies in Irish Literature and History*, pp. 280ff.
105 Carney, op. cit., p. 282, 286.
106 'Mongán Mac Fiachna and *Immram Brain*', *Ériu*, 23 (1972), 102–42, p. 122; 'On the 'Prehistory' of *Immram Brain*', *Ériu*, 26 (1974), 33–52; 'The Sinless Otherworld of *Immram Brain*', *Ériu*, 27 (1976), 95–115.
107 *Ériu*, 23 (1972), 138.
108 *Thesaurus Palaeohibernicus*, ed. W. Stokes and J. Strachan (Cambridge, 1903), II, 307–8.
109 J. O'Donovan, W. Stokes, *Cormac's Glossary* (Calcutta, 1868), pp. 94–5; W. Stokes, *Three Irish Glossaries* (London, 1862), p. 25; Meyer, *Archaeological Review*, I (1888), 303n., *Sanas Cormaic (Anecdota from Irish MSS.*, IV, Halle, 1912), no. 756. See also O'Rahilly, EIHM, pp. 323, 339f; Thurneysen, ZCP, 19 (1933), 163f.; N. K. Chadwick, 'Imbas Forosnai', *Scottish Gaelic Studies*, 4 (1935), 97–135; P. K. Ford, 'The Well of Nechtan and *La Gloire Lumineuse*' in Larsen, Gerald, ed., *Myth in Indo-European Antiquity* (Berkeley, 1974), pp. 67–74. Cf. Christian-J. Guyonvarc'h, 'Moyen-irlandais *imbas forosnai* "la grande science qui éclaire" ', *Ogam*, 19 (1967), 266–7.
110 According to O'Rahilly, op. cit., 337–9, who quotes earlier opinions, the meaning of *teinm laeda* is 'the chewing (or breaking open) of the pith'; see now Ford, op. cit., and also Christian-J. Guyonvarc'h, 'Moyen-irlandais *teinm laegda* "illumination du chant" ', *Ogam* 19 (1967), 267.
111 EIHM, pp. 323–24; Thurneysen, *Heldensage*, I, 421, 'bull-sleep'; O'Curry, *Manners and Customs*, II, 199; O. Bergin, *Irish Bardic Poetry*, ed., D. Greene, F. Kelly (Dublin, 1970), p. 10.
112 Keating, *The History of Ireland*, II, 348–50. It should be remembered that Brutus lies down on the skin of an old hind and falls asleep, whereupon the goddess Diana prophesies to him; H. Lewis, *Brut Dingestow* (Cardiff, 1942), p. 14; Geoffrey of Monmouth, *Historia Regum Britanniae*, ed. and trans. Lewis Thorpe (Harmondsworth, 1966), i, 11 (p. 65).
113 O'Curry, *MS. Materials*, p. 385ff.; Thurneysen, *Zu ir. Handschriften*, I, 48; ZCP, 20 (1936), 212–18; G. Murphy, *Ériu*, 16 (1952), 145–51.
114 Ed. by Meyer in ZCP, 3 (1901), 456–66. Also, O'Curry, op. cit., 618.
115 It includes a reference to Mael Sechlainn, who died in 1022. No doubt the *aisling* prophecy discussed in *Éigse*, 1 (1939), 42ff., was also characteristic of the *fili*-prophet.
116 O'Curry, *Manners and Customs*, II, 216f.; *The Book of Ballymote*, 13a; *Irische Texte*, III, 96f. But see the discussion in Howard Meroney, 'Studies in Early Irish Satire', *The Journal of Celtic Studies*, 1 (1950),

199–226, 2 (1953), 59–130, on satire and cursing, and F. N. Robinson, 'Satirists and Enchanters in Early Irish Literature', *Studies in the History of Religions*, ed. David Gordon Lyon and George Foote Moore (New York, 1912), pp. 95–130.

117 O'Curry, op. cit., II, 69, 70. Cf. K. Meyer, *Ancient Gaelic Poetry* (Lecture to Oss. Soc., Glasgow, 1906 [n.d.], 7, where the poet Aithirne is named.

118 O'Curry, 'The Fate of the Children of Lir', *Atlantis*, 4 (1863), 113–57.

119 Meyer, *Sanas Cormaic*, no. 698; Stokes, *Three Irish Glossaries*, xxxvi ff. Cf. Thurneysen, *Heldensage*, I, 523f.; O'Curry, *Manners and Customs*, II, 217. The same curse is found in the *Book of Ballymote* (294) as part of a procedure used by the *fili* against a noble man who refuses just recompense to him. The translation given is that of Liam Breatnach of the verse as found in *Uraicecht na Ríar* (Dublin, 1987), pp. 114–15.

120 'The Second Battle of Moytura', RC, 12 (1891), 91–2.

121 *Irische Texts*, III, 51ff., 117ff.

122 Ibid., III, 53f. The text and translation is also given by K. Meyer, *Learning in Ireland in the Fifth Century* (Dublin, 1913), p. 16ff. For more on this subject, see R. I. Best, 'Some Irish Charms', *Ériu*, 21, 1952), 27–32.

123 Douglas Hyde, 'Bards' in Hastings' *Encyclopaedia of Religion and Ethics*.

124 *Irish Literature* (Dublin, 1981), p. 11.

125 According to tradition, the legendary figure Amhairgin was both *fili* and *brithem*. Cf. O'Curry, *Manners and Customs*, II, 3, 20.

126 Binchy, 'The Linguistic and Historical Value of the Law Tracts', PBA, 29 (1943), 195–227.

127 *Laws*, I, 17. Cf. O'Curry, op. cit., II, 25; Mac Neill, *Studies*, 11 (1922), 23; *Celtic Ireland*, p. 84f.; Hull, *A Textbook of Irish Literature*, I, p. 179.

128 *Laws*, I, 18. Cf. O'Curry, MS. Materials, 45, 511. See also *Manners and Customs*, II, 20, 21; Hull, op. cit., I, p. 183.

129 Maud Joynt, *Tromdámh Guaire*, p. 3. See S. Ó Coileáin, 'The Structure of a Literary Cycle', *Ériu*, 25 (1974), 87–125.

130 ZCP, 5 (1904–5), 482ff., 8 (1911–12), 557. Cf. *Ségantus briathar*, referred to in 'Erchoitmed Ingine Gulidi', Meyer, *Hibernica Minora* (Oxford, 1894), pp. 65–69.

131 Ed. and trans. K. Meyer, *Archaeological Review*, 1 (1888); trans. Hull, *The Cuchullin Saga*, p. 57ff., and especially 69; Van Hamel, *Compert Con Culainn and Other Stories* (Dublin, 1933; rpt. 1956).

132 *Studies*, 11 (1922), 435ff. On the antiquity of these pieces, see ZCP, 18 (1930), 102.

133 M. Dillon, *Lebor na Cert* (Dublin, 1962), contains an edited text with a translation and supersedes the earlier edition by O'Donovan, *Leabhar na gCeart or The Book of Rights* (Dublin, 1847); see Mac Neill, *Celtic Ireland* (Dublin, 1921), chap. 6. Professor D. A. Binchy's opinion on the value of this source is to be found in Dillon, *Early Irish Society* (Dublin, 1954), p. 55.

134 See O'Rahilly, *Celtica*, 1, pt. ii (1950), 313–17.

135 The text was edited by Thurneysen in ZCP, 11 (1917), 80; for its date see

78–9, and ZCP, 13 (1921), 43ff.; J. Strachan, *Contributions to the History of the Deponent Verb in Irish* (rpt. *Trans. of the Philological Society*, 1894), 50; Meyer, *The Instructions of King Cormac mac Airt* (Dublin, 1909), v.

136 Cf. R. Flower, *The Irish Tradition*, 12f. It is sometimes attributed to Fithal; see Meyer, *Anecdota from Irish MSS*, III, 13; ZCP, 6 (1907–8), 216; Thurneysen, *Zu ir. Handschriften*, I, 16. The judge Fithal is described as a *fili* in *Echtra Cormaic i Tír Tairngiri*, *Irische Texte*, III, 157.

137 GL, I, 273.

138 Most of the poems published by K. Meyer in *Über die älteste irische Dichtung*, I, are genealogical. They contain the pedigrees of the kings of Leinster and Munster, and are dated as a class by Meyer to the seventh century. See D. Ó Corráin, 'Irish Origin Legends and Genealogy: Recurrent Aetiologies', in *History and Heroic Tales: A Symposium*, ed. Tore Nyberg et al. (Odense, 1985).

139 See ZCP, 8 (1911–12), 291–338, 411–18, 418–19; 9 (1913), 471–85; 10 (1914–15), 91–6.

140 Thurneysen, *Heldensage*, I, 36–46; GL, I, 283.

141 Ibid., I, 299f.

142 See O'Curry, *Manners and Customs*, II, 99.

143 See Máirín O Daly, 'The Metrical Dindshenchas' in James Carney, *Early Irish Poetry* (Cork, 1965), pp. 59–72 and T. Ó Concheanainn on 'Dinnshenchas Érenn' in JCS, 3 (1981–2), 88–131, *Ériu*, 33 (1982), 85–98. The names of known *filid* who wrote on the history and names of places in Ireland from the ninth century on are given by Mac Neill, *Celtic Ireland*, p. 39, and by E. J. Gwynn, *The Metrical Dindshenchas* (Dublin, 1935), V, 93. See also parts I (Dublin, 1903), II (1906), III (1913), and IV (1924). John V. Kelleher's statement in his 'Early Irish History and Pseudo-History', SH, 3 (1963), 113–27, is apposite: 'All of which should remind us that in medieval Ireland there were no categorical divisions between history and literature or between sacred and profane fictioneering.'

144 See Charles Bowen, 'A Historical Inventory of the *Dindshenchas*', SC, 10/11 (1975–6), 113–37.

145 GL, I, 283; Rolf Baumgarten, 'Placenames, Etymology and the Structure of *Fianaigecht*', in Bo Almqvist, Séamas Ó Catháin, Pádraig Ó Héalaí, edd., *The Heroic Process* (The Glendale Press, Dublin, 1987), 1–24.

146 It was Thurneysen's opinion that the poem could not be dated before the first half of the twelfth century (*Heldensage*, I, 20–21). Cf. GL, I, 282. In *Ériu*, 16 (1952), 151–5, G. Murphy argues convincingly that Cináed Ua hArtacáin was the real author of the poem and that it can therefore be dated in the tenth century. This article, 'On the Dates of Two Sources in Thurneysen's *Heldensage*', is important for its observations on the earliest writing of Irish texts. On the genre, cf. Thomas Jones, 'The Black Book of Carmarthen "Stanzas of the Graves" ', PBA, 53 (1967), 97–137.

147 *Irische Texte*, III, 285–444, 557; Thurneysen, *Heldensage*, I, 48–50; GL, I, 282f.; M. E. Dobbs, *Sidelights on the Táin Age* (Dundalk, 1917), p. 57ff.

148 GL, I, 595.
149 They were expected to know a great many of the tales as the second treatise on poetry in *The Book of Ballymote* shows; Thurneysen, *Mittelirische Verslehren*, pp. 50, 117. Cf. *Laws*, I, 44f.
150 P. Ó Riain, ed. *Cath Almaine* (Dublin, 1978); O'Donovan, *Annals of Ireland: Three Fragments* (Brussells 5301-20), pp. 32–51; Stokes, RC, 24 (1903), 41–70.
151 Cf. GL, I, 586f., where it is suggested that the combination 'poet-storyteller' was not restricted to the *filid*.
152 Vernam Hull, *Longes mac n-Uislenn: The Exile of the Sons of Uisliu* (New York, 1949).
153 Cf. G. Murphy, *Saga and Myth in Ancient Ireland*, p. 11.
154 ZCP, 18 (1930), 416.
155 Ed. by M. E. Byrne, *Anecdota from Irish MSS*, II, 42. For an analysis of the story, see O'Curry, *Manners and Customs*, II, 130, Thurneysen, *Heldensage*, I, 21, and Mac Cana, *The Learned Tales of Medieval Ireland* (Dublin, 1980).
156 979 in AU.
157 Mac Cana, op. cit., p. 38. Liam Breatnach, *Uraicecht na Ríar*, p. 91, believes that the final part of *Airec Menman U. M. C.* indicates that the main purpose of the text was to claim that the honour price of the poet should be the same as that of the king who appoints him.
158 Thurneysen, op. cit., I, 21–24 (the enumeration of 204 titles on p. 22 is not quite correct); M. E. Dobbs, 'Notes on the Lists of Historic Tales', JCS, 2 (1953), 45–8, and now Mac Cana, op. cit. For the minor list in the Advocates' Library, Edinburgh, see ZCP, 14 (1923), 1. For the suggestion that there is evidence that Irish poets were prepared to recite these lists or catalogues spontaneously when required to enumerate their repertoire for the benefit of a patron, see Rachel Bromwich, *Trioedd Ynys Prydein*, 2nd ed. (Cardiff, 1978), lxxii.
159 See O'Curry, *MS. Materials*, pp. 584–93.
160 Mac Cana, op. cit., p. 84.
161 Ibid., pp. 117–19.
162 Ibid., p. 87.
163 On the difficulty of distinguishing between various categories, see D. Dumville, 'Some Problems of Definition', *Ériu*, 27, (1976), 73–94.
164 In *The Book of Ballymote* (299, 45) there is an interesting treatise entitled 'Leabhar Ollamhan', i.e., 'the Book of the Ollavs'. See O'Curry, *Manners and Customs*, II, 171ff. for a summary of its contents; also Hull, *A Textbook of Irish Literature*, I, 189f., and *Encyclopaedia Britannica*, 14th ed., XII, 639.
165 Meyer, *Triads of Ireland* (Dublin, 1906), p. 9.
166 Dillon, 'The Archaism of Irish Tradition', p. 5.
167 Dillon, op. cit., 18, where Winternitz is quoted as saying, 'History in India was always only a branch of poetry . . . .'
168 O'Curry, *MS. Materials*, p., 593: '*Ni fili nadchomgne comatharnad scela uile.*'
169 *Celtic Ireland*, p. 37f.
170 '*Filidecht* and *Coimgne*', *Ériu*, 18 (1958), 139–52; he would read *ni fili nād*

comathar chomgne nād (na) scēla uile.

171 Art. cit., p. 150.
172 *Learned Tales*, p. 125.
173 Despite that, we must not forget the splendid poetry found in some of the tales, and that too was the work of the *filid*.
174 See Holder, *Altceltischer Sprachschatz* (Leipzig, 1891–1913), s.v. *bardos*.
175 ποιηταὶ μελῶν: according to H. M. and N. K. Chadwick, 'composers of songs'; in a footnote they add, 'We understand μελῶν to mean poetry accompanied by instrumental music', GL, I, 607.
176 *Athenaeus*, 4, 37; J. J. Tierney, op. cit., 248. See also Holder, op. cit., s.v. *Lovernios*, and cf. K. Meyer, *Ancient Gaelic Poetry*, p. 6.
177 *Éigse*, 2 (1940), 207. Cf. E. C. Quiggin, 'Prolegomena to the Study of the Later Irish Bards: 1200–1500', PBA, 5 (1913), 89–142, who gives a different view; for him, 'the humbler bard, advancing in dignity, assumed many of the functions of the learned order'. Professor D. Binchy, 'The Background to Early Irish Literature', SH, 1 (1961), 11, says of the *filid*, 'they had to compose praise-poems for their royal patrons, and also elegies after their deaths.'
178 *Éigse*, 2 (1940), 204ff.
179 'Amra Chonroi', *Ériu*, 2 (1905), 1–14.
180 For 'Amra Choluim Chille', see n. 95 above, and Máire Herbert, *Iona, Kells and Derry*, 9–12.
181 *Preuss. Akad. der Wissenschaften, 1919*: Abhand. Phil.-hist. Klasse. Nr. 7, Erster Teil (Berlin, 1919).
182 L. Renou, *Journal asiatique*, 231 (1939), 177–8.
183 *Servius et la Fortune* (Paris, 1943). For the Irish text see note 23 above.
184 Vernam Hull, 'Cairpre Mac Edaine's Satire upon Bres mac Eladain', ZCP, 18 (1930), 63–9; J. Travis, 'A Druidic Prophecy, the First Irish Satire, and a Poem to Raise Blisters', PMLA, 57 (1942), 912ff.; T. Ó Cathasaigh, 'Curse and Satire', *Éigse*, 21 (1986), 10–15. For a more general discussion see N. J. A. Williams, 'Gnéithe den Aoir i Litríocht na Gaeilge', SH, 20 (1980), 57–71; idem, 'Irish Satire and its Sources', SC, 12/13 (1977/78), 217–46.
185 RC, 8 (1887), 53–5.
186 Robert G. Elliott, *The Power of Satire: Magic, Ritual, Art* (Princeton, 1960), pp. 64–66.
187 E. J. Gwynn, *Ériu*, 13 (1942), 57–8.
188 Emile Benveniste, *Indo-European Language and Society* (London, 1973).
189 Morris-Jones, John and T. H. Parry-Williams, *Llawysgrif Hendregadredd* (Cardiff, 1932), p. 232.26. Cf. the equally significant line from *The Poetry in the Red Book of Hergest*, ed., J. Gwenogvryn Evans (Llanbedrog, 1911), col. 1219.21–2: *Gwnawn glot ynteu oth draws gampeu*, translated by J. Morris Jones in *A Welsh Grammar* (Oxford, 1913), p. 448, 'Let us fashion praise, then, of thy feats of arms', but we could substitute 'fame' for 'praise'.
190 J. E. Caerwyn Williams, *The Court Poet in Medieval Ireland* (Oxford, 1971), p. 18.
191 F. R. Schröder, 'Eine indogermanische Liedform. Das Aufreihlied',

Germanisch-Romanische Monatsschrift, N.F. 4 (1954), 179–85.

192 'Stylistic Repetition in the Veda', *Verhandelingen van de koninklijke Nederlandsche Akademie van Wetenschappen*, afdeling Letterkunde. Nieuwe reeks, 65/3 (1959), 51.

193 Ernout et Meillet, *Dictionnaire étymologique de la langue latine* (1939), s.v. *carmen*.

194 Rüdiger Schmitt, *Dichtung und Dichtersprache in indogermanischer Zeit* (Wiesbaden, 1967), 206–10.

195 *Servius et la Fortune* (Paris, 1943), chapter 1 (pp. 33ff) is devoted to 'La consécration du roi Pṛthu et la naissance du panégyriste', and chapter 2 (pp. 112ff) to 'L'élection du roi Servius et le premier *census*'.

196 Professor H. J. Rose has criticized Dumézil's use of the Roman evidence in *Servius et la Fortune*, and *Jupiter, Mars, Quirinus* (Paris, 1941) in *The Journal of Roman Studies*, 37 (1947), 183ff. For Dumézil's position *vis-à-vis* Rose's, see his *L'Héritage indo-européen à Rome* (Paris, 1949), 49ff.

197 H. H. Anton, *Fürstenspiegel und Herrscherethos in der Karolingerzeit* (Bonn, 1968).

198 A. D. Hellmann, *Texte und Untersuchungen zur Geschichte der altchristlichen Literatur*, xxxiv.15.

199 Fergus Kelly, ed., *Audacht Morainn* (Dublin, 1976), p. 7 for the translation and *passim* for discussion. Cf. R. Thurneysen, 'Morands Fürstenspiegel', ZCP, 11 (1917), 56–102; D. A. Binchy, *Celtic and Anglo-Saxon Kingship*, pp. 9–10.

200 Eoin Mac Neill, *Phases of Irish History* (rpt. Dublin, Sydney, 1968), p. 210.

201 *Ériu*, 31 (1980), 132–45. See also Myles Dillon, 'The Inauguration of O'Conor', in Watt, Morall, Martin, edd., *Medieval Studies Presented to Aubrey Gwynn* (Dublin, 1961)., pp. 186–202; *idem*, 'The Consecration of Irish Kings', *Celtica*, 10 (1973), 1–8.

202 E. O'Curry, MS. Materials, pp. 126, 542; J. O'Donovan, *The Genealogies, Tribes, and Customs of Hy Fiachra* (Dublin, 1844), p. 425.

203 'The Hindu Act of Truth in Celtic Tradition', *Modern Philology*, 44 (1947), 137–40; D. Greene, 'The "Act of Truth" in a Middle Irish Story', *Saga och Sed*, Kungl. Gustav Adolfo Academiens Års, Uppsala; A.-B. Ludequistska Bokhandeln.

204 GL, I, 4.

205 Ed. and trans. by K. Meyer, RC, 20 (1899), 7ff.; *Gaelic Journal*, 10, 613; also trans. by him in *Selections from Ancient Irish Poetry*, pp. 72f., and by Frank O'Connor, *Kings, Lords, Commons*, p. 41, whence the lines cited here.

206 GL, I, 350. On gnomic (instructional) poems, see ibid., 393–8.

207 Dillon, 'The Archaism of Irish Tradition', p. 18. See the thoughtful discussion of the oldest elements in the Irish tradition in P. L. Henry, *Saoithiúlach na Sean-Ghaeilge. Bunú an Traidisiúin* (Dublin, 1978), also his 'The Caldron of Poesy', SC, 14/15 (1979–80), 114–80, where he edits the text in four sections, three in verse which he dates to the seventh century, and one in prose of the eighth century. The same text is edited by Liam Breatnach, 'The Caldron of Poetry', *Ériu*, 32 (1982), 45–93, where it is given in sixteen sections, all dated to the eighth century.

It should be noted that our approach to early Irish Literature stressing its conservatism, its oral nature and its almost unbroken continuity with its pagan past, the approach associated with the names of Myles Dillon, D.A. Binchy, Kenneth Jackson and Proinsias Mac Cana, has recently been criticized by some of the younger generation of Irish scholars. See 'Medieval scholars and modern nativists' in Kim McKone, *Pagan Past and Christian Present in Early Irish Literature* (Maynooth, 1990), pp. 1–28.

CHAPTER 2

THE OLD AND THE NEW

§1

IT has been said that the earliest date about which there is any
certainty in Irish history is AD 431, the year the Christian
missionary Palladius came to Ireland.[1] The reason for this assertion is
quite fundamental: an accurate history is not possible without the use
of writing, and that did not really come to Ireland until Christianity
and its Latin culture arrived.[2] True, there was a method of writing
known in Ireland before the coming of Christianity, and there are
examples of it in the Ogam inscriptions that have survived on stone.[3]
Most of these are found in the south of Ireland, but there are some
also in Wales, Scotland, and the Isle of Man. The great majority of
them are dated (on linguistic evidence) to the fourth, fifth, and sixth
centuries, and their language is early Irish. In Wales it is not unusual
to find a Latin inscription cut in Roman letters side by side with the
Ogam inscriptions.

There are frequent references in the tales to the use of Ogam. We
are told often that the name of a hero was cut in Ogam on the occasion
of his burial. Ogam was used also to write charms sometimes on
weapons and sometimes on rods—birch, it appears. In *Táin Bó
Cúailnge*, Cú Chulainn uses Ogam to write messages on rods to the
men of Connacht,[4] and Fergus is the one who reads or interprets
them. Clearly, the *filid* were not the only ones skilled in Ogam,
although the knowledge of it, as we have seen, was a special part of
their training. In the text of *Scél Baili Meic Buain* ('The Story of Baile
Mac Buain'), a story set in the time of Art, father of Cormac, there is a
reference to the 'rods of the *filid*' upon which many tales of visions
and courtships were inscribed,[5] and in the *Immram Brain*, Bran writes
bardic poems in Ogam.[6] But in spite of all this, it is hard to believe that
such a clumsy form of writing was ever used widely for literary
purposes,[7] and there is no evidence that it was used to chronicle
events.

The native culture survived in an oral tradition before the coming
of Christianity, and there is no doubt that it retained its oral character
for a good while after AD 431. The name that was given to Christian
learning, *légenn* (Latin *legendum*), suggests the difference between it

and native learning. Parchment and ink were the chief instruments of transmitting the new learning; the old depended upon memory and speech for its transmission. But that was only one among many differences. There was plenty of room for disagreement and competition between the *filid* and the clerical scholars (known as *scribae* or *fir léiginn*), and one of the miracles in the history of Ireland is that the disagreement vanished and a remarkably well-matched and productive union of the old and the new occurred.[8] It has been suggested that one reason for the success of this union is that nowhere else in northern Europe were the clerical scholars of the Church confronted with a lay body like the *filid*. The *filid* could lay claim to a scholarship which (from the native standpoint) was of equal if not greater importance than ecclesiastical scholarship.[9] We should also keep in mind the great strength of the oral tradition in Ireland at the time of the introduction of literacy, that is, the ability to commit literature to writing. The oral tradition was thriving in Ireland at the time of the introduction of Christianity; left to its own devices, the native society was not likely to have developed the art of writing for a very long time, nor to experience any weakening of the oral tradition that such a development might have engendered.

As we have suggested, the natural loyalties of the *filid* were to the old pagan beliefs, and therefore they were the objects of suspicion and even enmity to the missionaries of the new faith. If the tradition referred to above is authentic,[10] Patrick attempted to distinguish between the religious functions and the cultural functions of the *filid*; he wanted to eliminate the former but to leave the latter alone. In a later age, Colum Cille, we are told, showed himself to be a friend to the order to which he was said to have once belonged, and because of that the *filid*, if we are to believe the tradition, were saved from extinction at the great conference of Druim Cetta.[11]

The result of the leadership of men like Patrick and Colum Cille was that the Church succeeded in doing in Ireland what it failed to accomplish in many another land, namely, to make a distinction between native religion and native culture. It is difficult to know whether the Irish clerics, and they alone, were responsible for that. It is very easy to over-emphasize the value and influence of the native culture, and the temptation is to idealize Irish society. But if the picture we attempted to sketch in the first chapter even borders on the truth, then it was a society whose civilization was fairly primitive, though that would not prevent its culture from being one with deep roots and extensive branches.

It could be that there was a special influence working on the Irish clerics and colouring their attitude toward the native culture and toward secular culture generally. The suggestion has been made—but there is no evidence to support it, and indeed the balance of probability is against it—that a school of literary men gathered in Ireland during the fifth and sixth centuries and perpetuated the Latin and Greek learning of Gaul for a while during the last years of the Roman Empire, and that 'Hisperic' texts (including the most famous of them, *Hisperica Famina*) represent one aspect of their activity.[12] These texts were probably written in a Christian community, but they are so secular in spirit that they cannot be ascribed to the monastic foundations that arose in Ireland in the fifth century and flourished there in the sixth. Ludwig Bieler believes that they were of British provenance. In any case it is easier to believe that they were the work of that literary society, whoever was responsible for its formation, that produced the rhetoricians who disparaged the 'uncouth' language of Patrick. Such a community, once the ties between it and Gaul, Spain, and Britain were severed, would be bound to vanish from the British Isles in the sixth and seventh centuries, leaving nothing but indirect traces of its influence upon the Latin literature of the monastic churches and upon the vernacular literature of the *filid*.[13]

Whatever the influence of that society on the native culture was, the Church became the great centre of intellectual activity in Ireland. It succeeded in uniting religious zeal with an enthusiasm for every kind of secular learning, and that is why the Irish in the Dark Ages became the chief custodians of the classical learning that had passed to Europe from Greece and Rome.[14] As one scholar has said, 'By the year 600, Ireland had not only caught up with the rest of the Roman world, but began to take the lead. For at least one century her Latin culture was remarkably superior to anything that could be found in Saxon England, Lombard Italy or Merovingian France. Even Caroline civilization owed not a little of its splendour to Irish learning.'[15] Indeed, 'during the centuries between Christian antiquity and the Carolingian revival, when the foundations of medieval Europe were being laid, only the Irish had something to contribute that was new as well as lasting.'[16]

Monasticism became the basis of the Irish ecclesiastical organization.[17] Every church of importance was a monastic church in the sense that it was a kind of hamlet enclosed by walls that contained monks or nuns living under ecclesiastical discipline and that served the spiritual needs of the people around it. Connected with every large church there would be a school. Toward the end of the sixth century, the most famous schools were those in Bangor (Bennchor), Armagh, Movilla and Derry in Ulster, Clonard in Meath, Clonmacnoise and Clonfert on the river Shannon, and Glendalough on the eastern side; but there were many others, and more still in the following centuries. In addition to the school, and probably connected with it, every large church had its *scriptorium*. Undoubtedly, much attention was given to the work of the writing room, for many manuscripts were produced, and the standard of writing and illumination was exceptionally high.

The Irish developed a distinctive Irish script. Its significance, according to Professor Bieler,

> emerges most clearly when its genesis is compared with that of the other 'national scripts' of the early Middle Ages. All the others — the Visigothic script in Spain, the Beneventan script in Southern Italy, the local types of the Merovingian kingdom, the Rhaetian and Alemannic scripts in the districts of Chur and St. Gall, and the less characteristic scripts of northern Italy and western Germany—can be understood as attempts at normalizing the degenerate cursive script of late antiquity in the hope of thus producing a serviceable book-hand. The Irish script, it seems, was a deliberate creation out of elements of the several scripts inherited from antiquity which the earliest missionaries had brought with them.[18]

And it is no wonder that Gougaud writes that

> The Irish of the Middle Ages nowhere displayed more manual dexterity, ingenuity, resourcefulness and invention than in the art of copying and adorning religious manuscripts, and many of their works deserve to be classed among the fairest specimens of calligraphy and illumination now extant.[19]

The splendour of the few specimens which have survived the ravages of time should not blind us to the fact that many of them must have been lost and that we should 'be careful not to postulate too close a connexion between those manuscripts which have happened to survive.' Among the latter, the most famous are *The Lindisfarne Gospels, The Book of Durrow,* and *The Book of Kells.* Only the first of these can be associated with certainty with the place-name it bears, although they are all examples of Irish calligraphy and illumination. It may have been *The Book of Kells* that Giraldus Cambrensis was describing as one of the wonders of Kildare in his *Topography of Ireland,* and even if this were not the case, his description is worth quoting as one which does justice to that book.

This book contains the four gospels according to the concordance of St Jerome, with almost as many drawings as pages, and all of them in marvellous colours. Here you can look upon the face of the divine majesty drawn in a miraculous way; here too upon the mystical representations of the Evangelist, now having six, now four, and now two, wings. Here you will see the eagle; there the calf. Here the face of a man; there that of a lion. And there are almost innumerable other drawings. If you look at them carelessly and casually and not too closely, you may judge them to be mere daubs rather than careful compositions. You will see nothing subtle where everything is subtle. But if you take the trouble to look very closely, and penetrate with your eyes to the secrets of the artistry, you will notice such intricacies, so delicate and so subtle, so close together and well-knitted, so involved and bound together, and so fresh still in their colourings that you will not hesitate to declare that all these things must have been the result of the work, not of men, but of angels.[20]

With the schools and libraries such an attraction, it is no wonder that students from everywhere came in droves to Ireland.[21] In a letter to Eadfrid, Bishop of Lindisfarne, St Aldhelm, Bishop of Sherbourne, says that the students from Britain go to Ireland in 'fleets',[22] and Bede testifies to the same thing.[23] It is an interesting fact that many of the students learned Irish, either from their teachers—as seems likely, or among the Irish students. We are told that Oswald, King of Northumbria, learned Irish perfectly and acted as interpreter between Aidan and his own noblemen when the saint was expounding Christian truths to them.[24] We find that Cedd, Bishop of London, also acted as interpreter by virtue of his knowledge of Irish.[25] King Oswy and his son Aldfrith were both skilled in the language,[26] and, as we have seen, the latter is said to have composed in Irish.[27]

But if students were pouring into Ireland, a great number of Irish—many of them scholars—were leaving their land to become missionaries and teachers in Britain and on the Continent.[28] There are too many of them to name and trace their careers one by one; we must be content to take one of the most renowned of them as representative.

Columbanus was born in Leinster around AD 530–45.[29] He became a member of the monastery at Bangor, which had recently been founded in Ulster on Belfast Loch by St Comgall, and which developed one of the most renowned of the celebrated monastic schools of Ireland. There the first annals to be compiled on mainland Ireland were kept, and there was the original place of writing and composition of the so-called *Antiphonary* of Bangor, which was taken from the Abbey of Bobbio to its present location, the Ambrosian

Library at Milan. The *Antiphonary*, according to Kenney, 'may be the oldest extant Irish manuscript: it is the oldest to which precise dates can—with probability—be assigned. Apart from some fragments it is the only record surviving of the old Irish church services unaffected by the seventh and eighth centuries, and is one of the very few western liturgical books of the seventh century which we possess.'[30] Among its treasures there is a hymn extolling the monastery of Bangor and its rule, *Benchuir bona regula*. It is of peculiar interest as an example of versification as well as for its content as a description of the monastic ideal at the time of writing:

> Benchuir bona regula,
> recta atque diuina,
> Stricta, sancta, sedula,
> summa, iusta ac mira.

> Munther Benchuir beata,
> fide fundata certa,
> Spe salutis ornata,
> caritate perfecta . . .

> Good rule of Bangor,
> straight and divine,
> holy, exact and constant,
> exalted, just and admirable.

> Blessed family of Bangor,
> founded on unerring faith,
> adorned with salvation's hope,
> perfect in charity.

> Ship never distressed
> though beaten by the waves;
> fully prepared for nuptials,
> spouse for the sovereign Lord.

> House full of delicious things
> and built upon a rock;
> and no less the true vine
> brought out of Egypt's land.

> Surely an enduring city,
> strong and unified,
> worthy and glorious,
> set upon a hill.

> Ark shaded by Cherubim,
> all overlaid with gold,

filled with the sacred things
and borne by four men.

A very queen for Christ
clad in the light of sun,
innocent yet wise,
from every side invulnerable.

A truly regal hall
with many jewels adorned,
of Christ's flock too the fold,
and kept by the great God.

A virgin fruitful she
and mother undefiled,
joyful and tremulous,
submissive to God's word.

For whom with the perfect
a happy life is destined,
prepared by God the Father,
to last to eternity.

Good rule of Bangor, [etc.][31]

Severe and hard though the 'good rule' of Bangor was, it was not hard enough for Columbanus. In the year 590 or a little earlier, when he was about fifty years old, he and twelve companions set out 'on his pilgrimage' passing through Britain (or Brittany) to western Gaul, and thence to Burgundy. The pilgrims settled first in Annegray, in a wooded district which forms the present *département* of Haute-Saône. Two other houses were established in the vicinity, one in Fontaine, the other in Luxeuil. This last became the chief monastery of the three. In no time at all, the whole neighbourhood was taking an interest in the new settlements, and their influence was soon felt in the ecclesiastical and political life of Gaul—an influence that was so unacceptable to the authorities that Thierry, King of Burgundy, sent an official to expel Columbanus and put him on a ship bound for Ireland. The last part of the assignment was not carried out, and the saint went from Nantes to the courts of Clothaire, King of Neustria, and Theodebert, King of Austrasia, and then up the Rhine to Switzerland. After endeavouring to preach the gospel to the natives there, he crossed the Alps and was welcomed in Milan by Agilulf and Theodelinda, the King and Queen of the Lombards. He received a strip of land from them, and upon it built the famous monastery of Bobbio.

Columbanus was fortunate to have the remarkably well-informed Jonas of Bobbio as his biographer.[32] Jonas tells us that Columbanus studied grammar, rhetoric and geometry before he came under the tutelage of first Senalus and then St Comgall at Bangor, and indeed his writings bear ample testimony to the fruits of this study. His letters are studded with quotations from the Scriptures and the five poems which can be attributed to him with reasonable certainty show that he had read not only Virgil but also Horace as well as Sallust and Ovid. Indeed, it is a remarkable fact that whereas the earliest Latin verses composed in Ireland show no familiarity with Latin texts other than the Scriptures, later verses and particularly those of Columbanus show a remarkable familiarity with some of the classical Latin poets and bear eloquent testimony to the type of training which the Irish schools quickly developed. It remains a mystery how these schools came into possession of the texts of Horace and Isidore of Seville, but it seems that Ireland played an important part in their transmission in Europe.[33]

Columbanus had a tremendous influence on the development of Western Europe, and traces of his work are evident in the Church of the Middle Ages. By adhering to the customs of his own land and struggling to keep the monasteries independent of the bishops, the saint began to shape the system that was to play an exceedingly important role in the life of the Church and the world for centuries. And that is but one example among many of his influence on ecclesiastical affairs.

There is not so much evidence available to measure his influence on the cultural life of Europe, but no doubt he did much to keep classical learning alive. We know that he was learned in the works of classical Latin authors. To find one who could equal him in learning, we would have to go back to the time of Sidonius Apollinaris or forward to the sixteenth century and the scholars of the Renaissance. He was a contemporary of Gregory of Tours, but the two were not in the same world culturally.[34] We get a glimpse of Columbanus's mettle as man of learning and scholar in these lines believed to have been composed for a companion of his called Fidolius:

Accipe, quaeso,   tuque frequenter
nunc bipedali   Mutua nobis
condita versu   obsequiorum
carminulorum   debita redde.
munera parva;   Nam, velut aestu,

flantibus austris,   missa frequenter
arida gaudent   laetificabit
imbribus arva   pagina mentes . . . [35]
sic tua nostras

This is in a metre called adonic: a simple dactyl is followed by a spondee or a trochee, – ˘˘ + – – or + – ˘ , used, e.g., as the fourth line of a Sapphic strophe. This poem alone would suffice to show that Columbanus was not only knowledgeable in prosody but also adept at putting his knowledge into practice. Of the five poems which can be attributed to him with reasonable certainty, four are epistolary in character, and as Kenney has rightly pointed out, they are 'valuable chiefly as first-hand evidence regarding the character of the literary training in the schools of sixth-century Ireland.'[36]

As we have selected one Irishman to exemplify the hundreds of *Scotti peregrini* who travelled on the Continent, let us also take one example of the many places upon which they left their mark. Here is what one scholar has said about the connection of the Irish with St Gall in Switzerland:

It will be seen that, quite apart from the continual stream of Irish pilgrims who passed through St. Gall on their journey to or from Rome, there were three successive waves of Irish immigration at St. Gall. First there was the seventh century, the age of missionary effort; second the ninth century, in which a general exodus from Ireland took place on account of the depredations of the Danes: this was the floodtide of Irish influence on the Continent. Lastly, in the twelfth century, the current flowed again, this time from the congregation of Irish monasteries in Bavaria. The first period is associated with Bangor, the second with Kildare and possibly Iona, the third with Ratisbon and Würzburg.[37]

Along with the missionaries and the scholars who left Ireland went many a manuscript, and in one sense we can be grateful for that. Because of the devastation wrecked upon monasteries in Ireland by the Vikings, hardly any of the manuscripts that were kept there through the end of the tenth century survived. In fact, apart from *The Book of Armagh* and *The Stowe Missal*, which are now in Ireland, and *The Southampton Psalter*, which is in England, the manuscripts that were written in Ireland in the eight and ninth centuries and are still extant are all on the Continent.

Latin is the language of these manuscripts and the theological and grammatical material in them, but in some of them, Irish glosses are found: words and an occasional sentence here and there translating the Latin and explaining it in Irish.[38] Some of these provide rather long passages of prose and sometimes even stanzas of Irish verse. Among them is one preserved in Milan (*Codex Ambrosianus C.* 301),[39] which contains a commentary on the Psalms in Latin with Irish glosses. It came to Milan from Bobbio, but it appears to have been written in Ireland in the first half of the ninth century. Another manuscript important for its Irish glosses is the *Codex Paulinus Wirziburgensis*, kept now in the University Library in Würzburg.[40] It contains the Latin text of thirteen epistles of St Paul and the Epistle to the Hebrews as far as chapter xii, verse 24. It appears that the copyist of the Latin text added some Irish glosses of his own, and then two other glossators did the same thing; the chief glossator was writing about the middle of the eighth century. One of the principal attractions of the manuscript *Codex Sancti Pauli* (kept in the monastery of St Paul in Carinthia) is the poetry in it.[41] The manuscript was written on the Continent by an Irishman in the second half of the ninth century, but the Irish verse is in language somewhat later than that. Even *The Book of Armagh*, which, as its name suggests, is preserved in Ireland, contains glosses and pieces of Irish prose; part of it was written before AD 807, the remainder by 846, the year in which the scribe died.

These Latin manuscripts that contain Irish glosses and a good many others were written by Irish clerics steeped in the Latin culture of the Church. Perhaps their main interest was theology and grammar—Latin grammar, that is—and their manuscripts reflect that interest, but we must not think of them as copyists who were content simply to pass on the treasures of the past to the future. Indeed, it has been possible to deduce something about the teaching methods used by Irish scholars from these manuscripts; under close scrutiny, a page of the St Gall Priscian yields a picture of an Irish teacher at work with his class, assisting them to grasp the structure of the Latin language as well as to understand the precise meaning of the text.[42] As the stanzas quoted from the work of Columbanus demonstrate, some of them were highly cultured in their adopted language, and must have been trained in schools where the teaching of grammar had reached a very high standard.[43]

They wrote a considerable number of Latin hymns: it has been suggested that the earliest Latin poem composed in Ireland was the hymn in honour of St Patrick attributed to Bishop Secundinus (d. 447),[44] and that we have in 'Sancti venite Christi corpus sumite,' found in the *Antiphonary of Bangor*, the oldest Eucharistic hymn in existence.[45] W. Meyer investigated the versification of these Hiberno-Latin hymns,[46] but not as much is known about it as about the versification of Continental Latin poetry. Although the metres themselves ignore the length of syllables, they are patterned on metres that depend on syllabic length. The basic element is the number of syllables and the rhythmic fall of cadences in line or half-line. Rhyme, assonance, and alliteration are important ornaments, but not indispensable. Another product of the Irish clerics was the Latin lives of the saints; for example, the life of Brigit by Cogitosus, lives of Colum Cille by Cuimíne Ailbe and Adamnán, works by Tírechán and Muirchú on Patrick, and the *Vita Tripartita*, which contains three homilies on the Saint.[47] This last has been dated in the ninth century, although in all probability it contains later material.

Besides the hymns, saints' lives, and various religious and theological works that comprise the corpus of these clerics' Latin works, we find an occasional composition that is on the borderline, as it were, between a religious tale and a secular romance. One such composition is *Navigatio Sancti Brendani*.[48] The *Navigatio* was written by an Irishman, almost certainly in Ireland, and its composition has been dated as early as the middle of the ninth century and as late as the first half of the tenth; but as Mac Cana has suggested, a date in the second half of the ninth century seems the most plausible.[49] The purpose of the voyage described is to search for *tír tairngiri* 'the land of promise', but in this story it is not Canaan or the Kingdom of Heaven which is meant by *tír tairngiri*, as was the case earlier when the Irish glossators used the phrase, but rather the Celtic Avalon of the West. For that reason the narrative contains many of the usual events that one encounters in the Irish voyage tales (*immrama*), such as *Immram Curaig Ua Corra* ('The Voyage of the Uí Chorra'), *Immram Snédgusa agus Maic Riagla* ('The Voyage of Snédgus and Mac Riagla'), and *Immram Curaig Maíle Dúin* ('Voyage of Mael Dúin').[50] But even though the author or authors have drawn their material rather broadly from the literature and folklore of Ireland and Europe and from what geographical knowledge was available, they did not lose sight of the religious intent of the story; against its diversified background, we are offered a view of the ideal monastic life.

It is not without reason that the *Navigatio Brendani* has been called an epic—if not an Odyssey—of the old Irish Church,[51] but the tale is

important from the standpoint of Irish literary history as well. For
one thing, it appears that the clerics adapted their native mythology
to their own purposes.[52] Furthermore, the *Navigatio* may be considered the last important composition written by Irish clerics in
Latin; from then on Irish was their main literary language. This was
to be expected, for, as suggested by more than one thing we have
already said, even those clerics who could glory in their Latin culture
were keenly interested in the native culture too. No doubt they used
Irish side by side with Latin even from the beginning, and, just as their
Latin compositions were enriched by their knowledge of Irish lore, so
were their Irish compositions influenced by their knowledge of Latin
literature.[53]

§2

The clerics began their work in the Irish language by composing
hymns. We do not know how early this development occurred, but it
could not have been later than the seventh century, and was possibly
as early as the sixth. Tírechán and Muirchú probably used metrical
compositions about Patrick, and Adamnán mentions the singing of
encomiastic hymns to Colum Cille as if it were an old custom.
Tradition assigns a hymn on Patrick to Fiacc, Bishop of Sletty and
contemporary of the saint, but it was composed probably about AD
800.[54] Linguistic evidence shows that this is also the time when the
Félire Oengusso ('The Martyrology of Oengus') was composed. The
body of the work is a calendar containing a four-line stanza for each
day of the year, giving the name of the saint to be commemorated on
that day. Usually only an epithet or conventional phrase is added to
the name, but sometimes reference is made to historical or legendary
material.[55] The chief literary interest of the work is that the author
used the Irish language and that he composed verses, presumably for
a mnemonic purpose, on a body of knowledge whose preservation he
considered important. To find a religious composition in an equally
ambitious metre, one has to wait until the last quarter of the tenth
century (about AD 987) when some scholar set forth a sacred history
of the world, as it occurs in the Bible and some apocryphal works, in a
hundred and fifty stanzas of *debhidhe* verse comprising the original
version of the *Saltair na Rann* ('Psalter of the Stanzas').[56] From
another standpoint, the *Martyrology of Oengus*, as well as the earlier
Martyrology of Tallaght, is important because it bears testimony to

the acquisition by the Irish Church of an ever increasing historical and cultural tradition in which a prominent part was given to its native aristocracy, its spiritual and its ecclesiastical leaders. The *Martyrology of Oengus* is a kind of *Who's Who* of the Irish Church and presupposes the existence of a school of Church historians whose professional activities have extended over a considerable period.

In a reference to the fragments of poetry collected by Kuno Meyer, Professor D. Binchy said that they showed 'that there was a native school of poetry with its own system of metrics before the syllabic metres, which afterwards developed into *Dán Díreach*, had been taken over from the Latin hymn sequences; hence the study of poetry must have been an old discipline.'[57] And Professor Calvert Watkins has since argued that the metrical systems of some archaic Old Irish metres had their origin in Indo-European metrics and that they existed as such 'in Proto-Goidelic and Common Celtic times'.[58] He discusses in particular the 'gnomic-epic' heptasyllabic line, the line of ten to twelve syllables with three cola, and, derived from it by the suppression of the middle colon, the basic Irish line of six to eight syllables and two cola. Professor Watkins's views have been challenged by Professors Wagner and Meid, but they have been accepted by Professor Dillon and others.[59]

Before Watkins had published his important paper, scholars tended to accept Thurneysen's suggestions regarding the development of the Irish metrical system, and in particular the suggestion that the Irish syllabic metres were more or less consciously developed by Irish poets from sources traceable ultimately to a Latin origin.[60] Indeed, Watkins does not deny Latin influence but contends that the native elements in the new metrical forms have been underestimated.

Very important in this connection are the poems discovered in the late 1950s by Professor James Carney and published by him in a volume in the Irish Texts Society series under the title, *The Poems of Blathmacc son of Cú Brettan Together with the Irish Gospel of Thomas and a Poem on the Virgin Mary*.[61] Blathmacc, apparently, was one of the Fir Roiss, a people living in the district which now forms the east of Co. Monaghan and part of Co. Louth. His father, Cú Brettan, is mentioned in the saga of the Battle of Allen, and his brother's name occurs both in the saga and in the Annals. Blathmacc, it would appear, lived in the eighth century and must have been a monk who had had some training in the composition of Irish verse. In the two poems which form the greater part of Professor Carney's volume, the poet does not seem to have been working to any structural plan and although the second poem refers back to the first there is no organic connection. Describing the events in the life of Christ, he gives them a social milieu similar to that with which he was familiar in Ireland. Thus, the Jews are in a bond of *célsine* or 'clientship' to God, who has endowed them with land only to find that they are not prepared to fulfil their obligations, thus illustrating the truth of the Irish proverb that it is wrong to improve the status of a slave. God, however, is the object of intense and sincere devotion. He is the sovereign Lord and Creator:

> It is He who makes heat and cold,
> The King who withers not;
> His is dew and mist,
> He is true ruler of a fair kingdom.
>
> It is He who raises wave from strand
> So that it drowns the tops of proud ships;
> It is He who overcomes the screech of tempest,
> Who casts a fair calm upon the sea.
>
> It is He who raises a sharp mighty wind
> That tears a forest from stout roots;
> It is He who pleasantly represses it
> So that it troubles not even a tiny pool.

In the poems of Blathmacc we have the beginning of that tradition which produced in the tenth century *Saltair na Rann*, and the poem which Professor Carney has called 'The Irish Gospel of Thomas' shows that that tradition was working on material peculiar to Ireland, for its author obviously had knowledge of the contents of a lost Latin apocryphon.

The Blathmacc poems are addressed to the Virgin Mary, and together with the anonymous poem to her published with them, give convincing proof that devotion to Our Lady was established in Ireland in the eighth century. In the first poem, Christ is dead and the poet asks Mary to come to him so that they may join together to keen him.

> Come to me, loving Mary
> That I may keen with you over your very dear one;
> Also the going to the cross of your Son,
> Who was a great Jewel, a beautiful companion.

Blathmacc is a good example of the Irish cleric making use of Latin learning to enrich the native tradition. It is unlikely that he was ever tempted to write Latin poetry; in any case he was writing for his native countrymen and it is significant that he chose the *debhidhe* metre.

No doubt the metrics of the Latin hymns influenced the Irish hymns, and through them Irish metrics generally.[62] According to K. Meyer, the earliest poetic forms were devoid of rhyme and rhythm and depended exclusively upon simple alliteration as a device to link small groups of words to each other.[63] Then a kind of irregular rhythm was developed. Examples of rhyme are found before the end of the sixth century. The following century, it seems, was a period of serious experimentation, but, alas, it is not easy to follow the developments. Rhythmic lines with and without rhyme were utilized; unrhymed varieties in short lines with unfixed stress in the first half, followed by a cadence, occur in the law tracts and sagas, even up to the Middle Irish period. Perhaps in the eighth century the poetic forms based on a specific number of syllables rather than rhythm won out over the others. In any case, stanzaic metres based on non-rhythmic lines of a set number of syllables and containing rhyme and alliteration were popular from the eighth to the sixteenth century, and on occasions were used even later than that.

Apparently, the *filid* were not prepared to use the ecclesiastical metres at first, and they were probably just as unwilling to accept the Church's poetic themes. *Núa chrutha* 'new forms'—that is how they described the majority of the syllabic metres, and it is no wonder that, at first, they considered them beneath the notice of their own lofty order and left them to the *baird*.[64] They were careful to point out that there was no fixed payment for a poem in the new metres. But despite that, *núa chrutha* became more and more popular, and by the ninth century they probably were fully cultivated by the *filid*.[65]

It is interesting to note that the poetry of the North, as represented by the poems of Cenn Faelad,[66] and the poems in *Immram Brain*, were all composed in stanzas of four lines, with regular rhyme and a fair amount of alliteration.[67] But in the South, the old forms were used: lines containing an irregular number of syllables, with accent the governing element and alliteration as the connecting link. These are the poetic forms that appear regularly in the genealogies of Leinster and Munster, and there is little doubt that they were the ones most used in the South.

We know of one poet in Munster who became a monk. Thurneysen collected what little of his poetry has survived, and he believed that it was handed down from the beginning in written form.[68] If that is true, then the tradition of writing in Irish had already begun in Munster by the year 600. Professor James Carney has argued, convincingly in our view, that Thurneysen was characteristically too conservative in his dating of this poetry.[69] Thurneysen accepted the annalistic obit for Colmán mac Lénéni's death *c*. 604–6, but he was unaware of the retrospective date for his birth, 530, in the *Annals of Inisfallen*, and so he resisted the conclusion that Colmán's floruit must have been earlier than *c*. 600. The Irish poem from which the stanza below is extracted was written, argues Carney, *c*. 565 to Domnall, king of Tara, for the gift of a sword. In any case, Colmán was a contemporary of Columbanus, and he is one of the first to use in the native language the kind of rhyme utilized by his saintly contemporary.[70] In the Latin poetry of the latter, the chief rhyme is in the final unaccented syllable, but a half-rhyme occurs sometimes in the other syllables as well. For example:

De terrenis eleva
tui cordis oculos;
ama amantissimos
angelorum populos.

Note the rhyme in *oculos, populos*. Compare this stanza from Colmán's panegyric to King Domnall:

Luin oc elaib
ungi oc dírnaib
crotha ban n-athech
oc ródaib rígnaib
Ríg oc Domnall
dord oc aidbsc
adand oc caindill
calg oc mo chailg-se.[71]

'Blackbirds (compared) to swans, ounces to pounds, the appearance of churlish women to proud queens,
    Kings to Domnall, mumbling to chanting, a taper to a candle, thus is any sword compared to my sword.'

This is the kind of rhyme that became standard in Irish poetry. Professor Carney argues that the rhyme was not originally a part of the metre, that it was added to the rhythm of the line of four stresses, and that this type of verse with its variations is probably the most basic form of Irish versification.[72]

But the change in poetic forms is nothing compared to the revolution in the content and spirit of the poetry; it is perhaps in these that the effect of Christianity on the mind and soul of the Irish can best be demonstrated. The coming of Christianity inevitably made a great difference to life in Ireland. The intellectual horizons of the Irishman were widened, his consciousness deepened, his spirit quickened, and he was imbued with a new sensitivity. This is nowhere reflected better than in the new poetry that came into being, the only poetry that is recognized as such today among the abundant poetic output of that period. To borrow a term used by H. M. and N. K. Chadwick, this is Archilochic poetry, that is, poetry designed to express personal feelings.[73] Remarkably enough, its most characteristic and most interesting pieces are those classified generally as nature poetry.

Professor Gerard Murphy showed that the old poetry of the *filid* exhibits no interest in nature and her beauty, nor is there any in the oldest tales.[74] Except for some later poems attributed to Deirdre, there is scarcely any of it in the Ulster Cycle or in the Mythological Cycle (that is, the cycle of tales about supernatural beings, the inhabitants of the fairy mounds), and it is very difficult to find any in the oldest tales of the Historical Cycle. Indeed, all those tales that exhibit any interest in nature are late: most especially in the tales that were constructed around Suibhne Geilt, the king who is said to have gone mad after being wounded in the Battle of Mag Rath, and in the tales about Fionn Mac Cumhaill in the ninth and following centuries—tales that developed from the folklore and traditions of various *fiana* or 'warbands'. It is worth noting that there was a close connection between these tales and the world of Christianity. In some of them, the saints, especially Patrick and Mo-Ling, play an important part, and in one of them the *fiana* are given a quasi-Christian appearance by being invested with the most gentle virtues, such as generosity, truthfulness, and love of learning. It is possible, therefore, to assert as a general truth that the oldest tales, those pagan in spirit, are devoid of any interest in nature, and that the later ones, Christian in background if not in spirit, evince it most.

Little is known about the personal lyric in the literature of this period, and there are not many examples of it except as part of dramatic poetry. In that respect, it is noteworthy that the poets who utilized the dramatic form in the ninth and following centuries put songs extolling the joys and pleasures of the open life almost exclusively into the mouth of some early monk or hermit like Colum Cille, Mo-Ling, Manchán, Ceallach or the legendary Marbán.[75] This suggests that in the poets' minds, nature poetry was linked with various monks and hermits of the sixth and seventh centuries. The saints' lives, of which there are, as one would expect, many, give a similar impression.[76] The early ones portray saints like Colum Cille and Columbanus as individuals very fond of nature and animals, and many of the later ones are little more than romances, ascribing to some of the saints an exceptional love of animals, both wild and domesticated. Mo-Ling is probably the most renowned of these. He is said to have raised animals in honour of God (*fera animalia et domestica consuebat in honoure conditoris suorum alere*).[77]

In view of all this evidence, Professor Gerard Murphy was probably correct when he insisted that it was Christianity and the belief in one God, creator of all things, together with monasticism which stimulated the Irish to value solitude, aroused their interest in nature, and induced in them an empathetic response to all her wildness as well as her placitude.

In a Latin manuscript preserved now in the Stiftsbibliothek in St Gall, Switzerland, but copied in the ninth century, were written a number of Irish glosses and a few stanzas of poetry.[78] One of the poems seems to describe the copyist at his work out in the open air:

> Dom·farcai fidbaidæ fál
> fom·chain loíd luin—lúad nad·cél—,
> húas mo labrán ind línech
> fom·chain trírech inna n-én.
>
> Fomm·chain coí menn—medair mass—
> hi m-brot glass de dindgnaib doss.
> dēbrad, nom·choimmdiu coíma,
> caín scríbaimm fo roída r(oss).[79]

The picture is charmingly recreated in English in Frank O'Connor's translation:

> A wall of woodland overlooks me; a blackbird's song sings to me (praise that I shall not hide). Over my lined book the trilling of the birds sings to me.
>
> A clear-voiced cuckoo sings to me in green cloak of bush-tops, a lovely utterance. The lord be good to me on Judgement Day! I write well under the woodland trees.[80]

In a manuscript preserved now in the Monastery of St Paul in Carinthia on the shores of Lake Constance (see above, p. 74), some peripatetic scholar from Ireland—from Leinster, presumably—wrote down things that struck his fancy; among these jottings are two remarkably interesting poems for which we are very grateful. One of them provides the first example in Irish manuscripts of the use of poetry to express wholly personal feelings. Not surprisingly, it deals with the author's cat:

Messe (ocus) Pangur bán,
cechtar nathar fria saindān;
bíth a menma-sam fri seilgg,
mu menma céin im saincheirdd.

Caraim-se fos, ferr cach clú,
oc mu lebrān lēir ingnu;
ni foirmtech frimm Pangur bán,
caraid cesin a maccdán.

Ó ru·biam—scél cen scís—
innar tegdais ar n-ōendís,
tāithiunn—dīchrīchide clius—
nī fris'tarddam ar n-áthius.

Gnáth-hūaraib ar gressaib gal
glenaid luch inna lín-sam;
os mé, du·fuit im lín chéin
dliged n-doraid cu n-dronchēill.

Fūachaid-sem fri frega fál
a rosc, anglése comlán;
fūachimm chēin fri fēgi fis
mu rosc rēil, cesu imdis.

Fāelid-sem cu n-dēne dul,
hi·n-glen luch inna gērchrub;
hi·tucu cheist n-doraid n-dil,
os mē chene am fāelid.

Cīa beimmi amin nach ré,
ni·derban cách a chēle.
máith la cechtar nár a dán,
subaigthius a óenurán.

Hē fesin as choimsid dáu
in muid du·n-gní cach ōenláu;
du thabairt doraid du glé
for mu mud cēin am messe.[81]

Here is O'Connor's translation:

Myself and white Pangur are each at his own trade; he has his mind on hunting, my mind is on my own task.

Better than any fame I prefer peace with my book, pursuing knowledge; white Pangur does not envy me, he loves his own childish trade.

A tale without boredom when we are at home alone, we have—interminable fun—something on which to exercise our skill.

Sometimes, after desperate battles, a mouse is caught in his net; as for me there falls in my net some difficult law hard to comprehend.

He points his clear bright eye against a wall; I point my own clear one, feeble as it is, against the power of knowledge.

He is happy and darts around when a mouse sticks in his sharp claw, and I am happy in understanding some dear, difficult problem.

However long we are like that, neither disturbs the other; each of us loves his trade and enjoys it all alone.

The job he does every day is the one for which he is fit; I am competent at my own job, bringing darkness to light.[82]

Above the other poem, on the left margin of the page, was written the name 'Suibne Geilt' (Mad Sweeney), the Irish king of the Dál nAraide whom we have said was wounded in the battle of Mag Rath (AD 637).[83] He is believed to have gone mad in that battle and to have dwelt subsequently in the wilderness, mostly in tree-tops. More poems dealing with life in the open air were attributed to him than to his counterpart in Welsh literature, Myrddin Wyllt (Mad Merlin); here is one of them:

M'airiuclán hi Túaim Inbir,
ni lántechdais bes sēstu:
cona rētglannaib a réir,
cona gréin, cona ēscu.

Gobbān du·rigni in sin—
co·n-ēcestar dūib a stoir—
mu chridecán, dīa du nim,
is hé tugatōir rod·toig.

Tech in-na·fera flechod,
maigen 'na·áigder rindi,
soilsidir bid hi lugburt
os ē cen udnucht n-imbi.[84]

My little oratory in Túaim Inbir: a whole house is not more fitting, with as many stars as one could wish, with its sun, with its moon.

The craftsman who made this—his story has been told to you—my beloved, God of heaven, He is the roofer who roofed it.

A house into which the rain does not come, a place where there is no fear of spears, as bright as in a garden yet there is no fence around it.

Before we leave nature poetry, we would like to quote at length from a tenth-century poem published by K. Meyer under the title

King and Hermit.[85] It is a dialogue between the legendary Marbán and his brother Guaire, seventh-century king of Connacht. Marbán became disaffected with the life of a nobleman and warrior and went off to become a hermit. His brother the king attempted to bring him back to the court. What follows is the conversation that ensued.[86]

> [Guaire] Hermit Marbán, why do you not sleep upon a bed? More often would you sleep out of doors, with your head, where the tonsure ends, upon the ground of a fir grove.
>
> [Marbán] I have a hut in the wood; only my Lord knows it: an ash-tree closes it on one side, and a hazel, like a great tree by a rath, on the other.
>
> Two heather doorposts for support, and a lintel of honeysuckle. The wood around its narrowness[?] sheds its mast upon fat swine.
>
> The size of my hut—small yet not small—a homestead with familiar paths. A woman in blackbird-coloured cloak sings a pleasant song from its gable.
>
> Long branches of a yew-green yewtree: glorious augury! Lovely is the place: the great greenery of an oak adds to that portent.
>
> There is an apple-tree with huge apples such as grow in fairy dwellings (great are these blessings), and an excellent clustered crop from small-nutted branching green hazels.
>
> Choice wells are there and waterfalls (good to drink)—they gush forth in plenty[?]; berries of yew, bird-cherry, and privet[?] are there.
>
> Around it tame swine, goats, young pigs, wild swine, tall deer, does, badger-cubs[?], and badgers have their lairs.
>
> Grouped in bands, at peace, a mighty army from the countryside, an assembly gathering to my house; foxes come to the wood before it: it is a lovely sight.
> Delightful feasts come . . . (swift preparing), pure water . . ., salmon and trout.
>
> Produce of mountain ash, black sloes from a dark blackthorn, berry-foods, bare fruits of a bare . . .
>
> A clutch of eggs, honey, mast, and heathpease (sent by God), sweet apples, red cranberries, whortleberries.
>
> Beer and herbs, a patch of strawberries (good to taste in their plenty), haws, yew-berries, nut-kernels.
>
> A cup of excellent hazel mead, swiftly served; brown acorns manes of bramble with good blackberries.

When summer comes—pleasant rich mantle—tasty savour: earth-nuts, wild marjoram, *foltain* from the stream (green purity);

Notes of gleaming-breasted pigeons (a beloved movement); the song of a pleasant constant thrush above my house;

Bees, chafers (restricted humming, tenuous buzz); barnacle geese, brent geese, shortly before Samain (music of a dark wild one);

A nimble linnet[?], active brown wizard, from the hazel bough; there with pied plumage are woodpeckers—vast flocks.

Fair white birds come, herons, gulls—the sea sings to them; not mournful is the music made by dun grouse from russet heather.

The heifer is noisy . . . in summer, when weather is brightest: life is not bitter nor toilsome over the rich delightful fertile plain.

The wind's voice against a branchy wood, on a day of grey cloud; cascades in a river; roar of rock: delightful music!

Beautiful are the pines which made music for me, unhired; through Christ, I am no worse off at any time than you.

Though you relish that which you enjoy, exceeding all wealth, I am content with that which is given me by my gentle Christ.

With no moment of strife, no din of combat such as disturbs you, thankful to the Prince who gives every good to me in my hut.

[Guaire] I will give my great kingdom and my share of Colman's heritage, undisputed possession of it till my death, to live with you, Marbán.

Dr Robin Flower believed that there was a close connection between the hermit reform movment (usually called the Culdee movement) in the late eighth and early ninth centuries and the appearance of this nature poetry, just as there was a connection between it and the efflorescence of Irish scholarship.[87] This has become more or less the accepted view, although a number of Irish scholars have entered caveats against such an acceptance. Among these may be mentioned K. H. Jackson, who thinks that a special group of seasonal poetry may perhaps have its remote origins in a pagan past;[88] David Greene and Frank O'Connor who gave their opinion that nature poetry developed at some time in the tenth century as a result of hints in contemporary Latin poetry;[89] and Donnchadh Ó Corráin who has argued that the so-called hermit poems 'belong to a genre of poetry well-known outside Ireland and represent a self-conscious hearkening back of monastic scholars to a simpler and an idealized way of life.'[90] But no amount of theorizing concerning the origins of the Irish hermit poems should distract us from appreciating their uniqueness in their time—Europe had to wait a very long time before the appearance of anything comparable to them in the vernaculars either in numbers or in artistry. They are characterized by the freshness of vision newly discovered and by an artistry which delights in its ability to express with the utmost economy and unfailing directness.

But to return to the work of the clerics who were composing in Irish, hymns were not the only things they wrote; they used Irish to compose prayers and other devotional works as well as saints' lives. Indeed, literary productivity in Latin diminished and gradually ceased; at the same time the history of literary activity in Irish shows steady growth. It has already been asserted that the *Navigatio Sancti Brendani* was the last Latin literary work of any importance to be produced in Ireland, and that, as we have seen, was very much indebted to the *immrama* of the *filid*.[91]

§3

The educational system of the *filid* was completely different from that of the Church.[92] The one was an oral tradition, the other was based on books. We know that writing carried the day in the course of the development of civilization, and no doubt the culture of the *filid* would have disappeared had they not taken advantage of the new means to transmit it.

We get a glimpse of what transpired in the history of Cenn Faelad, who died in the year 679.[93] It is said that he, like Suibhne Geilt, was wounded in the Battle of Mag Rath. After the battle he was brought to Tuaim Drecuin where he had an operation. Either because of the wound or the operation, he was deprived, says the story, of that part of the brain which enables a man to forget![94] In Tuaim Drecuin, there were three schools: a Latin school, a school of Irish law, and a school of Irish learning.[95] As nephew of the high king, Cenn Faelad was allowed to go to the three schools, where he remained for three years. This is what is recorded about him as a student: 'and everything that he heard uttered in the three schools he retained in his memory each night. And he cast those things in poetic form and wrote them on slate and tablets and copied them in a book of vellum.'[96] Now, as Mac Neill argued, the point of this memoir is undoubtedly to show that Cenn

Faelad had broken new ground in using writing as a means of learning in the Irish schools, and it is interesting to note that Binchy thinks that 'it must have been about Cenn Faelad's time that writing in the Latin alphabet spread to the native law schools.'[97] It was an old practice in the Latin schools, but in the schools that taught the native tradition it was revolutionarily new.

It is quite possible, however, that that is not Cenn Faelad's chief claim to fame. It is said that he wrote, among other things, an Irish grammar, and that parts of it are extant, preserved in *Auraicept na n-Éces*.[98] As those familiar with the literary output of Europe in the seventh century know, it is nothing short of a miracle to find a scholar in that period composing a grammar in any language other than Latin. Our admiration of Cenn Faelad would be greater still if it could be proven—as some insist it can—that he was a man well-versed not only in his own native language, but in the classical tradition of grammatical principles as well.

We do not know whether Cenn Faelad was a *fili* by profession, but there is no doubt about the fact that he had the knowledge and learning of a *fili*. In fact, he is the first poet whose work is quoted in the Annals, and it is interesting to note that all the poetry attributed to him deals with his kinsmen, the Northern Uí Néill. The title given to him in the Annals is *sapiens*, a technical term, it seems, used to designate a principal or teacher in a monastic school.[99] All this suggests that Cenn Faelad, whatever his official position, was able to bridge the gap single-handedly between the *filid* and the clerical scholars.[100]

There is no doubt that the clerical scholars were becoming more and more important in national life in this period. That is probably why the Annals begin to record the deaths of *sapientes* about this time.[101] Prior to AD 700, the *Annals of Ulster* (AU) record the following deaths: Cuimíne Fota of Clonfert[102] (d. 662; his teacher was Colmán moccu Chluasaig,[103] the man to whom one of the earliest Irish hymns is attributed); Sarán ua Critáin of Tisaran (d. 662); Aireran (Aileran) of Clonard, Co. Meath (d. 665); and Lochéne, Abbot of Kildare (d. 696). All these and others must have been active in the same century as Cenn Faelad.[104]

For these *sapientes* and the less conservative *filid*, it must have been quite a problem to decide what attitude they ought to take toward the tales which were such an integral part of native tradition, for it is important to remember that they were not simply stories to those who told or heard them, but true histories containing an account of the activities of the ancestors and forefathers of the Irish. The choice was between rejecting them as fabrications containing nothing but lies, or accepting them as part of the true history of the people. It takes a certain temperament to shatter idols, and apparently the scholars of that period did not possess it sufficiently to destroy those tales; they accepted them as history, and employed a conventional method of proving their authenticity: they brought some of the old heroes face to face with known historical personages.[105] That is what is behind the supernatural appearance of Cú Chulainn to Patrick,[106] the miraculous survival of Oisín, and Senchán's calling up of Fergus mac Roig from the dead.[107]

There are at least three versions of this last event.[108] In one of them, Senchán Torpéist sends his son Muirgein and Émine Ua Nínníne to search for the *Táin Bó Cúailnge*; they discover that the only extant copy has been carried abroad in exchange for the Cuilmenn (probably a copy of Isidore's *Origines*).[109] The two arrive at the grave of Fergus mac Roig, and there, in response to a *laíd*, Fergus appears and narrates the *Táin* to Muirgein alone for three days and nights in a kind of mist that enveloped the pair. That, in brief, is the first version in *The Book of Leinster* (LL).[110] In another version, found in Egerton MS 1782, neither Senchán nor his son Muirgein are mentioned—it is Nínníne who questions Fergus, and the event is dated in the time of Cormac mac Fáeláin.[111] According to the Four Masters, Cormac died in 751, and the death of his father, Fáelán Ua Silni, is dated in the year 710 (*recte* 711) by AU. This Nínníne, if he is identical with Nínníne Éces, is not entirely unknown. An old poem to Patrick in the *Liber Hymnorum* is attributed to him,[112] and there are references to him in the *Félire*. *The Annals of Tigernach* quotes two stanzas from his work under the year 621.[113]

For the third version we must return to *The Book of Leinster*. At the end of the version described above is another in which Fergus recites the *Táin* to Senchán himself after the poet has fasted upon the graves of saints in Fergus's line. This version is found in full in R.I.A. MS Stowe D. IV 2, f.49.[114] There, Guaire, king of Connacht, asks Senchán to recite the *Táin*. The poet asks for more time, and Guaire builds a house for him that stretches from Durlus to Clonfert. (This is a motif known from the tale of Cano mac Gartnáin.)[115] Senchán fasts on the grave of St Brendan of Clonfert; the latter, through a vision, sends him to the grave of St Ciarán of Clonmacnoise, and in a vision the saint sends him to the grave of the hero, Fergus, who narrates the tale to him.[116]

It was not enough to accept the stories as authentic history; they had to be brought into agreement with one another and afterwards harmonized chronologically within the framework of native and world history. The Church had its scheme of universal history in the Chronicle of Eusebius, as translated and continued by St Jerome and Prosper of Aquitaine.[117] The theory behind the system was that all the principal kingdoms—Assyria, Egypt, Palestine, Greece—through divine providence had culminated in the Roman Empire, and that, by the accord of Constantine and the Church, had become the Empire of Christ. The arrangement of the Chronicle of Eusebius was patterned on this concept. The whole history of the world was set forth in four parallel columns, and in this way one could get a synopsis of the chief events in the history of each important kingdom.

At one time it was held that the Chronicle of Eusebius, in one form or another, was the basis of the lost Irish World Chronicle—the document believed to lie behind the surviving Annals. It was thought that the Irish added a fifth column to the four of Eusebius, containing events in the history of Ireland and drawn, presumably, from the genealogies, local histories, and tales of all kinds; subsequently they set the original scheme aside and rearranged the history in the form of annals. The inclination now is to doubt that, for it appears that the material of Eusebius's Chronicle was not an integral part of the Irish World Chronicle, but that the Irish chronicle was influenced more by Bede.

However the earliest Irish chronicles were formed, they were clearly the fruits of the labours of scholars who, like Cenn Faelad, were able to synthesize the new and the traditional learning. The *filid* and the scholars seem to have done their best to assimilate one another's learning, and the evidence is that they were most successful in studying the history of the land.[118] Among the *filid* who took a special interest in historical traditions is Mac Liag (d. 1016),[119] the chief poet of Brian Bórumha; he appears to have incorporated the history of the Dál gCais into the framework that had been constructed by his predecessors. Another is Cúan Ua Lothcháin, poet of Meath, who died in 1024;[120] he wrote poetry on the antiquities of Tara and on subjects dealing with the high kingship. Gilla Caemáin (d. 1072) is the author of a long poem containing a synopsis of the history of Ireland from the creation to the time of Patrick.[121]

It is easy to cite examples of clerical scholars with similar interests. There is Cormac mac Cuilennáin, a bishop (in name if not in fact), who became king of Munster and was killed in 908. He is said to have been the author or compiler of *Sanas Cormaic*, 'Cormac's Glossary', perhaps the first etymological dictionary in any vernacular in Europe.[122] He is also credited with the *Leabhar na gCeart*,[123] a book already referred to, and a lost text, the *Saltair Caissil*, or 'Psalter of Cashel', which appears to have been a collection of poems on historical, genealogical, and other related subjects. *Saltair Caissil* was extant in 1453, when parts of it were copied into Laud MS. 610 (Bodleian Library).[124]

Eochaid Ua Flainn or Flannacáin (d. 1004), an *airchinnech*, that is, 'superior', of one of the establishments at Armagh and the church of Cluan Fiachna (Clonfeacle near Dungannon), must have been a man of similar purposes.[125] He is described as *sui* 'sage, learned man' in *filidecht* and *senchus*, and a number of his poems on pagan Ireland have been preserved.[126] Flann Mainistrech (d. 1056), as his name ('of the monastery') suggests, probably belonged to the same class of clerical scholars, although all his extant work falls neatly within the limits of the *filid*'s regular activity.[127] He was *fer léiginn* of Mainster Buiti (Monasterboice)—an interesting Irish title, for it supplanted Latin *scriba* as the official designation for the man who was in charge of the intellectual activities of an ecclesiastical school. The difference in titles probably reflects the changing interests in the various schools.

Fortunately, we have more than one text composed by a superior of these ecclesiastical schools that reflects the new interest taken in native culture. Under the year 1016, AU records the death of Airbertach mac Coisi-dobráin, *airchinnech* of Ros-Ailithir.[128] According to the *Annals of Inisfallen* (AI),[129] Norsemen destroyed Ros-Ailithir in 990 and took the *fer léiginn*, Mac Coss-dobráin, prisoner. Later, Brian Bórumha paid a ransom for him. It appears that this is the same Mac Cosse, *fer léiginn* of Ros-Ailithir, to whom *The Book of Leinster* attributes a topographical poem,[130] and Rawlinson MS B.502 the same poem together with religious and scriptural poems.[131]

We can safely assume that the change in the language of the manuscripts is another sign of the changing interests of the ecclesiastical schools. It has already been stated that manuscripts written up to the tenth century are mostly in Latin, with some Irish. In the period immediately following, the eleventh and twelfth centuries, Irish is the principal language of the manuscripts. And the change in language reflects, to a certain extent, a difference in content. The nature of the texts in Latin manuscripts is religious for the most part, but the content of the Irish manuscripts varies. Some of them contain nothing but religious material, but others have secular texts side by side with the religious. This distinction ought not to lead us into the erroneous conclusion that Irish subjects were not copied or studied before the eleventh century. It is evident that many of the secular texts that appear in Irish manuscripts are based on others which were unquestionably extant in the eighth and ninth centuries.[132]

Clerics were the scribes of both Latin and Irish manuscripts, but it appears that the Latin manuscripts did not come from the same centres as the Irish ones. As far as we can determine, those in Latin issued from schools in Leinster and South Ulster, but the Irish manuscripts came from schools more to the west, in that area along the Shannon between Loch Ree and Loch Derg, from Clonmacnoise and Terryglass. Generally speaking, then, Leinster and Munster were the centres of learning between the sixth and the twelfth centuries. When we run across centres outside their territory, such as Bangor and Iona, we can trace a connection between them and the South.

The monastery at Bangor was, as we have seen, an important centre; according to AU, it was established in 555 or 559 by St Comgall.[133] Not far from it was the Monastery of Movilla, founded around 540 by St Finnian. It is said that Colum Cille received part of his education in Movilla, and that St Comgall was with him as a missionary among the Picts. (It would be quite natural for St Comgall to have done that, for he came from the Pictish territory of Dál nAraide.) It is said also that St Comgall was the teacher of Columbanus. It seems, therefore, that some of the chief missionaries set out on their work from the area of Bangor and Movilla in Eastern Ulster.

This alone is evidence of the spiritual and intellectual vigour of the region, but there is additional evidence that Bangor was the centre of historical studies and that some of the earliest chronicles were produced there. It is believed that Sinlán (mo-Sinu) Moccu Mín,[134] the same Sinlanus referred to in the *Antiphonary* of Bangor as *famosus mundi magister*, founded the school of history there, after having spent some time, it seems, studying the *computus*—the basis of the science of *almanachus* in the Church at that time.[135] Mac Neill believed that Sinlanus was engaged in continuing the Chronicle of Eusebius (in Irish) down to the year 607, that the Old Irish Chronicle was composed around 717, and that that is what underlies all the

Annals now extant.[136] O'Rahilly was not prepared to follow Mac Neill; he believed that that chronicle ('The Chronicle of Ulster') incorporating an 'Iona Chronicle' was most likely composed in the Monastery of Bangor around 740.[137] It began with the year 431, the year Palladius came to Ireland. The compiler drew his materials mostly from local Irish sources, but he made use of foreign sources as well, e.g., the Chronicle of Marcellinus and a certain *Liber Pontificalis*. His work is best preserved in *The Annals of Ulster*,[138] but, naturally, with some additions, and it is represented also in other annals: *The Annals of Inisfallen* (AI),[139] *The Annals of Tigernach* (Tig),[140] *The Annals of Clonmacnoise* (AC),[141] *Cottonian Annals*,[142] and *Chronicon Scottorum* (CS).[143] In a later period—certainly not before the ninth century—another scholar from Eastern Ulster composed a chronicle ('The Irish World Chronicle') which began with the story of the creation and ended in 430. His materials were drawn from various Latin sources—Bede, Eusebius (in the Latin version), and Orosius, but some Irish pseudo-history was incorporated in it, such as the history of the conquests of Ireland (based on an early version of the *Lebor Gabála*), a list of the kings of Emain since its foundation, and a list of the kings of Tara from about the beginning of the Christian era. We can see, then, how closely Bangor and East Ulster were connected with the Irish chronicles.

A considerable amount of work has been done on the Irish Annals since the publication of O'Rahilly's *Early Irish History and Mythology*. In particular Professor John V. Kelleher has published some illuminating articles. Discussing 'Early Irish History and Pseudo-History' in 1963, he concluded that 'Apart from interpolations, it would appear that up to 910 all the annals are but selective versions of one common source, a text very likely composed in that year, and more national in its purview than any recensions derived from it.'[144] Dr Kathleen Hughes finds herself in general agreement with this statement. According to her:

> A comparison of *AU*, *Tig.*, *AI* and *CS* shows that there was a Chronicle of Ireland in existence at the beginning of the tenth century. This was conflated with Munster annals (possibly after 972) and was later savagely abbreviated. The abbreviated version is our *AI*. About 913 the texts of *AU* and *Tig.* diverge. One copy of the Chronicle of Ireland reached Clonmacnoise, where it was interpolated and became our *Tig*. In the seventeenth century Duald Mac Firbis made a copy of a MS of *Tig.*, which is now known as *Chronicon Scottorum*. Another copy of the Chronicle of Ireland, after a series of interpolations, became our *AU*.[145]

Dr Hughes agrees with O'Rahilly that an Iona/Ulster (Bangor) Chronicle formed the earliest stratum in the Chronicle of Ireland, but notes that the Iona/Ulster entries have been completely swamped by the rest, to some extent in the seventh century and increasingly so in the eighth century, as the records become fuller. As the Chronicle of Ireland does not reflect the Ulster interest which we would expect if it had been drawn up there, as O'Rahilly implies, Dr Hughes would look elsewhere for the centre where it was compiled.

The compiler of the Chronicle had an absorbing interest in the activities of the Uí Néill, and it is reasonable to look for the place where the annals were compiled not in east Ulster but in the territories of the Uí Néill, and more especially in that branch of the Uí Néill who figure most prominently in them: in the descendants of Aed Sláine. As the compiler was almost certainly a member of some monastic foundation, it is sensible to take his references to monasteries as an indication of his circle of interests. Examination of the entries show that the compiler probably had access to Kildare records and to Clonard records but most of the entries refer to houses further north, and Dr Hughes concludes that Professor Kelleher had more than a little justification in suggesting Louth in Brega as the place of compilation, but further consideration leads her to favour Armagh rather than Louth.

> I think that contemporary Uí Néill annals were being kept at least as early as the last quarters of the eighth century. These *may* at first have been kept at Louth. But the overwhelming weight of evidence from the late eighth century onward points to Armagh. There are fifty-eight entries in *AU* between 780 and 900, eight Louth entries in the same period.[146]

It is difficult to decide whether the *Lebor Gabála Érenn*, which itself is a kind of history book, underwent some of the stages in its development in the same district.[147] Indeed, among the men who composed the poems in it there were, so we are told, a cleric of Armagh and a lector of Monasterboice, but, unfortunately, we cannot rely on such statements as these because the work is, as Dillon characterized it, 'a collection of pseudo-historical poems by various authors, arranged in a pattern of invasions.'[148] O'Rahilly judges that the *Lebor Gabála* has seen a good deal of revision and expansion, and that the original composition—much smaller and corresponding better to its title than the present redaction—goes back at least as far as the beginning of the ninth century when the British historian, misnamed Nennius, refers to the invasions with the comment, 'Thus have the most learned of the Irish informed me'.[149] It was written, says O'Rahilly, to make the people forget their ethnic stratification and develop a consciousness of being one people and not a group of peoples.[150]

As it stands, the compilation cannot be earlier than the later eleventh century, and is clearly the product of monastic learning superimposed upon native learning. Some of the names are Latin or derived from Latin and the structure is based on Old Testament history—Gaedel is made a descendant of Japheth son of Noah and the ancestors of the Irish are made to set out, as did the children of Israel, from Egypt, and their destination is made into a kind of promised land, full of fruit, wheat and fish, with moderate heat and cold.

The imposition of the monastic on the native learning seems to be deliberate. Pagan elements in the native tradition are Christianized. Fintan, son of Labraid, was a year under the flood but survived until the coming of the saints, long enough to tell the early story of the Irish to Patrick, Colum Cille, Comgal and Finnian, by whom, we are told, it was written down. Since then saints and sages have co-operated to preserve it; indeed, they have 'stitched together all knowledge into it'.

In this sum of all knowledge, there is included a great deal of folklore as well as *senchas*, the traditional lore handed down from generation to generation; included in the latter, indeed, perhaps the foremost element in it, was genealogical lore.

Several collections of genealogies have been lost, others have survived. We know there was a collection of them in the lost Psalter of Cashel, compiled around 900,[151] but the oldest extant collection is in *The Book of Leinster*. Another very important element was the tales. Some of them, such as the Ulster Tales, and perhaps the stories about Mongán,[152] belong to the same area where the historians were so earnestly and seriously at work.

We do not know when the Irish tales were first written down, but we do know that some of them were set down on vellum during the first half of the eighth century. Reference has already been made to *Cín Dromma Snechta(i)* (Druim Snechta(i) = Drumsnat in Co. Monaghan),[153] a manuscript long since lost, but out of which lengthy excerpts were copied in the late Middle Ages. Using these excerpts, Thurneysen, who believed that the Book of Druim Snechta(i) could have been written in the first half of the eighth century, showed that it included *Immram Brain*,[154] *Compert Con Culainn* ('Birth of Cú

Chulainn'),[155] four stories about Mongán,[156] *Verba Scáthaige*,[157] *Echtra Machae* ('The Adventurous Journey of Macha'),[158] *Forfes Fer Fálchae* ('The Attack of the Men of Fálchae'),[159] *Echtra Conlai* ('The Adventures of Conla'),[160] *Togail Bruidne Dá Derga* ('The Destruction of Dá Derga's Hostel'),[161] *Baile Chuind Chétchathaig* ('The Frenzy of Conn the Hundred-Fighter'),[162] and *Tochmarc Étaíne* ('The Wooing of Étaíne').[163]

The next important piece of evidence for the tales is to be found in the aforementioned saga list which is preserved in two versions.[164] The earlier of them is in *Airec Menman Uraird Maic Coise*, a tale dated about AD 1000; the other is incorporated in *The Book of Leinster*. We know that there were tales in the Book of Dub-dá-leithe,[165] written in Armagh around 1050, but the knowledge does not count for much, because that book—like many another—has been irretrievably lost. Dub-dá-leithe was *fer léiginn* in Armagh during the years 1046–9, and superior of the monastery from 1049 to 1064.[166] The copyists to whom we are indebted for the tales are those referred to earlier, namely, the men who were engaged in that area of the Shannon between Loch Ree and Loch Derg, in Clonmacnoise and Terryglass. For example, the oldest collection of tales is found in *Lebor na h-Uidre* (LU), a manuscript written in the monastery of Clonmacnoise around 1100.[167] A part of Bodleian MS Rawlinson B.502 was produced in the same place;[168] the oldest part, which contains Fragment I of *The Annals of Tigernach*, was written about the same time as LU, and it is generally considered that the collection of religious texts which forms the largest part of it was written about 1120. Another manuscript that contains a collection of tales is *An Leabhar Laighneach*, that is, *The Book of Leinster* (LL), once thought to have been compiled by Aed Mac Crimthainn, abbot of Terryglass (Tír-dá-glas), at the request of Find, bishop of Kildare, who died in 1160; recent work has shown, however, that four main styles of writing are to be seen in that manuscript.[169] *An Leabhar Breac* (LB)[170] does not belong to the same period as the three other manuscripts, and the nature of its contents is religious rather than secular; still, it was written in the same neighbourhood as the others, and deserves to be counted as one of the Four Chief Books of Ireland.

It is not our purpose to discuss the stories in detail here, but it will be worthwhile to summarize the history of the principal story in the Ulster Cycle, *Táin Bó Cúailnge*, in order to exemplify the kind of development the tales underwent in the period.

It is believed that *Táin Bó Cúailnge* was written down for the first time toward the middle of the seventh century by a *fili* who may have had some of the Latin learning of the monasteries, and who also wished to record the native heroic tradition in a worthy form.[171] There are signs that either he or a later redactor was familiar with the *Aeneid*; Allecto (vii, 323ff) appears as Allechtu,[172] and it has been suggested that the boyhood deeds of Cú Chulainn were intended to correspond to the recital of Aeneas' feats in Books I and II. It has also been argued that the description of the watchman of the Ulstermen comes close to a feature that can be traced in *Iliad* III,[173] but the 'watchman-device' is not peculiar to Greek or even classical literature and in any case it is difficult to determine whether the reminiscences of the *Aeneid* some scholars have found in the *Táin* were in the seventh-century *Grundtext*.

The development of the epic has been explained in detail by Thurneysen and Cecile O'Rahilly.[174] The various stages are represented in three recensions. Recension I is found incomplete in the texts of the *Táin* in LU, Egerton MS 1782, *The Yellow Book of Lecan* (YBL) and O'Curry MS 1. None of these is a copy of the other. The LU text is the oldest but it contains interpolations and these, usually designated H, are also found in the Egerton and O'Curry texts but not in YBL.

Recension II is the version found in LL and in a modernized and expanded form in R.I.A. MS C VI. 3. Recension III is preserved in a fragmentary form in two late manuscripts, Egerton MS 93 and T.C.D. H2. 17. It agrees in many points with Recension II, but it contains passages which agree verbatim with the H-interpolations in the LU, Egerton, and O'Curry texts of Recension I.

It is generally agreed that Recension I in its uninterpolated form is the result of the conflation of two or more earlier versions: Thurneysen postulated the existence in the ninth century of two parallel versions. Apart from the contradictions and inconsistencies which arose from the conflation, it contained doublets and variants, i.e., incidents in which the same motifs and themes occur to a greater or lesser degree.

Recension II is based on Recension I shorn of its variants and doublets as well as its interpolations, but it draws also on a variant version now lost and designated *x*. The redactor responsible for this recension aimed at providing 'a full, accurate and definitive narrative to be the pattern of all future scribes'.[175] Naturally, he removed all or almost all of the inconsistencies and contradictions found in

Recension I. His style, rather florid and adjectival, became a pattern for later story writers.

It is easy to see that even the LU text is far from being a straightforward story written from sheer interest in the narrative, but rather a compilation made up of various traditions; indeed, the compiler shows his hand in comments such as *in aliis libris* (LU 244), *secundum alios* (LU 719), *atberat araili* (LU 2002). It is quite probable that the seventh-century *fili* postulated by Thurneysen as the one first responsible for committing the tale to writing was less an author than a compiler, for the elements of the story must be very old, and even the framework within which he gathered them, if it was, as we may well suppose, the story of a fight between two bulls, may reflect a cult of bull-gods of the kind which is found in the very earliest civilizations of the Mediterranean.

However much we may regret the loss of many of the early traditions which the compiler or rather compilers were forced to sacrifice for the sake of the consistency and the unity of the narrative—and one is forced to admit that they could have sacrificed more, for the story as a whole remains a hotch-potch to modern literary tastes—we cannot fail to be entertained by the art which is exhibited in some parts of the story. Our pleasure in the narrative does not depend on our knowledge or lack of knowledge as to which particular strata in the various stages of accumulation those parts belong to.

Thus we are told that the 'pillow-talk' between Ailill and Medb, which we quoted on pp. 15–16, is not part of the original story of the Táin, and—perhaps with more reason—that the account of Cú Chulainn's youthful exploits which is introduced as a 'flashback' and put into the mouth of Fergus is also an accretion. That consideration, however, does not detract from our pleasure in reading such episodes as 'How Cú Chulainn got his name', which we give here in a translation of the LU text.

> 'Come with me,' said Conchobor to Cú Chulainn. 'You will be a guest at this feast we are going to.'
> 'I haven't had my fill of play yet, friend Conchobor,' the boy said, 'I'll follow you.'
> Later, when they had all arrived at the feast, Culann said to Conchobor, 'Is there anybody still to come after you?'
> 'No,' Conchobor said, forgetting the arrangement that his foster-son was to follow them.
> 'I have a savage hound,' Culann said. 'Three chains are needed to

hold him, with three men on each chain. Let him loose,' he ordered, 'to guard our cattle and other stock. Shut the gate of the enclosure.'

Soon the boy arrived and the hound started out for him. But he still attended to his game: he tossed his ball up and threw his hurling-stick after it and struck it; the length of his stroke never varied. Then he would cast his javelin after both, and catch it before it fell. His game never faltered though the hound was tearing toward him. Conchobor and his people were in such anguish at this that they couldn't stir. They were sure they couldn't reach him alive, even if the enclosure gate were open. The hound sprang. Cú Chulainn tossed the ball aside and the stick with it and tackled the hound with his two hands: he clutched the hound's throat-apple in one hand and grasped its back with the other. He smashed it against the nearest pillar and its limbs leaped from their sockets. (According to another version he threw his ball into its mouth and so tore its entrails out.)

Then the Ulstermen rose up to meet him, some of them over the rampart, others through the gate of the enclosure. They carried him to Conchobor's bosom. They gave a great cry of triumph, that the son of the king's sister had escaped death.

Culann stood in his house. 'You are welcome, boy, for your mother's heart's sake. But for my own part I did badly to give this feast. My life is a waste, and my household like a desert, with the loss of my hound! He guarded my life and my honour,' he said; 'a valued servant, my hound, taken from me. He was shield and shelter for our goods and herds. He guarded all our beasts, at home or out in the fields.'

'That doesn't matter,' the boy said. 'I'll rear you a pup from the same litter. Until that hound grows up to do his work I will be your hound and guard yourself and your beasts. And I will guard all Muirtheimne Plain. No herd or flock will leave my care unknown to me.'

'Cú Chulainn shall be your name, the hound of Culann,' Cathbad said.

'I like that for a name!' Cú Chulainn said.[176]

The spirit of the Táin, however, is not conveyed by such episodes as the above but by the starkness of the fatal encounter between Cú Chulainn and Etarcomol. To gain time for the men of Ulster to recover from their mysterious illness called *noínden Ulad*, Cú Chulainn has proposed in an indirect way that he should fight the Connachtmen in single combat, and they have agreed in order to avoid the heavy losses which they were incurring at his hands.

Fergus went to Cú Chulainn therefore with the proposal. He was followed by Etarcomol, son of Eda and Léthrenn, a foster-son of Ailill and Medb.

'I would rather you didn't come,' Fergus said. 'Not that I dislike you, but for fear of strife between Cú Chulainn and you. With your pride and insolence, and the other's ferocity and grimness, force, fury and violence, no good can come from your meeting.'

'Can I not be under your protection?' Etarcomol said.

'Yes,' Fergus said, 'but only if you don't insult him while he is talking.'

They went to Delga in two chariots.

It happened that Cú Chulainn was playing *buanbach* with Laeg. Cú Chulainn was facing away from them and Laeg facing toward them.

'I see two chariots coming,' Laeg said. 'In the first chariot there is a great dark man. His hair is dark and full. A purple cloak is wrapped about him, held by a gold brooch. He wears a red-embroidered hooded tunic. He carries a curved shield with a scalloped edge of light gold and a stabbing-spear bound around from its neck to its foot. There is a sword as big as a boat's rudder at his thigh.'

'A big empty rudder,' Cú Chulainn said. 'That is my friend Fergus and it isn't a sword but a stick he has in his scabbard. I have heard that Ailill caught him off guard when he slept with Medb, and stole his sword and gave it to his charioteer to keep. A wooden sword was put in the scabbard.'

Fergus came up.

'Welcome, friend Fergus,' Cú Chulainn said. 'If the salmon were swimming in the rivers or river mouths I'd give you one and share another. If a flock of wild birds were to alight on the plain I'd give you one and share another, with a handful of cress or sea-herb and a handful of marshwort, and a drink out of the sand, and myself in your place in the ford of battle, watching while you slept.'

'I believe you,' Fergus said, 'but it isn't for food we came here. We know the style you keep.'

Then Cú Chulainn heard Fergus's message, and Fergus left. Etarcomol stayed, staring at Cú Chulainn.

'What are you staring at?' Cú Chulainn said.

'You,' Etarcomol said.

'You could take that in at a glance,' Cú Chulainn said.

'So I see,' Etarcomol said. 'I see nothing to be afraid of—no horror or terror or the grinding of multitudes. You're a fine lad, I imagine, for graceful tricks with wooden weapons.'

'You are making little of me,' said Cú Chulainn, 'but for Fergus's sake I won't kill you. If you hadn't his protection, you would have had your bowels ripped out by now and your quarters scattered behind you all the way from your chariot to the camp.'

'You needn't threaten me any more,' Etarcomol said. 'I'll be the first of the men of Ireland to come against you tomorrow under this fine plan of single combats.' And he went off.

He turned at Methe and Cethe, and said to his charioteer: 'I have sworn in front of Fergus,' he said, 'to fight Cú Chulainn tomorrow, but I can't wait so long. Turn the horses round from this hill again.'

Laeg saw this and said to Cú Chulainn: 'The chariot is coming back. He has turned the left chariot-board against us.'

'I can't refuse that,' Cú Chulainn said. 'Drive down to the ford to him, and we will see.'

'It's you who want this,' Cú Chulainn said to Etarcomol. 'It isn't my wish.'

'You have no choice,' Etarcomol said.

Cú Chulainn cut the sod from under his feet. He fell flat, with the sod on his belly.

'Go away now,' Cú Chulainn said. 'I don't want to wash my hands after you. I'd have cut you to pieces long ago but for Fergus.'

'I won't leave it like this,' Etarcomol said. 'I'll have your head or leave you mine.'

'It will be the latter for sure.'

Cú Chulainn poked at the two armpits with his sword and the clothes fell down leaving the skin untouched.

'Now clear off!' Cú Chulainn said.

'No!' Etarcomol said.

Then Cú Chulainn sheared off his hair with the sword-edge as neat as a razor, leaving the skin unscratched. But the fool stubbornly persisted and Cú Chulainn struck down through the crown of his head and split him to the navel.

Fergus saw the chariot passing him with only one man in it and he went back in fury to Cú Chulainn. 'Demon of evil,' he said, 'you have disgraced me. You must think my cudgel is very short.'

'Friend Fergus, don't rage at me,' Cú Chulainn said.

> 'You ran from Ulster
>   with no sword to your fame
> and menace me
>   like a rival or foe
> I honour mighty men
>   but vain Etarcomol
> bent under my yoke
>   gave up death flowers
> stretched in my strength
>   on the chariot cushion
> sleeping or eating
>   my heroic hard hand
> never at rest
>   don't chide friend Fergus.'

And he stooped humbly while Fergus's chariot circled him three times.

'Ask Etarcomol's charioteer was I at fault,' Cú Chulainn said.

'You were not, truly,' the charioteer said.

'Etarcomol swore', Cú Chulainn said, 'he wouldn't leave until he had my head or left me his own. Which would you say was easier, friend Fergus?' Cú Chulainn said.

Fergus pierced Etarcomol's two heels with a spancel-ring and dragged him behind his chariot to the camp. When they were travelling over rocky ground, the halves of the body split apart; when it was level the halves joined again. Medb saw this. 'That is brutal treatment for the unfortunate dog,' Medb said.

'I say he was an ignorant whelp,' Fergus said, 'to pick a fight with the irresistible great Hound of Culann.'

Then they dug a grave for him; his memorial stone was planted, his name written in ogam, and his lamentation made.

Cú Chulainn murdered no more that night with his sling.[177]

It will be instructive to compare this account with that of the LL or Recension II version. In the latter the style is freer and more flowing, admirably suited to the redactor's purpose of producing a harmonized narrative. To judge by the way it was imitated, it was immensely popular with the littérateurs of the time, but in less skilful hands, it became turgid and bombastic, and this perhaps has blunted our appreciation of its virtues.

Fergus's horses were harnessed and his chariot yoked, and his two horses were harnessed for Etarcumul son of Fid and of Lethrinn, a stripling of the household of Medb and Ailill. 'Where are you going?' asked Fergus. 'We are going with you,' said Etarcumul, 'to see the form and appearance of Cú Chulainn and to gaze upon him.' 'If you are to follow my counsel,' said Fergus, 'you would not come at all.' 'Why so?' 'Because of your haughtiness and your arrogance, and also because of the fierceness and the valour and the savageness of the lad against whom you go, for I think that there will be strife between you before ye part.'

[There follows an account of the meeting between Fergus and Cú Chulainn.]

Etarcumul remained behind him [Fergus] gazing at Cú Chulainn for a long while. 'What are you staring at, lad?' said Cú Chulainn. 'I am staring at you,' said Etarcumul. 'You have not far to look indeed,' said Cú Chulainn. 'You redden your eye with that. But if only you knew it, the little creature you are looking at, namely, myself, is wrathful. And how do you find me as you look at me?' 'I think you are fine indeed.

THE OLD AND THE NEW

You are a comely, splendid, handsome youth with brilliant, numerous, various feats of arms. But as for reckoning you among goodly heroes or warriors or champions or sledge-hammers of smiting, we do not do so nor count you at all.' 'You know that it is a guarantee for you that you came out of the camp under the protection of my master, Fergus. But I swear by the gods whom I worship that but for Fergus's protection, only your shattered bones and your cloven joints would return to the camp!' 'Nay, do not threaten me any longer thus, for as for the condition you asked of the men of Ireland, namely, single combat, none other of the men of Ireland than I shall come to attack you tomorrow.' 'Come on, then, and however early you come, you will find me here. I shall not flee from you.' Etarcumul went back and began to converse with his charioteer. 'I must needs fight with Cú Chulainn tomorrow, driver,' said Etarcumul. 'You have promised it indeed,' said the charioteer, 'but I know not if you will fulfil your promise.' 'Which is better, to do so tomorrow or at once tonight?' 'It is my conviction,' said the driver, 'that though doing it tomorrow means no victory, yet still less is to be gained by doing it tonight (for the fight is nearer).' 'Turn the chariot back again for me, driver, for I swear by the gods whom I worship never to retreat until I carry off as a trophy the head of yon little deer. Cú Chulainn.'

The charioteer turned the chariot again towards the ford. They turned the left board of the chariot towards the company as they made for the ford. Laeg noticed that. 'The last chariot-fighter who was here a while ago, little Cú,' said Laeg. 'What of him?' said Cú Chulainn. 'He turned his left board towards us as he made for the ford.' 'That is Etarcumul, driver, seeking combat of me. And I did not welcome him because of the guarantee of my fosterfather under which he came out of the camp, and not because I wish to protect him. Bring my weapon to the ford for me, driver. I do not deem it honourable that he should reach the ford before me.' Then Cú Chulainn went to the ford and unsheathed his sword over his fair shoulder and was ready to meet Etarcumul at the ford. Etarcumul arrived also. 'What are you seeking, lad?' asked Cú Chulainn. 'I seek combat with you,' said Etarcumul. 'If you would take my advice, you wouldn't come at all,' said Cú Chulainn. 'I say so because of the guarantee of Fergus under which you came out of the encampment and not at all because I wish to protect you.' Then Cú Chulainn gave him a blow and cut away the sod from beneath the sole of his foot so that he was cast prostrate with the sod on his belly. If Cú Chulainn had so wished, he could have cut him in two. 'Begone now for I have given you warning.' 'I shall not go until we meet again,' said Etarcumul. Cú Chulainn gave him an edge-blow. He sheared his hair from him, from poll to forehead and from ear to ear as if it had been shaved with a keen, light razor. He drew not a drop of blood. 'Begone now,' said Cú Chulainn, 'for I have drawn ridicule

on you.' 'I shall not go until we meet again, until I carry off your head
and spoils and triumph over you or until you carry off my head and
spoils and triumph over me.' 'The last thing you say is what will
happen, and I shall carry off your head and spoils and I shall triumph
over you.' Cú Chulainn dealt him a blow on the crown of his head
which split him to his navel. He gave him a second blow crosswise so
that the three sections into which his body was cut fell at one and the
same time to the ground. Thus perished Etarcumul, son of Fid and
Leithrinn.

Fergus did not know that this fight had taken place. That was but
natural, for sitting and rising, journeying or marching, in battle or fight
or combat, Fergus never looked behind him lest anyone should say
that it was out of fearfulness he looked back, but (he was wont to gaze)
at what was before him and on a level with him. Etarcumul's charioteer
came abreast of Fergus; 'Where is your master, driver?' asked Fergus.
'He fell on the ford just now by the hand of Cú Chulainn,' said the
driver. 'It was not right', said Fergus, 'for that distorted sprite [Cú
Chulainn] to outrage me concerning him who came there under my
protection. Turn the chariot for us, driver,' said Fergus, 'that we may
go and speak with Cú Chulainn.'

Then the charioteeer turned the chariot. They went off towards the
ford. 'Why did you violate my pledge, you distorted sprite,' said
Fergus, 'concerning him who came under my safeguard and protection?' 'By the nurture and care you gave me, tell me which you
would prefer, that he should triumph over me or that I should triumph
over him. Moreover, enquire of his driver which of us was at fault
against each other.' 'I prefer what you have done. A blessing on the
hand that struck him!'

Then two withes were tied round Etarcumul's ankles and he was
dragged along behind his horses and his chariot. At every rough rock
he met, his lungs and liver were left behind on the stones and rocks[?].
Wherever it was smooth for him his scattered joints came together
around the horses. Thus he was dragged across the camp to the door of
the tent of Ailill and Medb. 'Here is your youth for you,' said Fergus,
'for every restoration has its fitting restitution.' Medb came to the door
of her tent and raised her voice aloud. 'We thought indeed,' said Medb,
'that great was the ardour and wrath of this young hound when he
went forth from the camp in the morning. We thought that the
guarantee under which he went, the guarantee of Fergus, was not that
of a coward.' 'What has crazed the peasant-woman?' said Fergus. 'Is it
right for the common cur to seek out the bloodhound whom the
warriors of the four great provinces of Ireland dare not approach or
withstand? Even I myself would be glad to escape whole from him.'
Thus fell Etarcumul.

That is [the story of] the Encounter of Etarcumul and Cú
Chulainn.[178]

The language of Recension II is later than that of Recension I:
Thurneysen on internal evidence assigned the composition of

Recension II to the first third or even the first quarter of the twelfth century,[179] that of Recension I to the eleventh century.[180] It is now known that the Book of Leinster in which Recension II is found is not a lay patron's book but rather a scholar's volume written by ecclesiastics filled with the desire to preserve Irish secular learning. It is therefore very significant that the scribe who copied Recension II in it added this note in Irish:

> A blessing on everyone who shall faithfully memorise the Táin as it is written here and shall not add any other form to it.

and went on to write in Latin:

> But I who wrote this history or rather fable put no trust in this history or fable, for some of these things are the feats of devils, some poetic figments, some apparently true, some not, and some for the delectation of fools.[181]

In discussing these recensions, there is a tendency to lose sight of a very important consideration, namely the relationship between the written text and the oral narration. It would be naïve for us to assume that oral narration ceased as soon as a tale was recorded, and just as naïve to assume that any one written version of a tale corresponds exactly to a single oral narration of it. One must always assume that the writer would not as a rule be content simply to reproduce what he had heard, that he would at least be tempted to play the part of editor. After telling us that the written native lore (the sagas, etc.) are all of ecclesiastical provenance, Binchy reminds us that 'they received a dressing-up from scribes and redactors'.[182] Most scholars would agree that there was at least a measure of dressing-up, but they disagree in assessing its extent. Professor Carney seems to regard the recorded tales primarily as redactions produced by literary artists in and for a (Christian) literate community, and no doubt he is right in stressing the contribution made by the redactors to the tales in the form in which they are known to us. What is in dispute is the extent of that contribution. Although we must ascribe to them a degree of freedom and independence in the way they treated oral material, it is hardly likely that they enjoyed the same freedom as that claimed by writers in a society in which the oral tradition has been swamped by the written word. And it is probably true that even such written tales as have been transmitted to us were meant to be read aloud to an audience, and not simply enjoyed privately by an individual for his own enjoyment. Surely, the audience participation which is assumed for an oral performance was not completely absent at such readings. It is safe to assume that audience participation in the way of cheering and booing, handclapping and foot-stamping—perhaps to a degree difficult for us to imagine—would be expected in the reading as well as in the narration of certain parts of tales.

It has been demonstrated that the literature of Ireland in the early period that has been under scrutiny in these two chapters was the product of two groups, the *filid* and the clerical scholars. Perhaps it is meaningless to ask which of the two contributed most, although some scholars are inclined to favour one over the other. The late Robin Flower emphasized the contribution of the clerics at the expense of the *filid*.[183] Professor James Carney has followed his lead to judge from some of his statements.[184] But supporters of the *filid* are not scarce: they include H. M. and N. K. Chadwick,[185] MacNeill,[186] and others. However, the fairest assumption is that the two groups stimulated each other, sometimes through competition, sometimes through co-operation. And when they were in contention it was very difficult to settle the dispute between them, as two satirical tales show.

In one of these, a totally unhistorical tale from the late Middle Ages,[187] a controversy between the Church and the poets is depicted with the laurels going to the former. The representative of the Church is Marbán, an ascetic hermit, and Senchán, the chief *fili* whom we have already met, is the leader of the *filid*. The poets were assembling, and admittance was denied anyone who could not prove that there was a blood relationship between himself and poetry. Marbán gained entrance to the assembly because—and this is part of the satire—the grandmother of the wife of his dear servant was great-granddaughter to a poet! Once he got there, he had no difficulty in demonstrating that the *filid* were ignorant in every branch of knowledge, and even in that branch in which they were expected to excel, the traditional and historical lore of the land.

The other tale, *Aislinge Meic Con Glinne* ('The Vision of Mac Con Glinne'),[188] dates from the eleventh century, and its hero is the poet. His name is Mac Con Glinne, but he has a nickname, *Anier*, 'because there was not before him nor after him anyone whose satires and praises were more burdensome, and that is why he was called Anier, because he could not be refused.' At the beginning of the story, Mac Con Glinne is an ecclesiastical student in Armagh, but a passionate longing comes over him to give up his studies and pursue the profession of poetry. He considers where he ought to go on his first journey as a poet, and he decides to visit King Cathal mac Finguine,

who is on circuit in Iveagh in Munster, because he has heard that
there is enough and more than enough of fat meats to be had there,
and he has a lusty hunger for such things.

> The tale that follows is one long parody of the literary methods used by
> the clerical scholars. At every turn we recognize a motive or a phrase
> from the theological, the historical, and the grammatical literature. A
> full commentary on the Vision from this point of view would be little
> short of a history of the development of literary forms in Ireland. And
> it is not only the literary tricks of the monks that are held up to
> mockery. The writer makes sport of the most sacred things, not sparing
> even the Sacraments and Christ's crucifixion. He jests at relics, at
> tithes, at ascetic practices, at amulets, at the sermons and private
> devotions of the monks; the flying shafts of his wit spare nothing and
> nobody. It is little wonder that the monks were at odds with such poets
> as this. The point of the whole composition is the contempt of the
> monk for the poet and the way in which the poet turns the tables on
> him.[189]

Notes

1 M.A. O'Brien, 'Irish Origin-Legends', in M. Dillon, ed., *Early Irish
  Society* (Dublin, 1954), p. 36. For the uncertainty regarding 432, the
  year of St Patrick's arrival in Ireland, even in the sources, see J. V.
  Kelleher, 'Early Irish History and Pseudo-History', SH, 3 (1963), 126–7.
2 'No evidence has ever been produced to prove the existence of writing
  for literary purposes in Ireland before the coming of Christianity';
  Flower, *The Irish Tradition*, p. 73. And with one exception (*dubh* for
  'ink'), all the words for reading and writing in Irish are derived from
  Latin: *sgríobhaim* (*scrib-o*), *léighim* (*leg-o*), *penn* (*penna*), *litir* (*littera*);
  Dillon, op. cit., p. 16. But consider also Professor D. A. Binchy's
  remarks on 'The Background of Early Irish Literature', SH, 1 (1961),
  8–9.
3 Thurneysen, GOI, pp. 10–11; John Rhŷs, *Lectures on Welsh
  Philology* (1879), p. 272ff.; K. H. Jackson, 'Notes on the Ogam
  Inscriptions of Southern Britain', in *The Early Cultures of North
  West Europe* (H. M. Chadwick Memorial Studies, Cambridge, 1950),
  pp. 199–213. Much has been written on the origin of the Ogam alpha-
  bet: among the most recent contributions we may mention J. Carney,
  'The Invention of the Ogom Cipher', *Ériu*, 26 (1975), 52–65;
  Damien McManus, 'Ogam: Archaizing, Orthography and the
  Authenticity of the Manuscript Key to the Alphabet', *Ériu*, 37 (1986),
  1–31.
4 Windisch, *Táin Bó Cualnge*, 69.565, 71.582. C. O'Rahilly, *TBC from the
  Book of Leinster*, 11. 560–65 (pp. 16, 153).

5 Text and translation by O'Curry, MS. Materials, pp. 472ff.; cf. p. 464ff.; Meyer, 'Scél Baili Binnbérlaig', RC, 13 (1892), 220–27, Corrigenda, 17 (1896), 319.

6 Meyer and Nutt, The Voyage of Bran, I, 34.

7 Cf. GL. I, 484, 488ff.

8 E. Mac Neill, 'Beginnings of Latin Culture in Ireland', Studies, 20 (1931), 39–48, 449–60.

9 Cf. L. Bieler's comment, 'Ireland is unique in the medieval western world in having not only a native literature but also a native tradition of professional learning'; 'The Island of Scholars', Revue du moyen âge latin, 8 (1952), 213.

10 See above, pp. 31–2.

11 See above, pp. 26–7.

12 F. J. H. Jenkinson, ed., The Hisperica Famina (Dublin, 1908). More recently, ed. and trans. by Michael W. Herren, The Hisperica Famina: I. The A-Text (Toronto, 1974); The Hisperica Famina: II. Related Poems (Toronto, 1987). Bieler, art. cit., at 219, thought it 'utterly impossible that Continental scholars would have gone to Ireland before the middle of the fifth century.' (The dominicati rethorici of St Patrick's Confessio (c.13) are almost certainly to be sought outside Ireland.) See also Michael Lapidge, 'Latin Learning in Dark Age Wales: Some Prolegomena', Proceedings of the Seventh International Congress of Celtic Studies. Oxford, 1983, pp. 91–107, and especially pp. 96–7 where references to the latest work on the origin of the Hisperica Famina may be found.

13 Kenney, Sources, I, 257–8; cf. Thurneysen, Heldensage, I, 54; E. K. Rand, 'The Irish Flavor of Hisperica Famina' in Studien zur lat. Dichtung des Mittelalters, Strecker Festgabe, 1931, 134–42; L. Bieler, Ireland, Harbinger of the Middle Ages (London, 1963), p. 13.

14 H. Zimmer, The Irish Element in Mediaeval Culture, trans. by J. L. Edmunds (New York, London, 1891); S. J. Crawford, Anglo-Saxon Influence on Western Christendom (London, 1933), p. 88ff.; B. Bischoff, 'Il monachismo irlandese ne i suoi rapporti col continente', in his Mittelalterlichen Studien I (Stuttgart, 1966), 195–205. For a more general account see Bieler, Ireland, Harbinger of the Middle Ages.

15 Bieler, 'The Island of Scholars,' Revue du moyen âge latin 8 (1952), 213–31.

16 Bieler, Ireland, Harbinger, p. vii.

17 It is probably significant that although there are references to monks and nuns in the writings of St Patrick, there are no references to monasteries.

18 Bieler, Ireland, Harbinger, p. 17.

19 Dom L. Gougaud, Christianity in Celtic Lands (London, 1932), p. 361. On the significant development of the so-called Irish half-uncial, see H. Foerster, Abriß der lateinischen Paläographie (Stuttgart, 1963), pp. 141–53; B. Bischoff, Latin Palaeography (Trans. Dáibhí Ó Cróinín and David Ganz. Cambridge, 1990) 88–90.

20 Giraldus Cambrensis, Topography of Ireland, transl. J. J. O'Meara (Dundalk, 1951), p. 67. On the Book of Kells, see Françoise Henry, Art Irlandais (Dublin, 1954), p. 54.

21 This is how St Aldhelm described Ireland's reputation in the seventh century: 'Quamvis enim praedictum Hiberniae rus discentium opulens vernansque pascuosa . . . numerositate lectorum, quem admodum poli cardines astriferis micantium ornentur vibraminibus siderum . . . ' Migne, PL., LXXXIX, 94.

22 'Hibernia quo catervatim isthinc lectores classibus advecti confluunt,' Migne, loc. cit.

23 Beda, *Historia Ecclesiastica*, iii, 27.

24 Ibid., iii, 3.

25 Ibid., iii, 25.

26 Ibid.

27 See p. 34 ff., above.

28 L. Gougaud, *Christianity in Celtic Lands*, pp. 129–84; H. Zimmer, *The Irish Element in Mediaeval Culture*; G. Murphy, 'Scotti Peregrini: The Irish on the Continent in the Time of Charles the Bald,' *Studies*, 17 (1928), 39–50, 229–44; E. Cahill, 'Influence of Irish on Mediaeval Europe,' *The Irish Ecclesiastical Record*, v. ser., 46 (1935) 464–76; Bieler, *Ireland, Harbinger*; H. Löwe, *Die Iren und Europa im früheren Mittelalter* (Stuttgart, 1982); Próinséas Ní Chatháin and Michael Richter, *Irland und Europa. Ireland and Europe* (Stuttgart, 1984).

29 Kenney, *Sources*, I, 186ff.

30 Ibid, I, 712. A great deal has been written about St Columbanus since the appearance of Kenney's work. See, for example, the articles by A. Gwynn in *Studies*, 39 (1950) and M. O'Carroll, *Studies*, 42 (1953); numerous articles by Dr A. Maestri, published by the Oblates of St Columban at San-Columbano-al-Lambro; Perry F. Kendig, *The Poems of St Columban* (Philadelphia, 1949); Francis Mac Manus, *St Columban* (Dublin, London, 1963); E. Franceschini, *L'Antiphonario di Bangor* (*Testi e Studi di Storia e di Letteratura Latina Mediovale*, 4. Padua, 1941), and cf. F. E. Warren, ed., *The Antiphonary of Bangor: An Early Irish MS. in the Ambrosian Library at Milan* (HBS IV and X; London, 1893–1895).

31 Bieler, *Ireland, Harbinger*,p. 63. See also R. Culhane, 'The Bangor Hymn to Christ the King', *The Irish Ecclesiastical Record* 74, (1950), 207–19.

32 For the Life by Jonas of Bobbio, see Kenney, *Sources*, I, 203–05.

33 Bieler, 'The Island of Scholars', *Revue du moyen âge latin*, 8 (1952), pp. 227–34, esp. p. 225; *Ireland, Harbinger*, p. 106; *Mélanges colombaniens. Actes du Congrès international du Luxeuil* (Paris, 1951), p. 91; 'The Classics in Early Ireland', in R. R. Bolgar, ed., *Classical Influences on European Culture* (Cambridge, 1971).

34 Cf. Arbois de Jubainville, RC, 19 (1898), 73; 21 (1900), 339.

35 Grundlach, *Mon. Germ. Hist. Epistolae*, III (1892), 186, 'Accept now, I pray you, small gifts of little songs fashioned in lines of two feet; you in exchange give back to us often that which service obliges. For, as in the hot season when the south winds blow, the fields rejoice because of the showers, so your oft-sent pages will bring joy to our minds.' Cf. G. S. M. Walker, *Sancti Columbani Opera: Scriptores Latini Hiberniae*, II (Dublin, 1957), 192ff. See also Francis John Byrne, 'Latin Poetry

in Ireland', in James Carney, ed.,*Early Irish Poetry* (Dublin, 1965), 29–44.

36 Kenney, *Sources*, I, 190.

37 J. M. Clark, *The Abbey of St Gall* (Cambridge, 1926), p. 54.

38 See E. G. Quin, 'The Irish Glosses', in Próinséas Ní Chatháin and Michael Richter, *Irland und Europa. Ireland and Europe* (Stuttgart, 1984), 210–17. See K. Hughes, *Early Christian Ireland* (London, 1972), 199, for evidence that an Irish glossator differentiated between the literal meaning and its spiritual significance and moral application.

39 W. Stokes and J. Strachan, *Thesaurus Palaeohibernicus*, I (Cambridge, 1901; rpt. Dublin, 1975), Intro. xiv-xxi, 7–483.

40 Ibid., xxiii-xxv, 499–714.

41 Ibid., II (Cambridge, 1903; rpt. Dublin, 1975), Intro. xxxii-xxxiv, 293–95.

42 See Maartye Draak, 'Construe Marks in Hiberno-Latin Manuscripts', *Medelingen de Koninklijke Nederlandse Academie van Wetenschappen afd. Letterkunde*, Nieuwe Reeks XX (1957), 261–82, 'The Higher Teaching of Latin Grammar in Ireland during the Ninth Century', ibid., XXX (1967), 109–44.

43 For a discussion of the Latin grammars produced by Irishmen, see Bengt Löfstedt, *Der hiberno-lateinische Grammatiker Malsachanus* (Uppsala, 1965).

44 L. Bieler, 'The Hymn of St Secundinus', PRIA, 55 (1953), Sec. C, 117–27; C. Mulcahy, 'The Hymn of St. Secundinus in Praise of St Patrick', *Irish Ecclesiastical Record*, 1945, 145–49; Kenney, *Sources*, I, 258–60.

45 Ibid., I, 262; C. Mulcahy, 'The Irish-Latin Hymns "Sancti venite" of St. Sechnall (d. c. 447) and "Altus Prosator" of St Columba (521–597)', *Irish Ecclesiastical Record*, 57 (1941) 385–405.

46 'Die Verskunst der Iren in rythmischen lateinischen Gedichten', *Nachrichten v. d. kgl. Gesellschaft d. Wissenschaften z. Göttingen philol.-his. Kl.*, 1916, 605–44. See also Thomas FitzHugh, *The Old-Latin and Old Irish Monuments of Verse*, Univ. of Virginia, Bulletin No. 10 of the School of Latin (1919).

47 Kenney, *Sources*, I, 359–60; 428–33; 329–35. On the *Vita Tripartita* see Kenney, 342–5, and K. Mulchrone, 'Die Abfassungzeit und Überlieferung der Vita Tripartita', ZCP, 16 (1927), 1–94, 411–51; *Bethu Phátraic* (Dublin, London, 1939); Kenneth H. Jackson, 'The Date of the Tripartite Life of St Patrick', ZCP 41 (1984), 5–45.

48 Kenney, *Sources*, I, 411, 414–17; Carl Selmer, ed., *Navigatio Sancti Brendani Abbatis* (Notre Dame, 1959).

49 James Carney dates it *c.* 800 or some decades later (*Medium Aevum*, 32, 1963, 40); David Dumville prefers a date in the second half of the century (*Ériu* 27, 1976, 89, n.88).

50 The three were edited by A. G. Van Hamel, *Immrama* (Med. and Mod. Irish Series, xii, Dublin, 1941). See H.P.A. Oskamp, *The Voyage of Mael Dúin*, ed. and trans., prefaced by a study of Early Irish voyage literature, (Gröningen, 1970).

51 Kenney, *Sources*, I, 415.

52 Zimmer tried to show that *Immram Curaig Maíle Dúin* was the direct source of the *Navigatio*; see *Zeitschrift für deutsches Alterthum*, 33 (1889), 176ff. For the opposite view see James Carney, *Medium Aevum*, 32 (1963), 37–44, review of Selmer (see n. 48 supra). L. Bieler, 'Two Observations Concerning the *Navigatio Brendani*', *Celtica*, 11 (1976), 15–17, endorses Carney's view that the Voyage of Mael Dúin is a secular adaptation of the *Navigatio*, but while he agrees that the entire voyage literature is of monastic origins he is reluctant to state categorically that there was no Celtic belief in an Otherworld beyond the sea. See Christa Maria Löffler, *The Voyage to the Otherworld Island in Early Irish Literature* (Salzburg Studies in English Literature), vols. 1 and 2 (Salzburg, 1983); David B. Spaan, 'The Otherworld in Early Irish Literature' (unpublished diss. Univ. of Michigan, 1986).

53 E. Cahill, 'Irish in the Early Middle Ages', *The Irish Ecclesiastical Record*, 46, (1935), 363ff.

54 Kenney, *Sources*, I, 339–40.

55 Ibid., 479–81.

56 Whitley Stokes, *Saltair na Rann* (Oxford, 1883); D. Greene, Fergus Kelly, *The Irish Adam and Eve Story from Saltair na Rann*, I, Text and Translation; B. Muroch, *The Irish Adam and Eve Story from Saltair na Rann*, II, Commentary (Dublin, 1976). And see Gearóid Mac Eóin, 'The Date and Authorship of Saltair na Rann', ZCP, 28 (1960–61), where it is argued on linguistic, literary and other data that the poem was written in 988 by Airbertach Mac Coisse, *fer léiginn* of Ros Ailithir, Co. Cork, who died in 1016. It should be noted, however, that Professor James Carney held firmly to the view that the *Saltair na Rann* was a much earlier composition. see 'The Dating of Early Irish Verse Texts', *Éigse* 19 (1983), 177–216.

57 'The Background of Early Irish Literature', SH, 1 (1961), 11.

58 'Indo-European Metrics and Archaic Irish Verse', *Celtica*, 6 (1963), 194–249.

59 W. Meid, *Dichter und Dichtkunst in indogermanischer Zeit* (Innsbruck, 1978), 14; M. Dillon, *Celts and Aryans* (Simla, 1975), p. 53.

60 Thurneysen, 'Zur irischen Accent- und Verslehre', RC, 6 (1885), 309–47.

61 See also his 'Poems of Blathmac, son of Cú Brettan', in Carney, ed., *Early Irish Poetry* (Cork, 1965), 45–57, where the translations quoted are to be found.

62 Thurneysen, op. cit., and cf. Arbois de Jubainville and G. Paris, 'La Versification irlandaise et la versification Romane', *Romania*, 9 (1880), 177–191.

63 *Über die älteste irische Dichtung* (Abhandl. der kgl. Preuss. Akad. der Wissensch. 11, No. 10), 4. Perhaps it was only in Leinster that these arythmic forms were used. See op. cit., 1 (no. 6), 7 n.1.

64 The group of metres characteristic of the *baird*, indicated by the word *bairdne*, that are found in the Early Middle Irish tracts (Thurneysen, *Mittelirische Verslehren*, 6, 39, 107) contain almost all of the *dán díreach* metres that were normally used by the *filid* from the Old Irish period on.

65 G. Murphy, 'Bards and Filidh', *Éigse*, 2 (1940), 200–07.

66 Cf. Robin Flower, *The Irish Tradition*, p. 17f. The poetry of Cenn Faelad is quoted often in the Annals. It deals mostly with the wars fought by his kinsmen, the northern Uí Néill.

67 Meyer and Nutt, *The Voyage of Bran*, I, 4ff.

68 'Colmán mac Lénéni und Senchán Torpéist', ZCP, 19 (1933), 193–209.

69 See 'Three Old Irish Accentual Poems', *Ériu*, 22 (1971), 23–80, esp. 63–5.

70 Cf. G. Murphy, 'St Patrick and the Civilizing of Ireland', *Irish Ecclesiastical Record*, 79 (1953), 194–204; esp. 198–9.

71 ZCP, 19 (1933), 198.

72 *Ériu*, 22 (1971), 54–5.

73 GL, I, 595.

74 See G. Murphy, 'The Origin of Irish Nature Poetry', *Studies*, 20 (1931), 87–102. See also, K. H. Jackson, *Studies in Early Celtic Nature Poetry* (Cambridge, 1935). P. L. Henry, *The Early English and Celtic Lyric* (London, 1966), believes that the Old English elegies show the influence of Celtic penitential verse, whose main motifs are those of the religious exile and hermit with an emphasis on sea-voyaging.

75 On 'The Origin of Marbán', traced to an episode in the ninth-century *Vita Tripartita* of St Patrick, see P. Mac Cana, BBCS, 13 (1962), 1–6.

76 The most important collections of Lives of Irish saints are edited by Charles Plummer, *Bethada Náem nÉrenn*, vols. I and II (Oxford, 1922); idem, *Vitae Sanctorum Hiberniae*, vols I and II (Oxford, 1910); idem, *Miscellanea Hagiographica Hibernica* (Bruxelles, 1925).

77 Plummer, *Vitae SS. Hiberniae*, II, 201.

78 Codex Sangallensis 904; see *Thesaurus Palaeohibernicus*, II, Intro. xix-xxiii, 49–224.

79 Thurneysen, OIR, p. 39; *Thesaurus Palaeohibernicus*, II, 290.

80 D. Greene and F. O'Connor, *A Golden Treasury of Irish Poetry* (London, 1967), pp. 84–5. for other English translations, see R. Flower, *Poems and Translations* (London, 1931), p. 116; Murphy, EILs, p. 113.

81 Thurneysen, OIR, pp. 40, 41; *Thesaurus Palaeohibernicus*, II, 293, 294; *Irische Texts*, I, 316; Murphy, EILs, p. 2.

82 *A Golden Treasury*, pp. 82–3; Flower, *Poems*, p. 117.

83 See J. Carney, '"Suibne Geilt" and "The Children of Lir"', *Éigse*, 6 (1950), 83–110; *Studies in Irish Literature and History*, p. 129ff., 385ff.; R. P. Lehmann, 'A Study of *Buile Suibhne*', EC, 6 (1952), 289–311; 7 (1955), 115–36; P. Riain, 'A Study of the Irish Legend of the Wild Man', *Éigse*, 14 (1972), 179–206; and the notes by A. O. H. Jarman, *Llên Cymru*, 1 (1950–51), 201, and K. H. Jackson, 'A Further Note on Suibhne Geilt and Merlin', *Éigse*, 7 (1955), 112–16.

84 Thurneysen, OIR, pp. 39, 40; *Thesaurus Palaeohibernicus*, II, 294; *Irische Texte*, I, 318ff.; Murphy, EILs, p. 112.

85 *King and Hermit: A Colloquy Between King Guaire and His Brother Marbán* (London, 1901). See also 'Zwiegespräch zwischen König Guaire von Aidne und seinem Bruder Marbán, dem Einsiedler', ZCP, 3 (1900–01), 455–7.

86 Murphy, EILs, pp. 11–19.

87 'The Two Eyes of Ireland', in *The Church of Ireland AD 432– 1932*, ed. W. Bell and N. D. Emerson (Dublin, 1932), pp. 66–79; also *The Irish Tradition*, pp. 43–66; P. Mac Cana in B. Ó Cuív, ed., *A View of the Irish Language* (Dublin, 1969), pp. 40–41; K. Hughes, *Early Christian Ireland*, pp. 202–04.

89 *A Golden Treasury*, 14–15. James Carney would give a considerably earlier date to the nature poems—*Éigse*, 13 (1970), 292.

90 'Some so-Called Irish Hermit Poetry', unpublished paper, read at the Sixth International Congress of Celtic Studies, Galway, July 6–13, 1979. See now 'Early Irish Hermit Poetry?', in D. Ó Corráin, L. Breatnach, K. McKone, edd., *Sages, Saints, and Storytellers: Celtic Studies in Honour of Professor James Carney* (Maynooth, 1989), pp. 251–6. Seamus Heaney gives a refreshingly new appraisal of early Irish nature poetry in 'The God in the Tree', in Seán Mac Réamoinn ed., *The Pleasures of Gaelic Poetry*, pp. 25–45.

91 For a discussion of this kind of story, see H. Zimmer, *Zeitschrift für deutsches Alterthum*, 33 (1889), 129, 257.

92 Fergal McGrath. S.J., *Education in Ancient and Medieval Ireland* (Dublin, 1979).

93 E. Mac Neill, 'A Pioneer of Nations', *Studies*, 11 (1922), 13–28, 435–46; *Early Irish Laws and Institutions* (Dublin, n.d.), p. 84ff. Professor Binchy thinks that the legend about Cenn Faelad, 'like so many other legends, has a basis of fact'; 'The Background to Early Irish Literature', SH, 1 (1961), 7–18. See also P. Mac Cana, 'The Three Languages and the Three Laws', *Celtica* 5 (1970), 62–8.

94 *Laws*, III, 88; G. Calder, *Auraicept na n-Éces* (Edinburgh, 1917), 7.

95 See 'The University of Tuaim Drecuin' in O'Connell, *The Schools and Scholars of Breiffne*, p. 13–24.

96 Mac Neill, *Early Irish Laws and Institutions*, p. 84ff.; *Laws*, III, 88; O'Curry, *MS. Materials*, pp. 51, 513; *Manners and Customs*, II, 92ff.

97 SH, 1 (1961), 17. Cf. *Studies*, 11 (1922), 13–28, 435–46.

98 Calder, p. 6. Solid evidence that Latin grammar was studied in seventh-century Irish schools is provided by *Ars Malsachani*, the work of a seventh-century Irish grammarian, Malsachan, who probably made use of the work of another Irishman, Cuimnan. See Bengt Löfstedt, *Der hiberno-lateinische Grammatiker Malsachanus* (Uppsala, 1965). Anders Ahlquist, *An Early Irish Linguist. An Edition of the Canonical Part of Auraicept na nÉces* (Helsinki, 1983) stresses the importance of the canonical part of one of the very first texts in the western grammatical tradition to contrast the vernacular with a classical language.

99 His death is recorded in AU, s.a. 678 (*recte* 679; v. AU, iv, xcvi).

100 See O'Curry, *Manners and Customs*, II, 176ff., where it is demonstrated

that the profession of teacher was not restricted to clerics.

101 Flower, *The Irish Tradition*, p. 11.
102 Kenney, *Sources*, I, 420–1; AU s.a. 661 (*recte* 662).
103 Kenney, *Sources*, I, 726–7.
104 Ibid., 279–81; AU s.a. 664 (*recte* 665). For Lochéne, see AU s.a. 695 (*recte* 696).
105 On the use of this device generally, see Flower, *The Irish Tradition*, p. 6.
106 Thurneysen, *Heldensage*, I, 567.
107 Professor J. Carney has stressed the role of the clerics in the composition of tales. See his 'The Impact of Christianity' in Dillon, *Early Irish Society*, pp. 66–78, and his *Studies in Irish Literature and History*, passim. For their part in preserving the tales, see *Heldensage*, I, 72.
108 *Heldensage*, I, 251–67; H. Zimmer in *Kuhns Zeitschrift für vergl. Sprachforschung*, 28 (1887), 526ff. Also, see J. Carney, *Studies in Irish Literature and History*, p. 165ff., J. Mac Neill, *Celtic Ireland*, p. 16.
109 Thurneysen, op. cit., 252, n.4; Ó Máille, *Ériu*, 9 (1921), 71; O'Rahilly, *Ériu*, 10 (1926), 109.
110 See *Heldensage*, I, 111. But here is what Thurneysen says in ZCP, 19 (1933) 209: 'Aus dem Vorhergehenden ergibt sich, daß ich der freilich sagenhaften Überlieferung, Senchān Torpēist habe die Táin Bó Cuailnge zusammengefügt, nicht mehr dasselbe Mißtrauen entgegenbringe wie Ir. Helden- und Königsage, I, 111.'
111 Edited by K. Meyer in *Archiv für celtische Lexicographie*, III, 3f. This version is the basis of the later tale, *Tromdámh Guaire*.
112 *Thesaurus Palaeohibernicus*, II, 322.
113 RC, 17 (1896), 175; M. Dobbs, 'Nínníne Éces', EC, 5 (1949), 148–53.
114 Edited by Meyer, ACL, III, 4f.
115 *Anecdota from Irish MSS*, 1 (19), 9; see now D. A. Binchy, ed., *Scéla Cano meic Gartnáin*, MMIS xviii (Dublin, 1963).
116 Plummer, *Vitae SS. Hib.*, I, cxxxi.
117 Flower, *The Irish Tradition*, p. 4.
118 Kenney, *Sources*, I, 13–14; J. Mac Neill, *Celtic Ireland*: 'The Irish Synthetic Historians'; T. F. O'Rahilly, EIHM, pp. 410–18; S. Mac Airt, *The Annals of Inisfallen* (Dublin, 1951), xvi ff.
119 O'Curry, *Manners and Customs*, II, 114ff.; ZCP, 8 (1911–12), 119–20, 218–29; *Ériu*, 4 (1908), 72–3; Hardiman, *Irish Minstrelsy*, II; *Ossianic Soc. Trans.*, 5 (1860), 280–93. But see Ó Lochlainn, *Éigse*, 3 (1941–42), 208, 4 (1943 [1944]-45), 33 on Mac Liag and Mac Coisi; the author states his reasons there for believing 'that the poets Mac Coisi, Mac Liag, Flann, Mac Lonáin and his mother Laitheog are all literary figments.'
120 O'Curry, op. cit., II, 137ff.
121 O'Curry, *MS. Materials*, pp. 55, 56; Kenny, *Sources*, I, 154–5.
122 K. Meyer, *Sanas Cormaic* (Halle, 1912). For other editions, see above, p. 57, n. 109.
123 Mac Neill, 'The Book of Rights', *New Ireland Review*, 25 (1906), 65–80, 206–16, 348–62; *Celtic Ireland*, chap. vi.

124 Kenney, *Sources*, I, 15; Thurneysen, *Heldensage*, I, 19.
125 Kenney, *Sources*, I, 12–13.
126 Keating, *History of Ireland*, I, 170–3; ZCP, 14 (1923), 173–8.
127 O'Curry, *MS. Materials*, p. 53ff.; *Manners and Customs*, II, 149ff.; Mac Neill, 'Poems by Flann Mainistrech on the Dynasties of Ailech, Mide, and Brege', *Archivium Hibernicum*, 2 (1913).
128 W. M. Hennessy, *Annals of Ulster*, I, 540.
129 Ed. S. Mac Airt, p. 168.
130 LL, 135a 30.
131 But see Ó Lochlainn, articles cited above, n. 119, on the poet Mac Coisi.
132 See above on *Cín Dromma Snechta(i)*, p. 28 and n. 101.
133 Hennessy, *Annals of Ulster*, I, 54, 56, n.1.
134 He is identical with Sillan, Abbot of Bangor, according to the *Martyrology of Tallaght*. 'Perhaps the correct form of the name was Silnan. Cf. *Thes. Pal.*, II, 277, 282'—Kenney, *Sources*, I, 218, n. 168.
135 *Thesaurus Palaeohibernicus*, II, 285; Kenney, *Sources*, I, 218. Cf. Flower, *The Irish Tradition*, pp. 13, 14.
136 *Ériu*, 7 (1914), 30ff.; *Celtic Ireland*, p. 28, n.
137 *EIHM*, p. 253ff.
138 *Annals of Ulster*, I, ed. W. M. Hennessy (Dublin, 1887); II-IV, ed. B. Mac Carthy (Dublin, 1893, 1895, 1901); Seán Mac Airt, *The Annals of Ulster* (to AD 1131), Part 1. Text and Translation.
139 Ed. Seán Mac Airt, (Dublin, 1951).
140 Ed. W. Stokes, RC, 16–18 (1895–7).
141 Ed. D. Murphy, (Dublin, 1896).
142 Ed. A. M. Freeman (Paris, 1929); rpt. from RC, 41–44 (1924–27).
143 Ed. W. M. Hennessy (London, 1866).
144 SH, 3 (1963), 126.
145 Hughes, *Early Christian Ireland*, p. 114.
146 Ibid., p. 134.
147 Flower, *The Irish Tradition*, p. 14f.
148 See M. Dillon, 'Lebor Gabála Érenn', *Journal of the Royal Society of Antiquaries of Ireland*, 86 (1956), 62–72, esp. 66.
149 *Historia Brittonum*, iii, 13–15.
150 EIHM, p. 193ff., 263ff. See Thurneysen, *Heldensage*, I, 47f., where it is maintained that the *Lebor Gabála Érenn* in its present form is, for the most part, no more than a prose redaction of the 'historical' poems of Gilla Caemáin (d. 1072). See also the fine study 'Miotas na Gabhála: Leabhar Gabhála' by Mark Scowcroft in P. Ó Fiannachta, ed., *Éire Banba Fódla, Léachtaí Cholm Cille*, 13 (1982), 41–75; and idem, 'Leabhar Gabhála', *Ériu*, 38 (1987), 81–142, 39 (1988), 1–66.
151 *Saltair Caissil*; see p. 91 above and Kenney, *Sources*, I, 15; Thurneysen, *Heldensage*, I, 19.
152 Flower, *The Irish Tradition*, 16f.
153 Thurneysen, op. cit., 15–18; *Zu irisch. Handschriften.*, I, 23ff.
154 A. G. Van Hamel, *Immrama* (Dublin, 1941).
155 Van Hamel, *Compert Con Culainn and Other Stories* (Dublin, 1933), 3–15.
156 V. Hull, 'An Incomplete Version of Imram Brain and Four Stories Concerning Mongán', ZCP, 18 (1930), 409–19.

157 Van Hamel, *Compert*, pp. 57–60; K. Meyer, 'Verba Scáthaige fri Coin Culaind', *Anecdota from Irish MSS.*, V (1913), 28–30; Thurneysen, ZCP, 9 (1913), 487–88.
158 Van Hamel, op. cit., 33–5.
159 Thurneysen, *Zu irisch. Handschriften.*, I, 53–8; Meyer, ZCP, 8 (1911–12), 564–5.
160 Pokorny, J., 'Conles abenteuerliche Fahrt', ZCP, 17 (1928), 193–205.
161 E. Knott, *Togail Bruidne Dá Derga* (Dublin, 1936).
162 Thurneysen, *Zu irisch. Handschriften.*, I, 48.
163 Bergin and Best, *Tochmarc Étaíne* (Dublin, 1938; rpt. from *Ériu*, 12 (1938), 137–196.
164 P. 96 and n. 156.
165 Thurneysen, *Heldensage*, I, 318.
166 Kenney, *Sources*, I, 12.
167 Before 1106, the year that Mael Muire, chief copyist of the original book, died. According to its editors, R. I. Best and O. J. Bergin, 'As the volume now stands it will be seen that A contributed 16 pages, Mael Muire about 80, and the interpolations of H amount to 37 pages, most of which were no doubt originally contributed by Mael Muire . . .', *Lebor na Huidre* (Dublin, 1929), p. xxiii. See also H. P. A. Oskamp, 'Notes on the History of *Lebor na hUidre*', PRIA, 65 (1967), C., 117–37; R. Powell, 'Further Notes on *Lebor na hUidre*', *Ériu*, 21 (1969), 99–102.
168 *Rawlinson B. 502 . . . Facsimile . . . with an Introducton and Indexes*, by Kuno Meyer (Dublin, 1909). The interpolator's hand in *Lebor na hUidre* appears in the first item. See *Ériu*, 16 (1952), where B. Ó Cuív shows that a poem in the second part can be dated to *c.* 1120, so the second part must have been written after this date, probably soon after it.
169 *The Book of Leinster*, with introduction, analysis of contents and index, by Robert Atkinson (Dublin, 1880); R. I. Best, O. Bergin, M. A. O'Brien, *The Book of Leinster*, I–V (Dublin, 1954–67); VI ed. by Anne O'Sullivan (Dublin, 1983). Best maintained that *The Book of Leinster* was written entirely by one scribe, Aed Ó Crimthain. William O'Sullivan, however, has shown that the book is the work of several scribes: *A*, that of Aed himself; *F*, more probably that of Find's scribe than that of Find himself; *T*, the style common to the texts of *Táin Bó Cúalnge* and *Togail Troí*; and *U*, characterized by the frequent use of uncial *a* in medial position. See 'Notes on the Scripts and Make-Up of the Book of Leinster', *Celtica*, 7 (1966), 1–31, and Muireann Ní Bhrolcháin, 'Leabhar Laighean', P. Ó Fiannachta, ed., *Éire Banba Fódla, Léachtaí Cholm Cille* 13 (1982), 5–40. All parties agree that Aed wrote a considerable part of the MS.
170 *Leabhar Breac . . .*, preface by Samuel Ferguson (Dublin, 1872–76).
171 ZCP, 19 (1933), 209; *Kuhns Zeitschrift für vergl. Sprachforschung*, 59 (1932), 9.
172 Strachan and O'Keeffe, *Táin Bó Cuailnge*, p. 32; ZCP, 10 (1914–15), 207f.; Thurneysen, *Heldensage*, I, 144. On the general question of the influence of the classics, see W. B. Stanford, 'Towards a History of Classical Influences in Ireland', PRIA, 100 (1970), 13–91.
173 Windisch, *Táin Bó Cúalnge*, p. 710ff. See Carney, *Studies in Irish*

Literature and History, p. 305ff. on the 'Watchman device', but also Patrick Sims-Williams, 'Riddling Treatment of the "Watchman-Device" in *Branwen* and *Togail Bruidne Da Derga*', SC, 12/13 (1977/78), 83–7. See also P. Mac Cana's remarks in 'Conservation and Innovation in Early Celtic Literature', EC 13 (1972–3), 61–119, esp. 86–88 and the statement there that, 'the truth is, however, that there is no certainty that the items adduced by Thurneysen (reminiscences of the *Aeneid*) were ever in the *Grundtext* , whereas we know that versions of the classics became known in Ireland from the ninth or tenth centuries onwards.'

174 *Heldensage*, I, 96–248; ZCP, 19 (1933), 209; Cecily O'Rahilly, ed., *Táin Bó Cúalnge from the Book of Leinster* (Dublin, 1967), Introduction. In 'The Táin and the Annals', *Ériu*, 22 (1971), 107–27, J. V. Kelleher discusses the chronology of the Táin Age according to Irish tradition and suggests that a 'revision' of the TBC was undertaken in the ninth century, perhaps by Cuanu, abbot of Louth, who died in AD 825.

175 O'Rahilly, *TBC from the Book of Leinster*, p. xlv.

176 Text in O'Rahilly, *TBC Recension I*, ll. 564–604; trans. by T. Kinsella, *The Tain*, 82–4.

177 Text in O'Rahilly, op. cit., ll. 1289–387; trans. Kinsella, op. cit., 117–20.

178 Text in O'Rahilly, *TBC from the Book of Leinster*, ll. 1565–72; 1608–95; trans. ibid., 181, 183–5.

179 *Heldensage*, I, 115.

180 Ibid., 112–3.

181 O'Rahilly, op. cit., ll. 4919–25.

182 Binchy, 'The Background of Early Irish Literature', SH, 1 (1961), 7.

183 Flower, *The Irish Tradition*, p. 73.

184 Dillon, *Early Irish Society*, p. 70ff.

185 GL, I, 604ff.

186 *Early Irish Laws and Institutions*, p. 72ff., where the extent of the druids' culture is emphasized; according to Mac Neill (p. 82), *filid* was another name for druids.

187 M. Joynt, *Tromdámh Guaire*, p. 25ff.

188 K. Meyer, *Aislinge Meic Conglinne: The Vision of Mac Conglinne* (London, 1892); Kenneth Hurlstone Jackson, ed., *Aislinge Meic Con Glinne* (Dublin, 1990). There is a modern Irish version, *Aisling Mhic Conglinne* by Tomás Ó Floinn (Dublin, 1980).

189 *The Irish Tradition*, pp. 76–7.

CHAPTER 3

THE DEVELOPMENT OF PROSE

§1

Iᴎ the Middle Ages the work of preserving amd maintaining the literature passed into the hands of certain families—clanna Aodhagáin (the MacEgans), muintir Chléirigh (the O'Clerys), muintir Dhálaigh (the O'Dalys), muintir Dhuinnín (the Dinneens), muintir Mhaolchonaire (the O'Mulconrys), and others. These were the literary and intellectual families of the land, for they were the ones that gave the country not only its poets, but its historians, lawyers, and physicians as well, and by virtue of their interest in the written word they, more than anyone else, produced most of the manuscripts of the period.[1]

Dr Robin Flower drew attention to a very interesting fact in connection with these families, namely, that the most important of them can be traced back to districts in the centre of Ireland at the beginning of the Middle Ages, even though they were scattered throughout the land by the end of that period.[2] The reason for this may be closely linked to the rise of the famous Brian Ború (Bórumha). Dr Flower noted that, after making himself the undisputed king of Ireland, the first and last real 'High-King' of Ireland, Brian made expeditions to the north in 1002 and 1005 to take hostages and to secure recognition of his position.[3] In the course of his second expedition, in 1005, he came to Armagh, the chief centre of the Church since the time of Patrick, and there his secretary penned a note in *The Book of Armagh* acknowledging the supremacy of that Church. In the entry, Brian is described as *imperator Scotorum* 'emperor of the Irish'.[4] Elsewhere he is styled the 'Augustus of the West'. Note these titles (*Imperator, Augustus*) carefully, for they were used by Charlemagne as leader of the Holy Roman Empire, and, according to Dr Flower, in using them Brian wanted the world to know that he was performing the functions of a Charlemagne in Ireland,[5] as patron of learning and fosterer of intellectual pursuits of all kinds.

However, Flower's explanation of the rise of the learned families in the centre of Ireland has since been called in question. Professor P. Mac Cana has shown that not all the learned families in the medieval period originated in the midland area—in one or other of the monastic centres of learning—and that a goodly proportion of the post-Norman families of learned poets were descended from those hereditary officials who maintained possession of the old monastic termons after the monasteries themselves had been superseded. There seems to be no good reason, he argues, to suppose that this phenomenon was confined to the midlands. The important point to remember, according to Professor Mac Cana, is this:

> Until approximately the end of the eleventh century the monastic scholar was distinguished from his *fili* counterpart by his study of the 'synthetic' history which reached its fullest development in the twelfth-century compilation of *Lebor Gabála*, 'The Book of Conquest'; yet from the thirteenth to the seventeenth century *Lebor Gabála* received unquestioning acceptance from the schools of *filidheacht*—in Robin Flower's words, 'it became canonical.'
>
> The implication is clear: at the time of their reorganization in or about the twelfth century, the *filid* consciously took over the historical teaching elaborated by the monastic students of native tradition, or else, the total acceptance by the later *filid* of *Lebor Gabála* resulted from the gradual assimilation and, ultimately, the partial integration of the two classes. Indeed these alternatives are not mutually exclusive . . . .[6]

There is evidence that 'much of the initial impetus came from the midland area' and this should be taken in conjunction with the evidence that Brian Ború sought to play the part of a culture-king, i.e., a king who wished to foster, support and promote culture.

Indeed, Brian was not the first among the kings of Munster to take an interest in the national culture. We have seen that Cormac mac Cuilennáin,[7] one of the kings of Munster at the end of the ninth century, wrote books himself, and that these reflect an interest in the language, history, and antiquities of the land. He must have had an interest in its laws, too, for the first edition of the *Leabhar na gCeart* is attributed to him.[8] Brian is said to have had a second edition of it made; in his edition it was apparently deemed possible for a king of Munster, Leinster, Ulster, or Meath to be *ard-rí* ('high-king'), but a king of Connacht was denied that right. In the same way, the power of a king of Cashel in his own province was increased: he was given the right to service from the Irish of Ireland and Dublin, and when he was not king of all of Ireland, he was to be king of Mogh's Half (i.e., the southern half of Ireland).[9] However, *Leabhar na gCeart* is not as old as it claims to be. Professor Dillon, its latest editor, believes that the language of the main tract belongs to the late eleventh century, and that the compilation was made in the twelfth.[10] But on historical grounds it must belong to the period of Munster's greatness, and although its pronouncements on the rights of the kings of Munster are more a measure of their aspirations than of their achievements it reflects their powerful position at this time.

Of course, Brian's success against the Norsemen helped to secure the peace and calm so much needed in the land to develop its culture and civilization. Unfortunately, his untimely death prevented him from doing for Ireland all that he had dreamed, and none of his successors compared with him in ability or in vision. But it is more than likely that his court was a centre of great cultural activity and that the founders of the literary families named above were closely connected with it. Granting all of this, it is easy to see that the circumstances provided sufficient opportunity for the several families to secure their position as custodians of the literary tradition.

The old monastic Church, which had produced so many scholars for copying the Irish manuscripts and for sharing the burden of maintaining the tradition with the *filid*, was rapidly declining.[11] By the eleventh century it appears that the abbot of the ordinary monastic church, the *comarba* or 'heir' of the founder-saint, or, if the church was not the principal centre of the saint, the *airchinnech* ('superior'), had become a lay nobleman and his family kept that office and perpetuated it from generation to generation. The monk (*manach*) had become a landholder under the *airchinnech*, and the student (*scológ*) had become a labourer on the land. Of course, the major churches continued to be ecclesiastical institutions with many clerics and a school under the supervision of a *fer léiginn*, who was assisted by teachers and scribes. But these exceptions must have been few. We get a glimpse of the usual state of affairs when we note that the abbacy of Armagh had been uninterruptedly in the hands of one family, Clann Sinaig, for a century and a half after 957.[12] They would gain the position of *comarba* as layman, or as members of the minor orders, and then they would appoint some inconsequential person as bishop, or they would add that office to one they already held. Clearly, the possessions of the Church and most of its governance had passed into the hands of laymen, and it is no wonder that scholarship and literature passed into their hands as well.[13]

It is true that there were attempts to reform the native Church, but they had hardly succeeded at all by the time the universal reform movement came in the wake of the new Continental Orders. In 1142,

Máel-Máedoc Ua Morgair, better known as St Malachy, established the Cistercian monastery of Mellifont near Drogheda,[14] and with that the Continental Orders first set foot in Ireland. When the Anglo-Normans came, the movement to build monasteries for these Orders gained strength, and the old lords were vying with the new to give them space. A century after the Cistercians, the brothers of the Orders of Dominic and Francis arrived, and they were welcomed eagerly—especially the Franciscans, for many of the Irish saints had been unwitting forerunners, as it were, of the Saint of Assisi.

At first the attitude of the new Orders was to keep aloof from the native culture, but as more and more Irish joined their ranks, they came into a closer and closer relationship with it, and finally they were more representative of native than alien culture.

As we have said, the Franciscan friars won favour with the native population early, and their number increased rapidly. By 1282 their houses were incorporated in four districts (*custodia*), the Irish members outnumbered the foreign, and there was considerable enmity between the two factions. In the General Chapter that was held in Cork in 1291, the disagreements erupted into fist-fights, and some of the friars were killed. In 1325 there was an attempt to confine the Irish party to one district, the Nenagh District, including the houses in Nenagh, Athlone, Ennis, Clare-Galway, Galway, Armagh, Cavan, and Killeigh.[15] But every attempt to restrict the growth and influence of the Irish in the Order was in vain. Very soon, the 'Irish' district was the largest and most important, and the houses in the 'English' districts declined. In this way the Franciscans followed the usual path of foreigners in Ireland and became *Hibernis ipsis Hiberniores*.

The new Orders had a tremendous influence on the literature of the land. They were the channels along which the ideas and materials of continental literature flowed to the old tradition, and as they became more Irish in language and spirit, the part they played in shaping and handing on that tradition was not insignificant. Of course, their influence was not like that of the clerics in the earlier period, but just as those had co-operated with the *filid* in shaping the tradition, so members of the various Orders joined together with the literary families to support and foster it. In fact, many members of these families joined the Orders, and not the least valuable thing they brought with them was the training they had in the literature of their native land.

One of the most famous literary families in this period was the Mac

Aodhagáin clan (the MacEgans). A copy of its genealogy is found in Egerton 139.[16] It gave poets, judges, and clerics to the land, as well as copyists and keepers of manuscripts; it will suffice here to mention the work of the last. One of the oldest law manuscripts extant is that designated H. 2. 15a, preserved in Trinity College, Dublin.[17] The largest part of it was written in the fourteenth century, but some sections were copied around 1237, 'in the house of Cían Mac an Gabann in Ormond'. In a note written about 1350 by Aed Mac Aodhagáin, who died in 1359, it is said that the manuscript had belonged to his father Conchobar. In 1575 the manuscript was in Muilenn-Dúna-Daighre (Duniry), one of the family estates. Another famous manuscript must have been kept in the same place, because one of the lesser known names for the *Leabhar Breac*,[18] is *Leabhar Mór Dúna Daighre*. It was thought for a long time that the Mac Aodhagáin family's well-established connection with the *Leabhar Breac* extended to its writing and compilation, but there is evidence that it is in the hand of a scribe belonging to the Ó Cuindlis family who 'worked at Lecan, possibly also in other parts of Connacht, and in E. Ormond at the close of the fourteenth century and who is the only one known to have received his training at the school of Gilla Ísa Mór Mac Fir Bisig.'[19]

Another important literary family was the Mac Firbisigh (the MacFirbis).[20] Two very important books of the period are linked with them: *The Yellow Book of Lecan*[21] and *The Great Book of Lecan*.[22] *The Yellow Book of Lecan* is comprised of seventeen parts, put together by a later binder. The part that formed the original *Yellow Book* belonged, apparently, to a MacFirbisigh, and another part was written by Gilla-Iosa, son of Donnchad Mór Mac Firbisigh in 1380. Most of *The Great Book of Lecan* was written by Gilla-Iosa Mac Firbisigh in Lecan in 1416 with the assistance of other scribes.[23] Both *The Yellow Book of Lecan* and *The Great Book of Lecan* are compilations of older material—chronicles, legends and poems— which is of great value not only as literature but also as a source for the historian. It is said that the last representative of the family was Dubháltach Óg, author of *The Great Book of Genealogies*;[24] he was murdered by a member of an English family in 1671.

The Yellow Book of Lecan was connected with another famous literary family, muintir Mhaolchonaire (the O'Mulconrys):[25] one section of it was written by Seanchán, son of Máel-Muire Ua Maolchonaire in 1473, and another section by Iolland and Torna Ua Maolchonaire in 1572. In *The Great Book of Genealogies*, Dubháltach

Óg says that the O'Mulconrys were one of the families that took up the recording of history as a family profession. Records show that some of the members of this family became *ollaimh* (highest rank of *filidh*) in the Middle Ages. It is one of this family (Maolín Óg) who drew up the treaty between the Earl of Kildare and Mag Radnaill in 1530, and it was two cousins of his who copied Egerton MS 1782— one of the most important Irish parchment manuscripts extant in spite of its late date (*c.* 1517). Another member of the family was founder of the Monastery of the Holy Trinity on the island of Loch Cé in Roscommon County in 1215.[26] The chronicle of that monastery (B.M. Titus A. XXV = *The Annals of Boyle*)[27] was used by the scribe of *The Annals of Loch Cé*.[28] MS. Rawlinson B 512 was written by Dubthach Ó Duibhgeannáin (O'Duignan) for a member of this same literary family.[29]

This last copyist himself belonged to a very renowned literary family.[30] The greatest part of the *Book of Ballymote* (R.I.A. 23 P. 12) was penned by Magnus Ó Duibgennáin.[31] (We get a glimpse of the value placed on manuscripts of this kind in the period in the fact that the book just mentioned was sold by a member of the family that owned it, the MacDonaghs, to the family of O'Donnell for one hundred and twenty milch cows.[32] It is now kept in the Royal Irish Academy.) Another member of this family, Seán Mór Ua Dubhagáin, wrote the oldest part of the *Leabhar Uí Máine* (1360–1427).[33] According to Paul Walsh, O'Curry was correct in stating that the Annals of Loch Cé were no more than an incomplete abstract of the annals in the Book of the Ua Duibgennáin, that is, perhaps, of the *Annals of Connacht*.[34] One of the last official copyists in the family was David O'Duigenan (Dáibhí Ó Duibhgennáin), who was very active in the last half of the seventeenth century.[35]

An equally important literary family was the the O'Clerys (Ó Cléirigh).[36] We are indebted to one of them, Seán Buidhe Ua Cléirigh, for a very valuable manuscript of the period, Laud 610, written around 1453.[37] But this is not the place to discuss the O'Clery family; we will encounter more than one of its renowned scions further on.

We must be content to name one other scribe, Uilliam Mac an Lega— although he deserves more than passing comment, not only because he copied two important manuscripts of the period (B.M. Add. 30512 and 11809)[38] and part of another (Paris Celt. 1),[39] but also because he belonged to a literary family prominent for its physicians, a family of the same rank as Mac Duinn Shléibhe in Ulster, Ó hÍceadha in Thomond, Ó Callanáin in Desmond, and Mac Beatha in Islay and Mull.[40]

In discussing the literary families and the manuscripts they copied, we have named almost all the important manuscripts of the period: only three remain to be considered. Two of those were written in a monastery: T.C.D., F. 5. 3,[41] copied around 1454 in a monastery of the Order of St Francis in Clare, and an Irish MS in Rennes copied, it seems, for a monastery of the same order in Cell Créide (Kilcrea) near Bandon, Co. Cork.[42] T.C.D. F. 5. 3 is important because it contains material in both Latin and Irish, and even some in English, and because the Latin texts are frequently originals for the Irish translations. Furthermore, this manuscript belongs to the same class of which some have already been named: Add. 11809 and 30512, Laud 610, Paris Celt. 1, and Irish MS Rennes. Two manuscripts not yet named may be added to the group: Liber Flavus Fergusiorum,[43] which was copied by someone who was not a professional scribe, according to O'Curry[44] (the dates 1437 and 1446 are found on its pages), and R.I.A. 24 P. 25,[45] which is in three parts. The first part was written in the years 1513–14, the second not before 1532 nor after 1544, and the third part about the same time as the second.

A note found in Egerton MS 1781, 253a 20–253b 33, sheds some light on one of the habits of the scribes when they were at work. Here is a translation of part of it:

> This book was written in AD 1487 . . . .None other than Diarmaid becach mac Parrthaláin wrote this book . . . and in the house of Fingin half of this book was written, namely in Doire Cassain, and in the house of the son of Brian Tellach-Echach another part of it was written: namely, in the manor, to be sure, in the manor of Feilimid . . . and it was finished on Inis Brecmaigh on Thursday during the feast of St Catherine . . . And that Feilimid mac Tomáis meic Fergail meic Tomáis was lord of Tellach-Echach during the time this book was written . . . And may God's blessing be upon the souls of those who wrote this book.[46]

An examination of the contents of these manuscripts reveals that they are the product of two kinds of activity, the one supporting and building on the old native literature, and the other borrowing and adapting literary materials from the Continent. The latter activity shows that Ireland was second to no country of comparable size in the extent to which it participated in the literary tradition of the Continent and the former demonstrates that far from depending on the manuscript tradition deriving from the eighth and ninth century, the country's literary tradition continued to draw on the ever-developing living oral tradition.[47] However, it should perhaps be pointed out that it is in the later Middle Ages that Ireland became increasingly aware of the Continental tradition: in the earlier Middle Ages its main concern was with the native literary heritage.

In this connection, the Irish text *Cogadh Gaedhel re Gallaibh* ('The War of the Gaedhil with the Gall')[48] is of particular interest. Primarily, it is a chronicle of the Irish-Scandinavian wars. The first part is a chronological account of battles and settlements of the Norsemen in Ireland, but the second part, from chapter XXXV to the end, is not so much sober history as saga, and it reflects the development of legendary materials and popular traditions. It is a composition written in the same prose style as *The Book of Leinster* version of the *Táin Bó Cúailnge* and, to judge from its propagandist bias, it came from the same milieu as the *Leabhar na gCeart*. Although the writer has made use of some Norse traditions, he is typical of his period—the first half of the twelfth century—in that his interest is almost entirely confined to Irish affairs and that he makes extensive use of oral tradition.[49] Plainly modelled on *Cogadh Gaidhil re Gallaibh* and composed in a not dissimilar style, *Caithréim Cellacháin Caisil* 'The Battle Career of Cellachán of Cashel' tells of Cellachán, who was reigning as king of Cashel in 936 and died in 956. But its main events are almost entirely fictitious, and although it has the same theme as its exemplar—the oppression imposed on Munster and removed by a deliverer—it is less constrained both by historical events and by the growth of legend. It shows an author more or less in the modern sense achieving his object, the production of a work of art, dramatic in character and distinguished in diction, and in this respect anticipates the later (rather than reflects the early) Irish Middle Ages.[50] Since it claims for his predecessor the success achieved by Brian Ború, it has been suggested that it was composed sometime after the O'Brian ascendancy had waned, probably after 1118.

§2

Among the native tales that were copied and transmitted in this period were those of the Ulster Cycle, the Mythological Cycle, the Historical Cycle, and the Finn (or Fionn) Cycle, but this last was the most popular and it received the greatest development.[51] We know that tales about Finn and his men had been circulating in Ireland from the eighth century,[52] but no attempt was made to gather the tales into an actual corpus that could be compared with the *Táin Bó Cúailnge* and its fore-tales until the beginning of the thirteenth century, when some genius set himself to fill the need. He used the same device that was used to trace the true history of the *Táin*: he caused some of the *fiana* to survive their companions and to encounter Patrick on his travels through Ireland. The saint questions them eagerly, and the responses by Caoilte and Oisín resurrect the golden past in a spirit of noble melancholy. The ancient ones travel with Patrick throughout Ireland, and as they come to various places connected with the names and deeds of the *fiana*, the heroes and events that took place are commemorated in story and song, and at Patrick's urging, his secretary records them so that they might provide entertainment for lords and their noble retinues until the end of time. Of course, many of the stories were in existence earlier, but here (*c.* 1200) they are brought together to form a loose unity in the *Agallamh na Seanórach* ('Colloquy, Discourse of the Ancients').[53] The atmosphere and mood of the *Agallamh* is quite different from that of the old tales, but they must have been consistent with the taste of the age, for from that point on the saga of Finn was the favourite subject of storytellers and audiences alike, and the *Agallamh* exerted a great influence on the theme and style.

A brief excerpt will convey the atmosphere of the *Agallamh*. Caoilte has been asked by Patrick to find a well which may be used to baptize the peoples of North Dublin and Meath. He takes the saint to the well of *Tráig Dá Ban* ('The Two Women's Strand'):

Caoilte (then) began to tell its fame and qualities and made this *laíd*:

Well of Tráig Dá Ban,
Lovely is your pure-topped cress;
Since your verdure has become neglected
no growth has been allowed to your brooklime.

Your trout by your banks,
Your wild swine in your wilderness,
the deer of your crags fine for hunting,
Your dappled red-bellied fawns

Your mast on the tips of your trees,
Your fish in the mouths of your streams
lovely is the colour of your sprigs of arum lily,
green brook in the wooded hollow!

'Tis well,' Patrick said: 'hath our dinner and our provant reached us yet?' 'It has so,' answered bishop Sechnall. 'Distribute it,' said Patrick, 'and one half give to yon nine tall warriors of the survivors of the Fiana.' Then his bishops, and his priests, and his psalmodists arose and blessed the meat; and of both meat and liquor they consumed their full sufficiency, yet so as to serve their soul's weal.

Patrick then said: 'Was he a good lord with whom ye were; Fionn Mac Cumhaill that is to say?' Upon which Caoilte uttered this little tribute of praise:

> Were but the brown leaf,
> Which the wood sheds from it, gold,
> were but the white billow silver,
> Fionn would have given it all away.

'Who or what was it that maintained you so in your life?' Patrick enquired; and Caoilte answered: 'Truth that was in our hearts, and strength in our arms, and fulfilment in our tongues.'[54]

The saga of Fionn is recorded in two distinct styles: in the one we have prose tales interspersed with speech-poems instead of conventional dialogue; in the other we have poems (or ballads) that frame the dialogue between Patrick and those who address him—actually, by this time, Oisín (hence the designation 'Ossianic Poems'). But there is this difference: where there was perfect courtesy between the saint and the heroes in the *Agallamh*, in the later ballads there is a certain amount of antagonism, if not downright hostility, between them. A little later a number of these ballads were collected to form a new kind of *Agallamh* which was revised frequently in later manuscripts.[55]

These poems endured as part of the living inheritance of the nation, and it is not surprising to realize that they formed a body of poetry that was expanded continually as long as the Irish tradition remained active.[56] One of the most successful additions was a song by Mícheál Cuimín (1688–1760), *Laoidh Oisín*, describing the journey of Oisín to Tír na n-Óg ('Land of the Young').[57]

> Delightful land beyond all dreams!
>   Beyond what seems to thee most fair—
>   Rich fruits abound the bright year around
>   And flowers are found of hues most rare.
>
> Unfailing there the honey and wine
>   And draughts divine of mead there be,
>   No ache nor ailing night or day—
>   Death or decay thou ne'er shalt see!
>
> The mirthful feast and joyous play
>   And music's sway all blest, benign—
>   Silver untold and store of gold
>   Undreamt by the old shall all be thine!

A hundred swords of steel refined,
  A hundred cloaks of king full rare,
  A hundred steeds of proudest breed,
  A hundred hounds—they meed when there!

A hundred maidens young and fair
  Of blithesome air shall tend on thee,
  O form most meet, as fairies fleet
  And of song more sweet than the wild thrush free!

A hundred knights in fights most bold
  Of skilled untold in all chivalrie,
  Full-armed, bedight in mail of gold
  Shall in Tír na n-Óg thy comrade be.[58]

In describing the journey of Oisín to the Land of the Young, Mícheál Cuimín, as Corkery has suggested, undoubtedly did what thousands had wished to do—although they were probably not conscious of the urge—because,

the story was, it is likely, already in the possession of every Gaelic mind in Ireland: in some minds handsome and full, in others meagre and flat . . . The thousands of dwellers along the western seaboard had now one other lay in which to lose count of their miseries. Neatly packed in verse they could now easily memorize that story and carry it with them out to sea in their curraghs, or to the ploughing or the shearing, or on those slow pack-horse journeys of theirs along those bleak, treeless upland roads of Coimín's own countryside. It was their custom to sing such verses; and it is certain that they had scores of other lays in the self-same metre to test it by. O'Curry, who was himself a Clareman, tells us 'In Ireland, I have heard my father sing these Ossianic poems, and remember distinctly the air and the manner of their singing.' Then he gives account of a teacher named O'Brien, 'who spent much of his time in my father's house, and who was the best singer of Oisín's poems that his contemporaries had ever heard. He had a rich and powerful voice; and often on a calm summer's day, he would go with a party into a boat on the lower Shannon, at my native place, where the river is eight miles wide; and having rowed to the middle of the river, they used to lie on the oars . . . on which occasions O'Brien was always prepared to sing his choicest pieces, among which were no greater favourites than Oisín's poems. So powerful was the singer's voice that it often reached the shores at either side of the boat in Clare and Kerry, and often called the labouring men and women from the neighbouring fields at both sides down to the water's edge to enjoy the strains of the music.'[59]

One can hardly resist adding Corkery's further observation that, 'If O'Brien sang this lay of Oisín in Tír na n-Óg—"Comyn's Lay", as it was called—those happy ones in the boat, at the water's edge, had surely one magical hour at least to look back upon'.

Perhaps the most famous story in the Fionn Cycle is *Tóraigheacht Dhiarmada agus Ghráinne* ('The Pursuit of Diarmaid and Gráinne').[60] There must have been a version of it extant as early as the tenth century, for the title *Aithed Gráinne ingine Corbmaic la Diarmait ua nDuibne* ('The Elopement of Gráinne daughter of Cormac with Diarmuid') occurs in the tenth-century list of tales,[61] and a text from the same century describes an event in the course of the flight, *Uath Beinne Étair* ('The Cave of Benn Étair').[62] Despite that, the extant version of the *Tóraigheacht* is in Modern Irish, and the same is true of other stories in this cycle, such as *Feis Tighe Chonáin* ('The Feast of the House of Canán'), *Bruidhean Bheag na hAlmhan* ('The Little Battle of Allen'), *An Bhruidhean Chaorthainn* ('The Hall of the Mountain Ash'), *Cath Gabhra* ('The Battle of Gabhra'), and *Cath Finntrágha* ('The Battle of Ventry').[63]

Tóraigheacht Dhiarmada agus Ghráinne deserves a more detailed treatment than space allows here. The theme, the tragedy of a young girl betrothed to an old man and of the conflict between passion and duty on the part of her love, is the same as that of *Longes Mac nUislenn* ('The Exile of the Sons of Uisliu [or Uisnech]'),[64] which tells the tale of Deirdriu (or Deirdre), destined at birth to be the most beautiful woman in Ireland and to cause slaughter and devastation in Ulster. Reared by King Conchobar who had become her foster-father with the intention of making her his wife, she falls in love with Naoíse, son of Uisliu, whom she induces to elope with her by a mixture of cajolery and threats of everlasting shame.

> Once when Naoíse was outside alone Deirdriu slipped out to him as if she were going past him, and he did not recognise her.
>
> 'That's a nice heifer that is going by me,' he said.
>
> 'Heifers ought to be big,' she said, 'wherever there are no bulls.'
>
> 'You have the bull of the province,' he said, meaning the King of Ulster.
>
> 'I'd choose between you,' she said, 'and take a little young bull like you.'
>
> 'No,' he said, 'not after Cathbad's prophecy!'
>
> 'Are you saying that because you don't want me?'
>
> 'I am surely,' said he.
>
> She made a rush at him and grabbed his two ears. 'Then two ears of shame and mockery on you, unless you take me with you.'

'Go on, woman!' he said.
'You'll have it,' said she.[65]

It is unfortunate that the *Tóraigheacht Dhiarmada agus Ghráinne* has not come down to us in a form contemporary with that of *Longes Mac n-Uislenn* but in an Early Modern Irish form. The earliest text—in MS RIA 24 P 9, in the hand of Dáibhí Ó Duibhgeannáin—lacks the beginning and is still unpublished. The O'Grady text dates from the eighteenth century and like the other texts of the same period differs slightly from the older text, in particular in representing Gráinne as marrying Fionn after Diarmaid's death. Substantially, as we have said, its theme is that of the *Longes*, but here the heroine is Gráinne, daughter of Cormac mac Airt, who has promised to marry Fionn Mac Cumhaill at her father's bidding. The hero is Diarmaid Ó Duibhne who is forced by Gráinne to betray his leader and friend, and the story unfolds the elopement of the two lovers, Fionn's pursuit of them, the pretended reconciliation and the death of Diarmaid, not directly at the hands of Fionn but indirectly through his refusal to use his healing power. Compared with the *Longes*, the *Tóraigheacht* is perhaps not a major artistic achievement. It does not belong to the great age of Irish story-telling; it is less heroic and more romantic, but its main weakness is in its structure. No doubt the redactor was struggling to impose artistic order on an unruly mass of traditions, much of which was becoming unintelligible to his audience, and could not bring himself to jettison his superfluous material. Nevertheless, the story has compulsive fascination even for the modern sophisticated reader.

Although there are variations on the ending in the various texts of the *Tóraigheacht*, there is some justification for comparing the ending in O'Grady's text with that of the *Longes*. Peace had been restored between Fionn and Diarmaid, and even the memory of the estrangement had had time to be lost in oblivion. Then, one night as Diarmaid lay asleep he was awakened by the cry of a hound on the scent. Gráinne persuaded him to ignore the cry and to go back to sleep. The cry came a second time and Gráinne again laid hold of him and persuaded him not to go.

> Diarmaid lay down on the couch and a deep sleep and lasting slumber fell on him, and for a third time the bay of the hound awoke him. And day in its full light came to him afterwards, and he arose and said that he would go where the hound had bayed, since morning was come.
> 'Well then,' said Gráinne, 'take thou the Móraltach, even the sword of Manannán, and the Ga Dearg of Donn.'

'I will not,' said Diarmaid. 'I will take the Beagaltach and Ga Buidhe an Lámhaigh, and Mac an Chuill on the leash in my hand.'

Diarmaid went forth from Ráth Ghráinne, and he did not stay or rest until he reached the summit of Beann Ghulben. And he found Fionn there before him quite alone, and he gave no greeting, but asked him was it he that was holding the chase.

Fionn told him that it was not he, 'But', he said 'a company, with which I rode out awhile since; and one of our hounds that was running loose along with us chanced upon a spoor of wild pig and could not be caught. And it is the boar of Beann Ghulben that he met, and it is idle for the Fiana to pursue it since often aforetime it has escaped them, and it killing fifty warriors of the Fiana this morning. And it is coming up the Peak towards us with the Fiana in flight before it, so let us leave this hillock to it.'

Diarmaid said he would not leave the hillock . . . [66]

Now Diarmaid was under *gessa* ('taboos') not to hunt a pig. Fionn reminds him of the *gessa* but he fails to persuade him to abandon the hunt and leaves him alone on the hill. Diarmaid remembers Gráinne's warning and foresees his doom. His weapons prove useless against the boar and he is mortally wounded. Fionn and the Fiana come up and find him dying. Only a drink from Fionn's healing hands can save him now.

Then Oscar son of Oisín spoke:

'Fionn,' said he, 'knowest thou that I am more nearly akin to thee than to Diarmaid Ó Duibhne and that I would not suffer thee to withhold a drink from him.'

'I know not a spring on this peak,' said Fionn.

'That is not true,' said Diarmaid, 'for not nine paces from thee is the finest fresh-water spring that is best in all the world.' Then Fionn went to the spring and raised the full of his two cupped hands, but he let the water pass through his hands, and said he could not bring the water.

'I pledge my word', said Diarmaid, 'that it is of thine own will that thou dost so.' Fionn went to fetch the water again, and he had brought it no farther when he let it pass through his hands.

'I swear and my weapons are my witness,' said Oscar, 'if thou bring not the water speedily, Fionn, that only the stronger of us twain shall leave this place.'

Fionn at those words turned for the third time to fetch the water and he brought the full of his cupped hands of it, and as he was coming forward Diarmaid's spirit parted from his body. And then says the tale 'the company of the Fiana of Ireland that was in that place raised three grievous, exceeding mighty shouts of lamentation to the skies bewailing Diarmaid Ó Duibhne.[67]

Incidents in this story, as in other stories about the Fiana, have given rise to poems, many of which are preserved apart from the prose and in older forms of the language. Such is the sleep-song sung by Gráinne to Diarmaid with his reply, when they were in flight before Fionn and his men. It is dated 'c. 1150' and begins,

> Sleep a little, just a little,
> for there is nothing for you to fear,
> O lad to whom I have given love.
> Diarmaid son of Ua Duibhne.[68]

The poem and many others of the same kind are found in the early-seventeenth manuscript known as *Duanaire Finn*. Written in Ostend and Louvain by two scribes in 1626 and 1627 for Captain Sorley O'Donnell, one of the many Irish soldiers of fortune at the time on the Continent, it was in the Louvain collection of manuscripts, which was transferred to St Isidore's at Rome during the French Revolution. Later, in 1872, it was sent to the Franciscans in Dublin and it is now preserved in their Library, Dún Mhuire, Killiney, Co. Dublin.[69]

The most important development in the Mythological Cycle was the composition of *Trí Truaighe na Sgéalaigheachta* ('The Three Sorrows of Story-Telling').[70] The three stories resemble one another in style, a fact that suggests, as Thurneysen said, they share a common origin.[71] Support for this is found in the fact that the triadic nature of the common title is characteristic of the tales: there are three heroes in each. The manuscript tradition of one of the stories, *Oidheadh Chloinne Uisneach* ('The Tragic Death of the Children of Uisneach'), goes back to the first half of the sixteenth century, but it was clearly in existence before then. In fact, it is possible that it, like *Oidheadh Chloinne Tuireann* ('The Tragic Death of the Children of Tuireann'), was in existence in the second half of the fourteenth century. Thus the original version of the *Trí Truaighe na Sgéalaigheachta* could belong to this period. The denouement of the tale *Oidheadh Chloinne Lir* ('The Tragic Death of the Children of Lir') is set in Iorrus Domhnann and Inis Guaire, and this may suggest, as R. Flower said, that the story was composed in Uí Fiachrach Muaidhe, a district where Mac Firbhisigh was the chief literary family.[72] There is some evidence for connecting the two other stories with the same family. The oldest version of *Oidheadh Chloinne Tuireann* is in *The Book of Lecan*, a Mac Firbhisigh manuscript, and *Oidheadh Chloinne Uisneach* in one manuscript is joined to a recension of *Táin Bó Flidais*[73] which is found in a rather deteriorated form with Mac Firbhisigh manuscripts in *The*

Yellow Book of Lecan, and which demonstrates that its author or its editor was well-informed in the geography of Iorrus Domhnann.[74] Therefore, it is quite possible, though not certain, that these three tales took their present shapes in the second half of the fourteenth century and in the literary district of the Mac Firbhisigh family.

It appears that another class of tales distantly related to the Mythological Cycle was also evolved in the later Middle Ages, namely, the group of later 'romantic' tales: *Eachtra an Cheithearnaigh Chaoilriabhaigh* ('The Adventure of the Narrow-striped Soldier'),[75] *Eachtra an Ghiolla Dheacair* ('The Adventure of the Troublesome Lad'),[76] *Eachtra Chléirigh na gCroiceann* ('The Adventure of the Skin-clad Cleric'),[77] *Eachtra Bhodaigh an Chóta Lachtna* ('The Adventure of the Churl with the Grey-White Coat').[78]

A characteristic feature of these tales is that a visitor, one of the *Tuatha Dé Danann*, assumes a terrifying shape, and plays tricks by showing himself to a character or characters that belong to the stories of later cycles. The theme is not a new one: an example of it is found in a ninth-century adventure of Senchán Torpéist with the spirit of poetry, as found in Cormac's Glossary,[79] and another in the story of Fland mac Lonáin and Oengus.[80] As a rule, the visitor in these stories is Aongus an Bhrogha or Manannán mac Lir. It appears that *Eachtra an Ghiolla Dheacair* drew upon *Cath Finntrágha* ('The Battle of Ventry') for some details. *Cath Finntrágha* is found in Rawl. B. 487, a manuscript of the fifteenth century, the century in which, in all probability, it took shape. In that case, it may be that *Eachtra an Ghiolla Dheacair* was composed in the second half of the same century. One of the names that the Ceithearnach takes in *Eachtra an Cheithearnaigh Chaolriabhaigh* is *An Giolla Deacair*, suggesting, perhaps, that *Eachtra an Cheithearnaigh* is later than *Eachtra an Ghiolla*, and that it can be dated, perhaps, in the first half or middle of the sixteenth century.

§3

We can turn now to that literary activity which was concerned with making the literature of the Continent available to the Irish in their own language. This activity was not something entirely new to the Middle Ages, for it had already begun in the preceding age. Needless to say, what appealed to the Irish translators and adapters more than anything else were the stories of adventure and romance that were most popular on the Continent. It is customary to classify these into three 'matters', the Matter of Greece and Rome, the Matter of France, and the Matter of Britain; it will be convenient for us to follow this classification.

Kuno Meyer published an Irish text containing the story of Ulysses, *Merugud Uilix maicc Leirtis*, from Stowe MS 992 and *The Book of Ballymote*, and he surmised, 'that our author must have been acquainted, in ways still unknown, with the drift and main incidents of the Homeric poem, while this acquaintance was still so slight as to leave the play of his fancy free.'[81]

Virgil's *Aeneid* was translated before 1400; the only extant text, that in *The Book of Ballymote*, was published by George Calder.[82] In content it corresponds closely to the original, but the translator, a fine scholar in both Latin and Irish, takes advantage of the customary freedom of those translating into Irish by abbreviating and expanding whenever he presumed that that would add to the interest of the story as *scél*.

Sometime between AD 400 and 600 an unknown author composed *Daretis Phrygii de Excidio Troyae Historia* in Latin prose, asserting that he had translated it from the original Greek. His work was exceedingly popular in the Middle Ages. Fragments of an Irish translation of it are found in *The Book of Leinster*, but, according to Whitley Stokes, that text is not earlier than the eleventh century. Two fairly extensive fragments are also found in T.C.D.H. 2. 17.[83]

The history of Thebes was known on the Continent through the *Thebaid* of Statius, through the French poem *Roman de Thebes* (c. 1150) rather than any French prose version, and through the *Teseide* of Boccaccio, and it was loosely translated into Irish as well as into English.[84] The Irish version has been printed from two texts, one in Egerton 1781, the other in Advocates Library Gaelic MSS VIII, Kilbride Collection, No. 4.[85]

A free adaptation of the first seven books of Lucan's *Bellum Civile* was made—a poem that appealed greatly to the Irish imagination, not because of its excellence as poetry, but because of the tumultuous events it chronicles. As one can readily see, the adapter made use of every opportunity to augment these. In *Cath Catharda*[86] must have been quite popular, for several copies of it exist, in spite of the fact that it is the longest composition of the medieval period apart from *Táin Bó Cúailnge* and *Agallamh na Seanórach*.

Some of these texts influenced the native literature, the most conspicuous example of such influence perhaps being that exerted by

In Cath Catharda. It is obvious that Seán Mac Craith took the Irish adaptation of *Bellum Civile* as a model when he set about writing in the fourteenth century the history of the wars in Clare. His work, *Cathréim Thoirdhealbhaig*,[87] traces the history of Thomond under the lordship of Donough Cairbreach from 1204 on, and describes in detail the war between the Anglo-Norman family of De Clare and the family of O'Brien up to its bloody conclusion in the battle on the slopes of Corcomroe. To be sure, mere coincidence cannot account for the fact that this battle was called *cath catharda*.

The Matter of France is not well represented in the Irish literature of the period, although the stories about Charlemagne were quite well known.[88] Two of them in Latin are found in T.C.D. F. 5. 3: one is the *Chronicle of Turpin*, the other contains a unique and exceptional version of the *chanson* of Fierabras (Fortibras).[89] Translations of the two occur in Egerton MS 1781 and elsewhere. There are two versions of the *Chronicle of Turpin*. It could be that they represent two different translations, however the Latin text does not seem to be unlike the one found in T.C.D. F. 5. 3, and that in turn belongs to the same class as that represented by Harley 6358 and five others whose characteristics are described by H.L.D. Ward.[90] *The Tale of Fierabras* (*Fortibras*) was translated from a Latin version represented only, as far as we know, by the text in T.C.D. F. 5. 3.

The Arthurian tales form the substance of the Matter of Britain, and it has long since been recognized that many of the themes that occur in the tales about Arthur are found in Old Irish tales and can perhaps be traced to those tales. For example, Gertrude Schoepperle argued that the story about Gráinne in *Tóraigheacht Dhiarmada agus Ghráinne*—which typologically is but a variant of the Deirdre story in *Longes mac n-Uislenn*—represents a Celtic source of the story of Tristan and Isolt, and that it preserves many of the motifs that occur repeatedly in the French and German versions of that great romance.[91] Thurneysen believed that the tale of *Cano mac Gartnáin* contains parallel themes, and that even the name of the old king in that tale, Marcán, was consistent with the French tradition.[92] Binchy, however, could not agree: 'it would seem that apart from the universal and "eternal" triangle of aged husband, young wife, and youthful lover, the romance of Cano and Créd has little in common with the Tristan saga except the final *Liebestod*, for the identity of names between Marcán, Créd's husband, and Mark of Cornwall is doubtless fortuitous.'[93] From the same comparative standpoint, the text of *Altram Tige Dá Medar* ('The Fosterage of the House of Two

Milk Vessels') is just as interesting, because it appears to contain themes parallel with the French tale of the Holy Grail.[94]

The story of the Grail is the only major continental Arthurian tale to be translated into Irish. It was translated from a lost English version which seems to have been made in the fourteenth century. According to its editor, S. Falconer, the Irish translation was probably not made before the middle of the following century.[95] In drawing attention to the style of this translation, the editor emphasizes its difference from that adopted by most Irish translators of that period:

> In Irish the romance is simple and straightforward. This may be the outcome of a desire on the translator's part to recapture here, as with the grammar and orthography, the manner of the old heroic tales, or due to the fact that the original was followed with a degree of closeness incompatible with the ornate literary style much in vogue with prose writers from the 12th to the 17th century. Whatever the reason, it is particularly fortunate that the Quest, a work designed to attract in order to edify, should not have been burdened with the verbal extravagances of this style.

Clearly, some of the later Irish romances contain variations on some of the themes from Arthurian romances. For example, *Eachtra an Amadáin Mhóir* ('The Adventure of the Great Fool')[96] is a variation on the theme of the Foolish Knight. Furthermore, it commences with an episode based on some text of *Perceval le Gallois* and concludes with an adaptation of the tempting motif in *Sir Gawain and the Green Knight*.[97]

Eachtra an Mhadra Mhaoil ('The Adventure of the Blunt-Eared Dog')[98] was based on the motif of the man-turned-into-wolf, a motif discussed by G. L. Kittredge in *Arthur and Gorlagon*.[99] The 'Son of the King of India' is turned into a wolf by his step-mother, a wicked witch. He enlists the support of a knight of King Arthur's court in helping him find the Knight of the Lantern, son of the witch, since he is the only one able to turn him back into a man. Gwalchmai (Walwainus), here called Balbuaid and sometimes Ualbuaid (a form representing Walway, as Professor O'Rahilly demonstrated),[100] goes with him, and after a number of adventures, the pair succeed in accomplishing the purpose of the journey. The theme is also found in connection with an Arthurian tale in the *Lay of Melion* and in the Latin tale of *Arthur and Gorlagon*, which Kittredge traced through Welsh to an Irish source. Of course, the Arthurian link may be a later addition to the Irish tale, but it could be significant that it is

Gwalchmai who guides Arthur on his quest in the tale of *Arthur and Gorlagon* too. *Eachtra an Mhadra Mhaoil* was published by Macalister in his *Two Irish Arthurian Romances.*[101]

The other tale included in that volume is *Eachtra Mhacaoimh an Iolair* ('The Adventure of the Lad of the Eagle'). It was based on the theme of the child who is snatched away by an animal and who, having reached manhood, returns to avenge the wrong done to his mother, the same theme as that used in *Guillaume de Palerne* and other romances.[102] Not the least interesting thing in connection with all of this is that the name of the author and his method of composition have been recorded. The earliest extant copy is that in R.I.A. 24 P. 9, written in 1651 on an island in Lough Mask, Co. Mayo, by David O'Duigenan (Dáibhí Ó Duibhgennáin). It has been said that the author, Brian Ó Corcráin, is identical with a man of that name who was vicar of Claoininis (Cleenish on Loch Erne, Co. Fermanagh), and who died, according to the Four Masters, in 1487. But the suggestion made by Professor Bergin that the author was Brian Ó Corcráin, family bard to the Maguires (some of his poems are preserved in the Book of O'Conor Don), who lived *c.* 1600, is much more likely.[103]

In the introduction, Ó Corcráin says that he got the outline of the story from a nobleman who heard it in France. He enjoyed hearing the synopsis so much that he wrote it down, adding a few short poems. 'This story', he said, 'never existed in Irish'. This gives us some idea how the typical composer of Irish romances worked. He was always ready to take suggestions from foreign sources and to embellish them in the native style. Perhaps we shall never know what the original French tale was. As already suggested, the same theme is to be found in *Guillaume de Palerne*, in *Floriant et Florete* (but without the abduction by an animal), and in the French original of Alysaunder le Orphelyn (*Morte Darthur*, Book X; cf. ed. of O. Sommer, Appendix). Perhaps one of the additions of the Irish author was the part of the story in which Arthur appears; it is surely significant that it closely resembles other Irish tales that have an Arthurian framework.

It appears, too, that the Arthurian frame of *Eachtra Mhelora agus Orlando* is an addition.[104] The principal theme can be traced to the *Orlando Furioso* of Ariosto, canto III and IV, where Bradamant rescues Rogero from the castle Atlantis by getting the ring of King Agramant of Africa from Brunello. Dr Robin Flower noted that Sir John Harrington, the man who translated *Orlando Furioso* into

English during the reign of Elizabeth, brought his translation to the attention of Tyrone and his two sons in 1599, and that he came across a copy of it in Galway, 'where a great lady, a young lady, and a fair lady read herself asleep, nay dead, with a tale of it.'[105] Dr Flower concluded that the Irish story was probably the work of some Irishman living in the seventeenth century who knew of the *Orlando Furioso* either personally or at second hand. It was published with another Arthurian tale, the *Céilidhe Iosgaide Léithe*, which was probably composed in the fifteenth century.[106]

David O'Duigenan (Dáibhí Ó Duibhgennáin), who copied the oldest extant text of *Eachtra Mhacoimh an Iolair*, also preserved for us the Irish version of *Florent et Octavian*, a French tale similar to the *Eachtra*.[107] A theme similar to that found in these two stories occurs in *Eachtra Uilliam*, that is, the Irish version of *Guillaume de Palerne*. The way that this text is presumed to have reached the Irish is characteristic: it is a translation from an English prose version that was extant in the first half of the sixteenth century, itself based on an English metrical translation of a French poem similar to the *Roman de Guillaume de Palerne*, composed, presumably, at the end of the twelfth century. What distinguishes the translation of this tale from other Irish translations is that it adheres so closely to the original. 'Thus, the English tale, in all its essentials and most of its details, remains the same in the Irish version. It has, however, taken a completely Irish colour, and, as a good translation should, reads as if originally composed in Irish.'[108]

It is clear that several of these stories came to Ireland through the medium of English. The principal source of *Stair Ercuil ocus a Bás*[109] was the English translation made by William Caxton between 1 March, 1468 and 19 June, 1471 of a French work, *Recueil des Histoires de Troyes*, composed by Raoul Lefevre, and printed, probably, around 1478. The Irish versions of Guy of Warwick and Bevis of Hampton were probably taken from the English, too.[110] According to the editor, it is likely that

the Irish lives are free redactions of lost English versions. The assumed original of the 'Bevis' appears not to have differed in any important particulars from other existing forms of the story. In the case of 'Guy', on the other hand, the Irish text points to the existence in English of a combination, hitherto unknown, of the romantic material proper with the religious material originally distinct, of the *Speculum* Guy de Warewyke.[111]

Stair Ercuil ocus a Bás, Guy ocus Bevis, and *Beatha Mhuire Eigiptacdha* are texts extant only in the hand of Uilliam Mac an Lega, and G. Quin expressed the belief that Uilliam was both translator and scribe of these works.[112]

The Buke of John Maundeville was translated into Irish in 1475 by Fingin O'Mahony, an Irish lord who died in 1496.[113] In the introduction he says he made his version from sources in English, Latin, Greek, and Hebrew, but according to his editor it is clear that only an English text lay before him. The oldest and best copy is in the Irish Rennes Manuscript. In connection with the book of Maundeville, we must not neglect to mention the Irish abridgement of the Book of Ser Marco Polo.[114]

§4

Interesting though these tales are, we must remember that they were but a part of the literature of the period, and that the didactic literature which was produced—the religious, philosophical, and medical literature—took up just as much if not more space in the manuscripts. We cannot get a balanced view of the literature of the period without keeping that fact in mind.

Saints' Lives were a part of the religious literature that closely resembled the romantic tales. They became very popular in the later medieval period as reading materials in church services and in the monastic refectories. They were collected either in abbreviated form or *in extenso* in books of *legenda* 'things to be read'. The most widely known collection was the *Legenda Aurea* (*c.* 1260–70) of Jacopo de Voragine. Another important collection in these islands was that compiled in England in the fourteenth century by John of Tynemouth, the *Sanctilogium Angliae, Walliae, Scotiae et Hiberniae.* As the title indicates, this contains several Irish saints' lives.

The Irish were certainly busy in the same century—if not before—composing the same kind of *legendaria.* Their inclination was to restrict their parchment to the native saints, though they were not unwilling to give space to foreign saints who had won international fame. As a rule, the versions that were translated into Irish were those also found in the *Legenda Aurea* or those collected in the *Sanctuarium* of Mombritius. But quite often the Irish lives are completely independent of the Latin ones, and there is more than one version of some of them. Reference has already been made to the *Leabhar Breac,* written in 1411 or earlier. It contains Irish lives in the form of homilies on Patrick, Colum Cille, and Brigit. Apart from these and other homilies, it narrates the story of the sufferings of Christ, the apostles and the martyrs, and quite a number of Biblical and apocryphal stories. *The Book of Liss-mór* (Lismore)[115] was copied in the second half of the fifteenth century by a number of scribes, among them a certain Aonghus Ó Callanáin[116] and a brother of a religious order named Ó Buagacháin, for Finghin Mac Carthaigh *Riabhach* and his wife Catherine. It contains lives—many in the form of homilies—of Patrick, Brigit, Senán, Finnian of Clonard, Find-Chú of Brigown, Brendan of Clonfert, Ciarán of Clúain, and Mo-Chúa of Balla.[117]

There are two other large collections of Irish saints' lives extant.[118] One was compiled from older texts by Mícheál Ó Cléirigh between 1620 and 1635 when he was in Ireland, to send to Ward, Colgan, and the other antiquarians in Louvain. The other was put together by Domhnall Ó Duinnín in Cork during the month of June, 1627, for Francis Ó Mathgamhna (O'Mahony), who intended, perhaps, to pass it on to scholars in Louvain, although there is no evidence that anything came of that intention, for in 1776 it was in the possession of Charles O'Conor of Belanagare.

Among the lives of foreign saints are those of SS Alexius, Catherine, and Margaret. The Irish life of St Alexius is found in the *Liber Flavus Fergusiorum*, the same life, probably, as that found in R.I.A. 24 P 25, Egerton 1781, and Additional 30512. There is a later edition in Egerton 112 and Additional 18948.[119] It is claimed that the life in Egerton 136 is no more than a version of the ordinary life as printed in the Act. Sanct. Jul IV, p. 251.[120] The Irish life of St Catherine is in Egerton 1781; it is the same, no doubt, as that which tells the story of her martyrdom in T.C.D. H. 2. 17. The life in R.I.A. 24 P 25, said to have been translated from the Latin by Enog Ó Gilláin and Ciothruaigh Mac Fhionnghaill, appears to be different, as does that in Egerton 184.[121]

The Irish life of St Margaret occurs in Egerton 1781. It has been claimed that, 'The general aim is to turn the saint's life into a kind of bardic romance, and the language is the formal, adjectival style characteristic of these compositions.'[122] It appears to be a free translation of a Latin life such as that printed by Mombritius, *Sanctuarium*, 1910, ii, 190.[123] The translator was 'Philip Ó Dalaigh do muintir na Trínoídi', undoubtedly the man who was a canon in the Premonstratensian monastery on the Island of the Holy Trinity in Loch Cé, or in the monastery affiliated to it on the Island of the Holy

Trinity in Loch Uachtair, Co. Cavan. A copy of a life of the same saint found in MS Erlangen 1800 appears to be no more than a variant of the Egerton 1781 life.[124] Another recension in a similar style is represented apparently in the fifteenth-century life in Laud 610, f. 7. Finally, a translation by Tadhg Ó Neachtain from an unknown original occurs in Egerton 190.[125]

Reference was made earlier to Quin's conviction that Uilliam Mac an Lega translated the three texts *Stair Ercuil ocus a Bás*, *Guy ocus Bevis*, and *Beatha Mhuire Eigiptacdha*. He maintains furthermore that what can be said about the life of Mary of Egypt, 'in substance a romance and in manner an essay in style', is also true of the two romances.[126] But since they were produced, in a sense, by the same literary men, it was perhaps inevitable that some of the lives would be in the same style as the romances.

As one might expect, the Virgin Mary was a favourite subject of song and story. The apocryphal story *Transitus B. V. Mariae*, of which there is a Latin text in T.C.D. F. 5. 3, was translated and is found in *Liber Flavus Fergusiorum* and Laud 610.[127] There is also a translation of *Vita B. V. Mariae Rhythmica*, a life of the Virgin composed by a German in the thirteenth century; it too owes much to apocryphal sources.[128] The full translation is found in T.C.D. E. 8. 29, and a shortened translation is in Additional 11809. Each is followed in the manuscripts by a fifteenth-century translation of *Meditationes Vitae Christi*, a metrical version in Latin of the narrative of the Gospels, together with meditations, made by Tomás Ó Bruacháin, a canon in the cathedral church of Killala, Co. Mayo. The *Meditationes* was a very popular text in the later Middle Ages; it was attributed, incorrectly, to St Bonaventura.[129] The canonical gospels were not translated into Irish during this period, but there is a fair sampling of the apocryphal literature from both the Old and the New Testaments.

In *An Leabhar Breac* there is a fairly complete story-version of Holy Scripture, but the Old and New Testament come from different non-canonical sources.[130] The Old Testament part is from a prose version of the metrical narrative in *Saltair na Rann*,[131] which was composed in the tenth century, but the original is not followed faithfully and it has been expanded in places. There are two principal sources for the New Testament part, the first three books of Eusebius' *Historia Ecclesiastica*—probably from the Latin text of Rufinus of Aquileia, and apocryphal material drawn chiefly from the *Pseudo-Matthaei Evangelium* but in a version very different from the text printed by Tischendorf (*Evangelia Apocrypha*, 1876, p. 51) and from the original Greek (chapters i-xvii) of that text, the *Protoevangelium Jacobi*, as it is called. Copies of the New Testament part are found in Egerton 1781, T.C.D. H. 2. 17, R.I.A. 24 P 25, *Liber Flavus Fergusiorum*, and *The Book of Fermoy* (Fir Muighe).

There is a Latin text of the *History of the True Cross* (*Inventio Sanctae Crucis*) in T.C.D. F. 5. 3, and an Irish version of it is found in *An Leabhar Breac*; a version closer to the original is in Egerton 1781.[132] In the oldest manuscripts the Irish text is joined to the text of *Fierabras* (*Fortibras*), and it appears that it was translated in order to provide a preface to that story.

The fragments on The Passion of Christ and His Descent into Hell in *An Leabhar Breac* were based on the *Evangelium Nicodemi*, an apocryphal gospel of which there is an Irish version in *The Yellow Book of Lecan*, R.I.A. 24 P 25, and the *Liber Flavus Fergusiorum*. The story of Christ's Descent into Hell was popular in both prose and poetry. Dr Flower has drawn attention to a prose text describing the Descent in B.L. Additional 30512; it may be a version of an English poem not unlike *Ye Deuelis Perlament or Parlamentum of Feendis*.[133]

In light of the special contribution which the Irish made to vision literature in the Middle Ages, it would be surprising indeed if the *Visio Sancti Pauli* had not been translated into Irish. It was, of course, and we have a full version of it in R.I.A. 24 P 25 and a partial one in the *Liber Flavus Fergusiorum*.[134] There are later versions, one of which was published by Hyde in *Religious Songs of Connacht*, II, 319–49.

Among the original compositions in this particular area of religious literature that came directly or indirectly from Ireland are *Navigatio S. Brendani*, a work already referred to, 'The Vision of Fursa', 'The Vision of Adamnán', 'The Purgatory of St Patrick', and 'The Vision of Tundale'.[135] Latin was the original language of each of these visions except Adamnán's (*Fís Adamnáin*), but Irish versions were made later. An Irish version of the Latin life and visions of Fursa as given by Bede[136] is found in Egerton 180, MS Brussels Bibl. Roy. 2324–40,[137] and Stowe 9 (R.I.A. A. iv. I). The Visions of Fursa in Latin are the first of their kind in the Christian literature of Ireland, and they had a profound influence on the literature of Europe.[138] An Irish version of the *Vision of Tundale* occurs in T.C.D. H. 3. 18 and Stowe MS C. 11;[139] and Irish versions of the story of *St Patrick's Purgatory* were made, too.[140] And although there was no connection between the original Story of Guido and Ireland, it too was translated into Irish.[141]

This is not the place to discuss the wealth of devotional literature which was produced in this period, but perhaps we should summarize

Robin Flower's comments on its nature.[142] Irish religious thought during this period, he says, was affected by Franciscan influence, and many of the religious and theological texts represent the emphasis that the Brothers of the Order of St Francis put on sharing directly in the sufferings of Christ. Because of this emphasis, the image of the Virgin Mary standing at the foot of the Cross became the symbol of the grief of all mankind before the crucified Christ. It is no wonder that the famous Franciscan hymn, 'Stabat mater dolorosa', became the pattern and archetype of all that special poetry that developed the theme of the *planctus* or lament.

This Franciscan emphasis is visible in the *Meditationes Vitae Christi*, the Irish version of which has already been referred to, and in the *Dialogus de Passione Christi* wrongly attributed to St Anselm.[143] The *Dialogus* was translated by Seán Ó Conchubhair—probably the Roscommon man of that name who died in 1405. He could also be the one who translated the *Liber de Passione Christi*.[144] Another translation worth mentioning here is the one made by Uilliam Mac Duibhne of *De Contemptu Mundi*, the work of Pope Innocent III.[145]

Reference has already been made to the literary activity of the medical families in the Middle Ages, and especially to their work of copying manuscripts.[146] As might be expected, their chief interest was in those manuscripts that contained medical materials. Representatives of such families spring readily to mind. Such a one is Cormac Mac Duinn Shléibhe. We know that parts of Harl. 546 and Arundel 333, and maybe a part of Arundel 313, are in his hand.[147] And it was he who translated *Gualterus de dosibus* into Irish in 1459 for Diarmaid mac Domhnaill Ó Leighin.[148] Or consider the family of Ó hÍceadha: in Cotton App. LI there is a note saying that Tomás Ó hÍceadha wrote the 'book' for Maelachlainn Ó hÍceadha in 1589, though he wrote only a part of the manuscript as it is now.[149] In Egerton 89 there is a translation of the Aphorisms of Hippocrates, a translation said to have been done by Nicól Ó hÍceadha and Aonghus Ó Callanáin in 1403.[150] The family of Ó Callanáin was famous for its doctors, and two of its members—Diarmaid Ó Callanáin and Eoin Ó Callanáin—copied Cotton App. LI.[151] Another medical family was that of Mac Beatha.[152] Additional 15582, a manuscript containing medical matters, was written for one of them, Eoin Mac Beatha, in 1563,[153] and we know that the manuscript was in the possession of Fearghus mac Eoin mac Fhearguis mac Beatha later on in the century.[154] Medical memoranda by other members of the family are found in the manuscript.[155]

As S. H. O'Grady said, the literary physician in Ireland was steeped in scholasticism, and was in his heyday when the Arabic influence was one of the principal intellectual influences in Europe.[156] He wanted nothing to do with surgery: that was left to practical specialists whom he despised as his modern successor despises the unprofessional bone-setter. Nor was he, any more than his colleague in England and on the Continent, a scientific observer and recorder. He was neither investigator nor experimenter; indeed, he loathed every kind of originality. He was content to follow his predecessors, and his chief interest as a literary man was to collect materials that were already extant and to translate them when that was necessary. Since he was not a specialist, his interests could be broad, and he sometimes enlarged them to include metaphysics and philosophy; it is these interests that are represented in the treatises which he translated and wrote.[157]

Notes

1 *Irish Men of Learning* (Studies by Father Paul Walsh), ed. Colm Ó Lochlainn (Dublin, 1947). For Scotland use D. S. Thomson, 'Gaelic Learned Orders and Literati in Medieval Scotland', *Scottish Studies*, 12 (1968), 57–68.
2 Flower, *The Irish Tradition*, p. 85.
3 Ibid., pp. 88–93. On the 'High-Kingship' see J. V. Kelleher, 'Early Irish History and Pseudo-History', SH, 3 (1963), 113–127, esp. 119–20; D. A. Binchy, *The Origins of the So-Called High Kingship* (Statutory Lecture, Dublin Institute for Advanced Studies, 1959); F. J. Byrne, *The Rise of the Uí Néill and the High-Kingship of Ireland* (O'Donnell Lecture, Dublin, 1969), and *Irish Kings and High-Kings* (London, 1973).
4 Stokes, *Vita Tripartita: The Tripartite of Life of St. Patrick* (London, 1887), II, 336; J. Gwynn, *Liber Ardmachanus: The Book of Armagh* (Dublin, 1913), pp. cii, 32: *Ego scripsi, id est Calvus Perennis, in conspectu Briani imperatoris Scotorum et que scripsi finivit pro omnibus regibus Maeriae,* 'I, Calvus Perennis (trans. of Máel-Suthain), have written in the sight of Brian, emperor of the Irish, and what I have written he has confirmed for all the kings of Cashel.'
5 See also Kathleen Hughes, *Early Christian Ireland*, p. 293, on the tradition that Brian Ború sent scholars overseas to buy books to replace those destroyed by the Vikings.
6 Mac Cana'The Rise of the Later School of Filidheacht', *Ériu*, 25 (1974), 138–39.
7 Above, p. 91, and see Kenney, *Sources*, I, 11, 734–5.

8 Mac Neill, *Celtic Ireland*, chap. 6, 'The Book of Rights', and M. Dillon, *Lebor na Cert* (Dublin, 1962). Dr Kathleen Hughes, *Early Christian Ireland*, p. 285, believes that the preface to LC must have been written at the beginning of the twelfth century.

9 Cf. E. Curtis, *A History of Ireland* (London, 1950), p. 35.

10 M. Dillon, op. cit.; Kelleher, art. cit., 122, believes that LC was composed for Brian Ború's grandson 'and very likely dates from the first decade of the twelfth century'.

11 Kenney, *Sources*, I, 747ff.; Gougaud, *Christianity in Celtic Lands*, p. 394f. The situation was certainly much more complex than is suggested in this brief treatment, and the decline was perhaps neither as sudden nor as widespread as is presupposed here. See Máirtín Mac Conmara, ed., *An Léann Eaglasta 1000–1200* (Dublin, 1982) for a corrective description.

12 Curtis, op. cit., p. 38.

13 See Mac Cana, art. cit., 126–46.

14 Curtis, op. cit., p. 44; Kenney, *Sources*, I, 767.

15 E. B. Fitzmaurice and A. G. Little, *Materials for the History of the Franciscan Province of Ireland, AD 1230–1450* (Manchester, 1920), pp. xxv, 120.

16 Cf. *B.M. Cat. Irish MSS*, II, 91.

17 See Abbott and Gwynn, *Cat. of the Irish MSS. in the Library of Trinity College* (Dublin, 1921), pp. 90–92, and Best and Thurneysen, *The Oldest Fragments of the Senchus Már* (from MS H.2.15 in the Library, Trinity College, Dublin), Dublin, 1931.

18 Samuel Ferguson, *Leabhar Breac: The Speckled Book . . . now for the first time published from the original manuscript in the Library of the Royal Irish Academy* (Dublin, 1872–6).

19 Tomás Ó Concheanainn, 'The Scribe of the *Leabhar Breac*', *Ériu*, 24 (1973), 63–79.

20 Walsh, *Irish Men of Learning*, pp. 80–101.

21 *The Yellow Book of Lecan . . . now for the first time published from the original manuscript in the Library of Trinity College, Dublin, with Introduction, Analysis of Contents and Index* by Robert Atkinson (Dublin, 1896); H. P. A. Oskamp, 'The Yellow Book of Lecan Proper', *Ériu*, 26 (1975), 102–23. T. Ó Concheanainn, *Celtica* 18 (1986), 13–33, discusses the MS tradition of two Middle Irish Leinster tales, *Orgain Denna Ríg* and *Esnada Tige Buchet*, and after comparing the language and style of the different versions of the tales suggests that many important Middle Irish manuscripts were available to the north Connacht scribes of the Yellow Book of Lecan. See also W. O'Sullivan, 'Ciothruadh's Yellow Book of Lecan', *Ériu*, 18 (1980–81), 177–81.

22 *The Book of Lecan: Leabhar Mór Mhic Fhir Bhisigh Lecáin, With Descriptive Introduction and Indexes* by Kathleen Mulchrone (Dublin, 1937).

23 Tomás Ó Concheanainn, 'Gilla Ísa Mac Fir Bhisigh and a Scribe of his School', *Ériu*, 25 (1974), 156–71.

24 Walsh, op. cit., pp. 85–8.

25 Ibid., 34–48. Cf. *The Genealogies, Tribes and Customs of Hy Fiachrach,*

Commonly Called O'Dowd's Country, with trans. and notes by John O'Donovan (Dublin, 1844).

26 Flower, *The Irish Tradition*, p. 116.

27 *B.M. Cat. Irish MSS*, I, 4f.; Walsh, op. cit., p. 105.

28 W. M. Hennessy, *Annals of Loch Cé* (Rolls Series, London, 1871), I, II; (Reflex Process Facs., Dublin, 1939), I, II, (Text of T.C.D. H. i. 19).

29 R. I. Best, 'Notes on Rawlinson B. 512', ZCP, 17 (1929), 389–402; Stokes, *Vita Tripartita*, xiv-xlv; *The Academy*, 33 (1888), 191–2; Meyer, *Hibernica Minora* (Oxford, 1894).

30 Walsh, op. cit., pp. 1ff., 13ff., 25ff.

31 *The Book of Ballymote, with Introduction, Analyses of Contents and Index*, by Robert Atkinson (Dublin, 1887). See T. Ó Concheanainn, 'The Book of Ballymote', *Celtica*, 14 (1981) [1982], 15–25, where the north Connacht cultural background is described and the date of the manuscript is placed tentatively shortly before 1395. Two other scribes are named, Solamh Ó Droma and Robertus mac Sithigh. They and Magnus Ó Duibgennáin appear to have been students of a certain Domnal Mac Egan, and they penned the manuscript in 1400 or a little later.

32 *The Book of Ballymote*, 333a, Intro. 2.

33 *The Book of Uí Máine*, Collotype facsimile. Introduction and indexes by R.A.S. Macalister (Dublin, 1942).

34 Walsh, *Irish Men of Learning*, pp. 22–3; O'Curry, *MS. Materials*, p. 95. O'Curry describes it as 'a transcript' with a few additions (p. 113). A. M. Freeman, *The Annals of Connacht* (Dublin, 1944); compare Freeman's comments with those of Walsh, loc. cit.

35 Walsh, op. cit., p. 25ff.

36 P. Walsh, *The O Cléirigh Family of Tír Conaill* (Dublin, 1938).

37 J. H. Todd, 'Account of an Ancient Irish MS. in the Bodleian Library, Oxford', PRIA 2 (1842), 336–45.

38 *B.M. Cat. Irish MSS*, II, 470–505, 545–51.

39 H. Omont, 'Catalogue des MSS. celtiques et basques de la Bibliothèque Nationale', RC 11 (1890), 389–433.

40 Walsh, *Irish Men of Learning*, pp. 206–18.

41 Abbott and Gwynn, *Cat. of Irish MSS the Library of Trinity College, Dublin* p. 323ff.

42 G. Dottin, 'Notice du manuscrit irlandais de la Bibliothèque de Rennes', RC 15 (1895), 79–91.

43 E. J. Gwynn, 'The Manuscript known as the Liber Flavus Fergusiorum', PRIA 26 (1906); Sec. C, 15–41.

44 O'Curry, *MS. Materials*, p. 76.

45 P. Walsh, *Leabhar Chlainne Suibhne* (Dublin, 1920), xliv-lviii.

46 This note has been printed twice, first by G. Calder, *Togail na Tebe* (Cambridge, 1922), p. xxii, and then more accurately by Flower, *B.M. Cat. Irish MSS*, II, 538–539.

47 Thurneysen, holding that after the eighth and ninth centuries the Irish sagas were disseminated for the most part by manuscripts, errs in his belief that once a tale had acquired written form it was no longer influenced by oral tradition. For an example of a tale being influenced in

this way and developing as a result of that influence, see R. J. Cormier, 'Early Irish Tradition and Memory of the Norsemen in "The Wooing of Emer"', SH, 9 (1967), 65–75. See also G. Murphy, *Saga and Myth in Ancient Ireland* (Dublin, 1955), pp. 59–61.

48 Ed. and trans. J. H. Todd, Rolls Series (London, 1867).

49 See Kathleen Hughes, *Early Christian Ireland:* pp. 288–93; P. Mac Cana, 'The Influence of the Vikings on Celtic Literature', *Proceedings of the International Congress of Celtic Studies* (Dublin, 1962), pp. 84–6.

50 A. Bugge, *Caithréim Cellacháin Caisil* (Christiana, 1905). D. Ó Corráin, 'Caithréim Chellacháin Chaisil: History or Propaganda?', *Ériu*, 25 (1974), 1–69 argues that the author of *Caithréim* was an Irish secular who wrote to glorify Cellachán and thereby his descendants. He modelled his work on *Cogadh Gaedhel re Gallaibh*, a piece of Brian propaganda, which in turn may have been modelled on Asser's *Life of Alfred*.

51 For a general introduction to this extensive narrative cycle, with a close thematic analysis of the 'Boyhood Deeds' of Finn, see Joseph Falaky Nagy, *The Wisdom of the Outlaw: The Boyhood Deeds of Finn in Gaelic Narrative Tradition* (Berkeley, Los Angeles, London, 1985), and also Rolf Baumgarten, 'Placenames, Etymology, and the Structure of *Fianaigecht*', Alan Bruford, 'Oral and Literary Fenian Tales', and Proinsias Mac Cana, '*Fianaigecht* in the pre-Norman Period' in Bo Almqvist, Séamas Ó Catháin, and Pádraig Ó Héalaí, eds., *The Heroic Process* (Dun Laoghaire, 1987), 1–56, 75–99..

52 K. Meyer, *Fianaigecht* (R.I.A. Todd Lecture Series, XVI, Dublin, 1910), pp. xv-xxxi.

53 The text is found in *The Book of Lismore*, Laud 610, Merchants' Quay Franciscan Library A iv, and Rawl. B. 487. The most recent edition is that of Nessa Ní Sheaghdha, *Agallamh na Seanórach*, I, II (Dublin, 1942), III (1945).

54 *Agallamh*; S. H. O'Grady, *Silva Gadelica* (London, 1892), (Irish Text) p. 96; (Translation and Notes) pp. 103–4.

55 D. Hyde (An Craoibhín), 'An Agallamh Bheag', *Lia Fáil*, I (1924), 79–107; W. Pennington, 'The Little Colloquy', *Philological Quarterly*, 9 (1930), 97–100; Pádraig Ó Siochfhradha, *Laoithe na Féinne* (Dublin, 1941), p. 1ff.

56 See Meyer, *Fianaigecht*; E. Mac Néill, *Duanaire Finn*, I (London, 1908); G. Murphy, *Duanaire Finn*, II (London, 1933), III (Dublin, 1953); G. Murphy, *The Ossianic Lore and Romantic Tales of Medieval Ireland* (Dublin, 1955); Joseph F. Nagy, *The Wisdom of the Outlaw*; P. Mac Cana, '*Fianaigecht* in the Pre-Norman Period', J. F. Nagy, 'Fenian Heroes and their Rites of Passage' and other chapters on the Scottish Gaelic Ballads in Bo Almquist, Séamas Ó Catháin, Pádraig Ó Héalaí, edd., *The Heroic Process*.

57 One of the first editions is that of Bryan O'Looney in *Trans. Ossian. Soc.*, IV (1859).

58 Ed. and trans. by Tomás Ó Flannghaile, *The Lay of Oisín by Micheál Coimín* (London, 1896); anthologized in T. P. Cross and Clark Slover, *Ancient Irish Tales* (Chicago, 1936; rpt. with rev. bibl., 1969), pp. 439–56.

59 D. Corkery, *The Hidden Ireland* (Dublin, 1924; 1967), pp. 272–4.

60 S. H. O'Grady, *Tóruigheacht Dhiarmuda agus Ghráinne, or the Pursuit after Diarmuid Ó Duibhne and Gráinne* (= *Trans. Ossian. Soc.*, III, 1855) and Nessa Ní Shéaghdha, *Tóruigheacht Dhiarmadha agus Ghráinne* (ITS, 1967).
61 See above, chap. 1, p. 37ff.
62 K. Meyer, 'Uath Beinne Etair: The Hiding of the Hill of Howth', RC, 9 (1888), 125–34.
63 M. Joynt, *Feis Tighe Chonáin* (Dublin, 1936); N. Ní Shéaghdha, *Bruidhean Bheag na hAlmhan*, in *Trí Bruidhne* (Dublin, 1941); P. H. Pearse, *Bruidhean Chaorthainn* (Dublin, 1908); N. O'Kearney, *The Battle of Gabhra* (*Trans. Ossian. Soc.*, I, 1853); K. Meyer, *Cath Finntrága* (Dublin, 1885). For a discussion of these, see Dillon, *Early Irish Literature*, pp. 32–50.
64 Ed. Vernam Hull, (New York, 1949).
65 Irish text in Vernam Hull, 9 (p. 46).
66 The translation is by R. A. Breatnach, *Irish Sagas*, ed. Myles Dillon (4th edn., Dublin, 1985), pp. 143–4.
67 Ibid., pp. 144–5.
68 Murphy, *Early Irish Lyrics*, p. 161.
69 See n. 56 above.
70 O'Curry, 'Trí Thruaighe na Scéalaigheachta of Erinn', *Atlantis*, 3 and 4 (1862–63); S. Ua Ceallaigh, *Trí Truagha na Scéaluidheachta* (Dublin, 1927, 1932). Each of the three is the tale of an *oidheadh* or 'tragic death'.
71 *Heldensage*, I, 327.
72 *B.M. Cat. Irish MSS*, II, 347ff. But see also Carney, *SILH*, p. 158.
73 For *Táin Bó Flidais*, see *Irische Texte*, 2 ser., II; Thurneysen, *Zu ir. Handschriften.* (1912), pp. 95–6.
74 *B.M. Cat. Irish MSS*, II, 339ff., 350ff.
75 Enrí Ua Muirgheasa, *Ceithearnach Uí Dhomhnaill, nó Eachtra an Cheithearnaigh chaoil-riabhaigh do réir druinge* (Dublin, 1912); S. H. O'Grady, *Silva Gadelica*, I, 276–89.
76 Ibid., p. 257.
77 *B.M. Cat. Irish MSS*, II, 220, 367, 405; *Irisleabhar Muighe Nuadhat*, I (1907), 22–5.
78 O'Grady, op. cit., p. 289; P. H. Pearse, *Bodach an Chóta Lachtna* (Dublin, 1905).
79 *Anecdota from Irish MSS*, IV, 90, 1059; O'Donovan, Stokes, *Cormac's Glossary* (1868), pp. 135–8. And see now, P. L. Henry, *Saoithiúlacht na Sean-Ghaeilge* (Dublin, 1976), cap. VII: 'Na Filí: 3. Amargein agus Spiorad na hÉigse'.
80 *Anecdota*, I, 45.
81 *Merugud Uilix maicc Leirtis: The Irish Odyssey* (London, 1886), p. x. See also the edition by Robert Meyer, Dublin, 1958. On classical influence in general on Irish literature see W. B. Stanford, 'Towards a History of Classical Influences in Ireland', PRIA, 70 (1970), 13–91.
82 *Imtheachta Aeniasa: The Irish Aeneid* (London, 1907; = ITS VI); T. Hudson-Williams, 'Cairdius Aeneas ocus Didaine: The Love of Aeneas and Dido', ZCP, 2 (1899), 419–72.

83 Whitley Stokes, *Togail Troí: The Destruction of Troy* (Calcutta, 1881); *Irische Texte*, 2 Ser., I, 1–142.

84 Gröber, *Grundriß der romanischen Philologie*, II (Strassburg, 1902), 582; de Julleville, *Histoire de la Langue et de la Littérature Française* (Paris., 1896), I, 173, 252; *Encyc. Britt.*, 11th ed., *Thebes, Romances of.*

85 G. Calder, *Togail na Tebe: The Thebaid of Statius* (Cambridge, 1922). For a modern version see Tomás Ó Floinn, *Toghail na Téibe* (Dublin, 1983).

86 Whitley Stokes, *In Cath Catharda: The Civil War of the Romans. An Irish Version of Lucan's Pharsalia*, in *Irische Texte*, IV.

87 S. H. O'Grady, ed., *Caithréim Thoirdhealbhaigh* (The Wars of Turlogh) (ITS, XXVI, XXVII, London, 1929).

88 Douglas Hyde, *Gabhaltais Shearluis Mhóir: The Conquests of Charlemagne* (ITS, XIX, 1917 [1919]).

89 *B.M. Cat. Irish MSS*, II, 527–9. Cf. *Studies*, 8 (1919), 688.

90 *Catalogue of Romances in the Department of Manuscripts in the British Museum*, 2 vols. (London, 1883, 1893); I, 560–1.

91 Gertrude Schoepperle, *Tristan and Isolt* (London, 1913).

92 'Eine irische Parallele zur Tristan-Sage', *Zeitschr. f. rom. Phil.*, 43 (1923), 385–402; see also ZCP, 16 (1927), 280–82; J. Carney, SILH, 189f.; R. Bromwich, *Trans. Cymmr. Soc.*, 1953 (London, 1955), 33–60.

93 D. A. Binchy, ed., *Scéla Cano Meic Gartnáin* (Dublin, 1963), p. xvii. But see also the review by R. Bromwich in SC, 1 (1966), 152–5.

94 A. G. Van Hamel, 'The Celtic Grail', RC, 47 (1930), 340–82. The text was ed. and trans. by M. E. Dobbs in ZCP, 18 (1930), 189–230, and then in the light of Van Hamel's thesis (op. cit.) by Lilian Duncan *Ériu*, 11, pt. ii (1932), 184–225. And see ZCP, 13 (1921), 1; J. Vendryes, 'Les éléments celtiques de la légende du Graale', ÉC, 5 (1949), 1–50.

95 S. Falconer, *Lorgaireacht an tSoidhigh Naomhtha, An Early Modern Irish Translation of the Quest of the Holy Grail* (Dublin, 1953), pp. xxxi-xxxii.

96 T. Ó Rabhartaigh, 'Eachtra an Amadáin Mhóir', *Lia Fáil*, 2, 194–228.

97 See L. Mühlhausen, 'Neue Beiträge zum Perceval-Thema', ZCP, 17 (1928), 1–30; R. Flower, *The Irish Tradition*, p. 136.

98 *B.M. Cat. Irish MSS*, II, 271.

99 *Harvard Studies*, VII, p. 149.

100 *Gaelic Journal*, 19, 357.

101 ITS X (London, 1908). For a review of this volume, see *Gaelic Journal*, 19, 355.

102 *B.M. Cat. Irish MSS*, II, 353.

103 *Studies*, 10 (1921), 257.

104 M. Mhac an tSaoi, *Dhá Sgéal Artúraiochta Mar atá Eachtra Mhelóra agus Orlando agus Céilidhe Iosgaide Léithe* (Dublin, 1946), pp. 1–41.

105 *B.M. Cat. Irish MSS*, II, 339, n.

106 Mhac an tSaoi, op. cit., pp. 42–70. Cf. Maartje Draak, 'Sgél Isgaide Léithe', *Celtica*, 3 (1956), 232–40.

107 Ed. by Carl Marstrander, 'Sechrán na Banimpire', *Ériu*, 5 (1911), 164–99.

108 Cecile O'Rahilly, *Eachtra Uilliam* (Dublin, 1949), p. xvi.

109 G. Quin, *Stair Ercuil ocus a Bás: The Life and Death of Hercules* (ITS, XXXVIII, Dublin, 1939).

110 F. N. Robinson, 'The Irish Lives of Guy of Warwick and Bevis of Hampton', ZCP, 6 (1907–8), 9–104, 273–338, 556.
111 Ibid., p. 19.
112 Quin, op. cit., pp. xxxviii-xl.
113 Whitley Stokes, ed., trans., 'The Gaelic Maundeville,' ZCP, 2 (1899), 1–63, 226–312, 603–4.
114 Whitley Stokes, ed., trans., 'The Gaelic Abridgement of the Book of Ser Marco Polo', ZCP, 1 (1896–7), 245–73, 362–438. Corrigenda, 2 (1899), 222–3.
115 *The Book of Mac Carthaigh Riabhach, otherwise The Book of Lismore,* Collotype Facs. Introduction and Indexes by R. A. S. Macalister (Dublin, 1950).
116 On whom see *B.M. Cat. Irish MSS*, I, 222 and n. 1.
117 Whitley Stokes, *Lives of Saints from the Book of Lismore* (Dublin, 1890).
118 Kenney, *Sources*, I, 309. See in particular Charles Plummer, *Vitae Sanctorum Hiberniae*, 2 vols. (Oxford, 1910); idem, *Bethada Náem nÉrenn: Lives of Irish Saints*, 2 vols., (Oxford, 1922), and for a general surveys. L. Bieler, 'The Celtic Hagiographer', *Studia Patristica* 5 (1962), 243–65, and the introduction by P. Ó Riain to Máire Herbert, P. Ó Riain, ed., *Betha Adamnáin: The Irish Life of Adamnán* (ITS 54, 1988).
119 Printed by J. Dunn, RC, 38 (1920–21), 133–43.
120 See *B.M. Cat. Irish MSS*, I, 56; II, 457, 459, 503, 530, 555.
121 See ibid., II, 530, 575; G. Mac Niocaill, 'Betha ocus Bás Chaitreach Fina', *Éigse*, 8, pt. iii (1956–7), 232–6.
122 *B.M. Cat. Irish MSS*, II 531; and cf. Flower, *The Irish Tradition*, 117, 129–30.
123 *B.M. Cat. Irish MSS*, II, 531, 457, 461, 572–3.
124 See L. C. Stern, ZCP, 1(1896–7), 119.
125 *B. M. Cat. Irish MSS*, II, 586.
126 *Stair Ercuil*, p. xxxix. For *Beatha Mhuire Eigiptacdha* from B.L. MS. Add. 30512, see Martin Freeman, ÉC, 1 (1936), 78–113.
127 Martin McNamara, *The Apocrypha in the Irish Church* (Dublin, 1975), pp. 122–3; Charles Donahue, *The Testament of Mary* (Fordham UP, 1942). For a general survey of apocryphal literature in Irish, see McNamara, op. cit., and D. N. Dumville, 'Biblical Apocrypha and the Early Irish', PRIA, 73 (1973), Sec. C, No. 8, 299–338. For Biblical studies generally in Ireland during the Middle Ages see Martin McNamara, *Biblical Studies: The Medieval Irish Contribution* (Dublin, 1976).
128 McNamara, *The Apocrypha*, pp. 123–4; *B.M. Cat. Irish MSS*, II, 548.
129 C. Ó Maonaigh, *Smaointe Beatha Chríost* (Dublin, 1944). For the original, see P. Livario Oliger, '*Le Meditationes Vitae Christi*' Studi Francescani, 7 (1921), 8 (1922); Columban Fischer, 'Die *Meditationes Vitae Christi*', *Archivum Franciscanum Historicum*, 25 (1932).
130 *B.M. Cat. Irish MSS*, II, 534ff.
131 Whitley Stokes, *The Saltair na Rann* (Oxford, 1883), and McNamara, *The Apocrypha*, pp. 18–20.
132 McNamara, op. cit., pp. 78–9.
133 *B.M. Cat. Irish MSS*, II, 498, 499; McNamara, 68–74. Another version

of the Descent from The Book of Fermoy, 'The Harrowing of Hell', was
ed. and trans. by Bergin, *Ériu*, 4 (1908), 112–19.
134 J. E. C. Williams, 'Irish Translations of the *Visio Sancti Pauli*', *Éigse*, 6
(1950), 127–34. See also *B.M. Cat. Irish MSS*, I, 622; McNamara, pp.
105–9.
135 McNamara, op. cit., pp. 126–8.
136 *Historia Ecclesiastica*, iii, 19.
137 The Brussels text was published by Whitley Stokes, 'The Life of Fursa',
RC, 25 (1904), 385–404; see McNamara, 126.
138 C. S. Boswell, *An Irish Precursor of Dante* (London, 1908), pp. 166–9;
St. J. D. Seymour, *Irish Visions of the Other World* (London, 1930).
139 V. H. Friedel and K. Meyer, *La Vision de Tondale (Tnugdal)*, Textes
français, anglo-normand et irlandais (Paris, 1907).
140 T. Condún, 'Purgadóir Phádraig Naomhtha', *Lia Fáil* 1 (1924), 1–48.
141 K. Mulchrone, 'Spiritus Guidonis', *Lia Fáil*, 1 (1924), 131–52.
142 Flower, *The Irish Tradition*, p. 125ff. Cf. Ó Maonaigh, *Smaointe Beatha
Chríost*, pp. 323–5.
143 The translation is extant in *Liber Flavus Fergusiorum*, Laud 610, T.C.D.
H. 2. 17, H. 4. 22; McNamara, pp. 75–6.
144 Translations are found in *Liber Flavus Fergusiorum*, R.I.A. 24 P 25,
Egerton 136.
145 J. A. Geary, *An Irish Version of Innocent III's De contemptu mundi*
(Washington, 1931).
146 See P. Walsh, 'Notes of Two Irish Medical Scribes', *Irish Ecclesiastical
Record*, 20 (1922), 113–22; 21 (1923), 238–46; 'An Irish Medical
Family—Mac an Leagha', chap 14 in *Irish Men of Learning*, and John
Bannerman, *The Beatons: a Medical Kindred in the Classical Gaelic
Tradition* (Edinburgh, 1986).
147 *B.M. Cat. Irish MSS*, I, 171, 256–9.
148 Ibid., 177; S. Sheahan, *An Irish Version of Gualterus de Dosibus*
(Washington, 1938).
149 *B.M. Cat. Irish MSS*, I, 285–322.
150 Ibid, 222.
151 Ibid., 285.
152 Ibid., 262.
153 Ibid., 262, 276.
154 Ibid., 278–9.
155 Ibid., 276ff.
156 Ibid., 171ff.
157 The titles of a number of them will be found in a very interesting article
by Professor Francis Shaw on 'Medieval Medico-Philosophical
Treatises in the Irish Language', *Féilsgríbhinn Eóin Mhic Néill* (Dublin,
1940), pp. 144–57.

CHAPTER 4

THE DEVELOPMENT OF POETRY

§1

THE poetry of Ireland in the Middle Ages is freer of foreign influences than the prose and is much more a product of the peculiar circumstances of Irish society. It is important to remember that while the Viking raids had a devastating effect on that society, they did not succeed in paralysing its cultural life; indeed, as we have seen, cultural life was vigourous after the renowned BrianBorú defeated the Norse and their Irish allies at the Battle of Clontarf in 1014.

The arrival of the Anglo-Normans had, on the other hand, a deeper and more lasting effect.[1] They began their invasion of the land in 1169, and within seventy years of that time they had brought more than two-thirds of the country under their rule, nominally if not otherwise. But they succeeded only after fierce fighting. In fact, for the first 150 years of their ascendancy, destruction and waste were their chief contributions, and the country felt their effects. The old political and social order was thrown out of joint and cultural growth was impaired, especially in the field of art and architecture.

Naturally, the Irish learned a few things from their enemies, among them better methods of war. It was a lesson that paid off for them, and after about the middle of the thirteenth century they began to win back the land. By the middle of the fifteenth century it was evident that the lordship of the island was gradually returning to native hands, and from that time on, into the middle of the sixteenth century, the effective government of the conquerors was restricted to the confines of the 'Pale' and within the walls of the towns (boroughs).

The control of Ireland, then, was in the hands of three groups during this period: the Irish chieftains, the Anglo-Norman lords, and the citizens of the English towns. More than half of the island was under the control of native chieftains, and there is no doubt that they would have formed an invincible power if they had been able to agree with each other and unite in common cause. But the Anglo-Norman conquest had destroyed the system of provincial kings and overlordships, and the presence of invaders in the land holding the principal strategic places and fostering disunity on every side was bound to hinder any attempt to unify the land politically.

We get an idea of how much strength might have accrued to the Irish cause through unification when we remember that there were at least sixty native chieftains governing their own territories according to Irish law at the beginning of the sixteenth century.[2] Under these chieftains were lesser lords, each one with his own host of followers, and each owing loyalty to his own chief. The position of each chieftain depended on his ability to defend himself and the lords that owed homage to him: 'Every Iryshe captaine defendeyth all the subgetes and the comyn folke, wythin his rome [realm] fro ther enymyes asmuche as in hym is.'[3] It is no wonder, then, that making war had remained a way of demonstrating bravery and personal valour as well as a way of securing political victories.

Due in large part to the Anglo-Norman invasion, then, the beginning of the Middle Ages in Ireland was almost as warlike and turbulent as any period in the Heroic Age, and even at the end of the Middle Ages devastations and plunderings were common occurrences. Here is how R. Stanyhurst described the situation in his *Description of Ireland*, published in Holinshed's Chronicles:

> To rob and spoile their enimies they deeme it none offense, nor seekc anie meanes to recover their losse but even to watch the like turne; but if neighbors and friends [blood relatives] send their purveiors to purloine one another, such actions are iudged by the breighons [*breitheamhain* 'brehons', 'judges'] aforesaid.[4]

The Irish chieftains were not the only ones guilty of taking the law into their own hands. The Anglo-Norman barons did the same thing:

> Also, there is more then 30 greate captaines of th Englyshe noble folke, that folowyth the same Iryshe ordre, and kepeith the same rule, and every of them makeith warre and pease for hymself, wythout any lycence of the King, or of any other temperall person, saive to hym that is strongeyst, and of such that maye subdue them by the swerde.[5]

And yet, despite the superficial similarity between the Ireland of the Middle Ages and the Ireland of the Heroic Age, the difference between them was great and fundamental. For one thing, the *Weltanschauung* of the noblemen in the Middle Ages was much different from that of the heroes of the Táin Age, and they were less parochial. On the other hand, they had nothing like the colourful customs and ceremonies depicted in the royal court of Ulster in the Táin Age. The so-styled high kings and provincial kings had vanished, and with them had vanished the *raison d'être* of the national and local assemblies (Aonach Tailtean, Aonach Carman, and the others), where the *filid* had narrated *seanchas* ('history'), *dinnsheanchas* ('history of places'), and the *primscéla*, the 'principal tales' that gave the history of battles, plunderings, destructions, and the like. One of the signs of the changing times was that the *primscéla* were told but infrequently in the Middle Ages; these stories were valued by learned men in the manuscripts rather than by those who narrated them in the courts, because they no longer suited the pleasure or the taste of the audiences. These latter preferred stories about the adventures of Fionn and his ilk, stories that were half way between the historical tales set in the courts of kings and folktales set in the huts of labourers.[6]

Under the circumstances, it is no wonder that the *fili*, the chief figure in the literature of the Heroic Age of Ireland, was forced to divest himself of some of his offices; he was no longer called upon as narrator of sagas or as prophet and diviner. In fact, the only thing that remained to him was the composition of odes of praise and satire, the maintenance of pedigrees, and the chronicling of history.

The handbooks of Irish literature usually say that the *fili* ceased to exist, that he was replaced by the *bard* (pl. *baird*), but that is not entirely accurate. It is true that the word *bard* occurs in the heroic period as the name for a lower order of *fili*, and that the word *bairdne* is used in Middle Irish texts to describe a category of metres that was peculiar to the *baird*, and these metres included the metres of *dán díreach* almost exclusively.[7] It is also quite likely that the *bard* specialized in panegyric in the early period. But it would be a mistake to believe that the *bard* rose in the world and supplanted the *fili*. It would be more accurate to say that the *fili* suffered an eclipse, and then in the Middle Ages appropriated the genre of panegyric as a chief function rather than as something to which he occasionally turned, as in the early period.[8]

We know that the *fili* was prepared to adopt the *bairdne* metres, and it is only reasonable to suppose that he had used them from time to time even in the early period to sing the praise of a patron. But whatever the difference between *filidecht* (the poetry of the *fili*) and *bairdne* (the poetry of the *bard*) in the early period, there is virtually no difference between them in the later Middle Ages. The *fili* continues to be called by that name, however, and even though the nature of his poetry has changed it is still called *filidecht*; the term *bardaigheacht* is ultimately used to imply foul abuse. But since the *filidecht* of this period is different from that which preceded or followed it, it deserves separate consideration. Here are some of its standard features:

(i) This body of poetry was composed in the syllabic metres, that is, those metres defined by a regular number and class of syllables in the stanza.[9] The line must contain a special number of syllables and end on an accented word of a certain syllabic length; the metre is determined above all by the number of syllables in the line and by the syllabic length of the final word. There is no regular stress. In addition, the following rules are characteristic of all the metres of *dán direach* (strict versification) in the period 1250–1650: the last two stressed words in the stanza must alliterate; each line must end with a word bearing full accent; and the last words of a poem should echo its first words.

> Tánaig an tráth nóna,
>   a-nochd nóin ar saoghail;
> neimhiongnadh um nónaidh
>   ceiliobhradh dar gcaomhaibh.
>
> Is beag a fhios agam,
>   re hiarnóin dá n-anam,
> mh'aire cáit a gcuiream,
>   caidhe an áit a n-anam.
>
> Ná hanam re haidhchi,
>   budh aithreach dá n-anam;
> atá mar eachd oram
>   an lá do theachd taram.
> . . . .
> Sleagh do chur 'na chroidhe,
>   claon do bheith 'na bhraghaid,
> cách ní cóir nach smuainid
>   an nóin an tráth thánaig.[10]

(ii) Most of the poetry with which we are concerned here was composed between the end of the twelfth century and the middle of the seventeenth century, and between 1250 and 1650 little or no change or development in either language or versification can be observed. Naturally, one can find examples of it long before this period, even as early as the ninth century, and others a good deal after it. The tradition appears to have endured longer in Scotland than in Ireland:[11] in the Red Book of Clanranald there is a poem in the old style to Allan Clanranald, a man who was killed in Sheriffmuir in 1715, and an elegy in the same style to a man named James

MacDonald who died in 1738.[12] But however long the tradition of syllabic praise poems endured in Ireland, it would be a great mistake to suppose that there was no other kind of poetry there by 1650. *Amhrán* ('song') poetry, or 'free' poetry, was composed long before the beginning of the seventeenth century.

(iii) The most frequent element in the poetry is praise of the living or of the dead (elegy). Of course, other elements such as satire are found, and there are a few occasional poems that do not belong to the tradition, but these are rare, and by comparison with the poetic output of the Heroic Age, the work of these poets is isolated and rather restricted.

One of the earliest examples of this praise poetry is the song to a North Leinster chieftain, Aed mac Diarmada maic Muiredaig.[13]

> Aed oll fri andud nāne,
> Aed fonn fri fuilted féle,
> in deil delgnaide as choemem
> di dindgnaib Roerenn rēde.

'Aed, great at kindling splendor, Aed, joyous at increase of hospitality, splendid column most dear of the nobles of Roeriu's plain.'

The metrical translation of Dr R. Flower gives a better feeling for the poem, although it is quite free:

> Kindler of glory's embers,
> Aed, goodly hand of giving;
> Comeliest that song remembers
> By pastoral Roeriu living.
>
> A mighty shaft and loyal
> Whom glory overarches
> Of all men else most royal
> In grassy Maistiu's marches.
>
> My love—if such his pleasure—
> To Dermot's son I bring it;
> My song—more worth than treasure—
> To his high praise I sing it.
>
> Dear name! renowned in story,
> Aed! no man may decry him;
> Where Liffey flows in glory
> Fame's voice shall ne'er bely him.
>
> Grandchild of that fierce fighter
> Muireach, a cliff of splendours,

Honour—no fame is brighter—
To his race Cualu renders.

A stately tree, a glowing
Jewel whom strife embolden;
A silver sapling growing
From soil of princes olden.

Songs at the alefeast ringing,
Scales climbed of comely measures,
Bards with their heady singing
Acclaim Aed and his pleasures.[14]

Although this example is an early one, for it may have been composed at the beginning of the ninth century, its style is typical of hundreds, if not thousands, of praise poems sung during the following centuries:

> The style is always strict and concise; using metaphor in preference to simile; indulging in asyntactical constructions for which the exclamatory character of Irish sentence structure gives ample excuse; bold and barbaric in its terms and figures; and tending always to treat the chieftain eulogized as an abstract compendium of princely qualities rather than as a being subject to the ebb and flow of the more ordinary impulses.[15]

As a whole, this body of poetry is not likely to appeal to the tastes of modern readers. Indeed, there has been a great revolution in the world's attitudes toward poetry and poets since these poems were composed. Perhaps it would help to understand them if we believe with Bergin that their authors were fulfilling a function not unlike that of the newspaper reporters of our own day.[16] They served their society by chronicling the events of the day and making observations on them, sometimes adding a word of rebuke, but more often praising and approving. In addition to their other gifts, they might possess the gift of poetic inspiration, but inspiration or not, they wrote in verse.

§2

Poeta nascitur, non fit, said the Roman, but in Ireland in the Middle Ages *poeta nascitur et fit* would be much closer to the truth. A man was born a poet in the special sense that he was born to the same profession as his father. Just as the profession of law and medicine was restricted to certain families, so also was the profession of learning and poetry.[17] Thus, for the Middle Ages the same old family names keep recurring in the handbooks of literature. The poets, almost without exception, come from the Ó Dálaigh, Ó hUiginn, Ó Cléirigh, Mac an Bhaird and Mac Con Midhe families, plus a few others. And by virtue of their birth and their profession the bards were noblemen; that is why they are described as *generosi* frequently in official English documents.[18]

But if the man had to be 'born' a poet, he had to be 'made' one too, and it was necessary for him to go to one of the schools of poetry for the making. The best and in fact the only fairly complete description of one of these schools is that found in *The Memoirs of the Right Honourable The Marquis of Clanricarde*, a book first published in London in 1722, then in Dublin in 1744. The description was quoted by Professor Bergin in his lecture on 'Bardic Poetry', delivered before the Ivernian Society in 1912, and by Kenney (*Sources*, I, 36–7). It gives us an excellent sense of the schools as they were operated in the seventeenth century, and probably before that, for given the traditional conservatism of the poets, it is hardly likely that these schools had changed much during the four preceding centuries.

Apparently, the poets had a custom of maintaining 'inns' (*tighe aoigheadh coitchinne*) where the lodging was free.[19] No doubt these were places where men of learning met, where literary topics and events of the day were discussed.[20] But one ought not to confuse such inns with the schools of poetry, for, according to the description in the *Memoirs*, the schools were located in quiet places, 'in the solitary Recess of a Garden, or within a Sept or Enclosure, far out of the reach of any Noise, which an Intercourse of People might otherwise occasion'.[21] In every case the school was maintained by a poet-principal, and he was assisted, it seems, according to need, by other poets who were 'associate' professors. The school itself would be somewhere in the vicinity of the principal's home in a utilitarian building. 'The Structure was a snug, low Hut, and beds in it at convenient Distances, each within a small Apartment without much Furniture of any kind, save only a Table, some Seats, and a Conveniency for Cloaths to hang upon.' As we can see, the ordinary features of the building were not so much different from those of any modern conventional hostel, but the next feature mentioned makes it completely different from any modern boarding house or dormitory, and that, in one sense, was its most important and indispensable characteristic: 'No Windows to let in the Day, nor any Light at all us'd but that of Candles, and these brought in at a proper Season only'. The importance of this will be seen later on.

The schools were not open to just anyone, either: 'only to such as were descended of Poets and reputed within their Tribes'. Besides being the son of a poet, prospective candidates were expected to possess a good memory and be literate: 'The Qualifications first requir'd were reading well, writing the Mother-tongue, and a strong Memory.'

The students would bring gifts to the professor at the beginning of the season as payment for their education, it seems, rather than for maintenance during the term; for the latter they were fully dependent upon the generosity of neighbouring nobles.

> Every *Saturday* and on the Eves of Festival Days they broke up and dispers'd themselves among the Gentlemen and rich Farmers of the Country, by whom they were very well entertain'd and much made of, till they thought fit to take their leaves, in order to re-assume their Study. Nor was the People satisfied with affording this Hospitality alone; they sent in by turns every Week from far and near Liquors and all manner of Provision towards the Subsistence of the Academy, so that the chief Poet was at little or no Charges, but, on the contrary, got very well by it, besides the Presents made him by the Students upon their first coming, which was always at Michaelmas, and from thence till the 25th March, during the cold season of the Year only, did that close Study last. At that time the Scholars broke up, and repair'd each to his own Country . . .

The school term, then, lasted from the beginning of November until 25 March. There is independent testimony for this in the elegy that Tadhg Óg Ó hUiginn sang to his brother, a poet who kept a school:

> When November approached, there would be a meeting place for the adherents of poetry: if a certain man [i.e., the professor] had continued to live, they would not have been scattered. You, who in his house sought art and a place of abode, could easily hate the cry of the cuckoo. When the school was disbanded, each poet went to his homeland: never again will one come from his father's house to seek art.[22]

It is obvious from the elegy that Tadhg's brother, Fearghal, had been keeping a school for years. It may be that the Ó hUiginn family had kept one for generations, and that would not be an unusual thing for a bardic family to do.

At the end of each term the pupil would get some kind of certificate, 'an Attestation of his Behaviour and Capacity from the chief Professor to those that had sent him.' But he had to patronize the school for a number of years before finishing his course: 'it was six or seven Years before a Mastery or the last Degree was conferred, which you'll the less admire upon considering the great Difficulty of the Art, the many kinds of their Poems, the Exactness and Nicety to be observ'd in each, which was necessary to render their Numbers soft, and the Harmony agreeable and pleasing to the Ear.'

Another reason—and perhaps the most important—for the length of the course was that the student poet was expected to gain a thorough knowledge of the history and lore of his land. Furthermore, he had to learn to use a form of language that was basically artificial; indeed, one of the most striking characteristics of the language of court poetry is its homogeneity. Even though local dialects differed more and more from each other in the course of the Middle Ages, there is nothing in the language of any poem composed in the strict metres (dán díreach) to show that they were composed in Scotland, let us say, rather than in Ireland, or in the fifteenth century rather than in the thirteenth.[23]

Clearly, what the court poets did in Ireland was to create a linguistic medium for their own purpose by taking the unquestionably renowned language of the old poets as a standard, and rejecting everything that did not conform to that use and purpose. If evidence were needed to prove this, there are grammatical treatises extant from the Middle Ages that treat and discuss various features of the language (and especially the language found in the poetry) even down to such details as lenition and nasalization, and that legislate on doubtful points on the strength of evidence provided by a host of examples drawn from the works of the professional poets.[24] In one sense the authors of these treatises were scientific grammarians—witness their appeal to usage—but it is clear that it was practical interest rather than any scientific spirit which motivated them, and there is not any doubt that they wrote for student poets. As might be expected, the standardized literary language that was developed in this way produced a marked archaic quality, and yet there are elements in it that suggest a more modern flavour.

Let us return to the *Memoirs*, and a description of the method of instruction:

> The Professors (one or more as there was occasion) gave a Subject suitable to the Capacity of each Class, determining the number of Rhimes, and clearing what was to be chiefly observed therein as to Syllables, Quartans, Concord, Correspondence, Termination and Union, each of which was restrain'd by peculiar Rules. The said Subject (either one or more as aforesaid) having been given over Night,

they work'd it apart each by himself upon his own Bed, the whole next Day in the Dark, till at a certain Hour in the Night, Lights being brought in, they committed it to writing. Being afterwards dress'd and come together into a large Room, where the Masters waited, each Scholar gave in his performance, which being corrected or approv'd of (according as it requir'd) either the same or fresh subjects were given against the next Day.

Note carefully the method of composition: the shutting out of light, lying on the bed, wrestling with the subject throughout the day in darkness until the poem was composed, and then writing it, for this appears to have been the traditional means used by master poets as well as by pupils. There seems to be a reference to the process in the first line of one of the *Dindshenchas* poems: *Cid dorcha dam im lepaid* 'though I be in darkness upon my bed'.[25]

Professor Bergin drew attention to a poem composed by Ó Gnímh (probably Fear Flatha Ó Gnímh)[26] to mock Fearghal Óg (Mac an Bhaird) for breaking with convention and being so presumptuous as to compose a poem in the light of day and in the open air while riding his horse. The author himself was not accustomed to doing that: 'As for me, when I compose a poem, I am pleased—a thing that keeps me from straying—to take care to keep out the sun's light and have dark couches to make my vigil. If I could not get my eyelids between me and the bright beams as a protective shield from the light of day, my art would be destroyed.'[27] The masters, he says, did not compose in broad daylight either: Donnchadh Mór Ó Dálaigh, Giolla Brighde Mac Con Midhe, Aonghus Ruadh (the son of Cearbhall Buidhe Ó Dálaigh), Sgolb (a nickname of one of the sons of Cearbhall Buidhe Ó Dálaigh), An tÓrthóir (pseudonym of Eoghan Mág Craith), Gofraidh Fionn Ó Dálaigh, and Tadhg Óg Ó hUiginn, to name a few.

No doubt the practice of composing in a supine position and in the dark helped the bard to concentrate on his poem. It was also a way of impressing others with the fact that poetic composition was not child's play, and that the effort implied thereby fully merited the payment which was expected in exchange for it. But these considerations by themselves are not sufficient to explain a custom and practice which must have owed its origin to some pagan custom that prevailed when the poet was both magician and seer.[28]

In Scotland the method of composition was considerably more complex. This is what Martin has to say about it in his *Description of the Western Islands of Scotland* (London, 1703):

They shut their Doors and Windows for a Days time, and lie on their Backs with a Stone upon their Belly, and Plads about their Heads, and their Eyes being cover'd they pump their Brains for Rhetorical Encomium or Panegyrick; and indeed they furnish such a Stile from this Dark Cell as is understood by very few; and if they purchase a couple of Horses as the reward of their Meditation they think they have done a great Matter.[29]

After composing the poem, they had to present it to the nobleman who was praised therein.

The last Part to be done, which was the *Action* and *Pronunciation* of the Poem in Presence of the Maecenas, or the principal Person it related to, was perform'd with a great deal of Ceremony in a Consort of Vocal and Instrumental Musick. The Poet himself said nothing, but directed and took care that everybody else did his Part right. The Bards having first had the Composition from him, got it well by Heart, and now pronounc'd it orderly, keeping even Pace with a Harp, touch'd upon that Occasion; no other musical Instrument being allowed for the said Purpose than this alone, as being Masculin, much sweeter and fuller than any other.

This description makes it clear that it was not the author that delivered the poem but a performer referred to here as *bard*, although the usual name for him was *reacaire* (cf. *reacaim* 'I recite', *reacaireacht* 'recitation'). Professor Bergin published a poem by an anonymous bard that supports this. In it the *reacaire* is addressed, and he is given news to carry to the patron.

> Tríall, a reacaire, reac m'fhuighle,
>   imthigh go grod, ná gabh sgís
> gan dol d'fhéaghain chinn ar gcoimhghe:
>   fill ré sgéulaigh oirne arís.

Go, my speaker; speak my words; go quickly; let no weariness prevent you from going to see our lofty protector; then come back to me with tidings.[30]

We see, too, that the delivery is always accompanied by the harp. The *reacaire* could play the harp himself on occasion, but as a rule a harper (*cruitire*) would be on hand to do that. Thomas Smyth, in his *Information for Ireland* (1561), describes the work of the bard (*the Rymer*), the *reacaire* (*the Rakry*) and the harper in these words: 'Now comes the Rymer that made the Ryme, with his Rakry. The Rakry is he that shall utter the ryme: and the Rymer himself sitts by with the captain varie proudlye. He brings with him also his Harper, who please all the while that the raker sings the ryme'.[31]

Each poet belonged, in a special way, to one court or lord, and he had certain obligations to fulfill for that lord. The *Memoirs* says:

> As every Professor, or chief Poet, depended on some Prince or great Lord, that had endowed his Tribe, he was under strict ties to him and Family, as to record in good Metre his Marriages, Births, Deaths, Acquisitions made in war and Peace, Exploits, and other remarkable things relating to the Same. He was likewise bound to offer an Elegy on the Decease of the said Lord, his consort, or any of their children, and a Marriage Song when there should be Occasion.[32]

§3

Since singing praises accounted for the major part of the poet's activity, and since his livelihood depended, more or less, on the recognition he got, we should expect him to practice his craft every time there was a hope of generous reward. From that standpoint, there could not be a better oportunity than after a successful raid, when the lord would have booty to share. A poem by Tadhg Dall Ó hUiginn sheds some light on such occasions.[33] The poet describes a visit to Enniskillen. He had heard, no doubt, that the chieftain of that place, Cú Chonnacht Óg son of Cú Chonnacht, was about to carry out a raid, and for that reason he went to see him. He received a warm welcome, and spent a pleasurable day with the chieftain and his men. As might be expected, there was a great gathering there. That evening there was a feast, and the poet was seated next to the chieftain. We are not told in so many words, but it is likely that after the feast many old praise poems were recited, along with some new ones. Then everyone went to bed. At dawn, before the poet arose, the chieftain and his warriors set out on their raid. They returned in the evening, and the chieftain set about dividing gifts between his men and the poets. The nature of the gifts was determined by the nature of the spoil, of course, and normally most of that would be cattle. We can imagine Tadhg Dall setting out for home the next morning, driving a number of cows before him.

Such a raid and subsequent division of spoil would not be exceptional, either. In the year 1549, Mac Diarmada of Moylurg made a plundering raid on the family of Mac Goisdealbh and on clan Filip, and he is said to have gained (read 'rustled') 1,260 cows, and to have divided them all among the gathering of poets and scholars who had been entertaining and amusing him on the feast of St Stephen.[34] And that is not the only raid he made. Indeed, it was not possible to esteem any chieftain who could not lead such raids successfully, and thereby bring riches to his followers. Best of all would be those raids against foreign lords, but there was nothing extraordinary about native lords plundering one another in this way; on the contrary, they looked upon raiding as an entirely natural activity.

The poets profited (and sometimes, of course, suffered) under a system that permitted such depredations, and they do not appear to have raised their voices to attempt to change it. In fact, to the extent that they favoured the status quo, one can say that they were supporters of the old order. There is, therefore, a kernel of truth in the picture which Thomas Smyth gives in his *Information for Ireland*, though that kernel has been hidden under a mass of malicious distortions. This is what he says:

> The thirde sorte is called the Aeosdan, which is to saye in English, the bards, or the rimine sepctes; and these people be very hurtfull to the commonwhealle, for they chifflie manyntayne [*sic*] the rebells; and, further, they do cause them that would be true, to be rebelious theves, extorcioners, murtherers, ravners, yea and worse if it were possible. Their furst practisse is, if they se anye younge man discended of the septs of *Ose* or *Max*, and have half a dowsen aboute him, then will they make him a Rime, wherein they will commend his father and his aunchetours, nowmbrying howe many heades they have cut of, howe many townes they have burned, and howe many virgins they have defloured, howe many notable murthers they have done, and in the ende they will compare them to Aniball, or Scipio, or Hercules, or some other famous person; wherewithall the pore foole runs madde, and thinkes indede it is so. Then will he gather a sorte of rackells [rake-hells] to him, and other he most geat him a Proficer [prophet], who shall tell him howe he shall spede (as he thinkes). Then will he geat him lurking to a syde of a woode, and ther keepith him close til morninge; and when it is daye light, then will they go to the poor vilages, not sparinge to distroye young infants, aged people; and if the women be ever so great withe childe, her they will kill; burninge the houses and corne, and ransackinge of the poor cottes [cottages]. They will then drive all the kine and plowe horses with all other cattell, and drive them awaye. Then muste they have a bagpipe bloinge afore them; and if any of theis cattell fortune to waxe wearie or faynt, they will kill them, rather than it sholde do the honeur's [owners] goode. If they go by anye house of fryers or relygious house, they will geave them 2 or 3 beifs [beeves], and they will take them, and praie for them (yea) and prayes their doings, and saye his father was accustomed so to do; wharein he

will rejoise; and when he is in a safe place, they will fall to the devision of the spoile, accordinge to the dyscresion of the captin . . . Now comes the Rymer that made the Ryme, with his Rakry. The Rakry is he that shall utter the rhyme; and the Rymer himself sitts by with the Captain verie proudlye. He brings with him also his Harper, who please all the while that the raker sings the ryme. Also he hathe his Barde, which is a kind of folise fellowe; who also must have a horse geven him; the harper must have a new safern [saffron-coloured] shurte, and a mantell and a hacnaye; and the rakry must have XX or XXX kine, and the Rymer himself horse and harnes [suit of armour] with a nag to ride on, a silver goblett, a pair of bedes of corall, with buttons of silver; and this, with more, they loke for to have, for reducinge distruxione of the Comenwealth, and to the blasfemye of God; and this is the best thinge that yᵉ Rymers causith them to do.[35]

One has only to read the work of the poets to see that Thomas Smyth's commentary is largely baseless defamation, but alas! he was not the only one to produce propaganda for the foreign state against the ancient Irish civilization. It would be a mistake to suppose that the poets gathered only for an occasional destructive raid. Their presence very often has political significance, as we have demonstrated above in discussing the inauguration of Ó Dubhda (chapter 1, p. 48). It is no wonder, then, that the poets were present at every important event in the history of their patron's tribe. On the death of his father in 1432, Eoghan Ó Néill went to Tulach Óg, say The Annals of Ulster, and there he was made king through the will of God and men, bishops and chief poets.[36]

Securing the good will of the poets was as important to a chieftain in the Middle Ages in Ireland as securing the good will of the press is to the government in these days, and it is not surprising that an occasional chieftain would invite the country's poets to his house on special occasions. Such an event is chronicled in The Annals of Clonmacnoise (English translation of 1627):

1351 . . . William Ó [sic] Donough Moyneagh O'Kelly invited all the Irish poets, Brehons, bards, harpers, gamesters or common kearogs, Jesters and others of their kind in Ireland to his house upon Christmas this year, where every one of them was well used during Christmas holy Days, and gave contentment to each of them at the time of their Departure soe as every one was well pleased & extolled William for his bounty, one of which assembly composed certaine Irish verses in commendation of William and his house which began thus:
    Filidh Ereann go haointeach, etc.[37]

The poet who composed these verses was Gofraidh Fionn Ó Dálaigh, and his poem has been preserved.[38] It is to be compared with a poem sung by Tadhg Dall Ó hUiginn,[39] describing a Christmas feast that Toirdhealbhach Luineach Ó Néill gave for the poets of Ireland 'probably in order to ascertain his standing in public opinion, and increase popular opinion, and increase popular feeling in his favour.'[40]

In the year 1433, Margaret,[41] daughter of Tadhg Ua Cerbhaill, invited the poets and others to two different feasts at her house.

> It is shee that twice in one yeare proclaimed to, and comonly invited, (.i. in the darke dayes of the yeare) to wit, on the feast day of Dasinchell in Killaichy all persons both Irish and Scotish or rather Albians, to two generall feasts of bestowing both meate and moneyes with all other manner of guifts, whereinto gathered to receue gifts the matter of two thousand and seauen hundred persons, besides gamsters and poore men, as it was recorded in a Roll to that purpose, and that account was made thus, ut vidimus (viz.) the Chieftaine of each famelie of the Learned Irish, was by Gilla-na-naomh mac AEgans hand writen in that Roll, the chiefe Judg to O-Conner and his adherents, and kinsmen, so that the aforesaid number of 2700 was listed in that Roll with the arts of Dan or poetry, musick and Antiquitie. And Maelyn O-Maelconry one of the chiefe learned of Connaght, was the first writen in that Roll and first payed and dieted or sett to super, and those of his name after him, and so forth, every one, as he was payed, he was writen in that Roll, for feare of mistake, and sett downe to eate after-wards . . . And she gaue the second inviting proclamation (to very one that came not that day) on the feast day of the Assumpōn of our Blessed Lady Mary in haruest at, or in Rath-Imayn.[42]

No doubt it would have been impossible for Margaret to house such a number and to treat them in such a way had she not been married to Calbhach Ua Conchobhair, prince of Offaly, a man who had 'never refused the countenance of man, and who had won more wealth from his English and Irish enemies than any lord in Leinster,' according to the Four Masters in the entry for his death in 1458.[43]

Those who have maintained that poetry was a needless ornament in the courts of the Irish lords and that the society could have done without the bards altogether, have taken only a very superficial view. As is well known, that society was extremely aristocratic, and it was therefore inevitable that heavy stress would be laid upon descent. Like the Welshman, the Irishman was famous for boasting about his lineage. There is plenty of evidence for this, but it will be sufficient to quote one source: 'The Irishman standeth so much upon his gentilitie that he termeth anie one of the English sept, and planted [born and settled] in Ireland, "Bobdeagh galteagh" [*bodach gallda*], that is: "English Churle"; but if he be an Englishman borne, then he nameth him "bobdeagh saxonagh" [*bodach sacsanach*], that is: a "Saxon Churle"; so that both are churles, and he the onlie gentleman."[44]

Because preservation of pedigrees was a responsibility of the poets, one could say that it was they who maintained the nobility—and they were certainly not ignorant of that role. Here is a good example of the argument that poetry was necessary for the maintenance and validation of lineage:

> Dá mbáití an dán, a dhaoine,
> gan seanchas, gan seanlaoidhe,
> go bráth, acht athair gach fhir,
> rachaidh cách gan a chluinsin.
> . . . .
> Dá mbáití seanchas Clann gCuinn,
> agus bhur nduana, a Dhomhnuill,
> clann bhur gconmhaor 's bhar gclann shaor
> ann do ba comhdhaor comhshaor.
>
> Fir Éireann, más é a rathol
> ionnarbadh na healathon,
> gach Gaoidheal budh gann a bhreath
> gach saoirfhear ann budh aitheach.[45]

If poetry were suppressed, O people, so there was neither history nor ancient lays, every man for ever would be unheard of except for the name of every man's father.

If the lore of the Sons of Conn were suppressed along with your poems, O Domhnall, the children of your kennel-keeper and your noble progeny would be equally high born, equally base.

If it be the great desire of the men of Ireland to expel the poets, every Irishman would have an insignificant birth, every nobleman would be a churl.

The poets of Ireland were not alone in their boast that the nobility could not be maintained without them, as this excerpt from Spenser's *Ruines of Time* shows:

> But such as neither of themselues can sing,
> Nor yet are sung of others for reward,
> Die in obscure obliuion, as the thing
> Which neuer was, ne euer with regard

Their names shall of the later age be heard,
But shall in rustie darknes euer lie
Vnles they mentiond be with infamie.[46]

Of course, to the court poets nobility was synonymous with generosity. The more generous the nobleman, the more the poets sang to him, and the more the songs that were sung to him, the more noble he was considered to be. Every family of noble strain would keep a collection of the eulogies and elegies that were composed for various of its members. The size of the collection of such poems, called a *duanaire*, was indicative of the generosity of the family toward the poets and thus of its power and glory. In the death notices, one man is described as the proprietor of a great *duanaire*, and another is said to have possessed the largest *duanaire* in existence in his day.[47]

It has already been implied that the poets were not compelled to confine their odes to a single nobleman; in fact David Greene notes that the *duanaire* of Maguire is unique among the dozen or so *duanairi* that have survived in that all the poems in it are addressed to a single person.[48] For that matter, the works of almost every famous poet of the period under discussion show that a bard composed songs of praise to other nobles as well as to his own lord, the lord to whom he was official poet—*fili* or *ollamh*. In fact, the practice of singing to other noblemen was so widespread that a unique custom arose. According to the *Memoirs*, 'as to any Epick, or Heroick Verse to be made for any other Lord or Stranger, it was requir'd that at least a Paroemion, or Metre therein, should be upon the Patron, or the Name in general.' True, we do not have many examples of this custom, but then it is quite likely that the extra stanzas to the bard's own patron would be left out when the poem was copied into the *duanaire* of the family of the lord for whom the poem was made.

It was easy to accuse the poets of flattery and insincerity, and no doubt they were often guilty of that. In his lecture on 'Bardic Poetry', Professor Bergin drew attention to a poem attributed to one called *An Pearsún Riabhach*, that is, the Grey Parson.[49] The argument of the poem is that it will be very hard on the poets on Judgment Day on account of their lies. For example, he charges that the poets say a nobleman has curly locks when he is in reality bald, or that his skin is as white as the swan and his breast as white as chalk when in truth it is yellowed and burnt. But the Grey Parson was undoubtedly taking the poets' praises of the nobility much too seriously. Their encomiums were conventional, and what seemed excessive to the parson was, in reality, only the usual praise.

It should be pointed out too that much of the praise in these poems is for the family or the line rather than for any one individual. Reference has been made to the Christmas feast which Toirdhealbhach Luineach Ó Néill gave for the bards in the year 1577. After they arrived he sent to them to enquire what they had for him. They replied, 'a gift that is bound to reflect the highest honour upon him: songs that show he hails from the worthiest ancestors this realm has every produced.' But Ó Néill's answer was, 'What! so much about my family and nothing at all about me!' He saw to it that the poets were welcomed, but he himself did not appear. He had decided to teach them that he preferred to give fame to his family, not receive glory from it.[50]

Furthermore, there was a bit of intentional vagueness in the eulogy. In the first part of the poems, the nobleman is addressed and his ancestors are praised, but there is scarcely any reference to anyone outside his family. This means that the lord is praised *in vacuo* as it were. For example, he is honoured as a conqueror, but those he has conquered are not named. In other words, in these poems every noble is great and renowned, but none is compared with any other.

It is difficult to believe that this happened accidentally, and the evidence we have suggests just the opposite. Brian Ruadh Mac Con Midhe (fl. *c.* 1490) says:

> Dá fiafraigheadh duine dhe
> uaisle cháich tar a chéile,
> dlighidh file freagra mhall,
> d'eagla an tighe 'na thiomchall.[51]

If anyone should ask the poet about the nobility of one in comparison with another, he would have to be watchful for fear of the people around him.

In the same spirit, Maoilsheachluinn na nUirsgéal excuses himself from giving details about the military feats of Brian Ó Conor for fear of offending other noble families in Connacht. It is fair to assume that convention was involved here. The poets knew they must use discretion and the nobles themselves did not fail to understand that some things were better left unsaid.

The truth is, of course, that the poets were called upon to produce poems—eulogies and elegies, depending upon the occasion, and they could not ignore the summons without losing the reward, or what was worse still, without losing their position and support. Therefore, even when the patron's deeds were not such as might merit praise, the poet could not refuse it.

It is interesting to note that the lord who supported the English cause got his share of praise as well as the chieftain who upheld the Irish side, and there is undoubtedly an element of truth in these words of Gofraidh Fionn Ó Dálaigh:[52]

Dá chineadh dá gcumthar dán
i grích Éireann na n-uarán—
na Gaoidhilse ag boing re bladh
is Goill bhraoininse Breatan.

I ndán na nGall gealltar linn
Gaoidhil d'ionnarba a hÉirinn,
Goill do shraoineadh tar sál soir
i ndán na nGaoidheal gealltair.[53]

There are two races for whom poetry is composed in Ireland of the cold springs, the Irish, known in fame, and the English from the dewy isle of Britain.

In poetry to the English we promise that the Irish will be exiled from Ireland, and in poems to the Irish we vow that the English will be driven across the sea to the East.

But more than likely the poet uttered these words in a fit of pique, for it was not always easy to distinguish between the English cause and that of the Irish. It was certainly not easy to distinguish between the territory ruled by the barons and that ruled by the native chieftains. At the beginning of the sixteenth century an English official could send the following report to the English king: 'All the comyn peoplle of the saide halff countres [viz., of the Pale], that obeyeth the Kinges lawes, for the more parte ben of Iryshe byrthe, of Iryshe habyte and of Iryshe langage.'[54]

The poets went to the English as freely as to the native lords: 'Harpers, rymours, Irishe cronyclers, bardes, and isshallyn [i.e., aos ealadhan] comonly goo with praisses to gentilmen of the English pale, praysing in rymes, otherwise callid danes, their extorcioners, roberies and abuses, as valiauntnes, whiche rejoysith theim in that their evell doinges; and procure a talent of Irishe disposicion and conversacion in theme, which is likewyse convenient to bee expellid.'[55]

The nobility paid generously for these poems of praise, and the bardic profession was consequently a profitable one: from his own

lord the poet could expect land and cattle, protection and refuge.
Professor Bergin published a poem by the poet of the Maguire (Mág
Uidhir) family, probably composed sometime between 1589 and
1600, in which the poet acknowledges that he received a farm—free of
any payment or rent—from his lord. But because the farm was
located in a troubled district in which there were frequent battles, he
asks, or rather demands, a farm in a more peaceful neighbourhood.
The first stanza suggests the independent attitude of the poet toward
his patron:[56]

> T'aire riomsa, a rí ó nUidhir,
>   égnach cáigh ní cuirthi a suim,
> an uair nach éisde ret fhilidh,
>   a éisge shluaigh chinidh Chuinn.

Attend to me, thou chief of the descendants of Odhar; the rebuke of
others thou needst not heed, when thou dost not lend an ear to thy
poet, O moon of the host of Conn's race.

The poet, Eochaidh Ó hEoghusa, concludes very impatiently:

> Muna bhfagthar fearonn oile
>   d'áit innill ót érla nocht,
> dá ttí síon fhaobhrach an earraigh,
>   baoghlach díol an eallaigh ort.

> Tusa chuirfios crodh 'na n-ionadh,
>   a ua Mhagnuis nár mhaoith guin;
> munab olc leibhse a n-ég aguinn,
>   créd fá mbeinnsi ag cagaill chruidh?

> Uaid fuarus a bhfuil um urláimh,
>   ort iarrfad a n-iarrfa sinn,
> léig do chioth an cradh nó caomhnaidh
>   ní díoth dhamh gan aonbhoin inn.

If another farm in a secure spot be not obtained from the prince of the
bare locks, when the keen spring weather comes, I fear thou must pay
for the cattle.

'Tis thou that wilt put cattle in their place, O descendant of Maghnus,
whose strokes were ungentle; if thou carest not that they die in my
hands, why should I spare my cattle?

From thee I have got all that is mine: from thee I shall seek what I shall
seek. Let the cattle perish (?) or save them; it is no loss to me to be
without a single cow.

Besides acquiring farm and land from his own lord by virtue of his office, the poet could expect payment for every song he composed to other chieftains. And payment could run high. Tadhg Óg Ó hUiginn, who lived in the fifteenth century, says that he never received less than twenty cows from Tadhg Mac Cathal Ó Conor for a poem.[57]

The relationship between poet and patron is well represented in the story told by the Four Masters about Muireadhach Ó Dálaigh.[58] In the year 1213, it seems, a steward of Ó Domhnaill went to the home of the poet Muireadhach in Lissadell in Sligo to claim some tax for his master. The request was made in insulting language which so infuriated the poet that he seized a sharp axe and slew the steward on the spot. Then he fled for his life to the vicinity of Clanrickard, and appealed to Richard Fitz William Fitz Adelm de Burgo for protection. Ó Domhnaill pursued him, and the Four Masters say he was driven to Thomond, thence to Limerick, and finally to Dublin before crossing over to Scotland where he had to remain for years in exile. It was his years in Scotland that earned him the name Muireadhach *Albanach*. He appealed in vain for protection from every major family in Ireland, but in the end he won favour once again with Ó Domhnaill by composing three poems in his honour.

Muireadhach Ó Dálaigh's single axe stroke cost him years in exile, but as the following stanza shows, he considered the deed lightly at the time:

Beag ar bhfala risin bhfear,
bachlach do bheith dom cháineadh,
mé do mharbhadh an mhoghadh—
a Dhé, an adhbhar anfholadh?

Trifling is our difference with the man; that a churl was abusing me and that I killed the cad—God! is this a ground for enmity?[59]

This anecdote is but one of a number of strange deeds attributed to Muireadhach Albanach—he is even said to have made the journey to the Holy Land. Professor Brian Ó Cuív has examined the traditions which have come down to us concerning this thirteenth-century poet and has discussed the authenticity of the thirteen poems which bear his name. And though the Four Masters' account of his colourful career is not exactly what we would today call historical and owes much to legend, Professor Ó Cuív has determined that it is essentially consistent with the facts that can be gleaned from the poems themselves. If that account and the poems are the work of fabricators, then they deserve credit for not only the excellence of the poetry but for their skill and ingenuity in co-ordinating those two sources of Muiredach's life.[60]

The relationship between poet and patron was such that the one could not help but influence the other. As a man learned in the history and traditions of his country, the poet might venture to give advice to his lord, especially if the latter were young. For example, when the fourth Earl of Thomond took the title in 1580, Tadhg Mac Daire Mac Bruaideadha, the family poet, said that he could right then recite his duties to the new Earl, but that he would delay praising him until he had earned that praise.[61] It would be interesting to know what the poet thought about the later loyalty of this Earl to the cause of Elizabeth.[62] We know that he described the death of the Earl in 1624 as an unendurable loss.[63] But then, the departure of the fourth Earl of Clanricarde was lamented in the same terms,[64] even though when he was in the service of the English army of George Carew in the battle of Kinsale in 1601, it was said that 'he would not suffer any man to make prisoners of the Irish, but bade them kill the rebels . . . No man did bloody his sword more than his lordship did that day.'[65]

Naturally, our generalizations concerning the relationship between poet and patron tend to be misleading, as so much depended on the personalities and characters of the persons involved. We have referred to Eochaidh Ó hEoghusa grumbling request for a farm nearer his patron's own abode; but let us now consider a poem by Eochaidh, addressed to Aodh Mág Uidhir when he was campaigning in very inclement weather. It indicates how far the poet could identify himself with his patron in sympathy based on affection and a lively imagination.

Hugh Maguire

Too cold this night for Hugh Maguire;
I tremble at the pounding rain;
    Alas, that venomous cold
    Is my companion's lot!

It brings an anguish to my heart
To see the fiery torrents fall;
    He and the spikey frost—
    A horror to the mind!

The floodgates of the heavens yawn
Above the bosom of the clouds,
    And every pool a sea
    And murder in the air.

One thinks of the hare that haunts the wood,
And of the salmon in the bay;
    Even the wild bird; one grieves
    To think they are abroad.

Then one remembers Hugh Maguire
Abroad in a strange land tonight,
    Under the lightning's glare,
    And clouds with fury filled.

He in West Munster braves his doom,
And without shelter strides between
    The drenched and shivering grass
    And the impetuous sky.

Cold on that tender blushing cheek
The fury of the springtime gales
    That toss the stormy rays
    Of stars about his head.

I can scarce bear to conjure up
The contour of his body, crushed
    This rough and gloomy night
    In its cold iron suit.

The gentle and war-mastering hand
To the slim shaft of his sharp spear
    By icy weather pinned—
    Cold is the night for Hugh.

The low banks of the swollen streams
Are covered where the soldiers pass;
    The meadows stiff with ice;
    The horses cannot feed.

And yet as though to bring him warmth
And call back brightness to his face
    Each wall that he attacks
    Sinks in a wave of fire.

The fury of the fire dissolves
The frost that sheaths the tranquil eye,
    And from his wrist the flame
    Thaws manacles of ice.[66]

Of course, the most powerful weapon in the hand of the poet against friend and foe alike was his satire, for the belief that satire brought about death or other evil consequences persisted into our period. In the year 1414, the family of Niall Ó hUiginn satirized Sir

John Stanley, the Lord Lieutenant of Ireland, and that, it was believed, is what caused his death.[67] In chronicling the episode, the Four Masters comment that 'that was the second poetic miracle accomplished for Niall'. It is not surprising that one Elizabethan author writes 'The Irishmen will not sticke to affirm that they can rime either man or beast to death.'[68] According to Professor James Carney,

> It is possible, indeed, that the weapon of satire was as potent as excommunication with bell, book and candle. This is illustrated by a treaty made as late as 1539 between Manus O'Donnell and O'Conor Sligo. Representatives of the Church joined in this document, promising to excommunicate O'Conor if he broke any of its provisions. Similarly, representatives of the poets promised on behalf of the poets of Ireland that O'Conor would be satirised in the same eventuality. This document better than any other I know shows the poets as the functional heirs of the druids, and shows them as late as the sixteenth century acting as a corporate body.[69]

It was this power to satirize and the fact that the poets were eager to incite the nobles to rebellion that explains the irreconcilable hostility of the English toward them. The established judgment of the government toward the poets is no doubt expressed in the following memorandum: 'Bards. All their poetries tending to the furtherance of vice and the hurt of the English.'[70] No wonder the Commissioners of the King in Limerick ordained in 1549 that 'No rhymer [poeta] nor other person whatsoever shall make verses [carmina] or any other thing else called auran to any one after God on earth except the King, under penalty of the forfeiture of all his goods.'[71]

From time to time special campaigns against the poets were mounted. For example, in the year 1415 there is an account of Lord Justice Talbot (Lord Furnivall) organizing attacks on Diarmaid Ó Dálaigh, Dubhthach Mac Eochadha Eolaigh, and Muirgheas Ó Dálaigh.[72] In 1579, Sir Henry Harrington was appointed 'seneschal' and principal administrator of the land of Ó Byrne and other neighbourhoods. Here were some of his responsibilities:

> He shall make proclamation that no idle person, vagabond or masterless man, *bard, rymor, or other notorious malefactor*, remain within the district on pain of whipping after eight days, and *of death* after twenty days.
> He shall apprehend those who support such, and seize their goods, certifying the same to the lord deputy.[73]

In a district adjacent to County Kildare, Gerald, the Earl of Kildare, and Piers fitz James of Ballysonnon had a special commission, which included the following mandate:

> They are also to punish *by death*, or otherwise as directed, *harpers, rhymers, bards, idlemen, vagabonds*, and such horse-boys as have not their master's bill to show whose men they are.[74]

All this persecution took its toll, and a great number of poets came to a violent end—among them, Eoghan Ruadh Mac an Bhaird, Muiris Ballach Ó Cléirigh, Donnchadh an tSneachta Mac Craith, Cú Connacht Ó Cianáin, and Tadhg Dall Ó hUiginn.[75]

It is strange to think that all the powers of the government were not able absolutely to wipe out and annihilate the poets and the tradition they represented. And there is an irrepressible irony in the fact that Sir John Perrott hired bards to sing the praises of the English Queen[76] and that Lord Mountjoy and Sir George Carew bribed Aonghus Ruadh Ó Dálaigh to satirize the native families—if there is any truth in those allegations.[77]

§4

Those who are familiar with the *Gogynfeirdd* or the Poets of the Princes in Welsh tradition will immediately see a similarity between them and the Irish bards of the period. Both groups were craftsmen. They practised their craft in precisely the same way as carpenters and smiths, and like them they lived on the fees they received for their products. The knowledge that was the basis of this craft was, as in other crafts, the personal property of the craftsman, and it was handed on from father to son. In this way, the craft was kept within a small circle of families.

The society in which the poets functioned was rather loose in its organization, and the ties that kept it together were few in number. Most important was the loyalty of the lord to his subjects and their homage to him. One of the principal functions of the poets was to enthrone the lord as an object of loyalty. And since every lord depended upon two things for his position—his lineage and his bravery—the poets were expected to emphasize these heavily in their poems. Their poetry was thus thoroughly social: they were composed for social purposes, their contents were concepts and feelings relevant to the society, and they were proclaimed before that society.

It was poetry to be heard and not to be read; poetry for the ear not for the eye. It is important to remember this in considering both Irish and Welsh poetry in this period. As Thomas Parry has pointed out with reference to the latter:

> The tendency of modern criticism has been to consider primarily the thought expressed in a poem; as for the rhythm, the rhymes, the alliteration, they are desirable no doubt but are regarded as an adornment of the verse, additional elements, so to say, introduced to give beauty to the work. The poetry of today is read with the eye, and the eye is the door of the understanding. The poetry of old was heard with the ear, was recited or sung, and the ear is the gateway to the heart. The complex effect produced by the sound of answering consonants, rhymes floating on the hearing, old words bringing with them a fragment of the past into the memory and uniting yesterday and today (the 'aura' of which Mr. Saunders Lewis speaks), a feeling that all this glorifies the man who maintains life and society, guiding his subjects, the leader in the fullest sense of the word—that was the way in which poetry gave satisfaction to our fathers.[78]

We have to keep all this in mind before we can evaluate the poems of these bards, but their true worth cannot be realized without recreating in the imagination the circumstances that gave them life. For example, when Gofraidh Ó Domhnaill died in 1258, Cenél gConaill was left without a chieftain and in dire straits.[79] Ó Néill, the chieftain of Cenél nEoghain, was demanding that they submit to him, and was ready to attack. In their crisis, Cenél gConaill called a meeting to take counsel and to choose a new chieftain. While they were debating, Domhnall Óg, son of Domhnall Mór Ó Domhnaill, a young lad of eighteen years, just arrived from Scotland, appeared; he was chosen chief on the spot.

At that time there was a poet by the name of Giolla Brighde Mac Con Midhe living in Tír Eoghain. His lord was Niall Ó Goirmleadhaigh, a prince who owed homage to Ó Néill, the chieftain who was ready to attack Cenél gConaill, and the poet had sung to these two in the past. But he had also sung to the two brothers of Domhnall Óg, two brothers who had since died. Giolla Brighde heard about Domhnall Óg coming from Scotland and being proclaimed chieftain of Cenél gConaill, and he decided to compose a poem in praise of him.

We can imagine him retreating to the bedroom, shutting out the light, and then, stretched out on his bed, struggling with the poem. Domhnall Óg had been born after his mother died: *do fághbadh i mbroinn* ('relictus est in matrice'), but to the poet, this was a good sign, and he could cite the case of Tuathal Techmar, Fionn Mac Cumhaill, Cormac mac Airt and others as examples. Domhnall had no brothers living, but there again it might often be that *ferr begán cloinne iná clann* ('a few children are better than many') and *bídh mac nach mesa ináid meic* ('one son may be better than many'). The mother of Domhnall was a daughter of Cathal Croibhdhearg, a fact that secured the good will of Connacht for him; Munster, too, would be on his side because his maternal grandmother was daughter to Ó Briain. Those are some of the facts that the bard could make use of.

After composing the poem and perhaps taking a few days to refine and polish it, Giolla Brighde summons his *reacaire* or *bard* and has him learn the poem by heart. Afterwards he takes him and his harpist and goes to the court of Domhnall Óg. As a well-known poet, Giolla receives a princely welcome, and probably a banquet in his honour that evening. When the banquet is finished—except for the wines— the poet gives a sign to the harpist, who begins to play. The court falls silent, and the *reacaire* begins to chant:

> Do-fhidir Dia Ceinéal Conuill,
> do chur a n-imshníomh ar ais;
> táinig tre bháidh cridhe Colaim
> ar fine gcáidh gConaill chais.[80]

God knows Cenél gConaill. He has put an end to their concern. For love of his kinsmen, Colum has taken pity on the holy race of Conall the Curly-Haired. Because of the death of their king, the nobles of Erne were plunged into grief. A youth arrived at the bay outside, and lifted from the people the sadness that had paralysed them. When they heard that he had crossed the sea, hardly one of them stopped to put on his sword-belt. For the nobles of Erne, the tidings were as good as if his father had risen from the grave.

And so on, mentioning the young man's lineage on both his father's and his mother's side, what was expected of him, the heroes he might be likened to, and bidding him success.

It does not require much imagination to see that this encomium could make a deep impression on the mind of the young prince and on everyone who was listening. Each and every one of them would realize that the poem would exist long after they had passed on. And, in fact, the evidence is that songs like this were not only part of the tradition, they constituted that tradition. The proof is in the fact that the historians depended upon them for information.[81]

But despite every attempt to get the proper perspective for viewing and evaluating the glories of this poetic output, it is difficult for us to suppress fully our contemporary prejudices. It cannot be helped that the poems, which represent the interests and personalities of the poets, strike in us chords that were not plucked by others. Unfortunately, the official scribes did not treasure the songs that appeal most to us, and for that reason few of them were preserved. No doubt some, if not many, have been lost, for it is certain that the poets turned at times to the comfort of their craft in times of trouble, just as did Muireadhach Albanach Ó Dálaigh when he lost his wife Maol Mheadha (Maelva),[82] and Gofraidh Fionn Ó Dálaigh when he lost his son.[83]

Even in translation, Muireadhach Ó Dálaigh's poem 'On the death of his wife' shows some of the nobility of expression which resulted from the channelling of strong emotion into intricate metre made up of consonance, alliteration, and rhyme:

> I parted from my life last night,
>   A woman's body sunk in clay:
> The tender bosom that I loved
>   wrapped in a sheet they took away.
>
> The heavy blossom that had lit
>   The ancient boughs is tossed and blown;
> Hers was the burden of delight
>   That long had weighed the old tree down.
>
> And I am left alone tonight
>   And desolate is the world I see
> For lovely was that woman's weight
>   That even last night had lain on me.
>
> Weeping I look upon the place
>   Where she used to rest her head—
> For yesterday her body's length
>   Reposed upon you too, my bed.
>
> Yesterday that smiling face
>   Upon one side of you was laid
> That could match the hazel bloom
>   In its dark delicate sweet shade.
>
> Maelva of the shadowy brows
>   Was the mead-cask at my side;
> Fairest of all flowers that grow
>   Was the beauty that has died.

1.   Trinity College Dublin MS 58, *The Book of Kells*. (By courtesy of The
     Board of Trinity College Dublin.)

2. Dún Aonghusa from the air. (By courtesy of the Curator, Cambridge University Technical Services, Ltd.)

3. The Abbey of Clonmacnoise from the air. (By courtesy of the Curator, Cambridge University Technical Services Ltd.)

4. Trinity College Dublin MS 1282, *The Annals of Ulster*, fol. 46v. (By courtesy of The Board of Trinity College Dublin.)

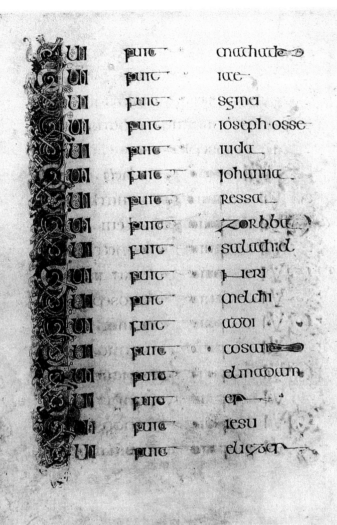

5. Trinity College Dublin MS 58, *The Book of Kells*, fol. 200v. (By courtesy of The Board of Trinity College of Dublin.)

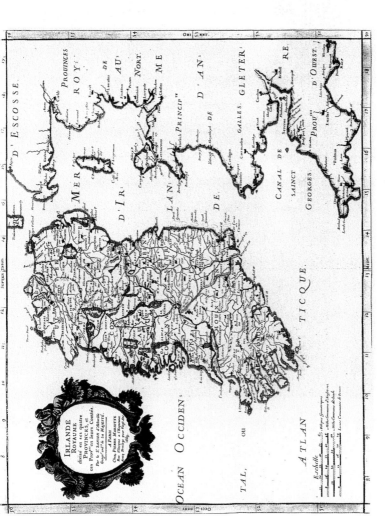

6. Samson's map of Ireland (1665). (By courtesy of Professor B. S. Mac Aodha and the Department of Geography, University College Galway.)

7.   Máirtín Ó Cadhain (1907–70). (By permission of *An Comhar*.)

8.   Seán Ó Ríordáin (1917–77). (By permission of *Gael Linn*.)

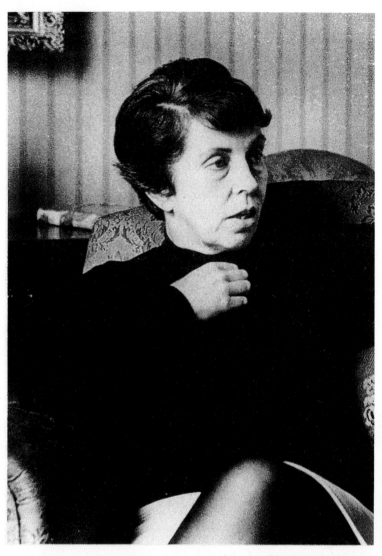

9. Máire Mhac an tSaoi (1922–   ). (By permission of the *Irish Times*.)

My body's self deserts me now,
　　The half of me that was her own,
Since all I knew of brightness died
　　Half of me lingers, half is gone.

The face that was like hawthorn bloom
　　Was my right foot and my right side;
And my right hand and my right eye
　　Were no more mine than hers who died.

Poor is the share of me that's left
　　Since half of me died with my wife;
I shudder at the words I speak;
　　Dear God, that girl was half my life.

And our first look was her first love;
　　No man had fondled ere I came
The little breasts so small and firm
　　And the long body like a flame.

For twenty years we shared a home,
　　Our converse milder with each year;
Eleven children in its time
　　Did that tall stately body bear.

It was the King of hosts and roads
　　Who snatched her from me in her prime:
Little she wished to leave alone
　　The man she loved before her time.

Now King of churches and of bells,
　　Though never raised to pledge a lie
That woman's hand—can it be true?—
　　No more beneath my head will lie.[84]

With the poets in such close contact with the nobles and sharing so many of their interests it is no wonder that they learned a great deal form each other. It is assumed that it was the nobles, in particular the descendants of the Anglo-Normans and those related to them by marriage, who first came to know of the love lyrics in which *amour courtois* was expressed, the lyrics which we think of as originating in Provence and as founding favour and imitation almost throughout Europe wherever there was appreciation of courtly behaviour and a love of poetry and music.[85] But once the poets had been introduced to them, they did not take long to show that they could give a thoroughly Irish and traditional as well as sophisticated expression to *amour courtois* although to use the French name for the sentiment is

probably misleading as a considerable number of the Irish love lyrics
that have survived were apparently written after the troubadour
influence had been long exhausted and owed less to French and
medieval continental influence than to Renaissance and English
influence.

T. F. O'Rahilly published under the title *Dánta Grádha* a number of
poems dealing with which in themselves constitute a literary treasure.[86]
Had the poets produced nothing more than these songs and those in his
Measgra Dánta their craft and art would merit studying.

> Lady, the meshes of your coiling hair
>   Hide like a mask my lovely one.
> And thro' that veil I guess at things more rare
>   Than Absalom, King David's son.
>
> A flight of cuckoos bursting from a curl
>   Do sing in every plaited tress,
> Whose silent tune sets many hearts a-whirl,
>   O'erborne with so much loveliness.
>
> The drooping ringlets of your long bright hair
>   Across your eyes their shadows fling,
> Those eyes that flash and glow like crystal there,
>   Or precious jewels in a ring.
>
> Like some strange beauty from an unknown land
>   In borrowed gems you ne'er were dressed.
> I see no golden bracelets on your hand,
>   A hundred rings upon your breast.
>
> Round your smooth neck the wreathed floods of gold
>   Coil from your brows above,
> And all your breast with jewelled chains enfold,
>   A breast for men to love.[87]

Once they were shown the art of clothing the stock themes of
courtly love poetry in Irish dress, more than a few of the nobility set
out to try their hand at it. And some were very successful, among
them the Earl Gerald (Gearóid Iarla, the third Earl of Desmond,
?1338–98),[88] Maghnus Ó Domhnaill (Lord of Tirconnell, *c.* 1440–
1563/4), Domhnall Mac Cárthaigh, and Piaras Feiritéir (*c.* 1610–53)
in Ireland,[89] and in Scotland the Earl and Lady Argyll and Duncan
Campbell of Glenorquhy.[90]   We close this chapter with a few
examples that show—even in the English translations offered here—
the degree of sophistication and eloquence achieved by these 'lay'
poets. The first is attributed to the remarkable Earl Gerald:[91]

Mairg adeir olc ris na mnaibh

Speak not ill of womankind,
    'Tis no wisdom if you do.
You that fault in women find,
    I would not be praised of you.

Sweetly speaking, witty, clear,
    Tribe most lovely to my mind,
Blame of such I hate to hear.
    Speak not ill of womankind.

Bloody treason, murderous act,
    Not by women were designed,
Bells o'erthrown nor churches sacked.
    Speak not ill of womankind.

Bishop, King upon his throne,
    Primate skilled to loose and bind,
Sprung of women every one!
    Speak not ill of womankind.

For a brave young fellow long
    Hearts of women oft have pined.
Who would dare their love to wrong?
    Speak not ill of womankind.

Paunchy greybeards never more
    Hope to please a woman's mind.
Poor young chieftains they adore!
    Speak not ill of womankind.

Soraidh slán don oidhche aréir[92]

'Tis goodbye then to last night,
Swift its flight and long our pain,
Tho' the morrow saw me hang
Would it ran its course again.

Two within tonight there chance
Whom a glance must give away,
Mouth to mouth they may not set,
But once met their eyes betray.

Keep we counsel—have a care
To that roving pair of eyes,
All our silence is small gain
When so plain they court surmise.

See these liars gathered here,
For their fear I ask no whit,
But my thoughts, which way they tend,
My eyes send you where you sit—

This night only keep for us
To be thus and then no more—
Here shall morning not make way;
Rise and turn day from the door!

Stand to me, Mother of God,
At your nod the wise obey—
Pity and redeem my plight:
Speed last night upon its way.

Not surprisingly, perhaps, in view of its content and context, the original of the following translation is not ascribed to any poet:[93]

Mo-chion dár lucht abarthaigh

Good luck to all who blame us
    Since you have made me rue;
They're welcome to defame us—
    Would only it came true!

A harmless dear adventure,
    It could not pass unheeded—
For all this smoke of censure
    A little flame is needed.

They hang you before trial—
    O neat anticipation!
To make their false espial
    My sorry consolation.

Why are we still delaying
    To prove what they repeat—
The chanter in the saying
    Could make the harsh bell sweet.

The lie has made good haste, love,
    You cannot now disclaim it
Quit toying with the taste, love,
    Take up the cup and drain it.

They'll not believe us honest,
    Then why not give them reason?
For what their colours promised
    We'll try them for a season.

Thro' me you suffer slander,
    Thro' me your name is lost,

Be careful how you squander
   The purchase with the cost.

Then ratify their lying,
   Their commentary invite—
We'll profit by their spying
   And love them for their spite.

Lady, my wits are astray and I may not recover
For the light of your delicate face where the warm
                     blushes hover,
My grief on the day when the tale-bearing rabble
                     discover
That binding our names in disgrace does not make me
                     your lover.

The original of the following translation has been described as one of the finest of this period; 'It is about a man so old and physically exhausted that he can no longer have sexual relations with the woman he loves. I doubt if an English Elizabethan would not have considered the subject comic rather than moving.'[94]

A bhean lán do stuaim

Woman full of wile
   Take your hand away,
Nothing tempts me now,
   Sick for love you pray.

But my hair is grey,
   And my flesh is weak,
All my blood gone cold—
   Tell me what you seek.

Do not think me mad,
   Do not hang your head,
Slender witch, let love
   Live in thought not deed.

Take your mouth from mine,
   Kissing bitterer still,
Flesh from flesh must part
   Lest of warmth come will.

Your twined, branching hair,
   Your grey eye dew-bright,
Your rich rounded breast
   Turn to lust the sight.

Yet but for the wild bed
   But for the body's flame,

> Woman full of wile,
> My love is still the same.

The Irish original is by Seathrún Céitinn (Geoffrey Keating, c. 1580–
c. 1644) and the translation is by Frank O'Connor, who has followed
the first editor of Céitinn's verse[95] by taking the word *stuaim* to mean
'wile'. It has been suggested that the editor chose that meaning under
the influence of the implication of the poem for the reader's view of the
life of the cleric-author. It is true that *stuaim* has the meaning 'self-
control, good sense, prudence' and thus translated would give the
reader an entirely different impression of the addressed lady's
character, but it also has the meaning 'ingenuity, steadiness, (patient)
skill', a meaning not all that removed from 'wile'.[96] Be that as it may, a
recent critic, Mícheál Mac Craith, no doubt reflecting his age just as
the editor reflected his, invites us to take a fresh look at the poem.

> The equation of '*stuaim*' with 'wile' seems to derive from an a priori
> condemnation of the lady addressed in the poem as the sort of woman
> who would dare seduce a priest. If, however, one abandons the
> interpretaion of this priest warding off temptations to his celibacy, it
> becomes much less a poem of renunciation than one of regret. It can
> easily be fitted into the framework of 'The Aged Lover Renounceth
> Love'—a pattern apparently initiated by Lord Vaugh in Tottel's
> Miscellany, and imitated by such famous poets as Ralegh, Campion,
> Sidney, and Donne.[97]

These love poems, like most of their kind, are based on the
expression of a great deal of conventional feeling, one of the
commonest being the profession of such a consuming passion for the
loved one that its outcome can be none other than the death of the
lover unless it is fully requited. But in Ireland as elsewhere this
exaggeration produced its antithesis in the avowal *not* to die for love.
The latter sentiment is well expressed here:[98]

> *Ní bhfuighe mise bás duit*
>
> O woman, shapely as the swan,
> On your account I shall not die:
> The men you've slain—a trivial clan—
> Were less than I.
>
> I ask me shall I die for these—
> For blossom teeth and scarlet lips—
> And shall that delicate swan-shape
> Bring me eclipse?
>
> Well-shaped the breasts and smooth the skin,
> The cheeks are fair, the tresses free—

And yet I shall not suffer death,
God over me!

Those even brows, that hair like gold,
Those languorous tones, that virgin way,
The flowing limbs, the rounded heel
Slight men betray!

Thy spirit keen through radiant mien,
Thy shining throat and smiling eye,
Thy little palm, thy side like foam—
I cannot die!

O woman, shapely as the swan,
In a cunning house hard-reared was I:
O bosom white, O well-shaped palm,
I shall not die!

Notes

1 See E. Cahill, 'Political State of Medieval Ireland', *Irish Ecclesiastical Record*, v Ser., 25 (1925), 245–65. For more information, see Michael Dolley, *Anglo-Norman Ireland* (Dublin, 1972), Kenneth Nicholls, *Gaelic and Gaelicized Ireland in the Middle Ages* (Dublin, 1972).

2 *State Papers, Henry VIII*, vol. II, part iiiA, 1–9.

3 Ibid., 17.

4 R. Holinshed, *Chronicles* (ed. 1583), p. 45: 2. The quotation and its glosses have been taken from S. H. O'Grady, *Silva Gadelica*, I, xxiii.

5 *State Papers*, II, part iiiA, 6.

6 On the Fionn Cycle, see chap. 3, n. 56.

7 Thurneysen, *Mittelirische Verslehren* (*Irische Texte*, III), 6, 39, 107.

8 'Under the stress of circumstances the *filidh* at the end of the twelfth century seem to have turned what had hitherto been a secondary function into a primary function, so that the once neglected praise-poems (originally doubtless considered typical only of bards, or of *filidh* assuming bardic functions) began to be preserved and held in honour'— G. Murphy, 'Bards and Filidh', *Éigse*, 2 (1940), 200–7; quotation from p. 207. See further J. E. Caerwyn Williams, *The Court Poet in Medieval Ireland* (PBA, 57 [1971], 1–51). Liam Breatnach, *Uraicecht na Riar* (Dublin, 1987) deals with the *filid* in the Old and Middle Irish periods. 'The Chief's Poet', by P. Breatnach, PRIA, 83, sec. C (1983), 37–79, deals with them in the Classical Modern Irish period. See also W. Gillies, 'The Classical Irish Poetic Tradition', *Proceedings of the Seventh International Congress of Celtic Studies* (Oxford, 1983), pp. 108–20; D. S. Thomson, 'The Poetic Tradition in Gaelic Scotland', ibid., 121–40.

9 See E. Knott, *Irish Syllabic Poetry* (Cork, Dublin, 1928); *The Bardic Poems of Tadhg Dall Ó Huiginn* (ITS, XXII), I, Intro., lxxxv ff.; O.J

188 THE IRISH LITERARY TRADITION

Bergin, 'Metrica', I, II, *Ériu*, 8 (1915–16), 161–69; III, IV, V, ibid., 9 (1921), 77–84. On the development of *dán díreach* metres see Brian Ó Cuív, 'Some Developments in Irish Metrics', *Éigse*, 12 (1968), 273–90, and A. Mac an Bhaird, 'Dán Díreach agus Ranna as na hAnnála 867–1134', *Éigse*, 17 (1977–79), 157–68, who argues that the origins of *dán díreach* are to be sought a good deal earlier than the widely accepted date of *c.* 1200.

10 Knott, *Irish Syllabic Poetry*, pp. 33–6.

11 See Knott, *The Bardic Poems of Tadhg Dall Ó Huiginn*, I, xxxviii; Dillon, *The Archaism of Irish Tradition*, p. 18. But note that Douglas Hyde in *A Literary History of Ireland* (London, 1901), p. 545, refers to a poem composed in the old style in Connacht in 1734.

12 A. Cameron, *Reliquiae Celticae* (Inverness, 1894), II, 248–58, 274–80.

13 *Thesaurus Palaeohibernicus*, II, 295. See also the Intro. to the work, p. xxxiv, where the editors say that we can safely assign a date earlier than the ninth century to the song. Professor Bergin was not prepared to agree; see *Éigse*, 2 (1940), 205, n. 8.

14 Flower *The Irish Tradition*, p. 27f.

15 Ibid., p. 28.

16 'He was, in fact, a professor of literature and a man of letters . . . He discharged, as O'Donovan pointed out many years ago, the function of the modern journalist. He was not a song writer. He was often a public official, a chronicler, a political essayist, a keen and satirical observer of his fellowmen'—Osborn Bergin, 'Bardic Poetry', *The Journal of the Ivernian Society*, 5 (1913), 154; this lecture was reprinted by the American Committee for Irish Studies, No. 3, and appears as the introduction to *Irish Bardic Poetry* (hereafter cited as IBP), compiled and edited by David Greene and Fergus Kelly (Dublin, 1970). This view of the poet's function has been well received, but some disagree. Frank O'Connor insisted that 'O'Donovan's remark is mere nonsense: there was nothing of the journalist, ancient or modern, about the Irish court poet'; *The Backward Look*, p. 86. There can be no doubt, however, that great emphasis was placed on the poet's learning. On the general question of the poet's place in the society, see James Carney, 'Society and the Bardic Poet', *Studies*, 62 (1973), 233–50.

17 Kenney, *Sources*, I, 20–21; Flower *The Irish Tradition*, pp. 85, 94. See Liam Breatnach, *Uraicecht na Ríar*, pp. 94–8, on the relevance of the families of the poets.

18 Knott, *Tadhg Dall Ó Huiginn*, I, xli.

19 Hennessy, *The Annals of Loch Cé*, II, 334, 378.

20 Knott, op. cit., I, xli; ZCP, 8 (1911–12), 109.

21 IBP, p. 6.

22 The poem was edited and translated by Professor Bergin in *Studies*, 13 (1924), 85–90 (= IBP, no. 38). Knott refers to the same poem, op. cit., I, xxxix.

23 See Bergin, IBP, p. 13, and his Sir John Rhŷs Memorial Lecture, 'The Native Irish Grammarian', PBA, 34 (1948), p. 5; Knott, op. cit., I, xxxviii; Brian Ó Cuív, *The Linguistic Training of the Mediaeval Irish Poet* (Statutory Lecture in the School of Celtic Studies,

1969), (Dublin, 1973), and *Celtica*, 10 (1973–4), 114–40 which gives an account of the principles on which the language of bardic poetry was normalized.

24 See Lambert McKenna, *Bardic Syntactical Tracts* (Dublin, 1944); Bergin, 'The Native Irish Grammarian', and his 'Irish Grammatical Tracts', supplements to *Ériu*, 8–10 (1915–18), and 'Metrical Faults', *Ériu*, 17 (1955), 259–92; Brian Ó Cuív, 'The Linguistic Training', and 'Linguistic Terminology in the Medieval Irish Bardic Tracts', *Trans. Philological Society*, (1965), 141–64.

25 E. Gwynn, *Metrical Dindshenchas*, III, 110; Knott, op. cit., I, xl.

26 B. Cunningham and R. Gillespie, 'The East Ulster Bardic Family of Ó Gnímh', *Éigse*, 20 (1984), 106–14, give an account of the canon of Ó Gnímh poetry (some twenty poems in all) and identify two members of the family, Brian, composing c. 1570–90, and Fear Flatha, composing c. 1607–c. 1638, probably father and son. See also Brian Ó Cuív, 'Some Irish Items Relating to the Mac Donnells of Antrim', *Celtica*, 16 (1984), 139–56.

27 IBP, no. 13.

28 Ibid., pp. 9–10. For further discussion of this practice in Ireland and some possible references to it in medieval Welsh poetry, see P. K. Ford, 'The Death of Aneirin', BBCS 34 (1987), 41–50.

29 IBP, pp. 8–9.

30 IBP, no. 55.

31 See Kenney, *Sources*, I, 30, 31; M. F. Hore, 'Irish Bardism in 1561', *Ulster Journal of Archaeology*, 6 (1858), 165–7. On 'The Performing of Dán' generally, see T. P. McCaughey, *Ériu*, 35 (1984), 39–57.

32 IBP, p. 7.

33 Knott, op. cit., I, 73–80.

34 W. M. Hennessy, *Annals of Loch Cé*, II, 354–6.

35 *Ulster Journal of Archaeology*, 6 (1858), 165–7.

36 AU, III, 119. In ' "Gabh umad, a Fheidhlimidh"—a Fifteenth Century Inauguration Ode', *Ériu*, 31 (1980), 132–45, K. Simms discusses a poem which is related to *Lebor na Cert* (*Leabhar na gCeart*).

37 *Ériu*, 5 (1911), 50 (quoted in Knott, op. cit.).

38 Ibid., 50–69. On 'The Ó Dálaigh Family of Bardic Poets 1139–1691', see James E. Doan, *Éire-Ireland*, 20 (1985), 19–23. On the several poets bearing the name Cearbhall Ó Dálaigh in fact or in tradition, see J. E. Doan, *Éigse*, 18 (1980), 1–24.

39 Knott, *Tadhg Dall Ó Huiginn*, I, 50; II, 34.

40 Ibid., II, 222.

41 See A. S. Green, *Old Irish World* (Dublin, London, 1912), p. 118.

42 All this is chronicled under the year 1451 in a collection of annals that have survived only in a translation that An Dubháltach Mac Firbisigh made in 1666. See *Miscellany of the Irish Archaeological Society* (Dublin, 1846), pp. 227–8; Kenney, *Sources*, I, 22–23.

43 FM, IV, 1000. Professor Bergin edited and translated an encomium to him composed by Seithfín Mór in *Studies*, 9 (1920), 416–20 (= IBP no. 40).

44 See the quotation in S. H. O'Grady, *Silva Gadelica*, I, xxii.

45 On the author, Giolla Brighde Mac Con Midhe (*c.* 1210–?1272) see N. J. A. Williams, ed., *The Poems of Giolla Brighde Mac Con Midhe* (ITS LI, 1980), Introduction and, for this poem, pp. 204–213; also see Knott, *Irish Syllabic Poetry*, pp. 78–80. For a metrical translation, see Thomas Kinsella, *The New Oxford Book of Irish Verse* (Oxford, NY, 1986), pp. 98–102.

46 *The Works of Edmund Spenser, The Minor Poems*, II (Baltimore, 1947), 46.

47 Knott, *Tadhg Dall Ó Huiginn*, I, xliv.

48 *Duanaire Mhéig Uidhir* ('The *duanaire* of the Maguire family'), ed. and trans. David Greene (Dublin, 1972), p. viii. The earliest of the songbooks is *The Book of Magauran*, ed. L. McKenna (Dublin, 1947), dating from the mid-fourteenth century; others include *The Book of O'Hara*, ed. L. McKenna (Dublin, 1951); *Leabhar Branach*, ed. S. Mac Airt (Dublin, 1944); the Book of O'Donnell's Daughter (in Brussells); the Songs of Dillon in R.I.A. A v 2. In 'A Feature of the Poetry of Fergal Óg mac an Bhaird', *Éigse* 15 (1973–4), T. Ó Concheanainn calls attention to the poet's practice of appending to every poem one, two or three extraneous stanzas expressing his devotion to one of his three patrons.

49 Ed. and trans. in *Irish Review*, September, 1912. Also ed. by T. F. O'Rahilly in *Measgra Dánta*, I (Dublin, Cork, 1927), who points out that in the manuscript the poem is attributed to Tadhg an Ghadraigh Mac Aodhagáin.

50 The incident is described in a very dignified poem, 'Nodlaig dochuamair don Chraoibh', by Tadhg Dall Ó hUiginn. See Knott, op. cit., I, 50ff.; II, 34ff. Cf. Hull, *A Text-Book of Irish Literature*, I, 201.

51 *Iomdha uirrim ag Ultuibh*, O'Conor Don MS. 172a. Quoted by Knott, op. cit., I, xlvi.

52 According to Bergin, ' "Ireland's arch-professor of Poetry" . . . He was professional poet to the Mac Carthys, to the Earls of Desmond, and to the O'Briens of Thomond'; *Studies*, 7 (1918), 97.

53 *Irish Monthly*, September, 1919, 513. Cf. Knott, op. cit., I, xlvii, and *Irish Classical Poetry* (Dublin, 1960), pp. 72–3. Note that *Gall* here is a nobleman whose speech and culture are Irish, although his origins are English; to translate it as *English(man)* is therefore misleading.

54 *State Papers, Henry VIII* II, part iiiA, 8.

55 Ibid., 450.

56 IBP, no. 33.

57 YBL, 375, 31ff., and cf. Knott, op. cit., I, xlii–xliii. Also *B.M. Cat. Irish MSS*, I, 474ff. where there is a summary of the rights demanded by Eochaidh Ó hEoghusa from his patron by virtue of his office as *ollamh*. On Eochaidh Ó hEoghusa, see James Carney, *The Irish Bardic Poet* (Dublin, 1967).

58 FM, III, 178ff.

59 Ed. and trans. by Bergin, IBP, no. 20.

60 See Brian Ó Cuív, 'Eachtraí Mhuireadhaigh Í Dálaigh', SH, I (1961), 59–69, and his 'Literary Creation and Irish Historical Tradition', PBA, 49 (1963), 233–62 (also printed separately).

61 *B.M. Cat. Irish MSS*, I, 389.

62 DNB, *s.n.* O'Brien, Donough Baron of Ibrickan and Fourth Earl of Thomond.

63 *B.M. Cat. Irish MSS*, I, 389.
64 L. M. McKenna, *Iomarbhágh na bhFileadh. The Contention of the Bards* (ITS, XX, XXI, London, 1918), II, 246.
65 *Cal. Carew MSS* (1601–03), 194; S. O'Grady, *Pacata Hibernia* (London, 1896), II, 61.
66 Transl. in Frank O'Connor, *The Book of Ireland*, pp. 85–6.
67 FM, IV, 818f.
68 Reginald Scot, 'Discoverie of Witchcraft', *Ulster Journal of Archaeology*, 6 (1858), 209.
69 Dillon, *Early Irish Society*, p. 73f.; J. Carney, *Studies in Irish Literature and History*, p. 263.
70 *Cal. Carew MSS* (1603–4), p. 449. Cf. *Spenser's Prose Works*, ed. R. Gottfried (Baltimore, 1949), p. 125.
71 *Cal. S.P. Ireland* (1509–73), p. 101.
72 FM, IV, 820.
73 Quoted by P. Walsh, *Gleanings from Irish Manuscripts* (Dublin, 1933), p. 186.
74 Ibid.
75 Kenney, *Sources*, I, 31–2.
76 Knott, *Tadhg Dall Ó Huiginn* I, xliv.
77 O'Donovan, *The Tribes of Ireland: a Satire by Aenghus O'Daly* (Dublin, 1852). See also *B.M. Cat. Irish MSS*, I, 341, 443–5; D. Mackinnon, *Cat. of Gaelic MSS. in . . . Scotland* (Edinburgh, 1912), 215, 320.
78 Thomas Parry, *History of Welsh Literature*, trans. by H. Idris Bell (Oxford, 1955), pp. 48–9.
79 FM, III, 364ff.; *B.M. Cat. Irish MSS*, I, 350–1; G. Murphy, *Glimpses of Gaelic Ireland* (Dublin, 1948), p. 37ff.
80 Fraser, Grosjean and O'Keeffe, *Irish Texts*, II, 22ff.; *Studies*, 35 (1946), 40–1. On Giolla Brighde Mac Con Midhe, see n. 45 above and G. Murphy in *Éigse*, 4 (1944), 90ff., and Anne O'Sullivan, 'Giolla Brighde Mac Con Midhe', in James Carney, *Early Irish Poetry* (Cork, 1965), pp. 85–98.
81 Murphy, *Glimpses*, pp. 42–3. Dr Katharine Simms is one example of a contemporary historian who uses bardic poems as historical sources.
82 IBP, no. 22. The poem is attributed to Muireadhach in *The Book of the Dean of Lismore*.
83 L. MacCionnaith, *Dioghluim Dána* (Dublin, 1938), p. 196. Professor T. F. O'Rahilly did us a great service when he collected the 'occasional' songs of the poets and published them under the title *Measgra Dánta*, I and II; see, for example, II, nos. 48, 49, 60–64, etc.
84 Trans. by Frank O'Connor, in John Montague, ed., *The Faber Book of Irish Verse* (London, 1974), 91–2.
85 For the status of French in Ireland during this period, see E. Curtis, 'The Spoken Languages of Medieval Ireland', *Studies*, 8 (1919), 234ff. Recently Mícheál Mac Craith, 'Gaelic Ireland and the Renaissance', in Glanmor Williams, Robert Owen Jones, edd., *The Celts and the Renaissance* (Cardiff, 1990) 57–89, has argued very convincingly that the *dánta grádha* are evidence of the growing influence of English culture on Gaelic literature in the period 1550–1650 and of the Renaissance mediated through English channels.

86 *Dánta Grádha* (Dublin, 1916; Dublin, Cork, 1926).
87 Ibid., p. 17; trans. by the Earl of Longford, *Poems from the Irish* (Dublin, 1944), p. 9.
88 Gearóid Mac Niocaill, 'Duanaire Ghearóid Iarla', SH, 3 (1963), 7–59. See also S. M. Mac Ateer, 'Gearóid Iarla, poète irlandais du XIV^c s., d'origine normande et son œuvre', EC, 15 (1978), 577–98; S. Ó Tuama, 'Traidisiún Iasachta sna Dánta Grá', *Éigse*, 17 (1977–80), 301–18; idem, 'Gearóid Iarla—"the first practitioner"?', S. Watson, ed., *Féilscríbhinn Thomáis de Bhaldraithe* (Dublin, 1986), pp. 78–86. On the theme of love etc. see Tomás Ó Concheanainn, 'Tréithe ar a Moladh Filí na Mná', op. cit., 70–77; P. Ó Fiannachta, ed., *An Grá i Litríocht na Gaeilge, Léachtaí Cholm Cille, 6, 1975)*, and especially S. Ó Tuama, *An Grá i nAmhráin na nDaoine* (Dublin, 1960), and his *An Grá i bhFilíocht na nUaisle* (Dublin, 1988). See Eiléan Ní Chuilleanáin, 'Love and Friendship', in Seán Mac Réamoinn, *The Pleasures of Gaelic Poetry* (London, 1982), pp. 49–62.
89 P. Ua Duinnín, *Dánta Phiarais Feiritéir* (Dublin, 1934).
90 Poetry by Earl Gearóid, Isobella, Lady of Argyll, Mac Cailin the Earl of Argyll, and Donncha Caimbeul mac Cailin and others will be found in *The Book of the Dean of Lismore*. See T. McLaughlan, *The Dean of Lismore's Book* (Edinburgh, 1862). See also E. C. Quiggin, *Poems from the Book of the Dean of Lismore* (Cambridge, 1937); W. J. Watson, *Scottish Verse from the Book of the Dean of Lismore* (Edinburgh, 1937).
91 On the attribution, see *Dánta Grádha*, p. 4. The translation is by the Earl of Longford, op. cit., reprinted in Montague, *The Faber Book of Irish Verse*, p. 101.
92 The original, by Niall Mór Mac Muireadhaigh, may be found in *Dánta Grádha*, p. 51; the translation is by Máire MacEntee, *A Heart Full of Thoughts: Translations . . . from the Irish* (Dublin, 1959), p. 4.
93 *Dánta Grádha*, p. 100; translated by MacEntee, op. cit., p. 9.
94 For the text with an additional two-verse *ceangal* see *Dánta Grádha*, p. 133–4, for the comment and the translation see Frank O'Connor, *The Backward Look*, pp. 106–7 (= *The Magic Fountain*, p. 43); *Kings, Lords, and Commons* (rpt. Van Nuys, 1989), p. 60.
95 Eoin Cathmhaolach Mac Giolla Eáin, *Dánta Amhráin is Caointe Sheathrúin Céitinn* (Dublin, 1900), 60–61, 191 ('ingenuity, wiles'). It is interesting to note that Eugene O'Curry did not believe that Céitinn was the author; ibid. 61.
96 Niall Ó Dónaill, *Foclóir Gaeilge - Béarla* (Dublin, 1977), s.v. *stuaim*.
97 Micheál Mac Craith, 'Gaelic Ireland and the Renaissance', Glanmor Williams, Robert Owen Jones, edd., *The Celts and the Renaissance* (Cardiff, 1990), pp. 57–59, 65.
98 Text in *Dánta Grádha*, p. 132; the translation is by Padraic Colum, in Montague, op. cit., p. 105; cf. *Kings, Lords, and Commons*, p. 59.

CHAPTER 5

THE DECLINE

§1

THE Battle of Kinsale (24–25 December 1601) was a fateful event for the Irish cause, because it resulted in the defeat of the armies of Ó Domhnaill and Ó Néill by the Elizabethan forces under Mountjoy and Carew, and because, as the poet and historian Lughaidh Ó Cléirigh (*c.* 1570–*c.* 1620) said, reflecting the sentiments of his colleagues, 'the authority and sovereignty of Gaelic Ireland has been lost *go foircheann an bheatha* ('till the end of time').'[1] Ó Domhnaill (Aodh Ruadh) went to the Continent to seek more aid from the king of Spain, and there he died—poisoned, they say, by an agent of the English. Lughaidh Ó Cléirigh wrote a biography of him. Five years later both Ó Néill, Earl of Tyrone, and Ruaidhri Ó Domhnaill, Earl of Tirconnell, had to flee to the Continent. The significance of that flight was immediately apparent; Fearghal Óg Mac an Bhaird (*c.* 1550–*c.* 1620) expressed the general feeling:

> All Ireland's now one vessel's company,
> And riding west by cliffs of Beare to sea.
> Upon the snowy foam of the ebbing tide
> Away in one frail bark goes all our pride.
> Now stolen is the soul from Éire's breast,
> And all her coasts and islands mourn oppressed.
> The great twin eagles of the flock of Con
> In perilous flight are in one vessel gone.
> For they whose pinions shaded Ulster's plain
> In their high bark have gone nor come again.
> Two last and yet most royal birds of all
> Fly westward to the sea beyond recall . . .
> Rory our darling, and our most gracious Hugh!
> And tho' we named no names beyond the two,
> Yet in this sailing have we lost a host
> Of men that fainting Ireland needed most . . .[2]

When their boat sailed from Loch Swilly on 14 September, 1607, it is said that the spectators on the shore heaved a sigh that echoed across the water. The feeling of all of Ireland could easily have been mustered in that one sigh, for from that time on a frequent lament by the poets and writers was that Ireland had been deprived of her leaders, that she was like Israel in Egypt but without any Moses to lead her.[3] There were other poets, of course, who believed that Ireland, like Israel, could look forward to deliverance from her Egypt. As Pádraigín Haicéad was to write:

> Clann Israel isí Éire;
> Éigipt eile a ghéibheann gann;
> A Mhuir Ruadh 's a fearta féile
> Bearta a buadh ar ghléire gall.[4]

The learned men of Ireland were not without their representatives among the ninety-nine aboard the ship: with the earls was the head of the Mág Uidhir family and its family chronicler, Tadhg Ó Cianáin (c. 1575–c. 1625). Tadhg stuck to the tradition faithfully and produced a history of the voyage.[5]

Of course, the bards could not stand idly by when their lords were being exiled from the land, and their poems display the measure of their concern and the extent of their sympathies. Professor Bergin published a number of poems by Eoghan Ruadh Mac an Bhaird (c. 1570–c. 1630), family poet to Ó Domhnaill.[6] Here is what he says about one he calls 'Looking Toward Spain', and which he believes was composed between 6 January 1902, when Ó Domhnaill sailed from Castlehaven, and 10 September of the same year, when he was poisoned in Simancas:

> With all his display of literary and antiquarian lore, a thing inseparable from his office, the poet is in dead earnest. He lets us feel the agony of suspense, the vain hopes and the well grounded fears with which the weary followers of O'Neill and O'Donnell looked towards Spain.[7]

Nuala, daughter of Aodh Dubh Ó Domhnaill, fled to the Continent with the Earls, and when she witnessed the death of her brother Ruaidhrí in Rome in 1608, the poet Eoghan Ruadh was moved to address her in one of his most famous poems, *A Bhean Fuair Faill ar an bhFeart*,[8] depicting her weeping and grieving over the grave, alone:

> O woman of the piercing wail
> Who mournest o'er yon mound of clay
> With sigh and groan,
> Would God thou wert among the Gael!
> Thou woulds't not then from day to day
> Weep thus alone.[9]

But perhaps the song that expresses best the feelings of Ireland during this period is one that has been attributed both to Aindrias mac Marcuis and to Eoghan Ruadh Mac an Bhaird, *Anocht as Uaigneach Éire.*[10]

> O'Donnell goes. In that stern strait
> Sore-stricken Ulster mourns her fate
> And all the northern shore makes moan
> To hear that Aodh of Annagh's gone.
>
> Men smile at childhood's play no more,
> Music and song, their day is o'er;
> At wine, at Mass the kingdom's heirs
> Are seen no more; changed hearts are theirs.
>
> They feast no more, they gamble not,
> All goodly pastime is forgot;
> They barter not, they race no steeds,
> They take no joy in stirring deeds.
>
> No praise in builded song expressed
> They hear, no tales before they rest;
> None care for books, and none take glee
> To hear the long-traced pedigree.
>
> The packs are silent, there's no sound
> Of the old strain on Bregian ground.
> A foreign flood holds all the shore,
> And the great wolf-dog barks no more.
>
> Woe to the Gael in this sore plight!
> Henceforth they shall not know delight.
> No tidings now their woe relieves,
> Too close the gnawing sorrow cleaves.[11]

That was the beginning of a century that saw the overthrow of Irish society. At its start, the Irish had possession of half the island, with the other half in the hands of the descendants of Roman Catholic Anglo-Normans. Three times during that century land was taken from the original owners and given to foreigners from Britain—foreigners indeed, even if a large number of them, the Scottish Presbyterians who came to Ulster, were mostly Gaelic speaking. Twice the Irish arose in a military campaign to regain their property, but they were unsuccessful on each occasion. By the end of the century that land had passed almost entirely into the hands of British Protestants, English law had displaced Irish law, and Protestantism was the only recognized religion. The lot of Catholics was persecution and punishment.

Cromwell and his followers brought a great deal of misery to the land. It was divided into two parts by them: in one part only—Clare and Connacht—were the Irish nobility permitted to hold land; the other part was given to officers in Cromwell's army and to others in payment for their services. Furthermore, citizens of such towns as Galway and Waterford were ordered to move their dwellings two miles outside the city limits to make way for the English.[12]

It is no wonder that the Irish embraced the Stuart cause at the end of the century. But it did them no good, for they were defeated in the Battle of the Boyne on 1 July 1690, and in the Battle of Aughrim on 12 July 1691. The most capable general on the Irish side was Patrick Sarsfield. He held the town of Limerick until he saw that the Stuart cause was utterly hopeless, then negotiated a treaty with the enemy (3 October 1691), securing for the Catholics the same freedom they had had under Charles II. Then he and most of his followers—around 20,000 it is said—sailed for the Continent. This exodus is referred to as the 'Flight of the Wild Geese'.

The Flight of the Earls at the beginning of the seventeenth century and the Flight of the Wild Geese at its end demonstrate clearly the process whereby Irish society was deprived of its traditional leaders and stripped of the tribal system that had been the foundation of the Irish way of life. On top of all that, a number of laws were passed at the beginning of the eighteenth century that were clearly designed to make life intolerable for Catholics. No Catholic was allowed to sit in Parliament or to carry arms; he was denied the right to maintain schools and forbidden to send his children to the Continent to be educated. No Catholic bishop remained in the land, nor any other person in religious orders who held an office higher than parish priest, and even the parish priest was denied freedom to do his work until he had sworn allegiance to the English throne. While it is true that similar laws were passed against Catholics in England, the important thing to remember is that in Ireland the laws punished a native majority and favoured a foreign minority.[13] It is no wonder that the condition of the people of Ireland in the eighteenth century has been described as one of the worst in all Europe.[14] And of course there was no difference between the condition of the common folk and that of the country as a whole, for—and the point must be stressed—the nobility had been deprived of most of its possessions. Its members were either in exile, serving as mercenaries in the armies of Europe, or labourers and beggars hovering like phantoms over the lands of their patrimony.

Those nobles who were able to keep their estates were rare exceptions, and they could not have done so had their lands not been in such remote and inaccessible places as the fastnesses of Kerry and Connemara. There, the house of the nobleman, 'the Big House', as it was called, continued to be the heart of the neighbourhood, and the family head the lord of the people. Consider the Martins: 'Within Connemara the Martins, from father to son, reigned with a sway that was absolute and supreme, they being not alone the owners of that huge tract, but also the only magistrates resident within its borders'.[15] Richard Martin, known as 'Humanity Dick', was asked if the law of the king 'ran' in Connemara; 'Egad, it does', was the answer, 'as fast as any greyhound if any of my good fellows are after it'.[16] The O'Connell family of Derrynane was not unlike the Martins.[17] Their homestead was the centre of a life, which, as regards organization, was virtually patriarchal. Their wealth was not in money but in flocks and herds, and their tenants paid the rent either in labour or in goods.

The houses of these noblemen were special in many ways, not the least interesting of which was their culture.[18] They were the ones who maintained Irish culture. They welcomed the poets who, in turn, paid for their welcome in the traditional way, by composing and reciting poems. To be sure, other bearers of the old tradition were welcomed too, the singers, harpists, and story-tellers, along with the representatives of that other tradition which was being inextricably bound up with the native culture during this time, the Roman Catholic priests. As we shall see further on, the poets and the priests kept company with each other often in this period.

The Irish 'Big Houses' took some interest in English culture also, although there was not much of it in Ireland at the time. In reality, their interest was slight compared with their interest in European culture, a fact that is not too surprising when we recall that these houses had many connections with the Continent. For one thing, many sons of the Big Houses spent time on the Continent as soldiers. At one time, for example, counting young and old alike, eighteen members of the O'Connell family of Derrynane were serving as soldiers in France, Spain and Austria.[19] From time to time there probably were families with even more members doing like service. Military service would have its appeal for those nobles who had been deprived of their patrimony, and best of all, of course, it might give them the chance to strike a blow against England.

It is no wonder, then, that the Irish took a personal interest in every battle fought on the Continent during this time; their brothers, sons, and husbands were fighting in them. When the news came that the Irish brigade under the command of Lally had conquered the strongholds of Fort Frederick-Henry, Lillo, and St Croix in Holland from the allies of England in October, 1747, a light was left burning in every window in Galway—their way of celebrating an Irish victory.[20]

Furthermore, very many sons of the Big Houses were priests or studying for the priesthood on the Continent. If some brothers were fighting with physical weapons against England, others were using spiritual weapons and playing a significant part in the Counter-Reformation. Flaithrí Ó Maolchonaire—in English, Florence Conry—(?1561–1629) is a good example of this latter group.[21] He founded the College of St Anthony in Louvain (1606), was an authority on St Augustine, wrote books on the doctrine of grace, and, as some believe, was an influence on his friend Jansen.[22] Nor did he neglect his mother tongue: he translated a devotional book from the Spanish under the title *Desiderius* or *Sgáthán an Chrábhaidh*, printed in Louvain in 1616.[23] It should be noted that he felt the need to explain that in the attempt to open the door of the true faith to the ordinary person in Ireland he had used the wooden key of the simple language rather than the golden key of the literary language of the bardic schools.

All of this goes to show that the Continent was nearer to Gaelic Ireland than were England and London—a fact worth remembering when reading the works of the poets. Aodhagan Ó Rathaille (Egan O'Rahilly, c. 1670–c. 1728) probably never went outside of counties Cork and Kerry during his lifetime, but we find him weighing the consequences of the death of the king of Spain in 1700.[24] Apart from one short visit, Seán Clárach Mac Domhnaill (1691–1754) spent his life on the border between counties Limerick and Cork, but we find him taking an interest in the death of the French Regent (1723), and in the Austrian war of succession. The poet-priest Liam Inglis (1709–78) showed himself to be remarkably well-informed in the events of the day, but then he had actually been on the Continent.[25]

Still, the number of Irish Big Houses were few, and they were found only in the remotest parts of the island. They knew that their continued existence was not secure, and that it depended upon keeping as far as possible out of sight of the English authorities. It is said that a certain historian by the name of Dr Smith visited the family of O'Connell in Derrynane, and was welcomed warmly. When the family discovered that he was collecting material for a book their warmth toward him declined considerably, and when he returned for a second visit, it was cooler still: they kicked him down the stairs![26]

These Big Houses, like the native culture itself, were part of the hidden Ireland, part of that life that had been prohibited by law. This was a time when it was an offence to possess a book or manuscript in the Irish language, the time when a manuscript containing poetry was hidden in the walls of Lismore Castle to be forgotten for decades and finally discovered damp and faded—*The Book of Lismore*.[27] It is not surprising that Irish culture tried to keep out of sight, and succeeded to such a degree that as enlightened a historian as Lecky knew almost nothing about it, though he wrote a history of Ireland in the eighteenth century.[28]

They say it was the Battle of Kinsale that broke the backs of the old native aristocracy and the Battle of the Boyne that smashed the old Anglo-Norman aristocracy. The fate of the court poets was tied to that of these two aristocracies, a fact it did not take long to realize. Many of the poets lost their lives exactly as did their lords. In 1671, Dubháltach Óg Mac Firbisigh (1585–1670), author of the magisterial *Genealogies of the Families of Ireland* or *Great Book of Genealogies*, who gave assistance to Sir James Ware, was murdered.[29] At about the same time, Tadhg Mac Dáire Mac Bruaideadha (1570–1652) was deprived of his land, though he was over eighty years of age. When the new owner, one of Cromwell's soldiers and an Irishman (alas!), came to take possession, the poet stayed in his house ready to argue his case. His adversary merely picked him up and threw him over the precipice into the sea below, shouting *Abair do rann anois, a fhir bhig* ('Say your verse now, little man').[30]

Even if the poet had been able to save his life and his land, he could not have maintained his profession in the old sense, for there were no longer any lords to sing to nor any lords to pay for the poetry. The poets were quick to see the implications of all this. 'Tell him' (viz., Gordún Ó Néill, *fl.* 1650–1704), says one of the poets, Diarmuid Mac Muiredhaigh, 'that I know well that Ireland's nobles, alas!, are giving up their right to the Irish of the glorious alliterations':

> Innsigh dhósan gur léur liom
> go bfuilid uaisle Éiriond
> mon-uar ag tréigin a gceirt
> san nGaeidhlig na n-uam n-oirrdheirc.[31]

No wonder, then, that one of the poets, Mathghamhain Ó hIfearnáin
(c. 1580–c. 1640), early in the reign of James I presumably, composed
a poem for his son that begins:

> A mhic ná mebhraig éigsi:
> cerd do shen rót rothréigsi . . .[32]

> My son, forsake your art,
> In that which was your fathers' have no part—
> Though from the start she had borne pride of place,
> Poetry now leads to disgrace.

> Serve it not then, this leavings of a trade,
> Nor by you be an Irish measure made, ,
> Polished and perfect, whole in sound and sense—
> Ape the new fashion, modish, cheap and dense.

> Spin spineless verses of the commonplace,
> Suffice it that they hold an even pace
> And show not too nice taste within their span—
> Preferment waits upon you if you can.

> Give no man meed of censure nor just praise,
> But if needs must your voice discreetly raise,
> Not where there's only hatred to be earned,
> Praising the Gael and for your labour spurned.

> Break with them! Reckon not their histories
> Nor chronicle them in men's memories,
> Make it no study to enrich their fame,
> Let all be named before an Irish name.

> Thus you may purge your speech of bitterness,
> Thus your addresses may command success—
> What good repute has granted, do you hide,
> Asperse their breeding, be their blood denied.

> The good that has been, see you leave alone,
> That which now goes for good dilate upon;
> Polish the praises of a foreign rout,
> Allies more likely as has come about.

> The race of Mílid and the sons of Conn,
> Who now maintains it, that their sway goes on?
> A lying prophet in men's eyes to stand,
> Proclaiming alien dynasts in the land!

> The tribe of Lord, proud Carthach's company,
> Be these your strangers come from oversea,

Over Flann's ground girt with the smooth sea-ring,
Let none who bore their name bear it as king.

Conn of the Hundred Battles be forgot,
The son of Eochaidh hold you now as naught:
The stock of Conn, modest and generous,
Who had deserved a better fate from us.

Drive out of mind thought of their excellence,
Gerald's king-blood, our store of recompense,
Whom might no man for love of self condemn—
No poem ponder thou in praise of them.

For, since none now care,
For knowledge and the comely things that were,
And were not then like fencing in a plot,
The making of a poem shall profit not.[33]

In the same vein, Fear Flatha Ó Gnímh (*fl*: 1602–*c*. 1640) sings:

Mairg do-chuaidh re ceird ndúthchais:
rug ar Bhanbha mbarrúrthais
nach dualghas athar is fhearr
i n-achadh fhuarghlas Éireann.

Alas for him who has followed his family profession: it has befallen
Banbha of the fresh soft surface that in Ireland's cool green field one's
father's natural calling is not the best.[34]

And as early as 1627, Conall Mac Eochagáin had this to say:

And now because they cannot enjoy that respect and gain by their said
profession as heretofore they and their ancestors received, they set
nought by the said knowledge, neglect their books, and choose rather
to put their children to learn English than their own native language,
insomuch that some of them suffer tailors to cut the leaves of the said
books (which their ancestors held in great account) and slice them in
long pieces to make their measures of, so that the posterities are like to
fall into mere ignorance of any things which happened before their
time.[35]

Because there was no call for poets as a professional class, there was
no call for the schools of poetic learning, and one might have expected
that these would disappear quickly from the land. But that was not
the case. Part of the reason must have been that these schools were not
dependent upon any institution but the poet-teacher himself for their
existence. As long as he was willing to teach, and as long as there were
pupils ready to learn, the work of the schools went on. Another

reason that the schools survived was precisely because they were schools of poetry and not prose. The prose of a people depends upon its institutions, both local and national; destroy these and you check the development of prose. And that is exactly what happened in Ireland and in Wales. But the Irish people continued to live, and the more misfortune overtook them the greater was their need for expression. The only means of expression left to them—as to every nation that has been conquered and deprived of its resources—was poetry and music.

Even when the bardic schools did finally disappear, the bardic families (or at least some of them) continued to interest themselves in their traditions and their national culture; they continued their interest in transcribing prose and poetry, and their services were called forth in a new field, that of ordinary, everyday education. As we have noted, Catholics were forbidden by the penal laws to keep schools. The implication is that the official schools were little more than implements to turn Catholics into Protestants and Irishmen into Englishmen.[36] Naturally, the Catholic authorities were not ready to submit to a system of education that aimed at the destruction of their faith. So, they made use of the resources at hand, that is, the two educated classes in the native society, the poets and the priests, and schools were convened in ditches and under hedges. Arthur Young, an Englishman travelling in Ireland in the years 1776–9, described them as follows:

> Some degree of education is also general: hedge schools,[37] as they are called (they might as well be termed *ditch* ones, for I have seen many a ditch full of scholars) are everywhere to be met with, where reading and writing are taught: schools are also common for men: I have seen a dozen great fellows at school and was told they were educating with an intention of being priests.[38]

The diary of Amhlaoibh Ó Súilleabháin (*c*. 1780–1837), written from January 1827 to December 1830 (although not published until 1936), is a testimony to the standard of the education which could be imparted even under the most difficult circumstances. In it he describes how he and his father started to teach in a sheep-shed before a schoolhouse was built for them at the crossroads in the parish of Callan in 1791:

> In truth, it was a small schoolhouse, some twenty feet by ten. The sod walls were put up on the first day, the timber roofing on the second, and the thatch on the third. Many a long uneventful year my father and I

spent teaching in this hovel, in another mud-walled cabin somewhat larger at the Tree of Killaloe, and in a good schoolhouse in Ballykeefe.[39]

Ó Súilleabháin's *Diary* must rank as one of the most significant of the non-imaginative Irish prose writings in the nineteenth century, and stands side by side with the *Fealsúnacht* or 'Philosophy' of Aodh Mac Domhnaill (1802–67) who although not a scholar had ambitions both as a prose and a verse writer and strove to overcome his educational disadvantages, disadvantages that remained for the bulk of the population despite the presence of hedge schools.[40]

The combination of poet and schoolmaster was probably fairly common. For example, Fiachra Mac Brádaigh, who lived near the village of Stradone in the parish of Larach, is described as 'a tolerably good poet' and as 'a witty schoolmaster'.[41] We know that Eoghan Ruadh Ó Súilleabháin, too, kept a school at times in spite of his distaste for the profession. Among other teachers were Aindrias Mag Craith ('An Mangaire Súgach', ?1708–c.1795) and Donnchadh Ruadh Mac Conmara (1715–1810).[42] But since Catholics were forbidden to keep schools, it appears likely that many a poet-teacher was content to be recognized as poet alone, or as poet and harpist, for there was a great demand for harpists to teach dancing.[43] Says Young: 'Dancing is so universal among them that there are everywhere itinerant dancing masters to whom the cottiers pay sixpence a quarter for teaching their families'.[44]

The quality of education that could be obtained in these unofficial schools would vary from place to place. In some areas a learned priest would be allowed by the Protestant nobles to maintain a school; sometimes the permission would be willingly given because of the need for a classical education for their own children, and so occasionally a very good school is found. One such was maintained by Father John Garrigan in the parish of Moybolge and Kilmainham Wood.[45] There remains a description of the school that some traveller got in 1780 from a brother of Dr Thomas Sheridan, friend of Swift and great-uncle of the dramatist, R. B. Sheridan:

> Father Garrigan taught Latin in a corner of that church at the age of eighty. I read Livy under him, and can repeat some of the speeches at this time. We had no translations of the Classics in those days. (The Latin tongue) . . . formed almost the whole of our education—the very shepherds could speak Latin . . . We had many who excelled in the study of the Irish Language too.[46]

There is some degree of support for what he says about Latin in an observation recorded by Dr Thomas Sheridan in a letter to his friend, the Reverend John Magill. He says that he saw the following lines on the window of a house in Dungarvan that sold eggs: *Si sumas ovum, Molle sit atque novum.*[47]

It is no wonder, then, that some of the bards were so well educated in the classical languages. There is a wonderful story about the poet Aodhagán Ó Rathaille entering a book shop in Cork and picking up a book in one of the classical languages—holding it upside down. The shopkeeper told him that it was not his sort of book, but if he could read it, he could have it for nothing. After getting the shopkeeper to repeat his offer in earnest, the poet turned the book right side up and began to read it and translate it easily into English.[48] Another bard, Seán Clárach, is said to have proposed translating Homer into Irish.[49] On his gravestone he is described as *vir vere Catholicus et tribus linguis ornatus nempe Graeca Latina et Hybernica non vulgaris ingenii poeta.*[50] And still another, Donnchadh Ruadh Mac Conmara, composed a Latin elegy for his friend Tadhg Gaedhealach Ó Súilleabháin (1715–95).[51]

But these were undoubtedly exceptions. We must remember that, after all, the poets of this later period were not noblemen as were their predecessors in the Middle Ages. Indeed, in their impoverished state was reflected the fate of the entire race. They were reduced to be 'hewers of wood and drawers of water'; they were labourers for the most part, living with the common people and sharing in their experiences. We will marvel at some of the subjects of their poems unless we remember that, for they include mourning the loss of a sheep, the death of a horse, and searching for a new shovel handle among their themes.[52] But even though Eochaidh Ó hEoghusa, who was at one time poet to Mág Uidhir in Fermanagh, had foreseen the change as early as 1603 (the year he composed *Ionmholta malairt bhisigh* 'A change for the better is to be commended'), the special standing of the bards declined slowly, and the literary tradition weakened only gradually.[53]

In this context, the poem published by T. F. O'Rahilly in *Ériu*, 13 (1942), 113–18, is extremely important, despite its corrupt text. In it, the poet Piaras Feiritéir either names or refers to many of the places where professional bards were living. In the process, he provides evidence for the state of literature in the period. Although the bardic schools could not help being in a wretched state of decline at that time, the poem shows that they were far from having vanished

completely. As Professor O'Rahilly says, here is further testimony
that validates the belief that the poets succeeded in eking out a living
after the Elizabethan Conquest, and that they were not completely
destroyed until the oppression that followed the wars of 1641–50.

§2

Contrary to what one might expect, the beginning of the seventeenth
century was a period of extraordinary literary activity.[54] Indeed,
paradoxically this century was to prove itself one of the richest in the
history of Irish literature—both in prose and poetry.[55] Confronted
with the misfortunes of the period, the literary men seem to have
worked all the harder to keep alive as many elements of the old
tradition as they could. Undoubtedly, the spirit of the Renaissance,
which proved to be such a singular force in the native literatures of
Europe in the fifteenth and sixteenth centuries, was one of the stimuli,
although it, like every other influence from the Continent, was rather
late in reaching Ireland. That produced a remarkable situation: 'In
Europe the Reformation preceded the Counter-Reformation; in
England they synchronized, but in Ireland the Counter-Reformation
was established before the Reformation had made any real headway.
Religious issues were strongly coloured by the new learning, so that
the religio-cultural conflicts were sharper than anywhere else in the
British islands.'[56]

We have already mentioned the work of Flaithrí Ó Maolchonaire,
who translated the Spanish *El Desseoso* into Irish under the title of
Desiderius or *Sgáthán an Chrábhaidh* ('Mirror of Piety'). It was he
who founded the Franciscan College of St Anthony in Louvain in
1606, thus providing a centre for Irish intellectual activity on the
Continent. The establishement of an Irish press there in 1611 was an
important moment in the propaganda war between Catholics and
Protestants. One of the first students of the new college was Giolla
Brighde (Bonaventura) Ó hEoghusa (O'Hussey; *c.* 1575–1614), scion
of a bardic family that had been in the service of Mág Uidhir
(Maguire) of Fermanagh in the sixteenth century.[57] The poetry he
wrote reflects his sorrow at having left Ireland and his friends in the
bardic schools there. As a brother of the Order of St Francis he
became warden of the College and published a didactic volume
entitled *An Teagasg Críosdaidhe* (Christian Doctrine, Catechism), the
first Roman Catholic publication in the Irish language.[58] As it was

written strictly to provide for the spiritual needs of the common people, it marks an important departure from all previous use of the Irish language. Sometime between 1614—the year of his death—and 1619, three of Ó hEoghusa's poems were published in Louvain; there is but one copy extant, preserved in the Cambridge University Library. It is significant that he felt the need to apologise to his erstwhile fellow poets for adopting a simple diction:

> Lé hóradh briathar dá mbeinn,
> mór dhobh fá chiaigh dho chuirfinn . . .
>
> Were I to set about gilding words,
> I should obscure many of them . . .[59]

Another man who played an important part in the early history of the College was Aodh Mac Cathmhaoil (in English, Hugh Mac Caughwell or Caghwell, later MacAingil), (1571–1626).[60] He toiled in Louvain until 1623, when he was summoned to Rome. In June, 1626 he was anointed Bishop of Armagh, but he died the following September before setting out for Ireland. He wrote *Scáthán Shacramuinte na hAithridhe* ('Mirror of the Sacrament of Penance') in 1618, a popular work of Christian doctrine. His style is straightforward and solemn, but rises occasionally to the level of passionate rhetoric.

There were many other Irish books published on the Continent in this period; among them we note:[61]

Catechismvs, seu Doctrina Christiana, Latino-Hibernica . . . Adhon, an Teagasc Críostuí iar na fhoillsiu à Ladin & à Ngaoilaig by Father Theobald Stapleton, a catechism in the form of a dialogue between master and pupil, in both Latin and Irish. It is significant that Stapleton forcibly argued the case for the use of the vernacular to instruct the poor simple lay Irishman; he regretted the fact that so many Irish speakers were taught to say their prayers in broken Latin and to repeat them like parrots, not knowing what they were saying. The *Catechismus* was published in Brussels in 1639—the first Irish (as opposed to Scottish Gaelic) book to be printed in Roman letters, and the first notable attempt at planned simplification of the orthography to reach a wider public.[62]

Parrthas an Anma by Brother Antoin Gearnon (Anthony Gearnon), Louvain, 1645, is largely a simplification of the 1611 Ó hEoghusa catechism, but it proved to be one of the most popular publications in Irish in the seventeenth century.

Suim bhunudhasach an teaguisg chríosdaidhe a bpros agus a ndán by

Father Seán Dubhlaoch (John Dowley), a summary of Christian doctrine with a form of service and prayers; Louvain 1663.

Lóchrann na gCreidmheach or *Lucerna Fidelium* (Rome, 1676) by Froinsias Ó Maolmhuaidh (Francis O'Malloy), the publisher of the *Grammatica Latino-Hibernica* of 1677, which Edward Lhuyd used when he was writing *Archaeologia Britannica*. These works may be considered the product of the Catholic Counter-Reformation. Several of them have been reprinted in the *Scríbhinní Gaeilge na mBráthar Mionúr* series of the Dublin Institute for Advanced Studies.

We owe the translation of the Bible, not surprisingly, to the Protestant Reformation. Five hundred copies of the New Testament in Irish were printed in 1602. A number of scholars are said to have begun the work of translation, but it appears that Uilliam Ó Domhnaill, one of the first students to enroll in Trinity College Dublin (1592) and to be promoted to a Fellowship, took over the responsibility for the translation in the last decade of the sixteenth century. It was he who saw it through the press, although he had the assistance of Domhnall Óg Ó hUiginn with the Irish, and the cost of publication was borne by William Ussher. This was followed by Ó Domhnaill's translation of the Book of Common Prayer in 1608 (he had been made Archbishop of Tuam in 1595), and a new edition of the New Testament in 1681. It was not until 1685 that an edition of the Old Testament in Irish appeared. William Bedell, Bishop of Kilmore, and a number of assistants were responsible for the Old Testament translation, although he had been long dead (7 February 1641/2) before it was published. Irish was not Bedell's native tongue, and that may explain the fact that the Old Testament translation is inferior to that of the New Testament.[63] The Old and New Testaments were published together in 1690.

Most of the Catholic books were published in Louvain, and it is appropriate to refer to their authors as *literati* of the 'Louvain School'. Some of them were descended from the bardic families, and they were all connected with the tradition those families represented. But unlike the literary men of that tradition, these authors addressed the public rather than members of the nobility. They avoided scholarly ambiguity and attempted to be intelligible to all. It is true that their idiom smacks of learned literary prose, but on the whole their attitude was to use the more homely forms of colloquial speech. They borrowed words from Latin when that was necessary, but they refrained from using too many adornments—such as alliteration, and they kept to the point. Modern Irish prose, in fact, begins with them.

If Louvain was the home of a literary school, it was even more so a centre for scholars; one might even say fairly that Louvain was the 'University of Ireland' in the seventeenth century.[64] In 1626, Father Aodh Buidhe Mac an Bhaird (Hugh Ward; 1592/3–1635) was appointed warden of St Anthony's College. He, like Flaithrí Ó Maolchonaire and Giolla Brighde Ó hEoghusa, came from a bardic family and was educated in one of the bardic schools. He conceived the plan of collecting and publishing the Lives of the Saints, but died before the project was completed. His colleague, Father John Colgan (1592–1658), another descendant of a bardic family, carried on the work and published two thick tomes. The first of these sets out the lives of the saints whose feast days occur during the first three months of the year (*Acta Sanctorum . . . Hiberniae . . . tomus primus*, 1645), and the second (*Trias Thaumaturga*) gives the stories of Patrick, Brigit, and Colum Cille.[65] Even though the work of Aodh Buidhe Mac an Bhaird and Colgan was new from the standpoint of its overall plan and style, we must remember that scholars in Ireland had been for some time engaged in the activity of collecting the old materials and imposing order upon them. Maghnus Ó Domhnaill, for example, compiled materials for a life of Colum Cille (*Betha Colaim Chille*) in 1532.[66] We can perhaps view that biography as a typical product of the Renaissance, and Maghnus Ó Domhnaill as a typical Renaissance man.

On the other hand, it must not be assumed that the work of salvaging the native lore from oblivion was left entirely in the hands of the Franciscans after their appearance on the scene. Pádraig de Brún notes that, from the earliest times, Irish scribes seem to have preferred to use their art to preserve material of a ponderous and learned nature rather than material of immediate or (to their mind) transitory interest.[67] He estimates that of some 4,250 Irish manuscripts which have been preserved, hardly 400 were written before the middle of the seventeenth century. At that time, the old learning seems to have been cultivated most assiduously in north Connacht and south-west Ulster, but the tradition there seems to have been weakened gradually. During the two centuries between the coming of Cromwell and the Famine it was in Munster, south-east Ulster and Dublin where scribes began to congregate, that it was most flourishing. Few parts of the country, however, were entirely without scribes. For example, a manuscript was written in Kildare in 1759–60, and a scribe called Séamus Ó Murchú was active in Loch Garman as late as 1799 at least, and, as we shall see, there were districts in the island where scribes were busy up to the time the language revival movement got under way.

Brother Mícheál (Mícheál Ó Cléirigh, 1575–c. 1645), the best known—if the most humble—of a renowned family of historians,[68] was sent back to Ireland by Father Aodh Mac an Bhaird to gather materials for himself, Colgan, and their fellow workers. Contemplating their project, Charles Plummer wrote: 'There is, indeed, hardly to be found in the history of literature a more pathetic tale than that of the way in which Colgan and his fellow workers . . . strove, amid poverty, and persecution, and exile, to save the remains of their country's antiquities from destruction'.[69] Nevertheless, Ó Cléirigh did his job thoroughly. The copies of old manuscripts which he made and sent to Louvain are extant in two thick manuscripts, Brussels Bibl. Roy. 2324–40, and 4190–200; they are the most extensive collections ever made of the lives of Irish saints. But Ó Cléirigh's interests were broad, and it is clear that he worked with the pace of a man who was buying time. After wandering around Ireland for fifteen years collecting historical materials of every kind, he and three others who shared his interests settled into a cottage not very far from the Fanciscan religious house in Drowes in Donegal in 1632 to sort out and arrange the materials.[70] At the end of four years, they gave Ireland the *Annála Rioghachta Éireann*, or as it is more generally known, *The Annals of the Four Masters*.[71]

And that was not Ó Cléirigh's only work. With the help of his colleagues he wrote *Réim Rioghraidhe* ('The Succession of Kings'), *Félire na Naomh nÉrennach* ('Calendar of the Saints of Ireland'), a new edition of *Leabhar Gabhála*, and *Foclóir nó Sanasán Nua* ('Lexicon or New Dictionary')—the only one of his compositions published during his lifetime (in 1643).

The priest Séathrún Céitinn (Geoffrey Keating), c. 1580–c. 1644, was another industrious scholar of the period. In addition to his devotional works,[72] he wrote a history of Ireland called *Foras Feasa ar Éirinn* ('Elements of the History of Ireland'),[73] because it was not fitting, he said, for 'a land as honourable as Ireland and hosts as grand as those that dwelt there to vanish (*dul i mbáthadh*) without a word or mention of them.' Keating is no scientific historian, but he is a master of Irish prose, and the spirit of national pride courses through his entire work. It is no wonder that the *Foras Feasa* has become a classic in the language. Keating spent some time on the Continent, in Bordeaux and perhaps in Rheims as well, and graduated as a Doctor of Divinity. He returned to Ireland about 1610, and it was while he was discharging the duties of a priest that he wrote his celebrated *Foras Feasa*. There is evidence that he travelled the length and breadth of the land in search of material and that he completed the work about 1633 or 1634.

It seems likely that Keating was educated in Irish (in a school of poetry) and in Latin, and that he was made a priest before he left the shores of Ireland. In any case, he gained sufficient mastery over the syllabic metres to compose in them, even if his grasp of them was not completely secure. It is significant that he was a better poet in those new metres that were crowding out the old. In fact, he was one of the poets that gave a big boost to composing *amhráin* in the seventeenth century.[74] If the ascription to him is correct, Keating was the author of the well-known poem 'A bhean lán do stuaim', quoted on p. 185 above.[75] And he would not have been the only one of the friars or priests to compose love songs: others were Pádraigín Haicéad, Liam Inglis, An Caisideach Bán, Uilliam Mac Gearailt and Mánas Ó Ruairc.[76] They say that it was in Louvain that Pádraigín Haicéad (*c.* 1600–54) learned the syllabic metres.[77] Be that as it may, it was at Louvain that he was trained for the priesthood and it was there, after serving in Ireland for a while, that he died, an exile from the land he loved passionately, to judge from his poetry. Indeed, it is fitting that his poetic art reached its zenith in expressing his love for Ireland in 'Chum na hÉireann Tamall roimh Thriall dá hIonnsaighe', or 'Cuirim Séad Suirghe', as it is sometimes called. His experience was truly miserable if the following stanza reflects his true feelings:

> Isan bhFrainc im dhúscadh dhamh,
>   I nÉirinn Chuinn im chodladh;
> Beag ar ngrádh uaidh don fhaire—
>   Do thál suain ar síorfhaire.[78]

Awake I am in France, asleep I am in Ireland; little do I care to be awake, I always try to cultivate longer sleep.

It is likely that this and a few other poems from France were composed after he had received holy orders and was on his way back to Ireland, perhaps in 1632 when he was in Brittany and may have had to tarry there for some time. When he heard that the friars in Ireland had been forbidden to compose poetry of any kind, he composed a song in defence of the poets and their muse.[79]

It appears that the poets of Ireland, like the scholars both at home and abroad, were very conscious of the fact that the old traditions could not be kept alive without a concerted effort. Either in an attempt to breathe new life into the old order or as a challenge to the new, the poets who lived at the beginning of the seventeenth century doubled their efforts and produced what is called *Iomarbhágh na bhFileadh* ('The Contention of the Bards').[80] There was hardly any political design of the old sort behind this debate, such as urging the chieftains of the North and South to compete with one another in doughty deeds against the common enemy. Rather it began when Tadhg mac Daire Mac Bruaideadha (1570–1652) contradicted a boast set forth in two poems by Torna Éigeas, a poet said to have lived in the fifth century (!), and asserted the superiority of the South (*Leath Mogha*, or 'Mug's half') over the North (*Leath Chuinn*, or 'Conn's half'). He, in turn, was answered by Lughaidh Ó Cléirigh, defending the North. Other poets joined in and before it was over, nearly seven thousand lines had been written, and the entire mass of current traditional learning had been paraded before the public. but if the poets' purpose had been to keep the old tradition alive, it was all in vain, and we can sympathize with the bard who wrote an epigram on the 'Contention':

> Lughaidh, Tadhg agus Torna,
>   filí eólcha bhur dtalaimh,
> coin iad go n-iomad bhfeasa
>   ag gleic fan easair fhalaimh.[81]

Lughaidh, Tadhg, and Torna, pre-eminent bards of your land; they are like dogs endowed with great learning, quarrelling over an empty kennel.

Clearly, this poet and many another must have thought that it was absolutely pointless to argue over the superiority of the South or the North when the whole country was fast falling into the hands of the English. Of course, it was inevitable that the poets should renew their interest in their traditions and in the history of the country. The circumstances compelled them to do that, and it would have been remarkable indeed had they been able to compose their poetry without any thought for the condition of the people.

Between June of 1650 and February 1653, the poem *An Síoguidhe Rómhánach* was composed by some anonymous bard who was probably a priest.[82] The poem is cast in the form of a vision, and tells the history of Ireland in that period, mentions the death of Eoghan Ruadh Ó Néill, details various other misfortunes that have befallen the people, and their expectations of deliverance. The most noticeable characteristic of the poem is its simplicity and directness of expression, and the clarity of its vision.

A short time later (between 1655 and 1659), and perhaps in imitation of *An Síoguidhe Rómhánach*, Seán Ó Conaill wrote the historical poem *Tuireamh na hÉireann*.[83] It begins with the story of the flood, but it is clear that the poet was motivated by the hardships which the Irish suffered and to which he was witness.

The scathing satire called *Páirlement Chloinne Tomáis* has been described as 'one of the most important and influential prose compositions in Irish. Its continued popularity throughout the seventeenth, eighteenth, and nineteenth centuries meant that it was assiduously read, copied, and adapted by generation after generation of scribes'.[84] In its best versions it falls into two parts. The first, about twice the length of the second, was written, according to N. J. A. Williams, in Co. Kerry *circa* 1615. The second part, he believes, was written by a different author in or near Co. Westmeath, *circa* 1665.

> The author appears to have been so well acquainted with Irish literature that as well as much else, the *Parliament* is, as it were, the author's personal gloss upon the entire literary tradition up to the early seventeenth century.[85]

Its framework is a burlesque parody of the prose romances, and probably derives in part from the earliest burlesque tales *Bodach an Chóta Lachtna* and *Eachtra an Cheithearnaigh Chaoilriabhaigh*. Much work has been done on its literary debts and its Irish and European analogues since Professor Bergin wrote on it, but his words on the standpoint of the 'author' are still well worth quoting:

> Its author was evidently one of the many men of letters who suffered so severely as a result of the wars and confiscations of the time. After years of careful training in the schools they found their profession had disappeared. The old aristocracy, with whom all Irish learning and literature had been bound up from the start, were gone. Their places were taken by foreign settlers, men from a different world, or by what the student from one of the bardic schools—the nearest thing in the Ireland of that day to the university graduate—looked upon as coarse and brutish peasants, gluttonous and quarrelsome, aping the gentry, trying to dress fashionably, too low to understand the meaning of refinement, and lost in admiration of a man who could talk broken English.[86]

A satire similar to the *Páirlement* is the *Eachtra Chloinne Tomáis Mhic Lóbuis nó Tána Bó Geannain*, a composition dated in the eighteenth century.[87]

There is only a superficial resemblance between *Páirlement Chloinne Tomáis* and *Párliament na mBan* by Domhnall Ó Colmáin, a work which went through several versions between 1670 and 1703. The latter pretends to describe the activities of a 'Parliament of Women', but in fact it is a treatise dealing with lust, anger, jealousy, slander, sloth, drunkenness, false witness, and other sins, and it has now been shown that it is in the main a translation.[88]

In summary, despite the poems of *Iomarbhágh na bhFileadh* and other poems that demonstrate a sensitivity to the condition of the society and a longing to change it, we must acknowledge the fact that the bardic tradition had lost its footing in the seventeenth century. Even so, the practice of composing for the nobility stayed alive nearly throughout the century; strangely enough, one of its last gasps was heard in Central Ulster, an area that had been almost totally possessed by foreigners. There, a eulogy was sung to Cormac Mac Airt Óig Ó Néill by Tadhg Ó Rodaighe (c. 1610–1710) in the year 1680, as the Book of Clanaboy (*Leabhar Cloinne Aodha Buidhe*) shows.[89] Of course, we must remember that the most prolific poets at the end of the sixteenth century were those of the North, and they continued to be so—especially in the counties on the border between Ulster and Leinster—right down to the eighteenth century.[90]

§3

The reversal of the social position of the poets can be traced in the history of such men as Dáibhí Ó Bruadair (c. 1625–1698), Séafradh Ó Donnchadha an Ghleanna (c. 1620–78) and others. The most interesting of these—and the most important in many ways—is Dáibhí Ó Bruadair. At the beginning of his career, he could depend on the nobility for support; at the end, he was compelled to work as common labourer for his livelihood.[91] It is no wonder he felt that fate had played a trick on him, nor are we surprised to hear him say: 'Is mairg nach bhfuil 'na dhubh-thuata'[92] (Woe to him who is not a gloomy boor). He deplores the fact that the old lords have been obliged to flee to the Continent:

> Do chealg mo chom go trom le haicídíbh
>   aistear na gcodhnach lonn do leasaigheadh sinn:
> 'snach faicim ar bonn 'san bfonn do thathuighidís
>   gan easbaidh gan fhoghail acht moghaidh is maistínidhe.[93]

> Pierced hath been my breast severely with full many a disease
>   At the journey of those gallant chiefs who laboured for our weal

For in the land they loved to dwell in now so far as I can see
No one hath been left unrobbed or free from want but serfs and curs.

He pokes fun at those who are trying to speak English:

> Nach ait an nós so ag mórchuid d'fhearaibh Éireann
> d'at go nó le mórtus maingléiseach,
> giodh tais a dtreoir ar chódaibh gallachléire
> ní chanaid glór acht gósta gairbhBhérla.[94]

> How queer this mode assumed by many men of Erin,
> With haughty, upstart ostentation lately swollen,
> Though codes of foreign clerks they fondly strive to master,
> They utter nothing but a ghost of strident English.

But he soon began to realize that it was the English speakers who were getting ahead. He is said to have composed this stanza when the Earl of Ormonde became Lord Lieutenant in 1643/4:

> Mairg atá gan Béarla binn,
> ar dteacht an iarla go hÉirinn;
> ar feadh mo shaoghail ar Chlár Chuinn
> dán ar Bhéarla dobhéaruinn.[95]

> Woe to him who cannot simper English,
> Since the Earl hath come across to Erin;
> So long my life upon Conn's plain continues,
> I'd barter all my poetry for English.

He wrote an eloquent political poem on *Longar Langar Éireann* ('Hurly-Burly of Ireland'), and the final stanza gives us a pretty good idea of the poet's frame of mind:

> Gé shaoileas dá saoirse bheith seasgair sodhail
> im stíobhard ag saoi acu, nó im ghearra-phróbhost,
> ós críoch dhi mo stríocadh go seana-bhrógaibh
> fínis dom sgríbhinn ar fhearaibh Fódla[96]

Here is James Stephen's translation of this and the preceding four verses:

I will sing no more songs! The pride of my country I sang
Through forty long years of good rhyme, without any avail;
And no one cared even the half of the half of a hang
For the song or the singer—so here is an end to the tale!

If you say, if you think, I complain, and have not got a cause
Let you come to me here, let you look at the state of my hand!
Let you say if a goose-quill has calloused these horny old paws,
Or the spade that I grip on, and dig with, out there in the land?

When our nobles were safe and renowned and were rooted and tough,
Though my thought went to them and had joy in the fortune of those,
And pride that was proud of their pride—they gave little enough!
Not as much as two boots for my feet, or an old suit of clothes!

I ask the Craftsman that fashioned the fly and the bird;
Of the Champion whose passion will lift me from death in a time;
Of the Spirit that melts icy hearts with the wind of a word,
That my people be worthy, and get, better singing than mine.

I had hoped to live decent, when Ireland was quit of her care,
As a poet or steward, perhaps, in a house of degree,
But my end of the tale is—old brogues and old breeches to wear!
So I'll sing no more songs for the men that care nothing for me.[97]

In addition to the change in the social status of the poets, Dáibhí Ó Bruadair saw changes in their poetry, too. Remember that the language of the bards up until this period had been a uniform literary language without any dialectal variances. The bardic schools had undoubtedly been responsible for this fact, but the schools had ceased to exist, and in a very short time the linguistic uniformity began to be eroded, and dialectal forms began slowly to creep into the poetry.

Another effect of the closing of the schools was the abandonment of the old metres and the adoption of new ones—namely, the folksong metres, the *amhráin*, which the traditional bard had been loath to accept.[98] They began to appear towards the end of the sixteenth century in the work of Eoghan Mac Craith, Tadhg Dall Ó hUiginn, Keating and Haicéad.[99] But these and later poets were conscious of being the heirs of another tradition, and they retained too much love for their finely cultivated art and too much fondness for precise craftsmanship to adopt the *amhrán* metres unchanged. They first had to experiment in the new metres, and before long they had modified and transformed them into metres adorned with melodious alliteration and ingenious rhymes, and full of unrivalled musical beauty.

But the new metres were not adopted without protest from the conservative members of the older tradition. Dáibhí Ó Bruadair says he is broken-hearted because there is no more true poetry; he goes on to complain that knowledge is so corrupted in Munster that only the lowest, most common poetry can be understood:

Is fusaide féire i bhféith na fochaille fis
nach tuigthear acht sméirlis éigse i bhforba Cuirc.[100]

'Tis easy for their muse to blunder, knowledge now is so corrupt
That in Corc's land nought but vulgar poetry is understood.

Similarly, Aindrias Mac Cruitín (*c.* 1650–1738) complains to James Mac Donnell of Kilkee that he has been constrained to compose 'a left-handed, awkward ditty of a thing, but I have had to do it, to fit myself in with the evil fashion that was never practised in Éirinn before'.[101]

The innovations in language and metre were not simultaneous developments. For example, Seán Ó Neachtain (?1655–1728),[102] a poet who was born in Co. Roscommon and who spent most of his life in Meath, and Séamus Dall Mac Cuarta (?1647–1732),[103] who lived for a while in the same district, both used the standard literary language, but composed mostly in the *amhrán* metres.

It has been said that Séamus Dall Mac Cuarta may be called the father of the Northern School of new poets, a school that had changed its locale, as it were: at the beginning of the seventeenth century, Tirconnell was the home of the majority of these poets, but by the end of that century they were more numerous in South Ulster. Pádraig Mac a Liondain (Mac Giolla Fhiondáin: 1665–1733) is said to have had a 'school' for some time in Cnoc Chéin Mhic Chainte near Dundalk where people learned to read and write Irish manuscripts.[104] Among the most famous of the later bards of the North were Art Mac Cobhthaigh (?1715–73)[105] and Peadar Beag Ó Doirnín (*c.* 1700–69).[106]

Aodhagán Ó Rathaille (*c.* 1670–?1728), already mentioned, may be looked upon as the father of the new poets in Munster.[107] He was but a young man when Dáibhí Ó Bruadair was singing *Longar Langar Éireann*, and the syllabic metres had been almost completely abandoned by the time he began to write. He witnessed the Flight of the Wild Geese, the transplanting of Irishmen to make room for foreigners, the penal laws, and the general subjugation of his people. Among his more notable songs are his elegies and the two poems in which he bemoans the fate of Ireland, 'Créachta Crích Fódhla' and 'An Milleadh d'Imigh ar Mhór-Shleachtaibh na Tíre'. It is no wonder that his poems grow increasingly sadder as he grows older, and if what they say about poets is generally true—that 'their sweetest songs are those that tell of saddest thought', then the poems of Ó Rathaille are among the sweetest in the language.

It would be a mistake, however, to conclude that Ó Rathaille's songs are sentimental or maudlin, for there is an undertone of indignation, of savage indignation, in most of them, and a quiet dignity.

I shall not call for help until they coffin me.
What good for me to call when hope of help is gone?
Princes of Munster that would have heard my cry
Will not rise from the dead because I am alone.

Mind shudders like a wave in this tempestuous mood,
My bowels and my heart are pierced and filled with pain
To see our lands, our hills, our gentle neighbourhood
A plot where any English upstart stakes his claim.

The Shannon and the Liffey and the tuneful Lee,
The Boyne and the Blackwater a sad music sing,
The waters of the west run red into the sea—
No matter what be trumps their knave will beat our king.

And I can never cease weeping these useless tears,
I am a man, oppressed, afflicted, and undone,
Who where he wanders mourning no companion hears
Only some waterfall that has no cause to mourn.

Now I shall cease, death comes and I must not delay
By Laune and Laine and Lee, diminished of their pride,
I shall go after the heroes, ay, into the clay—
My fathers followed theirs before Christ was crucified.[108]

It was Ó Rathaille who made famous the *aisling* type of poem
(a 'dream' or 'vision') that was so popular among his successors.[109]
The basic form of the genre is simple enough. As the poet is
alone, meditating, a beautiful girl approaches him, a maiden
whose beauty absolutely dazzles him. The poet asks her which of the
comely ones of the world she is: Helen of Troy? Deirdre? Cearnait or
Fand? The beauty then reveals herself to be none other than Éire,
that is, Ireland herself, distressed and sorrowed by her great
tribulations.[110]

Some of the *aisling* poems end with the identification of the maiden
as the sorrowful Éire, but others—especially the later ones—go on to
prophesy that the trials and tribulations of Éire will come to an end,
and that her true spouse will come back to her from across the sea.
For most of the Ulster poets, this 'true spouse' was a representative of
the Uí Néill line, but as a rule he was envisioned as one of the Stuarts.
Therefore, the *aisling* developed into a kind of Jacobite song, though
that genre never became in Ireland what its counterpart did in
Scotland. For one thing, there was no reference at all to the Stuarts in
the early *aisling* poems; the only figure in them was the stunningly
beautiful Éire. Secondly, even in the later *aisling* poems in which the

Stuarts are accomodated, Éire continues to be the principal figure, and certainly the only one who arouses love and admiration. And this is an important distinction between the Irish and Scottish attitudes toward the Stuarts: in Scotland the Stuarts in themselves stirred feelings of affection and loyalty; in Ireland they were merely symbols of the hope of deliverance. Éire, the queen that remained captive, was the foremost object of their feelings.[111]

The convention that underlies the *aisling* poems can be traced back to the Old Irish period; it is, in fact, a quite common theme in Celtic stories. A man sees a beautiful woman in his sleep, falls helplessly in love with her, and seeks everywhere for her until he finds her. It is the theme that underlies the Welsh 'Dream (*breuddwyd*) of Macsen Wledig' and the Irish 'Dream (*aislinge*) of Oengus'. And that is merely the reverse of another theme wherein a woman of the fairy folk loves a mortal and entices him to accompany her to the Otherworld, to the land of magic. In that fashion did Fand love Cú Chulainn and Rhiannon Pwyll.[112]

An even closer parallel occurs in those early tales in which the hero meets a woman of the fairy people who prophesies to him. The earliest of these, perhaps, is the *Baile in Scáil* 'Frenzy [in fact, a frenetic vision] of the Phantom', in which the king—Conn Cétchathach—visits the Celtic Otherworld and receives a prophecy concerning his descendants from the god Lugh and a beautiful gold-crowned maiden called *Flaith Érenn* 'the Sovereignty of Ireland'.

Professor O'Rahilly has shown how in earlier times in Ireland the elevation of a man to the kingship was viewed as a marriage with Éire, that is with the earth mother embodied in the land.[113] The marriage of the king with Éire was certainly theoretically a practice designed to assure abundance and success during his reign. The notion is used figuratively by the poets of the nobility when they refer to their patrons as 'worthy spouse of Éire'. On the other hand, Seán Ó Tuama has argued that the pattern of the political *aisling* followed by Eoghan Ruadh and others was influenced by the learned form given to the *reverdie* among the *dánta grádha* at the beginning of the eighteenth century.[114]

James II appears to have been the first foreign king to be accepted as 'true spouse of Éire'. Since he was descended from the Scots, the Irish could consider him as one of their own race; furthermore, the sad fact is that Ireland produced not a single native leader between the fall of Limerick and the time of Daniel O'Connell, a period of over a hundred years. Therefore, the only flag that portended a continuation of the struggle if not fresh hope, was the Stuart flag. Aodhagán Ó Rathaille was one of the first to see hope for deliverance in James II, but there is a mournful, melancholic note in his *aisling* poems, a note heard distinctly in the most famous of them, *Gile na Gile*.

The Brightest of the Bright

The Brightest of the Bright met me on my path so lonely;
    The Crystal of all Crystals was her flashing dark-blue eye;
Melodious more than music was her spoken language only;
    And glorious were her cheeks, of a brilliant crimson dye.

With ringlets above ringlets her hair in many a cluster
    Descended to the earth, and swept the dewy flowers;
Her bosom shone as bright as a mirror in its lustre;
    She seemed like some fair daughter of the Celestial Powers.

She chanted me a chant, a beautiful and grand hymn,
    Of him who should be shortly Éire's reigning King—
She prophesied the fall of the wretches who had banned him;
    And somewhat else she told me which I dare not sing.

Trembling with many fears I called on Holy Mary,
    As I drew nigh this Fair, to shield me from all harm,
When, wonderful to tell! she fled far to the Fairy
    Green mansions of Sliabh Luachra in terror and alarm.

O'er mountain, moor and marsh, by greenwood, lough and hollow,
    I tracked her distant footsteps with a throbbing heart;
Through many an hour and day did I follow on and follow,
    Till I reached the magic palace reared of old by Druid art.

There a wild and wizard band with mocking fiendish laughter
    Pointed out me her I sought, who sat low beside a clown;
And I felt as though I never could dream of Pleasure after
    When I saw the maid so fallen whose charms deserved a crown.

Then with burning speech and soul, I looked at her and told her
    That to wed a churl like that was for her the shame of shames
When a bridegroom such as I was longing to enfold her
    To a bosom that her beauty had enkindled into flames.

But answer made she none; she wept with bitter weeping,
    Her tears ran down in rivers, but nothing could she say;
She gave me then a guide for my safe and better keeping—
    The Brightest of the Bright, whom I met upon my way.[115]

When the Stuart flag was flown over Scotland a new hope
sounded, clearly audible in the poems of Seán Clárach Mac
Domhnaill, one of the most talented poets of the early eighteenth century.[116] But it was a short-lived hope, and its demise
can be glimpsed in the songs of Eoghan Ruadh Ó Súilleabháin.
When it finally died at the end of the eighteenth century, the whole
raison d'être of the *aisling* type of poem was lost, and the
genre survived only as a hackneyed convention. It was said earlier
that Aodhagán Ó Rathaille was father and master of the Munster
school of bards, and that Eoghan Ruadh was the last poet of that
school. But we must remember that the term 'school' here is used
in a very broad sense, and is not to be confused with the schools
of the court poets. And yet it is amazing to contemplate the part
it played in the tradition during this last period, and how influential one poet was upon another. At times, the relationship was quite
personal. For example, Seán Ó Tuama An Ghrinn (*c.* 1708–75)[117]
and Aindrias Mag Craith (An Mangaire Súgach), who died in 1795,
were friends; they in turn were acquaintances of Seán Clárach
(1691–1754). When the latter died, Seán Ó Tuama composed an
elegy to him, and wrote a *barántas* (mock warrant in verse)
calling on his fellow poets to do everything in their power to dam
the English flood, undertaking thereby the responsibility of leading
them. Seán Clárach seems to have been a kind of leader of the
bards' assemblies at his farm in Charleville or in Bruree, Co.
Limerick; when he died Seán Ó Tuama became head of the poets of
Limerick and North Cork. Ó Tuama was one of a remarkable group
of poets living in that part of Co. Limerick called Coshma or Cois
Máighe after the river Máighe or Máigh, a tributary of the Shannon,
which runs through it. Another member was Aindrias Mac Craith.[118]

Seán Ó Tuama became the proprietor of an inn at Croom, perhaps
through marriage. Over its door he put up a sign offering in verse
welcome and hospitality to all true Irishmen even when they were
short of money:

> Níl fánach ná sáir-fhear ar uaislibh Gaoidheal,
> Bráthair den dáimh ghlic ná suairc-fhear groidhe
> I gcás go mbeadh láithreach gan luach na dighe
> Ná go mbeadh fáilte ag Seán geal Ó Tuama roimhe.[119]

> There is neither a wanderer nor a fine fellow of the
> noble race of Gaels,
> Neither a member of the ingenious (bardic) party nor a
> hearty joyous man

> If he happened to be present without the price of a drink
> That would not be welcomed by good Séan Ó Tuama.

It is no surprise that the inn came to be patronized by poets, many of whom could not pay for their drinks, rather to the disgust of Ó Tuama's wife, as we deduce from the following verse:

> Mo mhuirinn-se Muirinn tar muirinnibh áilne críoch;
> Mo mhuirinn do Mhuirinn do mhuirinn ag tál na dighe;
> Cé muirinn le Muirinn mo mhuirinn chun cláir ag suidhe
> Ní muirinn le Muirinn mo mhuirinn gach tráth gan díol.[120]

Muirinn is my love beyond the beautiful Muirinns of the country; my love to Muirinn pouring out drink to a company; though Muirinn delights in my company sitting at the table, she is not pleased at my company's not paying on every occasion.

It is not surprising either that Croom came to be the meeting-place of a bardic court (*Cúirt Éigse Cois Máighe*): it was already the site of four annual fairs, one of which Seán Ó Tuama has described with great detail (*Aonach Chromaidh an tSubhachais*). A modern poet, Robert Farren, has imagined the scene at the inn:

> The bungs are out from Seán Ó Tuama's barrels,
> And Seán sees port like Homer's 'wine-dark seas'
> Go pouring down the poets' open hatches
> And roll the poets round like wrecked triremes.[121]

Drinking there was, of course, but it was not the only pleasure; Ó Tuama, indeed, enumerates others in his quatrain:

> Do b'ait liom-sa ceólta na dteampán,
> Do b'ait liom-sa spórt agus amhrán,
> Do b'ait liom-sa an gloine ag Muirinn dá líonadh,
> Is cuideachta saoithe gan meabhrán.[122]

> I liked the resonant sounds of the drums,
> I liked the sporting and the song,
> I liked the glass with Muirinn filling it
> And the company of wisemen without insobriety.

Seán Ó Tuama and Aindrias Mac Craith had both attended hedge schools and had come away with sufficient knowledge of English and Latin to take up the work of teaching, although Seán does not seem to have taught anywhere except at Croom and there, it is suggested, inside a building. For their time and society they have to be accounted educated men, and one is not surprised that they were joined in their 'court' of poetry by such people as Father Seán Ó Ceallaigh, the parish priest of Ráth Loirc, and Father Nioclás Ó Domhnaill, OFM, a native of Coshma in all probability and the 'Guardian' of the suppressed Franciscan convent of Áth Dara (Adare); indeed, Father Ó Domhnaill is said to have been the 'Sheriff' of the court at one time. Of course, there were other poets with less education, including a tailor and a stone mason. The latter, Brian Ó Flatharta of Brú na nDéise, is said to have been refused admission to the court on his first application, but he was successful on his second, having written in the meantime a poem or song on Binnlisín, a well-known *lios* on the banks of the river Camhaoir near Brú na nDéise:

> Lá meidhreach dá ndeaghas-sa liom féin
> Ar Bhinnlisín aerach an Bhrogha,
> Ag éisteacht le binnghuth na n-éan
> Ag cantain ar ghéagaibh cois abhann.
> An breac taibhseach san linn úd faoi réim,
> Ag rinnce san ngaortha le fonn,
> Más tinn libhse radharc, cluas ná béal
> Tá leigheas ón éag daoibh dul ann![123]

> One jolly morning I went on my own
> On pleasant Binnlisin an Bhroga,
> Listening to the sweet voice of the birds
> Singing on tree-branches by a river.
> The showy fish in that water flourishing,
> Dancing on the river bed with delight,
> If you are sick of seeing, of hearing and of talking,
> It's a cure for your numbness to go there.

Enough has been quoted of the lighter aspect of Seán Ó Tuama's (and his companions') work to explain why Seán himself was nicknamed *An Ghrinn* 'The Joker' or 'The Witty One', 'The Merriman', and why Aindrias Mac Craith was nicknamed *An Mangaire Súgach* 'the Jolly Pedlar'. But there was a more serious side to their work, for although they did not disdain to use their poetry to make fun of one another and to amuse each other, they used it also in the performance of their role as custodians of their country's honour and self-respect.

Mac Craith already had a reputation for wenching and drinking when he made pretence of leanings towards Protestantism, doubtless for some material advantage. Though he later disavowed his pretended conversion, he had already incurred the wrath of both the Protestant minister and the Catholic priest of the district; he wrote humorously

to Seán Ó Tuama that now his only recourse was to become an
Arian or a Calvinist. In his reply Seán Ó Tuama reminded his
friend:

Má's aineamh ort bheith greannamhar i ráidhtibh suilt
Feasach fuinte fearamhail 's go fáilteach fliuch
Geala-spirid na fairsinge bheith táithte libh—
Is fada tusa ceangailte insna cáilibh sin.[124]

If it is a blemish on you to be merry at times of gaiety,
To be wise, firm, manly and with a well-oiled welcome,
And the fine spirit of generosity joined with you,
Long have you been bound in those qualities.

But at the same time he says:

Geallaim duit, a dhalta dhil, 's a ghrádh mo chuirp,
An ceangal tugas cheana dhuit, an pháirt 's an cion
Go mairfid sin go scarfa thusa an bás is mé
Bí it mhangaire, it phrotestan, nó it phápaire![125]

I promise you, my dear lad and all my love,
The bond that I made with you, the partnership and the
friendship,
That will last until you part death and me,
Be you a pedlar, a Protestant or a Papist.

On the other hand, when a Dominican friar named Denis
Hedderman went over to the Protestant fold, no less than two or three
poets felt it incumbent upon them to address poems to Seán Ó Tuama
expressing their indignation and their concern for the present and
future of their people. He replied in a poem, perhaps the most
vigorous to come from his pen, and certainly one composed with a
seriousness that showed that he appreciated the gravity of the
implications for his country.

It is poems like this that prompted Daniel Corkery to claim for
the work produced by the poets of the Maigue that they were classical because they were truly natural and truly national, expres-
sive in every way of the feelings of the community and characterized
by a perfect blending of form and content. Corkery refers to
Brunetière's opinion that a classical literature is natural, national and
exemplary and quotes the passage in which he defines what makes a
classic:

Un classique est classique parce que dans son œuvre toutes les facultés
trouvent chacune son légitime emploi,—sans que l'imagination prenne

le pas sur la raison, sans que la logique y alourdisse l'essor
de l'imagination, sans que le sentiment y impiète sur les droits du
bon sens, sans que le bon sens y refroidisse le chaleur du sentiment,
sans que le fond s'y laisse entrevoir dépouillé de ce qu'il doit
emprunter d'autorité persuasive au charme de la forme, et sans que
jamais enfin la forme y usurpe, un intérèt qui ne doit s'attacher qu'au
fond.

One feels that Corkery is making rather extravagant claims for
the work of the poets of the Maigue, for he does not seem to notice
the unevenness and occasional trivialness. But at the same time one
has to admit that working within a tradition and under a discipline imposed by it, weak though it had become (compared with its
power in earlier ages) these poets achieved a degree of perfection
in form far above that which one expects from peasant or folk poets.
Of their poetry as of Irish poetry in preceding centuries, it can
be said that its beauty is derived as much from the excellence
of the tradition which conditioned it as from the genius of the
individual poets who composed it. The truth is that the poets of
the Maigue were almost as much school poets as their predecessors
had been since the dawn of Irish literature, evidenced among other
things in the way they parade their learning and regard it as
indispensable.

That quality is apparent when we compare their work with that
of Aodh Ó Domhnaill, a cobbler in An t-Áth Leacach (Athlacca,
Co. Limerick) who died in 1845. His work remained for the most
part unpublished and unstudied until fairly recently. His command
of language and metre is not comparable to that of his predecessors in Coshma. Besides being a poet he was a scribe, and it is
thought that he had some manuscripts belonging to Seán Clárach
and Aindrias Mac Craith in his possession when he died. It is certain that he had some manuscripts of his own, but they were
burnt sometime in the early years of this century by the last
member of the family when she left An t-Áth Leacach to enter a
convent. No doubt she thought that no one would ever again be
interested in the manuscripts or in the language in which they were
written.

Sometimes the relationships within traditional boundaries were
more social. There is no better example than that provided by the
history of the poets of Blarney and Whitechurch, Co. Cork.[126] Clan
Cárthaigh (the McCarthys), perhaps the oldest noble family in
Ireland, had a residence near Blarney. In the same vicinity was a

family that had provided poets for the McCarthys for centuries. But like other members of the nobility, the McCarthys fell upon hard times and their last local poet was Tadhg Ó Duinnín. When there was no longer any place for him, he says,

> Mo cheard ó mheath le malairt dlighe i nÉirinn,
> Mo chrádh go rach gan stad le bríbhéireacht.

> Because my craft has faded in the wake of a new order
> in Ireland, alas, I must now take up brewing forthwith.

As a response to this, Eoghan Ó Caoimh (1656–1726), a poet from Duhallow, proclaims:

> A Thaidhg, ó bhraithim go rachair le bríbhéireacht,
> Rachad-sa sealad ag bearradh gach cíléara.[127]

> Tadhg, now that I see you taking up brewing,
> I will take up skimming cream for a while.

What really happened was that Tadhg took up farming. As for Eoghan Ó Caoimh, when his wife and child died he took holy orders and died a priest in the parish of Doneraile.[128]

When Tadhg Ó Duinnín turned to farming, the bardic school of Blarney (*Damhscoil na Blarnann*) was doomed; the tradition, however, was carried on in a different form. As might be expected, the poets that had enjoyed the warm society of their own schools were bound to want some kind of relationship with one another, and they did succeed in holding assemblies. Interestingly enough, the name they gave to these assemblies was *cúirt*, that is, a law court or court of judgment, and the notion of giving a verdict, passing judgment is implicit in every reference to the *cúirt* found in poems. The bard who presided over such a meeting was called 'sheriff' or 'high sheriff'. It was his responsibility to call the poets together, although he received help in doing that from another officer of the *cúirt*, the 'registrar'. Earlier, the expression used for a summoning of the bardic school was *gairm scoile*, but in the eighteenth century the summons was called *barántas*, a borrowing from English *warrant*, and it began usually with the English 'Whereas'. The *barántas* was often full of humour, and it would be easy to misjudge the role the *cúirt* played in the poet's life if we did not keep in mind that the *barántas* itself was no more than an invitation passed from hand to hand, much like the invitations used by some artists' associations.

A number of these *barántaisí* are extant, many of them, as already suggested, jocular and sportive in tone, like this one by Seán Clárach:

Whereas this day a great complaint is come before me
By our friend Diarmuid, an file aniar ó Bhun Leacaí
That Seón Gallda millteoir mealltach de shíol na Seoirsí
Ba mhinic i dteannta tré a chuid geallta 's ag siubhal póirsí
Most felonious and erroneous *contemptor Juris*
Do ghoid an fleascach iubhrach leastair do bhí i gcumhdach
Ag Neilli insa bhfeircín i gcóir an chonntais . . .[129]

There are others more serious in nature, such as that sent by Seán Ó
Tuama and addressed to those who wanted to see the old Irish order
preserved (*do gach aon ler mian athnuadhadh na sean-nós
nÉireannach*), urging them to attend a meeting in Croom in memory
of Seán Clárach. In it the poet insists that what little Irish remains is
sure to vanish utterly, 'unless we do our very best to help each other
willingly and with singleness of purpose to preserve it' (*muna
bhféacham meón-dícheallach le cuidiughadh go caoin caomhchumaim
le chéile go toileamhail re n-a coiméad ar bun*).[130]

Why was the assembly of poets called a 'court'? The reason that has
been suggested—and there does not appear to be a better one—is this:
in Gaelic Ireland in the eighteenth century, the court of law was the
only institution graced by tradition and dignity. The old nobility with
their castles and palaces had vanished, and the Catholic Church had
been deprived of its edifices and its colourful and musical ceremony.
The law court, therefore, despite the fact that it was by this time quite
alien from the standpoint of language, spirit, and atmosphere, was
the only institution that could—in the eyes of the poets—rejoice in its
tradition and dignity. And that is why the poets modelled their
assemblies on it. Furthermore, the concept of judging between good
and bad, which is a basic principle in the law court, was germane to
notions of excellence in the poetic art.

The *cúirt* was held in the local 'Big House', if that happened to be in
the possession of an Irish family, or in the house of the chief poet (the
'sheriff' or 'high sheriff'), or in some historical spot in the
neighbourhood. Later on, the practice of holding the *cúirt* in a tavern
became widespread. The assembly would usually coincide with some
important event, such as a fair, a marriage, or the burial of some
highly respected personage. In fact, any occasion that brought
together people from the nearby districts would suffice. During the
meeting, the poets would recite the poems they had composed since
the last *cúirt*; songs that, for the most part, were about events and
things of local interest.

The first bard to preside over the *cúirt* of the Blarney poets was

Diarmaid Mac Seáin Bhuidhe Mhic Cárthaigh (c. 1630–1715).[131] He was educated in the bardic tradition, but was not blessed with much poetic inspiration; most of his work consists in elegies on members of the McCarthy clan who died during his lifetime. One of his poems, however, deserves special attention, because it provides some insight into these new poets and their times.

When he was old and in poor health, his horse died. Naturally, this was a severe loss for him, and he composed a poem about it entitled *An Fhalartha Ghorm* ('The Black Palfrey').[132] The argument of the poem depicts the bard as old and decrepit, and now without his horse. Because of this terrible misfortune he can no longer traverse the mountains, he cannot go to Mass, he cannot attend funerals. Therefore, his friends had better give him a new horse, or he will satirize them before the poets. There are those living across the sea, he says, who would gladly give him a new horse and a saddle as well—if they had the opportunity. And here he takes off on his favourite theme, the flight of the nobles across the sea.

The poem encouraged other bards in the district to write, and some 200 lines in all were produced. The gap between the young and the old is very apparent in the poetry: the old are looking back with longing to the good old days when there was an aristocracy that maintained the bards in a dignified fashion. The young had never seen those days and they are impatient with the old for looking backwards.

An Fhalartha Ghorm is typical of many poems composed during this period. For one thing, it was based on an actual event; furthermore, it was composed for a society of poets. Though its emotions are rather naïve, it is not without artistic merit. Diarmaid Mac Cárthaigh (to use the short form of his name), like Dáibhí Ó Bruadair before him, realized that the old order had passed. He saw the bardic school of Blarney reduced to a bardic court, he saw the old metres and diction relinquished. In fact, he himself used the new metres and the everyday language of the people (*caint na ndaoine*).

When James II succeeded to the throne and Irish Catholic soldiers were made officers in the army in Ireland, Irishmen believed that a new world was dawning on them. Diarmaid Mac Cárthaigh believed it too, and composed a spirited poem expressing the hope of his people.

> Céad buidhe re Dia in ndiaidh gach anfaidh
> 'S gach *persecution* chugainn dár bagradh,
> Rí gléigeal Séamus ag Aifrionn
> I Whitehall is gárda sagart air . . .

'You Popish rogue!' ní leomhaid labhairt rinn;
Ach 'Cromwellian dog!' is focal faire againn
Nó 'Cia súd thall?' go teann gan eagla.
'Mise Tadhg,' géadh teinn an t-agallamh.

'A hundred thanks to God after each fearful storm
And each persecution that menaced us heretofore.
James, the illustrious sovereign, is hearing Mass
In Whitehall, surrounded by priests as bodyguards . . .

'You Popish rogue!' they won't dare say to us;
But 'Cromwellian dog' is the watchword we have for them
Or 'Cia súd thall' [who's there], said sternly ánd fearlessly,
'Mise Tadhg' [I am Tadhg—sobriquet for an Irish
          Catholic], though constrained the dialogue.[133]

Needless to say, this hope like so many others was dashed to the ground.

We do not know whether Diarmaid Mac Cárthaigh was anything besides a poet, but his successor as president of the *cúirt*, Liam an Dúna Mac Cáirteáin (*c.* 1670–1724), was a soldier. He served in one of the armies of James, and when the war was over, he settled in Whitechurch, a few miles from Blarney, and farmed there. He, in turn, was succeeded by Liam Ruadh Mac Coitir (d. 1738),[134] and then by Seán na Ráithíneach. Seán was born in 1700 and lived in the shadow of the McCarthys; at one time he served them in the capacity of clerk. It appears that he was bailiff to the civil court for a time, but could not endure the work for long.

Ó's duine dhen dáimh sinn tá síos d'easbhaidh na dtriath,
Gan tideal in n-árd dhlighe d'fhagháil puinn eatortha riamh,
Rithfead dom gháirdín, ránn mhín glacfad mar riaghail,
Is cuirfead an bháillidheacht fá thrí i n-ainm an diabhail.[135]

Since I am one of that company that is impoverished from
the lack of nobility, not permitted under the mighty law to
receive anything from them, I will run to my garden, take
shovel in hand, and the devil with being a bailiff.

The death of Seán na Ráithíneach in 1762 marks the end of the court of bards in Blarney and Whitechurch. Of course, there were other courts, but not apparently outside Munster. Cúirt na mBúrdún, also called Cúirt Eigse Uí Macoille, deserves to be mentioned if only for the colourful accounts of it which have been preserved in popular memory.[136] Held in the eastern part of Co. Cork at a place where three parishes meet, Baile Mhac Oda (Ballymcoda), Cill Liath and Cluain Prochais, it was established about 1744 and continued to meet until about 1795. Although the president or *ard-fhile* was appointed initially for only three years, he remained in office until someone superior to him in poetry appeared or until he moved away from the district or died. For most of the time the Cúirt was in existence, its president was Piaras Mac Gearailt (1709–?1791),[137] the author of *Rosc Catha na Mumhan* ('The Munster War-Song'). The symbol of his office and the sign that the Cúirt was in session was the *bata na bachaille*, a crozier-like staff, although shorter than a bishop's crozier, painted yellow and white apart from the crook, which was decorated. There was, according to tradition, some writing on it. There was a 'ceangal na cúirte' which ran

> Gléasfam Cúirt cois abhann ag Fannuisc air,
> Agus cuirfeam ina suí i ag Bata na Bachuille;
> Ansan gheobhaidh trial i measc trí ceathrar,
> Agus más daor é—a chúis i láthair boird,
> Le feidhm go dtachtfam é.

The condition of Irish literature during this period is clearly reflected in the condition of the men who produced it. Whereas the literary men of the Middle Ages were wealthy men who insisted upon and received support and respect from the society, those of the later era were hardly able to sustain themselves at all. Most of them spent their lives in abject poverty. Aodhagán Ó Rathaille, Brian Merriman, and Piaras Mac Gearailt all died poor. Eoghan Ruadh Ó Súilleabháin and Cathal Buidhe Mac Giolla Ghunna not only died in poverty but in the loneliness of a sick-house.

Moreover, the poets of the Middle Ages worked within a very strict tradition, composing their songs with a near fanatical reverence for literary convention—so much so that we are more concerned with the tradition that underlies their work than with the poets as artists. The later poets, on the other hand, were compelled to stand on their own feet, and it is no wonder that their personalities are more evident in their works than were those of their predecessors.

One of the first to use poetry extensively as a vehicle of personal expression was Dáibhí Ó Bruadair; Eoghan Ruadh Ó Súilleabháin (1748–84), who came later, was another. It is difficult to imagine a more colourful character, or one whose career was more wretched, than the poet Eoghan Ruadh. For details of his life we are indebted apart from folklore to his poems. In early manhood he seems to have been a *spailpín*, a migrant worker, and intermittently a schoolmaster. He seems to have gone to England some time before the beginning of 1777, to have joined the army or the navy—there is a suggestion that he was 'pressed' to join—and to have remained there until 1778. The following year he was back in Ireland earning a living as a migrant worker and a schoolmaster, but the wanderlust must have seized him again for he took part as a sailor in the naval battle between the English and the French off Port Royal in the West Indies on 12 April, 1782. He celebrated the English victory by composing an English song in praise of Admiral Rodney, 'Rodney's Glory', hoping, thereby, to obtain his discharge.

There is a story that he eventually got his discharge by wounding himself, and that he returned to Kerry to open a school in Knocknagree, a village only a few miles away from his birthplace, but it did not last long. In the summer of 1784, so the story goes, he visited Colonel Daniel Cronin (Dónal Ó Cróinín) of Park, near Killarney. Cronin had just been promoted colonel, and Eoghan Ruadh seized the opportunity to compose a praise poem in his honour in English. For some reason, Cronin paid no attention to the poem, and the poet therefore received nothing for it. That angered him so that he made a scathing satire against Cronin. A short time afterwards, we are told, Eoghan Ruadh encountered some of Cronin's men in a Killarney tavern. There was a quarrel, and a fight ensued. Cronin's coachman is said to have struck the poet with a pair of fire tongs. One blow was sufficient, and Eoghan Ruadh returned to Knocknagree, his head swathed in bandages. By the time he arrived there he was in the throes of a fever. He was removed to a sick-house about 200 yards from the village, with no one to wait upon him but an old woman—a kind of visiting nurse—who used to look in on the invalids there. Finally, his temperature abated and he was recuperating, but, it is said, 'an act of self-indulgence brought on a relapse from which he never rallied'. As the end drew near, he sat up in bed, called for pen and paper, and began to write his death-bed song—a song of repentance, as was the custom of the Irish poets. But, alas, he was weaker than he supposed: the pen slipped from his hand and tumbled to the floor as he softly whimpered:

> Sin é an file go fann
> Nuair thuiteann an peann as a láimh.

> There's a weak poet for you
> When the pen falls out of his hand.

And he lay back to die silently.[138] As Daniel Corkery observed, Eoghan Ruadh was a poet at heart until the end, 'no matter to what misguided uses the rough racket of the world had put him while he lived'.[139]

Eoghan Ruadh's *An Spealadóir* ('The Mower') has been described as a masterpiece of the *aisling* form, and although we know nothing of the circumstances in which it was composed (beyond a laconic note in the manuscripts that the poet was working as a harvest labourer at the time on the banks of the Blackwater near Mallow, in Co. Cork), the imaginative introduction by Donal O'Sullivan to his translation of the poem seems very much to the point:

> The day's mowing is over, and the harvesters are gathered for an evening's diversion in the spacious farmhouse kitchen, Owen among them: a stocky figure in his frieze coat and knee-breeches, the handsome, intellectual face somewhat out of harmony with a pair of hands that have been roughened and reddened by the scythe. There is ale for those who call for it, and whiskey as well; and the night is spent in singing and story-telling, the gossip of the countryside and dancing with the girls.
>
> There have been jigs, reels, set-dances, and now the fluter starts a hornpipe. The couples move to take the floor, but not Owen. He sits pensive in a corner by the turf fire, wondering where has he heard that captivating melody before. He remembers now. It was on the fo'c's'le deck of his ship as she lay in the Downs, the night before they set sail for the West Indies. The sailors were dancing to it clumsily, most of them three sheets in the wind, having spent their last shore-leave as sailors do.
>
> A queer name it had too, if only he could recall it. Was it not—? Yes, it was! 'Come ashore, Jacky Tar, with your trousers on!' He laughed to himself as he thought of the time they lay off Port Royal on the morrow of Rodney's victory over the French: how he swopped his working dress of short skirt and peaked cowl for his bell-bottomed trousers and round cap (number one rig, the English sailors called it) before taking the liberty-boat to meet the girls waiting on the steps at the end of the old mole. Good times, those were!
>
> The music continues, but now his face grows graver beneath his flaming hair. What is making him so mind-weary and heart-sore? Not mowing to be sure, for he is used to physical labour and doesn't mind it. No, but the knowledge that he and his like—poets, men of learning, heirs of an ancient and honourable tradition—are condemned to a degraded existence by the tyrannical rule of the upstart and ignorant foreigner. And so, almost without conscious effort on his part, his thoughts shape themselves to the rhythm of the melody:

Mo léan le lua 'gus m'atuirse!
'S ní féar do bhuain ar teascannaibh
D'fhúig céasta buartha m'aigine
Le tréimhse go tláth.

My grief to mention, and my affliction!And it is not the journey-work of making hay/That has left my mind troubled and in anguish/And weak for a spell . . .

> Alas! alack! and well-a-day!
> 'Tis not the task of mowing hay
> Has left my mind so sad to-day,
>   Dejected and sore.
> But the thought of those I hold most dear,
> The bard and sage, in bondage drear,
> Despised and mocked both far and near
>   On Erin's green shore.

And the noble band of heroes grand whose fathers came from Spain,
That on the field would never yield but proudly fought amain,

> By treacherous wiles of knavery
> All sunk in darkest slavery,
> Their lands, their homes, once fair and free,
>   Now know them no more!.

> Yestreen I lay in pensive mood,
> My thoughts on men of Gaelic blood,
> The race that rightly held each rood
>   Of famed Inisfáil,
> Now brought to such a grievous pass
> By English whelps and thieves, alas!
> The churls that falsely spurn the Mass,
>   The priesthood, and all:

Now sore distressed, by grief oppressed, aye, hungry and athirst,
The wretched pawn of devil's spawn, by aliens accursed.

> As on our woes my thoughts I kept,
> With breaking heart salt tears I wept,
> Till magic slumber o'er me crept
> And held me in thrall.

> As in my dream I wandered far,
> Upon my path I met a star,
> More fair than earthly maidens are,
>   More gracious, more kind:
> Her glossy tresses, flowing free
> Like spume upon a troubled sea,
> Came tumbling downward to her knee,

And streamed in the wind.
Upon her snood blithe Cupid stood, his quiver full of darts,
As poets tell, with intent full to penetrate the hearts
      Of all who, greatly venturesome,
      To greet this lovely maid might come,
      Whence heroes bold were stricken dumb,
         To death were resigned.

      Her gentle voice was soft and low,
      Like harmonies of long ago
      On harp or magic viol, though
         'Tis wildly I speak:
      Her skin the lily put to shame,
      Her posture that of swan on stream,
      Her chiselled brows a classic frame
         For roses in cheek:
Her shapely breast still unconfessed to lovers who deceive,
Her fingers deft at warp and weft a tapestry would weave.
      Emboldened by her gracious mien,
      I ventured on the tranquil scene,
      And modestly approached my queen,
         Her lineage to seek.

      'Art thou the lady whom to gain
      Dread Tailc Mac Treóin crossed o'er the main,
      When thousands were in battle slain,
         And died in their gore?
      Or Helen fair, the Grecian bride,
      Who, ravished to Scamander-side,
      Brought down on Troy destruction's tide,
         So famous in lore?
Or Deirdre frail who set her sail from Alba o'er the sea,
For whom were slain on Navan's plain the noble brothers three?
      Or the light-o'-love called Dervorgill,
      A name that history echoes still,
      For 'twas through her that foreign ill
         First touched on our shore?'

      She answered me between her sighs,
      But gently still, with limpid eyes,
      'I'm none of those whom you surmise,
         Famed though they be:
      Behold in me the rightful Queen,
      The spouse of Charles, though now, I ween,
      You see in mine a tragic mien,
         With my hero o'er sea.

But God is good and, by the rood on which He died for men,
He soon will chase the foreign race out our land again.
I'll pity not the treacherous horde
When once they're smitten by the Lord,
My harp will sound a joyful chord
For the Gaels will be free!

'As ancient seers and prophets tell,
Who con and read the omens well,
A fleet will brave the ocean swell
On Saint John's Day;
From Munster's lands 'twill put to rout
Each portly, thieving English lout,
They'll one and all be driven out
And swept far away.
The gleaming spears, the gun that sears, will banish them at last,
The greedy swine who swilled their wine and scorned the Friday fast.
And when at last the Gaels arise,
The music of the Saxon sighs
Will bring more gladness to mine eyes
Than the mower's sweet lay!'[140]

Eoghan Ruadh won a special place for himself in the affections of the people of his district. Stories were woven around him, and some of his songs—and it should be remembered that most of his compositions were written to be sung—were popular with the Irish speakers of Munster down to the beginning of the present century. To his own people he was a master craftsman, Eoghan an Bhéoil Bhinn—Eoghan Sweet-Mouth—and there was something in the pathetic misadventures of his life that endeared him to them.[141]

Later critics differ in their estimation of his work. To some of them Eoghan Ruadh was nothing more than a poet working at the end of a tradition, content to use old themes and old ideas, and without a spark of originality in his work. His one virtue, they admit, is his mellifluousness. To others, his work offers much more. As Daniel Corkery observes:

Eoghan Ruadh's gifts, then, were manifold: there was that intellectuality that so effectually staved off the sentimental; there was that intuitional sense of form which accounts for the perfect articulation of his most winged lyrics; there was that freshness of vision which accounts for his daring epithets; there was, above all, his thirst for music, his lyric throat. Of these great gifts he did not make the most; but how could he have done so, even were his passions less violent and his will-power greater, in the Irish Munster of his day?

What was all that land but a death-stricken country, an outland, one might say, far from the stir of life? In such a land he could have done nothing were it not for those thousands of other Gaelic poets who for a thousand years had been using the Gaelic language and enriching the Gaelic mind.[142]

Eoghan Ruadh is considered to be the last of the poets of Munster. With him the procession of poets to which Aodhagán Ó Rathaille may be seen as progenitor comes to a halt, and the bardic tradition is ended.

About the time that Eoghan Ruadh died, Antoine Rafteirí (c. 1784–1835) was born in Co. Mayo, but he spent most of his life in Co. Connacht composing verses and playing his violin. His verses were remembered by the people, and perhaps it seems fitting that they were collected and published by one of the architects of the revival of the Irish language and its literature, Douglas Hyde.[143]

Brian Merriman (c. 1748–1805) stands rather outside the tradition. He was born in Ennis, Co. Clare, and died in Limerick where he taught mathematics. About twenty-five years before his death he composed *Cúirt an Mheadhon Oidhche* ('The Midnight Court'), a poem of 1,026 lines.[144] In it he describes a parliament of women discussing an issue very dear to their hearts: that the young men of Ireland are hesitant to marry, and when they do they marry the old for their money and property. In the course of the discussion and debate—for the men are represented too—some very revolutionary ideas are proposed. For example, the notion of clerical celibacy is challenged: why should not priests be allowed to marry, for they are as capable as anyone of keeping a woman and raising children.

> What is the use of the rule insane
> That marriage has closed to the clerical clan
> In the church of our fathers since first it began.
> It's a melancholy sight to a needy maid
> Their comely faces and forms displayed,
> Their hips and thighs so broad and round,
> Their buttocks and breasts that in flesh abound,
> Their lustrous looks and their lusty limbs,
> Their fair fresh features, their smooth soft skins,
> Their strength and stature, their force and fire,
> Their craving curbed and uncooled desire.
> They eat and drink of the fat of the land,
> They've wealth and comfort at their command,
> They sleep on beds of the softest down,
> They've ease and leisure their lot to crown,

They commence in manhood's prime and flood,
And well we know that they're flesh and blood!
If I thought that sexless saints they were
Or holy angels, I would not care,
But they're lusty lads with a crave unsated
In slothful sleep, and the maids unmated.
We know it is true there are few but hate
The lonely life and the celibate state;
Is it fair to condemn them to mope and moan,
Is it fair to force them to lie alone,
To bereave of issue a sturdy band
The fruit of whose loins might free the land?
Tho' some of them ever were grim and gruff,
Intractable, sullen and stern and tough,
Crabbed and cross, unkind and cold,
Surly and wont to scowl and scold,
Many are made of warmer clay,
Affectionate, ardent, kind and gay;
It's often a woman got land or wealth,
Store or stock from a priest by stealth,
Many's the case I call to mind
Of clergymen who were slyly kind,
I could show you women who were their flames,
And their children reared beneath false names;
And often I must lament in vain
How they waste their strength on the old and plain
While marriageable maids their plight deplore
Waiting unwooed thro' this senseless law;
'Tis a baleful ban to our hapless race
and beneath its sway we decay apace.[145]

The work has been praised more than once as an example of a poem by a bard rebelling against tradition in order to introduce an element of realism into his native literature.[146] But it would be easy to overemphasize the novel in Brian Merriman's poem. It is true that naturalism was sweeping the Continent in the eighteenth century and that Merriman may have known about the ideas of Voltaire and Rousseau. But the source of realism in his poetry may have been much closer to home; it may have been in the life of the country people. After all, there is considerable realism in many a ballad, and, in fact, strains of it may be traced from the beginnings of Irish literature. Consider the passage in which Merriman describes an illegitimate child:

Ní seirgtheach fann ná seandach feósach,
Leibide cam ná gandal geóiseach,
Meall gan chuma ná sumach gan síneadh é,
Ach lannsa cumusach buinneamhach bríoghmhar
Ní deacair a mheas nach spreas gan bhrígh
Bheadh ceangailte ar nasc ar teasc ag mnaoi,
Gan chnámh gan chumus gan chumadh gan chom,
Gan ghrádh gan chumann gan fuinneamh gan fonn,
Do scaipfeadh i mbroinn d'éan mhaighre mná
Le catachus draghain an groidhre breágh.[147]

He isn't a dwarf or an old man's error,
A paralytic or walking terror,
He isn't a hunchback or a cripple
But a lightsome, laughing gay young divil.
'Tis easy to see he's no flash in the pan;
No sleepy, good-natured, respectable man,
Without sinew or bone or belly or bust,
Or venom or vice or love or lust,
Buckled and braced in every limb
Spouted the seed that flowers in him.

Despite the directness of these lines, its tone is not more realistic than that of *An Chailleach Bhéara*, a poem that belongs to the eighth or early ninth century.[148] 'The Old Hag of Béare' was probably a mythological figure at first, but in the poem, which constrasts the exuberance of youth with the inevitable mortification of years and the decrepitude of old age, the poet adapts her to his own purposes. He has her speak as an old woman who has become a nun in her last days after a reckless and extravagant youth. Throughout the poem he stresses mutability and the inevitable death that overtakes man in old age. The old woman's life is at ebb, but unlike the ebb of the sea, this one will never flow again:

Céin mair insi mora máir
dosn-ic tuile íarna tráig;
    os mé, ní frescu dom-í
    tuile tar éisi n-aithbi.

Happy island of the main:
To you the tide will come again
But to me it comes no more
Over the blank, deserted shore.[149]

An Chailleach Bhéara reminds us that women figure only rarely among historical poets and authors of the medieval and modern literature, even though—as in the case of the mythical Cailleach Bhéara—they are sometimes represented as the speakers of dramatic lyrics. Thus some of the tenderest love songs were put in the mouths of women.

> Lad of the curly locks
>   Who used to be once my darling.
> You passed the house last night
>   And never bothered calling.
> Little enough 'twould harm you
>   To comfort me and I crying,
> When a single kiss from you
>   Would save me and I dying.
>
> If only I had the means
>   'Tis little I'd think of giving
> To make a land of my own
>   To the place where my lad is living.
> Trusting in God that I'd hear
>   The sound of his hasty paces,
> For I'm many a night awake,
>   Longing for his embraces.
>
> I thought you were sun and moon
>   When first I met you, my darling.
> And then you seemed to me
>   Like snow on the hills at morning.
> And after that I was sure
>   You were God's own lantern swaying
> Or the North Star over my head
>   To keep my foot from straying.
>
> You said I'd have shawls and shoes,
>   Satin and silk hereafter,
> And said if I went away
>   You'd follow me through the water.
> But now an old bush in a gap
>   Is all that you are leaving.
> As I mind my father's house
>   At morning and at evening.[150]

But in Ireland, as in many another land, the woman's lot was to look after her husband and family, and when disaster struck—as it often did—the greatest share of the anguish fell to her. At least one of these turned her grief into poetry: when Art Ó Laoghaire was killed by an Englishman in 1773 for refusing to sell his champion racehorse for five pounds (under the Penal Laws, no Irishman was allowed to own a horse of greater value than that), his wife Eibhlín Dubh Ní Chonaill composed an elegy to him, *Caoineadh Airt Uí Laoghaire* ('The Lament for Art O'Leary').[151] There is some doubt about the nature of its textual tradition, but the *Caoineadh* breathes a certain sincerity from beginning to end. Eibhlín tells the story of their marriage, and describes how her husband pampered her in their new household:

> Do chuiris gan dearmad
> Párlús d'á ghealadh dham,
> Rúmanna d'á mbreacadh dham,
> Bácús d'á dheargadh dham,
> Bric d'á gceapadh dham,
> Rósta ar bhearaibh dham,
> Mairt d'á leagadh dham,
> Cóir mhaith leapthan dam
> Codladh i clúmh lachan dam.

> You gave me everything.
> There were parlours whitened for me,
> Bedrooms painted for me,
> Ovens reddened for me,
> Loaves baked for me,
> Joints spitted for me,
> Beds made for me
> To take my ease on flock . . .[152]

Despite the magnitude of her grief, Eibhlín Dubh does not lose sight of her nobility. In fact, pride and grief come together in this sad song, and there is a special significance in the conclusion:

> Stadaidh anois d'bhúr ngol,
> A mhná na súl bhfliuch mbog,
> Go bhfaghaidh Art Ua Laoghaire deoch
> Roimh é dhul isteach 'sa sgoil—
> Ní h-ag foghlaim léighinn ná port
> Ach ag iomchar cré agus cloch.

> But cease your weeping now,
> Women of the soft, wet eyes
> Till Art O'Leary drink
> Ere he go to the dark school—
> Not to learn music or song
> But to prop the earth and stone.[153]

As Daniel Corkery observed, the punning reference to the bardic schools and the practice of composing in the dark shows that even in this poem there are traces of a tradition that spans the history of literature in Ireland. Rachel Bromwich goes so far as to say that the poem itself is representative of a tradition of 'unofficial' poetry that stretches back to the early period, although not much place was given to it in the manuscripts.[154]

But it was in the poetry of the bardic courts or, outside Munster, of the bardic associations that the main body of the tradition was kept alive, and there it seems to have survived into the nineteenth century. In this connection, the following note is interesting because it shows how the poets consciously strove to keep the tradition alive.

> The last *Iomarbhaid* or Bardic Contention, known to be held in Ireland took place in Dundalk in the year 1827. There were several competitors for bardic honours, but they dropped off one by one and left the prize to be contended for by Arthur O'Murphy of Grotto Castle and James Wood, Esq., M.D.[155]

James Wood, or as he is known in Irish, Séamus Mac Giolla Choilleadh, wrote an elegy on Art Mac Cobhaigh (Cumhaidh) who died in 1773, and bridged the gap between the latter's generation of poets and the new school of poets who continued the tradition into the nineteenth century.[156] The man who won the 'Contention', Arthur or Art Murphy (Ó Murchadha), was younger than Wood, and seems to have kept a school for poets at Thomastown, near Dundalk. Among his pupils probably the most notable was Nicholas Kearney, the author of the poem *Cumha na mathara fén leanbh*, adjudged by some to be the best poem written in the nineteenth century in Ireland in either English or Irish. Kearney was active in the cultural movements of the day. He edited the first two volumes of its transactions for the Ossianic Society. Unfortunately, he published in 1856 a volume entitled *The Prophecies of Columbkille* which purported to be an old text predicting the events which had occurred during the previous couple of decades, including the famine and the mass emigration, as well as events which would occur soon, culminating in the final overthrow of the English, which Kearney calculated would take place in 1862. This was an obvious forgery and was denounced as such by some of the leading Irish scholars of the day. After this Kearney did not have the heart to publish anything else although he continued to collect and transcribe Irish material. Among his surviving manuscripts, some of them large tomes, there is one inscribed *The Bardic Remains of Louth*. A personal note from his pen gives us an insight into the man's interests and into the state of the Irish tradition:

During the scanty moments of leisure which my usual rustic employment afforded me in transcribing MSS, many of which are worn by the corroding rust of age, and in making more ample collections of the remains of the most celebrated bards of my own country . . . As for me who have spent all my leisure and even underwent expenses far beyond my abilities in collecting and transcribing the reliques of Irish Antiquity and Song without the remotest hope of encouragement, I shall cease to exist when I forget that I am an Irishman and that I should blushingly and effeminately recede from my attachment to the antiquities of my native land.[157]

Kearney's activities as a scribe and as a poet were apparently more than matched by those of Mícheál Óg Ó Longáin (1766–1837), who spent most of his life in Co. Cork and who was described by Standish Hayes O'Grady as 'the most prolific of later scribes'.

In being a scribe as well as a poet, Kearney was faithful to the Irish tradition (remember Eoghan Ruadh's reference to his pen: *Sin é an file go fann/'Nuair thuiteann an peann as a láimh*). Almost all the eminent poets of this period were also scribes. Dáibhí Ó Bruadair, Piaras Mac Gearailt and Peadar Ó Doirnín have left us manuscripts in their own hands, and a few of them holograph copies of their poems. Aodhagán Ó Rathaille, Seán Clárach Mac Domhnaill, Andrias Mac Cruitín and Seán Ó Tuama have left us copies of Keating's *Foras Feasa ar Éirinn*. Ó Rathaille had a copy of *Agallamh na Seanórach* in his possession, and has left his signature in another parchment manuscript now to be found in the National Library of Ireland. And this tradition of copying manuscripts either to be sold or to be kept continued among the Irish peasants down to modern times. The Revd James Alcock's daughter, writing in the year 1887 but referring to a time some sixty years prior to that, tells us:

Already amongst the Celtic, and exclusively Irish-speaking population, there existed a class called MS. men, whose pride it was to read, to study, to transcribe, and to preserve, any writings they could find in their beloved native tongue. These were generally old legends, bits of Irish history, or sometimes fragments of the classics.[158]

In the year that was written, Jeremiah Curtin, in his search for folk tales (or 'myths' as he called them), met a schoolmaster near Caisleán Nua in Co. Limerick.

He brought with him a manuscript a hundred and twenty years old. After patiently listening to a long story about the manuscript, I asked the old man if he could tell me a Gaelic myth. His answer was: 'I don't care to be telling lies that have been handed down from father to son. I care only for things that have been recorded and are authentic.' I told him that the manuscript contained myths which had been handed down for a thousand years or more, but I couldn't reason with him. 'What was written was true.'[159]

Notes

1 Lughaidh Ó Cléirigh, *Beatha Aodha Ruaidh Uí Dhomhnaill*, Transcribed ... by Revd. Paul Walsh and prepared for press by Colm Ó Lochlainn, part I (ITS XLII, Dublin, 1948). Lughaidh was the father of Brother Mícheál Ó Cléirigh, the principal scholar of the Four Masters. For the history of Ireland after 1600 we can thoroughly recommend R.F. Foster, *Modern Ireland 1600–1972* (London, 1988, 1989).
2 Earl of Longford's version; see John Montague, ed., *The Faber Book of Irish Verse* (London, 1974), p. 124.
3 Cf. these lines from the textbook of World Geography written in 1701 by Tadhg Ó Neachtain (R.I.A. Cat. Fasc. XX. 2482): ' ... the Jewish race being the children of God and His own people, He did not let them be until He had given them a mighty overthrow which He did not give to any other people but the Irish alone. Hence it is understood that there is no people in Europe dearer to God than the Irish . . '; trans. by R. A. Breatnach, 'End of a Tradition', SH, 1 (1961), 128ff.; quotation from p. 131.
4 Máire Ní Cheallacháin, *Filíocht Phádrigín Haicéad* (Dublin, 1962), p. 40 (XXXVI.65).
5 Tadhg Ó Cianáin, *Flight of the Earls*, ed. P. Walsh (Dublin, 1916), and Pádraig de Barra, Tomás Ó Fiaich, *Imeacht na nIarlaí* (Dublin, 1972). Cf. also 'Cín Lae Ó Mealláin' (ed. T. Ó Donnchadha), *Analecta Hibernica*, 111 (1931), 1–61, on the Ulster Rising in 1641.
6 IBP, nos. 1–4.
7 IBP, p. 31.
8 T. Ó Raghallaigh, *Duanta Eoghain Ruaidh Mhic an Bhaird* (Galway, 1930).
9 Translation by Mangan in Eleanor Hull, *The Poem Book of the Gael* (London, 1912), pp. 176–81.
10 B.M. Cat. Irish MSS., I, 397; *Ériu*, 8 (1915–16), 191–94; *Catholic Bulletin*, 18 (1928), 1074–80 (ed. from Brussels MS. 6131–3), where it is attributed to Eoghan Ruadh Mac an Bhaird.
11 Translation by Robin Flower, *Poems and Translations* (London, 1931), pp. 169–70.
12 This transplanting engendered widespread hatred of the English. For a poetic expression of it at the time of the first Ulster transplant, see the

poem of Lochlainn Óg Ó Dálaigh, 'C'áit ar ghabhadar Gaoidhil?' ('Where have the Irish gone'), *B.M. Cat. Irish MSS*, I, 54, 374f.

13 Here is what the historian Lecky had to say about these laws: ' . . . but it is not the less true that the code, taken as a whole, has a character entirely distinctive. It was directed not against the few, but against the many. It was not the persecution of a sect, but the degradation of a nation . . . And, indeed, when we remember that the greater part of it was in force for nearly a century, that its victims formed at least three-fourths of the nation, that its degrading and dividing influence extended to every field of social, political, professional, intellectual, and even domestic life, and that it was enacted without the provocation of any rebellion, in defiance of a treaty which distinctly guaranteed the Irish Catholics from any further oppression on account of their religion, it may be justly be regarded as one of the blackest pages in the history of persecution'; W. E. H. Lecky, *A History of Ireland in the Eighteenth Century* (London, Bombay, 1906), I, 169–70. See also R. Dudley Edwards, 'History of the Penal Laws against Catholics of Ireland from 1534 to the Treaty of Limerick, 1691', *Institute of Historical Research Bulletin* 11 (1934), 185–9, and E. Cahill, 'The Penal Times (1691–1800)', *The Irish Ecclesiastical Record*, v. Ser., 54 (1939), 483ff. Lecky shows a Lord Chancellor (Bowes) and a Chief Justice (Robinson) asserting in the days of the eighteenth-century penal laws that, 'The law does not suppose any such person to exist as an Irish Roman Catholic'. For the modern view of what the Penal Laws meant in actuality see R.F. Foster, *Modern Irland 1600–1972* (London, 1989), 205ff.

14 Curtis, *History of Ireland*, p. 286ff.

15 J. M. Callwell, *Old Irish Life* (Edinburgh, London, 1912), p. 200.

16 Ibid., p. 211.

17 See Mrs. Morgan John O'Connell, *The Last Colonel of the Irish Brigade*, I, II (London, 1892).

18 For bardic descriptions of the 'Big Houses', see P. S. Dinneen, *The Poems of Egan O'Rahilly* (ITS III, London, 1900), pp. xxiv, 36f, 70ff.; also Corkery, *The Hidden Ireland* (²Dublin, 1941), 30–58.

19 *The Last Colonel*, I, 68.

20 Callwell, op. cit., p. 76.

21 T. Ó Cléirigh, *Aodh Mac Aingil agus an Scoil Nua-Ghaedhilge i Lobháin* (Dublin, 1935), p. 35ff (a new edition prepared by T. de Bhaldraithe was published in Dublin in 1985); L. F. Renehan, *Collections on Irish Church History*, I, 395; D.N.B., *s.n.* Florence Conry and Hugh MacCaghwell.

22 Ó Cléirigh, op. cit., pp. 44–5.

23 Ed. T. F. O'Rahilly (Dublin, 1941). On Ó Maolchonaire's 'Catechism of Christian Doctrine', see Brian Ó Cuív, *Celtica*, 1 (1950), 161–206.

24 P. S. Dinneen, T. O'Donoghue, *Dánta Aodhagáin Uí Rathaille*, New Edition . . . (ITS III, A, 1909), p. xv.

25 Risteárd Ó Foghludha, *Seán Clárach* (Dublin, 1933, reprt. 1935 and 1944), pp. 54, 69; Liam Inglis, *Cois na Bride*, ed. R. Ó Foghludha (Dublin, n.d.), p. xviii f.; D. Corkery, *The Hidden Ireland*, pp. 54–5.

26 Corkery, op. cit., p. 31.

27 O'Curry, MS. Materials, p. 196; Kenney, *Sources*, I, 308.

28 Lecky, op. cit.; on 'Hidden Ireland', see Corkery, op. cit., and cf. L. M. Cullen, 'The Hidden Ireland: Re-assessment of a Concept', SH, 9 (1969), 7–47; Seán Ó Tuama, 'Dónal Ó Corcora agus Filíocht na Gaeilge', SH, 5 (1965), 29–41.

29 O'Curry, MS. Materials, p. 122; Walsh, Irish Men of Learning, p. 80.

30 O'Flanagan, Transactions of the Gaelic Society (1808), 29. But see Éigse, 4 (1943), 60–3, where reasons for doubting the story are advanced.

31 P. Walsh, Gleanings from Irish Manuscripts (Dublin, 1933), p. 90.

32 B. M. Cat. Irish MSS, I, 392f.

33 Translation by Máire Cruise O'Brien (= Máire Mhac an tSaoi); see John Montague, ed., The Faber Book of Irish Verse, pp. 128–9.

34 IBP, no. 28.

35 Quoted by Pádraig de Brún, 'Gan Teannta Buird ná Binse. Scríobhnaithe na Gaeilge c. 1650–1850', Comhar, Samhain, 1972, 15–22; quotation on p. 17.

36 See E. Cahill, 'English Education in Ireland During the Penal Era (1691–1800)', The Irish Ecclesiastical Record, v. Ser., 54 (1939), 627–43; O'Connell, Schools and Scholars of Breiffne, chaps, 3 and 5.

37 'The name (sc. Hedge School) was generally applied to every school conducted under Catholic auspices and where the Catholic Catechism was taught . . .The Hedge Schools were also known as "Cabin Schools" and sometimes as "Catholic Pay Schools" . . .,' O'Connell, op. cit., p. 357; see esp. chap. 9: 'A Century of Popular Education', pp. 357ff.

38 Arthur Young's Tour in Ireland (1776–9), ed. A. W. Hutton (London, New York, 1892), II, 147.

39 M. Mac Graith, Cinnlae Amhlaoibh Uí Shúilleabháin. The Diary of Humphrey O'Sullivan (ITS, London, 1936), 2 vols.; quotation is from I, vii. See B. Ó Madagáin, An Dialann Dúlra: Cinn Lae Amhlaoibh Uí Shúilleabháin agus Scríbhinní Dúlra an Bhéarla (Dublin, 1978).

40 C. Beckett, Fealsúnacht Aodha Mhic Dhomnaill (Dublin, 1967); F. W. O'Connell, 'The Philosophy of Aodh Mac Domhnaill', Louth Archaeological Journal, 3 (1915), 311ff. The adventures of Tomás Ó Casaide (fl. c. 1750) are written in a mixture of prose and verse and make interesting reading; see Mairghréad nic Philibín, Na Caisidigh agus a gCuid Filidheacht (Dublin, 1938).

41 O'Connell, op. cit., p. 204; Dictionary of National Biography, s.n. Mac Brady; B. M. Cat. Irish MSS, III 142–3, 151, 172–3.

42 R. Ó Foghludha, Éigse na Máighe (Dublin, 1952), pp. 64ff.; idem, Donnchadh Ruadh Mac Conmara (Dublin, 1933), p. 10.

43 O'Connell, op. cit., p. 203f. On dancing as the chief relaxation of the poor, see E. Mac Lysaght, Irish Life in the Seventeenth Century (Cork, 1950), p. 36.

44 Arthur Young's Tour, II, 147; cf. I, 366, 446, and Mac Lysacht, loc. cit.

45 O'Connell, op. cit., 259ff.

46 Quoted in O'Connell, p. 263f. Note that Campion reports that in the mid-sixteenth century Latin was spoken fluently in the native schools: 'Without either precepts or observation of congruity they speake Latine like a vulgar language, learned in their common Schools of Leach-craft and Law'. Quoted by Francis Shaw in B. Ó Cuív, ed., Seven Centuries of Irish Learning: 1000–1700 (Dublin, 1961), p. 96.

47 O'Connell, op. cit., p. 295.
48 P. S. Dinneen, *The Poems of Egan O'Rahilly*, p. xxx; Dinneen and O'Donoghue, *Dánta Aodhagáin Uí Rathaille*, pp. xxviii-xxix.
49 P. Ua Duinnín, *Amhráin Sheagháin Chláraigh Mhic Dhomnaill* (Dublin, 1902), p. xvi.
50 Ibid., p. xxi.
51 Ó Foghludha, *Donnchadh Ruadh Mac Conmara*, p. 18.
52 See the collection of poems written to lament the loss of Father Nicholas O'Connell's horse in Duinnín, *Filidhe na Máighe*, pp. 48ff.
53 IBP, no. 30; see also James Carney, *The Irish Bardic Poet* (Dublin, 1967).
54 See E. Cahill, 'Irish Poetry and Traditional Literature, 1540–1690', *The Irish Ecclesiastical Record*, v. Ser., 54 (1939), 337–54.
55 Proinsias Mac Cana, *Literature in Irish* (Dublin, 1980), 44, 46.
56 John J. Silke, 'Irish Scholarship and the Renaissance', *Studies in the Renaissance*, 20 (1972), 169–206; the quotation is from p. 169. See now Mícheál Mac Craith, 'Gaelic Ireland and the Renaissance' in Glanmor Williams, Robert Owen Jones, edd., *The Celts and the Renaissance. Tradition and Innovation* (Cardiff, 1990) 57–89.
57 T. Ó Cléirigh, op. cit., pp. 28–34. See James Carney, *The Irish Bardic Poet*, for references to the O'Husseys and their patrons, the Maguires of Fermanagh. See also the articles by Paul Walsh in *Irish Historical Record* 31 (1928) and *Irish Book Lover* 18 (1930).
58 The Scots were the first to print a book in Gaelic—John Carswell's translation of Knox's Liturgy: *Form na n-urrnuidheach agas freasdal na Sacramuinteadh*; this they did in 1567, using ordinary Roman type with *h* as the sign of aspiration of consonants. This was followed by Seán Ó Cearnaigh's *Aibidil Gaoidhilge 7 Caiticiosma*, printed in Dublin in 1571. See N. Williams, *I bPrionta i Leabhar* (Dublin, 1986) on Seán Ó Cearnaigh and on the earliest printing in Dublin.
59 This couplet occurs in 'An Teagasg Críosdaidhe i n-dán' (The Metrical Creed). It is one of eleven poems ascribed with certainty to Giolla Brighde Ó hEoghusa, edited by Cuthbert Mhag Craith in *Dán na mBráthar Mionúr*, pt. 1 (Dublin, 1967). Mag Craith translates the two verses preceding our verse as follows: 'We have not given them a tempering in grand, literary language—no defect that!—what a cleansing they have received in God, the source-water of precious stones! I have not—it would not have been right for me—dulled, with the shine of words, the glistening array sparkling with gems, from heaven—the radiant words of the Creator.' It should be noted that Stapleton in his *Catechism* blames the Irish literati for stifling the language *verborum obscuriorum varietate* and the nobility for neglecting the native tongue in favour of foreign ones. That the Irish Franciscans wished to defend their language as well as their faith was understood at the time. Thus Father Risteárd Ó Fearghal writes to the *Congregatio de Propaganda Fide*: 'Contra ignorantiam et ad augendam perfectionem, et conversandam linguam Patriae mirum in modum contulerunt Iberniae tres libri: Doctrina Christiana, Speculum Paenitentiae, et Speculum Vitae Religiosae Ibernicis typis publicati a Fratribus Minoribus

Lovenii . . . '; R. O'Connell, R. O'Ferrall, *Commentarius Rinuccinianus* 1645–9, 6 vols. (ed. S. Kavanaugh, Dublin, 1932–1949), v. 490.
60 T. Ó Cléirigh, op. cit., pp. 46ff. See also Anraí Mac Giolla Chomhaill, *Bráithrín Bocht ó Dhún: Aodh Mac Aingil* (Dublin, 1986). On the history of Louvain in this period, see Léon van der Essen, *L'Université de Louvain 1425–1940* (Brussels, 1945), pp. 17–61. On the part played by the St Anthony's College in the making of the 'golden age' of Irish Franciscanism (1615–1650), see C. Mooney, 'The Golden Age of the Irish Franciscans', *Measgra Mhichíl Uí Chléirigh* (Dublin, 1944), pp. 21–33, idem, 'St. Anthony's College, Louvain', *Donegal Annual*, 8 (1969), 14–48, and more generally Cathaldus Giblin, 'The Contributions of Irish Franciscans in the Seventeenth Century' in Michael Maher, *Irish Spirituality* (Dublin, 1981), 88–103.
61 See E. R. McC. Dix and J. Cassedy, *List of Books, etc. Printed . . . in Irish* (Dublin, 1905); for a history of the presses that printed them, see the article by T. W. Lynam, *The Library* (Trans. of the Bibliographical Society), 1924, 286. For a general discussion, see C. Ó Maonaigh, 'Scríbhneoirí Gaeilge Oird San Froinsias', *Catholic Survey* (Galway, 1951), vol. I, no. 1; 'Scríbhneoirí Gaeilge an Seachtú hAois Déag', SH, 2 (1962), 182–208.
62 The work was republished in Reflex Facsimile (Dublin, 1945).
63 N. Williams, *I bPrionta i Leabhar*, gives a detailed analysis of Protestant writing from the sixteenth to the eighteenth century.
64 Kenney, *Sources*, I, 38–53.
65 See Ludwig Bieler, 'John Colgan as Editor', *Franciscan Studies*, 8 (1948), 1–24; C. Mooney, 'Father John Colgan, O. F. M.: His Work and Times and Literary Milieu', in T. O'Donnell, ed., *Father Colgan, O. F. M.* (Dublin, 1959).
66 R. O'Kelleher, G. Schoepperle, *Betha Colaim Chille* (Chicago, 1918). See Brendan Bradshaw, 'Manus "the Magnificent": O'Donnell as Renaissance Prince', in Art Cosgrove, Donal McCartney, eds., *Studies in Irish History Presented to R. Dudley Edwards* (Dublin, 1979), pp. 15–36.
67 'Gan Teannta Buird ná Binse: Scríobhnaithe na Gaeilge. c. 1650–1850', *Comhar*, Samhain, 1972, 15–22.
68 P. Walsh, *The Ó Cléirigh Family of Tír Conaill* (Dublin, 1938). See also Brendan Jennings, *Michael Ó Cléirigh, Chief of the Four Masters and his Associates* (Dublin, Cork, 1936).
69 Quoted by Pádraic de Brún, 'Gan Teannta Buird ná Binse. Scríobhnaithe na Gaeilge. c. 1650–1850', *Comhar*, Samhain, 1972, 15–22; quotation is from p. 17.
70 It was Colgan who gave the work the name *Annála na gCeithre Máistrí* 'Annals of the Four Masters'; the four were Brother Mícheál, Cúchoigcríche Ó Cléirigh, Fearfeasa Ó Maolchonaire and Cúchoigcríche Ó Duibhgeannáin. P. Walsh, *The Four Masters and Their Work* (Dublin, 1944). Walsh shows that the scholars did not work uninterruptedly for the four years, as is usually supposed, and that they had the help of two other writers for a brief period. On the prose of the historical and devotional works of the period, see Brian Ó Cuív, 'The

Irish Language in the Early Modern Period', T. W. Moody, F. X. Martin, and F. J. Byrne, eds., *A New History of Ireland*, 3 (Oxford, 1976), pp. 529–34.

71 Ed. John O'Donovan, *Annála Ríoghachta Éireann*, I–VII (Dublin, 1848–51).

72 *Eochairsgiath an Aifrinn* ('An Explanatory Defence of the Mass'), *Trí Bior-Ghaoithe an Bháis* ('Three Shafts of Death'). See Bernadette Cunningham, 'Geoffrey Keating's *Eochair Sgiath an Aifrinn* and the Catholic Reformation in Ireland', W. J. Shiels and Diana Wood, eds., *The Churches, Ireland and the Irish* (Oxford, 1989), pp. 133–43.

73 Keating, *History of Ireland*, I, ed. D. Comyn, II, III, IV, ed. P. Dinneen (ITS IV, VIII, IX, XV). On Keating, see W. P. Burke, 'Geoffrey Keating', *Waterford Arch. Soc. Journal*, 1 (1894–5), 173–82; E. C. Mac Giolla Eáin, *Dánta, Amhráin is Caointe Shéathrúin Céitinn* (Dublin, 1900); R. Ó Foghludha, *Saoghal-ré Sheathrún Céitinn* (Dublin, 1908) [= *Irisleabhar na Gaedhilge*, 18 (1908), 3–12, 47–57]; idem, *Duanarán ré 1600–1700* (Dublin, 1935), 5–18. On Keating as a historian, see Bernadette Cunningham, 'Seventeenth-Century Interpretations of the Past: The Case of Geoffrey Keating', *Irish Historical Studies* 25 (1986), 116–28. For an important contribution outlining the literary and historical contexts to the composition of the *Annála Ríoghachta Éireann* and Keating's work see B. Ó Buachalla, '*Annála Ríoghachta Éireann* agus *Forus Feasa ar Éirinn*: An Comhthéacas Comhaimseartha', SH, 22/23 (1982–3), 59–105.

74 See Mac Giolla Eáin, op. cit.

75 The original may be found in Pádraig de Brún, Breandán Ó Buachalla, Tomás Ó Coincheanainn, *Nua-Dhuanaire*, 1 (Dublin, 1971).

76 See S. Ó Tuama, *An Grá in Amhráin na nDaoine* (Dublin, 1960), p. 260, n. 52.

77 T. Ó Donnchadha ('Tórna'), *Pádraigín Haicéad, cct.* (Dublin, 1916); Máire Ní Cheallacháin, *Filíocht Phádraigín Haicéad* (Dublin, 1962); Art Ó Beoláin, 'Páidrigín Haicéad', *Brian Merriman agus Filí Eile* (Dublin, 1985), 50–64.

78 M. Ní Cheallacháin, p. 10. See also de Brún et al., *Nua-Dhuanaire*, p. 19, and pp. 21–2 for an edition of 'Cuirim séad suirghe . . .' On the theme of the exile's *Sehnsucht* for Ireland, see J. Carney, *Early Irish Poetry*, 26–27.

79 M. Ní Cheallacháin, op. cit., p. 63.

80 Ed. Lambert McKenna, *Iomarbhágh na bhFileadh*, I, II (ITS XX, XXI, London, 1918).

81 *B. M. Cat. Irish MSS*, I, 617; II, 61–62, 98; T. F. O'Rahilly, *Dánfhocail* (Dublin, 1921), p. 31. The stanza is attributed to Flaithrí Ó Maolchonaire, founder of the College of Saint Anthony and later Archbishop of Tuam; see O'Rahilly, p. 81.

82 C. O'Rahilly, *Five Seventeenth Century Political Poems* (Dublin, 1952), pp. 17–32.

83 Ibid., pp. 59–82. The poem was first edited by Douglas Hyde in *Lia Fáil*, 2 (1932).

84 N. J. A. Williams, 'Irish Satire and its Sources', SC, 12/13 (1977/8), 217–

46; quotation is from p. 217. Ed. by Osborn Bergin in *Gadelica*, I (1912), 33–50, 127–31, 137–50, 220–36 (see also *B. M. Cat. Irish MSS*, II, 423ff.) and by N. J. A. Williams, *Pairlement Chloinne Tomáis* (Dublin, 1981), who holds that of the two distinct sections of this text, the first was probably written in Kerry, the home county of Muirid Mac Dáibhí Dhúib, shortly before 1615, and the second in the period 1662–5. See also N.J.A. Williams 'Nótaí Éagsúla ar Phairlement Chloinne Tomáis', SH 16 (1976) 73–108, 17 and 18 (1977–88) 71–90. T. de Bhaldraithe, *Ériu*, 33 (1982), 172–3, comments on the date of the text and on some words in it.

85 N. J. A. Williams, 'Irish Satire and its Sources', SC 12/13 (1977/8) p. 2í7.

86 *Gadelica*, I, 35–6.

87 Ed. by Máiréad Ní Ghráda, in *Lia Fáil*, I (1924), 49–78.

88 Brian Ó Cuív, *Párliament na mBan* (Dublin, 1952). James Stewart has recently proved that the account of the first two sessions in *Párliament* is in the main a translation of one of Erasmus's *Colloquia Familiaria*. See SH, 7 (1966), 135–41.

89 T. Ó Donnchadha, *Leabhar Cloinne Aodha Buidhe* (Dublin, 1931), p. 279.

90 *B. M. Cat. Irish MSS*, II, 50.

91 It is only fair to point out that his situation may have been due rather to general economic hardship (the year 1674 was memorable for the failure of the corn harvest) than to lack of patronage.

92 J. C. MacErlean, *Duanaire Dháibhidh Uí Bhruadair* ITS XI, XIII, XVIII (1911–17); vol. I, 130. It has been suggested that it was in 1674 that Ó Bruadair fell on hard times. See Art Ó Beoláin, 'Dáibhí Ó Bruadair', *Comhar*, Feabhra, 1970, and *Brian Merriman agus Fili Eile*, pp. 65–76.

93 MacErlean, III, 184; cf. *B. M. Cat. Irish MSS*, I, 521.

94 MacErlean, op. cit., I, 18, and cf. *B.M. Cat. Irish MSS*, I 522, n. 2.

95 MacErlean, op. cit., I, 18; *B. M. Cat. Irish MSS*, I, 522.

96 MacErlean, op. cit., III, 180; *B.M. Cat. Irish MSS*, I, 569. For a study of the poet's work, see G. Murphy, 'David Ó Bruadair', *The Irish Ecclesiastical Record*, v Ser., 78 (1952), 340–57. See also *Selected Poems of Dáibhí Ó Bruadair*, trans. and introduced by Michael Hartnett (Dublin, 1985); Pádraig Ó Fiannachta, 'Dáiví Ó Bruadair', idem, ed., *Éire Banba Fódla, Léachtaí Cholm Cille* 13 (Maynooth, 1982), 130–50.

97 See J. Montague, ed., *The Faber Book of Irish Verse*, pp. 131–2.

98 'The principles of this great change may be summed up in two sentences; first *the adoption of vowel rhyme in place of consonantal rhyme*; second, *the adoption of a certain number of accents in each line in place of a certain number of syllables*'—Douglas Hyde, *A Literary History of Ireland*, p. 541. See O. Bergin, 'On the Origin of Modern Irish Rhythmical Verse', *Mélanges offerts à H. Pedersen* (Copenhagen, 1937).

99 For Eoghan Mac Craith's use of the *amhrán* metre, see James Carney, *Poems on the Butlers of Ormond, Cahir, and Dunboyne (AD 1400–1650)* (Dublin, 1945), xvi, xix, and notes, and for Tadhg Dall's *amhrán* poem composed sometime before 1579, see Knott, *Bardic Poems of Tadhg Dall Ó Huiginn*, I, 255ff., II, 277; it and another (no. 41) by Aonghus Dubh Ó Dálaigh, composed about 1594, are found in *Leabhar Branach* (ed. S. Mac Airt).

100 MacErlean, op. cit., III, 194.
101 Hyde, op. cit., p. 546.
102 *B.M. Cat. Irish MSS*, II, 88–90; U. Ní Fhaircheallaigh, *Filidheacht Seagháin Uí Neachtain* (Dublin, 1908); E. Ó Neachtain, *Stair Eamuinn Uí Chléire* (Dublin, 1918). In spite of the title, C. G. Ó Háinle's 'Neighbours in Eighteenth Century Ireland: Jonathan Swift and Seán Ó Neachtain', *Éire-Ireland*, 13 (1978), 106–21, deals mostly with Ó Neachtain's poetic school.
103 *B.M. Cat. Irish MSS*, II, 117–18. See Seán Ó Gallchóir, ed., *Séamas Dall Mac Cuarta, Dánta* (Dublin, 1971); Lorcan Ó Muireadaigh, ed., *Amhráin Shéamais Mhic Cuarta* (Dublin, 1925). Cf. Éamon Ó Tuathail, ed., *Rainníní agus Amhráin* (Dublin, 1923).
104 *B.M. Cat. Irish MSS*, II, 118. See now. S. Mag Uidhir, ed., *Pádraig Mac a Liondain* (Dublin, 1975).
105 *B.M. Cat. Irish MSS*, II , 125. Art Mac Cobhthaigh wrote with deep feeling: *Tá mo chroí-se réabtha ina míle céad cuid/'s gan balsam féin ann a d'foirfeadh dom phian/nuair a chluinim an Ghaeilge uilig á tréig bheáil/is caismirt Bhéarla i mbéal gach aoin* ('My heart is torn into a thousand hundred pieces/and without a balm at all that would ease my pain/ when I hear all Gaelic a-fading/and conflict of language on everyman's tongue'). See Énrí O Muirgheasa, ed., *Abhráin Airt Mhic Chubhthaigh agus Abhráin Eile* (Dublin, Dundalk, 1916; Dundalk, 1926). There was an important bardic family bearing the name Ó Cobhthaigh that had settled in Westmeath during the fifteenth and sixteenth centuries. Among its best known poets were Diarmaid, Domhnall, Muircheartaigh and Tadhg, whose poem 'Corrach do chodlas a-réir' (see T. O'Rahilly, *Danta Grádha* [Dublin, 1916; Cork, 1926]) was rewarded with a mare for each of its lovely verses by Maghnus Ó Domhnaill.
106 *B.M. Cat. Irish MSS*, II, 123f. Seán de Rís, ed., *Peadar Ó Doirnín* (Dublin, 1969); Breandan Ó Buachalla, 'Peadar Ó Doirnín agus Lucht Scríte a Bheatha', SH, 5 (1965), 123–54. Ó Buachalla thinks that most of Ó Doirnín's poetry was composed in Co. Armagh and Co. Louth; see op. cit., p. 154. S. Watson has written on women and love in Ó Doirnín's poetry in 'Mná agus Grá i bhFilíocht Uí Dhoirnín' in Micheál Ó Máirtín, ed., *Meascra Ulad* (Belfast), II, 31–9.
107 P. S. Dinneen and T. O'Donoghue, *Dánta Aodhagáin Uí Rathaille* (ITS IIIa, 1909); Dáibhí Mac Conmara, *Aogán Ó Rathaille Dánta* (Dublin, 1969); Art Ó Beolain, 'Aogán Ó Rathaille', in *Merriman agus Filí Eile* (Dublin, 1985), pp. 77–87; John Jordan, 'Aogán Ó Rathaille', in Seán Mac Réamoinn, ed., *The Pleasures of Gaelic Poetry*, pp. 81–91.
108 Trans. by Frank O'Connor, *Kings, Lords, and Commons* (Van Nuys, Ca., 1989), p. 107.
109 G. Murphy, 'Notes on *Aisling* Poetry', *Éigse*, 1 (1939), 40–50; Tomás de Bhaldraithe, 'Notaí ar an Aisling Fháithchiallaigh', *Measgra i gCuimhne Mhíchíl Uí Chléirigh*, ed. S. O'Brien (Dublin, 1944), p. 210ff. B. Ó Buachalla, 'An Mheisiasacht agus an Aisling', *Folia Gadelica* (Cork, 1983), pp. 72–87; 'Na Stíobhartaigh agus an t-Aos Léinn: Cing Séamas', PRIA, 83 (1983), sec. C., 81–134.

110 There are two *aisling* poems by Tadhg Dall Ó hUiginn in which he describes the maiden—herself one of the fairy folk visitors—who enticed Conla and Bran. But she does not claim to be Éire. See Knott, op. cit., I, nos. 39, 40.

111 G. Murphy, 'Royalist Ireland', *Studies*, 24 (1935), 589–604.

112 See Rachel Bromwich, 'The Continuity of the Gaelic Tradition in Eighteenth-Century Ireland', *Trans. Yorkshire Society for Celtic Studies*, 4 (1947–8), 2–28; 14.

113 'On the Origin of the Name *Érainn* and *Ériu*', *Ériu*, 14 (1943), 7–28. See also R. A. Breatnach, 'The Lady and the King', *Studies*, 42 (1953), 321–36.

114 Ó Tuama, *An Grá in Amhráin na nDaoine*, p. 190.

115 Trans. by J. C. Mangan, in Montague, *The Faber Book of Irish Verse*, 142f.

116 R. Ó Foghludha, *Seán Clárach*. See now Breandán Ó Buachalla, 'Na Stíobhartaigh agus an t-Aos Léinn: Cing Séamas', PRIA, 83 (1983), Sec. C, No. 4., 81–134.

117 See the introductions by Ó Foghludha to *Éigse na Máighe* and *Seán Clárach*; P. Ó Duinnín, *Filidhe na Máighe* and *Amhráin Sheagháin Chláraigh Mhic Dhomhnaill*.

118 Their poems and those of their fellow poets have been published twice, the first time by Father Pádraig Ua Duinnín *Filidhe na Maighe* (Dublin, 1906), the second time, and more correctly and completely, by Risteárd Ó Foghludha, *Éigse na Máighe* (Dublin, 1952).

119 *Éigse na Máighe*, p. 41. See the verse which Seán Ó Tuama made on himself as a tavern keeper, quoted ibid., p. 61, and in Mainchín Seoighe, *Cois Máighe na gCaor* (Dublin, 1965), p. 139.

120 *Éigse na Máighe*, pp. 42, 73.

121 *Rime, Gentlemen, Please*, quoted by Mainchín Seoighe, op. cit., p. 132.

122 *Éigse na Máighe* , p. 128.

123 Seoighe, op. cit., p. 85.

124 *Éigse na Máighe*, p. 199.

125 Ibid.

126 T. Ó Donnchadha, *Dánta Sheáin Uí Mhurchadha na Ráithineach* (Dublin, 1907), pp. xx-xxiv; also his *Seán na Ráithineach* (Dublin, 1954), pp. xix-xxiii.

127 *Dánta Sheáin Uí Mhurchadha*, p. xxi.

128 *B. M. Cat. Irish MSS*, I, 528; Tórna, 'An t-Athair Eoghan Ó Caoimh: a Bheatha agus a Shaothar', *Gadelica*, 1, 10ff., 101ff., 163ff., 251ff.

129 Ó Foghludha, *Seán Clárach*, pp. 98–100. Compare the *barántas* published by Pádraig Ó Fiannachta in *Éigse*, 16 (1973), 7–12, a satire on Seán Míodhach, who, according to the poet, was acting above his station in life. See also Ó Fiannachta, 'An Barántas. Genre Grinn agus Gairsiúlachta', *Feasta*, 30.6. 7–12, 18, 7. 5–8.

130 Ó Foghludha, *Éigse na Máighe*, p. 215. Professor Brian Ó Cuív has published from RIA 23, H. 39 the 'Rules' of a *cúirt éigse* in Clare; see *Éigse*, 11 (1965–6), 216–18. It is in the hand of Tomás Ó Míocháin, called 'Teacher of Accompts and Mathematics' (*B. M. Cat. Ir. MSS*, II, 185), and was drawn up in 1780; the rules prescribe that no language

THE DECLINE   251

except Irish is to be used in the *cúirt*, that books and mss. are to be kept
for the use of members, and that historical knowledge and old songs are
to be preserved.

131 Tadhg Ó Donnchadha, *Amhráin Diarmaid Mac Seáin Bhuidhe Mac
    Carrthaigh* (Dublin, 1916). See also *Journal of the Ivernian Society*,
    1914–15 for his life and work.
132 Op. cit., No. 28, July–Sept., 1915.
133 Published in MacErlean, *Duanaire Dháibhidh Uí Bhruadair*, III, 94ff.
134 Ó Foghludha, *Cois na Cora* (Dublin, 1937).
135 T. Ó Donnchadha, *Dánta Sheáin Uí Mhurchadha*, p. xxvii, and *Seán na
    Ráithíneach*, pp. xiii, 239. See the introductions to the two works and *B.
    M. Cat. Irish MSS*, II, 384.
136 Pádraig Ó Nuatain, 'Cúirt Éigse Uí Macoille', *Feasta*, Lúnasa, 1967, 19–
    20. See the letter published by Brian Ó Cuív, *Éigse*, 11 (1965), 100, and
    the reference to the custom of holding a *cúirt na mbúrdánach* in every
    district in Ireland.
137 Risteárd Ó Foghludha, *Amhráin Phiarais Mhic Gearailt* (Dublin, 1905).
138 See the introduction to P. Ua Duinnín, *Amhráin Eoghain Ruaidh Uí
    Shúilleabháin* (Dublin, 1901), esp. pp. xxii-xxiii, and Art Ó Beoláin,
    'Eoghan Rua Ó Súilleabháin', in *Merriman agus Filí Eile*, pp. 88–98.
139 *The Hidden Ireland*, p. 215.
140 Donal O'Sullivan, *Songs of the Irish* (Dublin, 1960), pp. 136–8.
141 P. S. Dinneen, *Four Notable Kerry Poets (Filidhe Mhóra Chiarraighe)*
    (Dublin, 1929), p. 25.
142 *The Hidden Ireland*, pp. 233–4.
143 D. de hÍde, *Abhráin agus Dánta an Reachtabhraigh* (Dublin, 1933). See
    also Aine Ní Cheannain, *Raifteirí an File: the Strolling Bard of Mayo*
    (Dublin, 1984); Ciarán Ó Coigligh, ed., *Raiftearaí, Amhráin agus Dánta*
    (Dublin, 1987).
144 Ed. by R. Ó Foghludha, with an Introduction by Piaras Béaslaí (Dublin,
    1912, 1949); the 1912 ed. was rev. by T. F. O'Rahilly in *Gadelica*, I
    (1912), 190–204. Also ed. by L. C. Stern, 'Brian Merrimans Cúirt an
    Mheadhoin Oidhche', ZCP, 5 (1904–5), 193–415. Though we place him
    somewhat outside the tradition, no less a scholar than T. F. O'Rahilly
    insisted that this poem was 'in fact an ordinary aisling with its "as-I-
    roved-out-one-morning-early type" somewhat expanded and with some
    borrowings from the English poet Savage.'
145 Arland Ussher's translation, John Montague (ed.), *The Faber Book of
    Irish Verse* (London, 1974), pp. 168–9.
146 See Máirín Ní Mhuirgheasa, 'Cúirt an Mheán-Oíche Agus Finnscéal an
    Róis', in *Feasta*, 4 (1951), 7–9, where the relationship between the *Cúirt*
    and *Le Roman de la Rose* is discussed; H. R. McAdoo, 'Notes on the
    "Midnight Court" (Merryman)', *Éigse*, I (1939), 166ff. For a fuller
    study, see Seán Ó Tuama, 'Cúirt an Mheán Oíche', SH, 4 (1964), 7–27,
    Seán Ó Tuama, 'Brian Merriman and his Court', *Irish University
    Review*, 11 (1981, 149–64, G. Ó Crualaoich, 'The Vision of Liberalism in
    Cúairt an Mheán Oíche', *Folia Gadelica* (Cork, 1983), 95–104, Art Ó
    Beoláin, *Merriman agus Filí Eile* (Dublin, 1985), pp. 7–23, who stresses
    Merriman's debt to elements in the native tradition rather than to any

external influences, and Cosslett Ó Cuinn, 'Merriman's Court' in Seán
Mac Réamoinn, *The Pleasures of Gaelic Poetry* , pp. 113–26.

147 Ó Foghludha, op. cit., ll. 619ff; translation is by Frank O'Connor, *Kings,
Lords, and Commons* (London, 1962), p. 154.

148 Text and trans. in G. Murphy, 'The Lament of the Old Woman of
Beare', PRIA, 55 (1953), 83ff (revised in EILs, pp. 74–82); and see A.
Haggerty Krappe, 'La Cailleach Bheara. Notes de Mythologie
Gaélique', EC, 1 (1936), 292–302; Hull, 'The Old Woman or Nun of
Beare', ZCP, 19 (1933), 174–76. Trans. by S. O'Faolain, *The Silver
Branch* (London, 1939), pp. 103–7, and F. O'Connor, *Kings*, pp. 34–8.

149 Trans. O'Connor, op. cit., p. 38

150 O'Connor, op. cit., p. 129. The original, 'A ógánaigh an chúil
cheangailte', will be found in Dubhglas de h-Íde, *Abhráin Grádha Chúige
Chonnacht* (Dublin, 1950), pp. 34–35.

151 Three versions of the *Caoineadh*—each differing slightly from the
other—have been published: Mrs Morgan John O'Connell, *The Last
Colonel*, II, 327–40; O. Bergin, *The Gaelic Journal*, 7 (1896), 18–24; Seán
Ó Cuív, *Caoine Airt Uí Laoghaire* (Dublin, 1923). Trans. by O'Connor,
op. cit., pp. 109–19. O'Connor hears a defensive note throughout the
Caoineadh and it has been held that Eibhlín Dubh gives a more
favourable version of her own conduct than was warranted. Be that as it
may, the 'Caoineadh' is a fine poem. It has been called 'a classic' and 'one
of the world's great poems' (Thomas Kinsella, 'Another Country' in
Mac Réamoinn, *The Pleasures of Gaelic Poetry* , p. 186) and illustrates
well the remarkable support the 'occasional' poet or poetess can draw
from an exceedingly strong poetic tradition.

152 Bergin's ed., p. 18; O'Connor, op. cit., p. 110.

153 Bergin ed., p. 22; O'Connor, op. cit., p. 119.

154 'The Continuity of the Gaelic Tradition in Eighteenth-Century Ireland';
see also her article 'The Keen for Art O'Leary', *Éigse*, 5 (1948), 236–52,
and B. Ó Madagáin, ed., *Gnéithe den Chaointeoireacht* (Dublin, 1974);
Seán Ó Coileáin, 'The Irish Lament: An Oral Genre', SH, 24 (1984–8)
97–117.

155 *Collectanea Grahamea, or Bardic Remains of Louth*, quoted in É. Ó
Muirgheasa, *Amhráin Airt Mhic Chubhthaigh agus Amhráin Eile*
(Dundalk, 1926), II, 76.

156 For the history of an interesting experiment that was made in
Músgraighe Uí Fhloinn (Muskerry, Co. Cork) during this century, see
Domhnall Ó Caocháin, *Saothar Dhámh-Sgoile Mhúsgraighe* (Dublin,
1933). Wood's poetic work has been recently published; see S. Ó
Daithginn, *Séamas Mac Giolla Choille* (Dublin, 1972). His work is
discussed by Tomás Ó Fiaich, 'The Ulster Poetic Tradition in the
Nineteenth Century', in P. Ó Fiannachta, ed., *Litríocht an 19ú hAois*,
Léachtaí Cholm Cille 3 (Dublin, 1972), pp. 20–37.

157 Quoted by Tomás Ó Fiaich, art. cit., 17–28.

158 Quoted by Pádraig de Brún, 'Gan Teannta Buird ná Binse', *Comhar*,
Samhain 1972, 15–22; quotation on p. 15. Kenney, *Sources*, 54–5,
writes: 'Of the hundreds of Scribes, the majority farmers and labourers
who in their scanty leisure copied their country's records and literature,

the names of only a few can be mentioned . . . ' goes on to mention some twenty by name. Cf. Douglas Hyde, *A Literary History of Ireland* (London, 1901), p. 616. Breandán Ó Conchúir, *Scríobhaithe Chorcaí 1700–1850* (Dublin, 1982), has a fine study of Co. Cork scribes in the period under discussion, over 200 of them.

159 Séamus Ó Duilearga, ed., *Irish Folk-Tales. Collected by Jeremiah Curtin* (Dublin and Cork, 1944), p. xi.

CHAPTER 6

THE REVIVAL

§1

IT has ever been the policy of empires to undermine and traduce the languages of conquered peoples. 'The mighty state', said St Augustine speaking of Rome, 'has been able to impose not only its yoke but its language upon the nations it has subdued.'[1] The English poet Spenser approved precisely the same policy in Ireland a thousand years later: 'for it hathe bene ever the vse of the Conquerour to destroy the language of the Conquered, and to force him by all meanes to learne his.' This he justifies as follows: 'the speache beinge Irishe the harte muste nedes be Irishe for out of the abundance of the harte the tonge speakethe.'[2] It was clearly in the spirit of such a policy that Henry VIII wrote to the inhabitants of Galway in 1536, 'that every inhabitaunt within the saide towne indevor theym selfe to speke Englyshe, and to use theym selffe after the Englyshe facion; and specyally that you, and every of you, do put forth your childe to scole, to lerne to speke Englyshe.'[3]

It falls to the political historian rather than to the literary historian to trace English policy in Ireland; suffice it here to say that that policy reached its most heinous level in the penal laws of the eighteenth century, and that the effects of those laws, coming on top of the political misfortunes that were suffered in the seventeenth century, severely crippled and nearly killed national tradition altogether. Despite those adverse circumstances, there were four million speakers of Irish out of a population of five million at the beginning of the nineteenth century in Ireland. That is, Ireland was for the most part Irish in language and custom as late as that. But by the first year of the present century, only a little over 641,000 could speak the language.[4]

This sudden shrinking of the number of Irish speakers was surely the result of a policy that had been set in motion and prosecuted closely before the beginning of the century, but it was abetted by two events that occurred during that century. One of these was the establishment of the National Educational Board of Ireland in 1831.[5] The Board was so reactionary that it banned the teaching of Scott's patriotic lines:

> Breathes there a man, with soul so dead
> Who never to himself hath said,
> This is my own, my native land!

and instead urged the adoption of the following lines penned for the purpose by Archbishop Whateley:

> I thank the goodness and the grace
> Which on my birth have smiled,
> And made me in these Christian days
> A happy English child.[6]

There is no doubt at all that the education policies of the Board turned an Irish-speaking nation into an English-speaking one. But in all fairness, one must add that their work was greatly facilitated by certain political leaders, such as Daniel O'Connell, who almost without exception turned their backs on Gaelic. They were supported by Catholic clerics who backed the English language partly, so it is claimed, for the remarkable reason that the Protestants used the Irish language! But a more likely reason might be that they believed the material condition of their people would be improved and the influence of the Church expanded through the use of English. In any case, the 'national' system of education was accepted quite generally by the Irish leaders, and as long as it did not interfere with the faith, they were content with Anglicization.[7]

The other event that drastically affected the use of the Irish language was the Great Famine of 1846–7. The effects of that disaster were felt most severely in the less productive districts of western Ireland, from Donegal in the North as far as Cork in the South, districts that had always been strongholds of the Irish language. The Famine was directly responsible for the deaths of 729,000 people, and indirectly responsible for the start of a massive emigration to America and England: between 1846 and 1901, some 4,976,462 Irish men and women, it is said, left their native land.[8]

While Irish as a spoken language was declining, interest in it by the intellectual and literary classes was growing. There were three principal factors responsible for this new interest, which began to make itself felt in the 1780s: political, antiquarian, and literary. The establishment of the Irish Parliament in 1782 did little to secure freedom for the people as a whole—apart from the governing class, that is—but it did help create a national feeling, a desire to know the pre-Anglo-Norman history. And that history could not be known without studying the manuscripts and, of course, the language they were written in, Irish. Strangely enough, one of the earliest partisans of the movement to cherish and preserve Irish manuscripts was an English military engineer of French Protestant background. Colonel Charles Vallancey (1721–1812) was little more than a dilettante antiquarian who, despite all his work and enthusiasm, was unable to learn enough Irish to interpret the old manuscripts. In his series *Collectanea de Rebus Hibernicis* (1770–1804), however, he began the work of examining the manuscript materials with the help of such native scholars as Charles O'Conor and Bishop John O'Brien. As will become apparent further on, the state of scholarship in the land was not as impoverished as the history of Vallancey would indicate; among other things, there were a good many Irishmen hard at work copying manuscripts (the press was still too costly for most).[9]

In the literary world generally, the Romantic Movement had gained a foothold in Great Britain, and the Ossianic forgeries of Macpherson, *Fragments of Ancient Poetry* (1760), and Bishop Percy's *Reliques of Ancient English Poetry* (1765) had appeared. To anyone familiar with the Irish manuscripts, the fictitious element in Macpherson's work must have been apparent from the first. In B.M. Add. MS 21121, f.8, there is a letter from Charles O'Conor listing the arguments against the authenticity of the Ossianic poems under six headings. But to the public, Macpherson's forgeries were as convincing as the equally romantic theories of Vallancey, and, moreover, they stimulated a renewed interest in the original documents. It was these alone, after all, that could prove or disprove the claims advanced for them by Macpherson and Vallancey. In the same way, the Percy volumes stirred scholars to begin searching for a body of poetry in Irish to rival that in English.

The first work to make any significant contribution was Charlotte Brooke's *Reliques of Irish Poetry* (1789).[10] It was Percy's work that motivated Miss Brooke, and we find her expressing her intention to publish the poetry in a letter to him in 1787.[11] Most of the poems she published are Ossianic, and they are rendered in a style reminiscent of Thomas Gray, but she also gives a few poems in the folk idiom, a sixteenth-century bardic poem, and a love song. She got her manuscripts from J. C. Walker, author of *Historical Memoirs of the Irish Bards*, Sylvester O'Halloran of Limerick, the author of numerous books on the early history of Ireland, Theophilus Ó Flannagáin, a scholar of Trinity College, Dublin, a Co. Clare man, and first secretary of The Gaelic Society of Dublin, and Maurice O'Gorman, the best-known teacher of Irish in Dublin in his time and the most diligent of the scribes of the North between 1745 and 1794, the year he is said to have died. It is O'Gorman's northern compatriots who can claim the distinction of having published the first ever Irish language magazine, *Bolg an tSolair*, a 120–page miscellany of grammar, dialogue, poetry, prayers, and translations, produced by the newspaper office of *The Northern Star* in 1795. Unfortunately only one number appeared.

The new interest in things Irish Gaelic was responsible for the foundation of various societies. In 1772, the Dublin Society appointed a committee to investigate Irish antiquities. The committee was short-lived, but some of its members assisted Vallancey in the publication of his *Collectanea*. Then, in 1782, a small society comprised mostly of members of Trinity College was formed to promote and facilitate scholarship in the land; it was that small group that founded the Royal Irish Academy in 1785.

The first society formed to protect the welfare of the Irish language was The Gaelic Society of Dublin (1807). As a society it did next to nothing (a volume of 'transactions' was published in 1808 under the editorship of Theophilus Ó Flannagáin), but the individual members were most industrious. Four of them, Paul O'Brien, William Neilson, Patrick Lynch and W. Haliday, published grammars, and another, Denis Taafe, wrote a grammar that can be found in Egerton MS 116. Edward O'Reilly, another of the Society's members, published a dictionary, and Patrick Lynch compiled a list of Irish manuscripts in Trinity College and in the libraries of various members of the Society.[12]

In 1818, The Iberno-Celtic Society was founded, but it only published one volume of transactions (1820). One of the most active members of the Ulster Gaelic Society, established in 1830, Robert MacAdam, collected a considerable number of Irish manuscripts and much Irish folklore. He published a collection of Irish proverbs in the *Ulster Journal of Archaeology*,[13] a periodical which he not only founded but also edited for some ten years, from 1852 to 1862. In 1840, The Archaeological Society was formed and, five years later, The Celtic Society; the two merged in 1853, the same year that the The Ossianic Society was founded. These organizations, apart from the Belfast Ulster Gaelic Society, had their headquarters in Dublin, where they performed a very valuable service through the publication of ancient Irish texts. Fortunately, by then a number of good Irish scholars had appeared on the scene.

The greatest of this new breed were undoubtedly Eugene O'Curry

(1796–1862) and John O'Donovan (1809–61).[14] They and their contemporaries were the last of the old native Irish scholars. During their lifetimes they witnessed the establishment of the new system of education, the Great Famine, and the beginnings of emigration. They also saw the language and native traditions wither and fade. The scholars who succeeded them had to learn the language for the most part, and even when they knew it from the cradle they did not have the opportunity to inherit with it that traditional knowledge that was the heritage of *file, seanchaidhe*, and professional scribe. But in O'Donovan and O'Curry, fortunately, traditional knowledge survived long enough to come into contact with the modern linguistic and historical knowledge that issued from the universities of Europe.

In 1853, the year The Ossianic Society was formed, Zeuss published his *Grammatica Celtica*—the foundation stone for the modern study of Celtic—and scholars on the Continent began to study Irish. Strangely enough, it was through the interest of these continental scholars that the desire to keep the Irish language alive gained strength. In the meantime, Thomas Moore had published his *Irish Melodies* (1834), and had rekindled the interest of the nobility in the west of Ireland. As Douglas Hyde said, 'he had rendered the past of Ireland sentimentally interesting without arousing the prejudices or alarming the upper classes.'[15]

The first society established for the sole purpose of rescuing the spoken language was The Society for the Preservation of the Irish Language, founded in 1876.[16] Among its early members were Father John Nolan, David Comyn, and T. O'Neill Russell. Among its many accomplishments was persuading the National Education Board and the Intermediate Education Board to put Irish on the list of subjects in the year 1878,[17] the year Douglas Hyde joined the Society. But alas, in the same year a disagreement arose among the members, with the result that the most active (those just named) withdrew; later (1880) they formed The Gaelic Union. This new society concentrated its efforts on keeping the spoken language alive. It succeeded in publishing a monthly, *The Gaelic Journal (Irisleabhar na Gaedhilge)*,[18] the first issue of which appeared on the first of November, 1882. Although it cannot claim to be the first Irish language monthly (*An Gaodhal. The Keltic Journal and Educator* was published in Brooklyn, New York, in October, 1881, and continued in existence until 1904), *The Gaelic Journal* was a remarkable achievement considering that those years between 1878 and 1893 were not exactly favourable to such an enterprise: they were the years of the Land League, Home

Rule measures, the Parnell split, etc. The journal contained original compositions in Irish and articles, commentary, and correspondence in both Irish and English, discussing the problems of the Irish language and its literature.

But in spite of the great efforts made by these several societies, the language continued to decline, and the official census of 1891 registered a further fall in the number who could speak it. The official accounts enumerated both monoglot Irish speakers and those who spoke both Irish and English from 1851 on, and the revelation was less than promising—even for those diehards who continued to look on the bright side.[19]

Year	Irish only	Irish & English	Population
1851	319,602	1,204,684	6,552,385
1861	163,275	942,261	5,798,967
1871	103,562	714,313	5,412,377
1881	64,167	885,765	5,174,836
1891	38,192	642,053	4,704,750

These figures were no doubt known to the members of The Gaelic Union and to the members of the new society that succeeded it and assumed publication of its monthly. The Gaelic League (Connradh na Gaedhilge) was founded on July 31, 1893, under the leadership of Eoin Mac Néill and Douglas Hyde. In contrast to the other organizations that had been more or less content to headquarter in Dublin, the new society sought to embrace all of the people by establishing branches throughout the land. Its growth was slow until Mr D. P. Moran, a journalist who had been working in London, started editing a weekly called *The Leader* and began to teach people how essential their language was to their nationalism. With that, the League began to sweep the land. By 1897 only 43 branches had been formed, but by 1902 there were 227 branches, and by 1904 a spectacular increase to nearly 600 had occurred, with a total membership of around 50,000. But Moran's influence must not be allowed to obscure the contribution made by the scores of idealistic and enthusiastic language teachers who frequently taught more than one class on the same evening, and often in remote and out of the way places in very inclement weather.[20]

The general aims of the League may be summarized in four points: to keep the language alive in those areas in which it was spoken (*Gaeltacht*), to support and strengthen it where it was losing ground (*Breac-Ghaeltacht*), to restore it to the new English-speaking districts

(*Galltacht*), and to foster the growth of literature in it. In order to attain this last goal, the *Oireachtas* was established. Miss A. W. Patterson had, in October 1884, put before the League a plan for 'the revival of the ancient Gaelic musical and literary festivals', with the result that an annual *Feis Ceoil* ('Musical Festival') was instituted. But by August of 1896 it had become clear that the *Feis Ceoil* was not fulfilling the League's expectations of it, and it was decided to establish 'an *Oireachtas* or public assembly on behalf of the Irish language'. The first *Oireachtas* was a very modest affair held on the day before the *Feis Ceoil* in 1897, and the few competitions it organized were all literary—except for one competition for a song or anthem to be sung by members of the League at its meetings. However, this first meeting was regarded as a success, and a more ambitious programme was prepared for the next one; the *Oireachtas* continued to flourish until the enthusiasm for it was dissipated in the political dissensions of the early 1920s.[21]

In 1895 the Gaelic League had taken over responsibility for the editorship of *Irisleabhar na Gaedhilge* and it set about publishing its own paper. On 6 January 1898, the first number of *Fáinne an Lae*, the first Irish weekly, was published, and on 18 March 1899, the first number of another weekly, *An Claidheamh Soluis*. These two weeklies were combined in August 1900, under the name of the latter, and it was to remain the official organ of the League for more than thirty years.[22]

The League took another important step in 1900 when it decided to establish its own publishing board, Coiste na gClódhanna or Coiste na bhFoilseachán, with Patrick Pearse as its first secretary and J. Lloyd as general editor. This decision, needless to say, was of far reaching significance, for the Coiste published not only pamphlets and other materials in English explaining the League's aims and activities but books in Irish as well.[23]

An Intermediate Education Commission had been set up in 1898 to examine intermediate education in Ireland, and one of the questions raised and debated before the Commission was the place which was to be accorded to the Irish language in the schools. Among the leaders of the opposition to the inclusion of Irish in the curriculum was Robert Atkinson, an Englishman who had been educated at Trinity College, Dublin, and was Professor of Comparative Philology and Sanscrit there from 1871 till 1907. Strangely enough, although he knew more about Irish and its literature than any others in his camp (he was president of the Royal Irish Academy from 1901 to 1906), Atkinson was the most formidable opponent to its inclusion. Among the Old Irish texts that had been published, he said, 'it would be difficult to find a book in which there was not some passage so silly or so indecent as to give you a shock from which you would not recover for the rest of your life'.[24] But against his testimony, the Gaelic League brought the statements of such renowned Celtic scholars as Heinrich Zimmer, Ernst Windisch, L. C. Stern, Holger Pedersen, Georges Dottin, John Rhŷs, and others, and they carried the day. In 1908, the League won its most important victory: it succeeded in making Irish a compulsory subject for Irishmen in the entrance examination for the newly established National University.

The president and leader of the Gaelic League from the beginning had been Douglas Hyde, and much of its success is to be attributed to his energy and his vision. But in 1915, he resigned his post, saying that there were many in the organization who now felt that it ought to work not only for preservation of the language but to win independence as well. Since he had always fought to keep the League non-partisan and apolitical, he felt that he could no longer serve it as president. But although the organization had restricted itself in the early period to the language issue, it had indeed nurtured most of the leaders of Sinn Féin and the other nationalist movements that led to the 1916 Rebellion and culminated in the Irish Free State (Saorstát Éireann) in 1922. Patrick Pearse, who was former editor of the League's paper, An Claidheamh Soluis, and who was to be 'president' of Ireland during Easter week, 1916, said with some justification:

> The Irish Revolution really began when the seven proto-Gaelic Leaguers met in O'Connell Street . . . Whatever happens to the Gaelic League it has left its mark upon Irish history and the things that will be dreamt of and attempted in the new Ireland by the men and the sons of the men that went to school to the Gaelic League will be dreamt of and attempted—yea, and accomplished—just because the Gaelic League has made them possible.[25]

If it can be truly said that the Revolution began in 1893 with the establishment of The Gaelic League and that it was fulfilled by proclaiming the Irish Free State (established in 1922), and a Republic in all but name in 1937, then it is fitting indeed that on 6 May 1938, Douglas Hyde was elected the first president of the Republic of Ireland.

From the very beginning, various governments (first, that of the Free State, then that of the Republic of Ireland) have pledged themselves to do as much as possible for the Irish language. Steps were taken to make the language more or less a compulsory subject in the schools, for every school that received a government grant was obliged to teach Irish a specified number of hours every week. If the quota was surpassed, more money was received, and still more money was made available if other subjects were taught through the medium of Irish. Furthermore, prospective candidates for posts in the Civil Service were required to demonstrate some degree of proficiency in the language. Unfortunately, it soon became clear that more was expected of the schools than they could achieve in the context of the increasing apathy of the people in general regarding the language; their own failure and that of the politicians to halt the decline of the language in the Gaeltachts (a decline not compensated for by the increase in the number of people learning the language) led to further disillusionment.

The Irish government has tried to help the language outside the classroom, too. In 1926, it set up An Gúm, a company that has since published hundreds of books in Irish. It is true that many of these are translations and many of the rest are either school books or books without any real literary merit, but at least the Gúm provided for the first time a substantial body of reading matter in Irish, much of it written by native speakers of the language.

In the matter of language, as in other matters, the government in power in Ireland is swayed by public opinion. During the war for independence there was widespread enthusiasm for the language: the ideal was a Free Ireland and an Irish-speaking Ireland. But alas, many of the leaders were lost in the 1916 Rebellion and more still in the Civil War of 1921–22, and the people became apathetic. For that reason, although no political party can afford to neglect the Irish language, none goes so far as to proclaim boldly the ideal of an Irish-only Ireland. The goal, rather, is a bilingual country.[26] Even so, hitherto the pattern in Ireland has been as follows: the grandmother and grandfather are monoglot Irish; the father and mother bilingual: Irish speakers who can speak English; the children are bilingual, speaking English but able to speak Irish also; the grandchildren are monoglot English.

It would be fair to say that most of the movements fighting for the survival of the language today are led by men who have learned it as a second language. This alone reflects the fact that Irish-speaking Irishmen are relatively indifferent to their language—and that is not an inexplicable attitude. For centuries Irish was regarded as the language of the oppressed—both politically and economically, and the economic prospects of a monoglot Irishman even in the Ireland of today are not at all as good as those of his English-speaking brothers and sisters. The latter can learn Irish as a cultural activity, their interest in it being heightened because of its national significance. But to the former, if learning English is not a matter of life and death, it is the means of raising him from the level of farm labourer or fisherman and of escape from those Gaeltacht districts that are proverbial for their barrenness.

Such indifference to the language was perhaps at its greatest during the twenties and thirties of this century, in the period immediately following the Civil War. It seemed during those years that the initial enthusiasm for the language had either dissipated or had been lost in the effort to gain political independence and in the Civil War that resulted from that struggle. In those years more than one Irish periodical fell by the wayside, and even the Gaelic League's periodical ceased publication in 1932.

But by the beginning of the forties, the old interest had been revived. In 1939, the first *Oireachtas* since 1924 was held, and it has continued annually since then. Two years later, the Gaelic League began publishing its journal again, this time under the name *An Glór*. It changed name and format again in 1948, and now *Feasta*, as it is called, is one of the most interesting periodicals in Ireland. It is an Irish-only publication, devoted especially to problems of language and culture. Another important periodical, sponsored by the Gaelic societies of the universities and issued monthly is *Comhar*. It welcomes all sorts of contributions, but favours those dealing with contemporary social and economic problems and the practical arts, such as architecture. Then there are other periodicals, more parochial in appeal and circulation: *Agus* in Munster, *An tUltach* in Ulster; *Ar Aghaidh*, which served Connacht, and *Amárach*, which catered to all the Gaeltachts, have not survived.

In March, 1943, *Inniu*, the first Irish-language weekly newspaper appeared. At one time it achieved a circulation of over ten thousand, and there was talk of making it a daily newspaper, but then its circulation decreased, and it finally ceased publication on 24 August 1984; its place was taken by *Anois*, which began in mid-September of that year. In addition, the chief daily papers of Ireland have columns in Irish, appearing either daily or two or three times a week.

Perhaps one of the most important events of recent times was the founding of An Club Leabhar ('The Irish Books Club') in 1948. Its membership slowly but steadily grew, so that by the mid-fifties, it had distributed more than 73,000 books. There is no doubt that the very fact of its existence has encouraged new writers to use Irish as a literary medium, and has shown that there is a future for Irish book publishing.

§2

Generally speaking, there are two distinct bodies of literature in Ireland today: Anglo-Irish literature coming from the Galltacht, and Gaelic literature issuing ultimately (though not directly) from the Gaeltacht. In a primitive society (as the Gaeltacht was until fairly recently) and an impoverished one (as it still is to some extent today), the literary tradition is of necessity an oral tradition. In the oral tradition of the Gaeltacht the most important element was the folktale; folktales were numerous and their materials varied. One cannot overemphasize the role these played in the culture that was transmitted from generation to generation by Irish speakers. There is not a country in Europe (some would say none this side of Russia) that can compare with Ireland in the matter of folktales.[27] One has only to think about the fact that there were hundreds of tales not unlike those made famous by the brothers Grimm in Germany and by C. Perrault in France alive in the mouths of story-tellers up to the beginning of this century to get some idea of the wonders that have survived in Irish oral tradition. And yet their worth went unrecognized for a long time—almost too long! They were part of a way of life that was fading fast, and that by now has nearly vanished; there is no doubt at all that an enormous number of those tales has been lost.

Dr Douglas Hyde (1860–1949) was one of the pioneers in the work of collecting that material.[28] To him and his successors Séamus Ó Duilearga (Delargy), Fionán Mac Coluim, and Pádraig Ó Siochfhradha, we owe the establishment of the Folklore Commission (supported by the Government), which was the means of rescuing thousands of these tales from oblivion. It made possible the development of one of the largest folklore collections in the world, a collection that now, since the merging of the Commission with the Department of Irish Folklore at University College Dublin, forms a part of that department's resources. The material has not yet been studied in depth, but there is every expectation of reaping a great harvest from such study. The Sir John Rhŷs Memorial Lecture on 'The Gaelic Story-Teller', which Professor Ó Duilearga delivered before the British Academy in 1945, is a well-spring of knowledge on the subject, but no one was more willing than Ó Duilearga himself to admit that it barely scratched the surface of a subject that is bound to be very revealing in the future.

Ó Duilearga gives us a glimpse of the way in which the oral traditon worked in the picture he sketches for us of the district of Teilionn in south-west Donegal. A century or so ago only a handful of people there received any education, and yet there existed a popular culture of very high calibre. There was not a village there without a house to which the same company would go night after night throughout the winter to revel in the sounds of story and song. The chief entertainer at these gatherings seems to have been the story-teller. For some reason or another, these story-tellers preferred not to tell their stories in their own homes, and so they would go to some other house, where, free of the distractions of their children and amidst a gathering that treasured their gift, they would apply themselves to the practice of their art.

Invited guests made up the greatest part of the audience, of course, and they paid for the privilege of being present by helping with the household chores, such as carrying in peat, fetching water from the well, and arranging stools and chairs. When everything and everybody were in place, the man of the house would light his pipe and puff on it. Then he would pass it to the most venerable man among the guests, who would take a puff and pass it back. The man of the house then passed it to someone else, and so on, until each had smoked. In the meantime, the company made small talk. After this prelude of smoking and light conversation, they would come to the main business of the evening, the stories. Every story-teller seems to have specialized in one of two kinds of story: the long tale (*scéalaíocht*), especially those about the ancient heroes (*scéalta gaiscígh*) or tales about specific persons and places (*seanchas*). To be sure, there was room for other entertainers, too, such as those who could sing or who knew the words to various songs. But there was never any doubt about who commanded the greatest respect: it was he who could recite the tales about Fionn and the other ancient heroes.

One of the best storytellers Ó Duilearga ever met was Seán Ó Conaill of Kerry. Seán was seventy years old at the time of their first encounter, and he had only once been away from the district in which he was born. He could neither speak nor understand English. He was illiterate in one sense, and yet he knew scores of tales by heart, that is to say he could recite them almost word for word in the same way each time. His almost incredible feats of memory are exemplified in the following incident. When he was a boy, he twice heard the same section of O'Grady's edition of *Diarmaid and Gráinne* read. Fifty years later, he could tell the story word for word as he had heard it read. Ó Duilearga published the stories he got from Seán Ó Conaill in a thick tome entitled *Leabhar Sheáin Í Chonaill* (Dublin, 1949). The tales, along with some poetry, fill nearly four hundred printed pages.[29]

It was Douglas Hyde who did most to alert the public to the value of the folktales preserved by the people of the Gaeltacht. His first book, *Sgéulaigheachta* (1889) was a collection of folktales. It was followed by others, *Beside the Fire* (London, 1890), *Cois na Teineadh* (Dublin, 1891), and *Sgéalta Thomáis Uí Cathasaigh* (Dublin, 1939). In addition to being a scholar, Hyde was a littérateur. Among his original compositions in Irish are ten short plays (four of which Lady Gregory translated into English) and a number of simple yet attractive poems.[30] Perhaps it was the artist in him who saw and appreciated the special virtues of the poetry that was on the tongues and in the minds of the Irish speakers he met in the Gaeltacht. Some of these he published with translations in his *Love Songs of Connacht* in 1893. It is difficult to overemphasize the impact which this collection made on the public. Not only did it open the eyes of the Irish people to the beauty of Gaeltacht literature, it also exercised a profound influence on Anglo-Irish writers, such as J. M. Synge and others. Indeed, it is said of Synge that the '*Love Songs of Connacht*, which is little more than the living tradition set down in print, was ever in his hands'.[31]

The word 'song' in the book's title reminds us vividly that, like every other country, Ireland has its body of folk music and verse, the result of a corporate urge for self-expression either in its creation or in its preservation and perhaps to some extent in both, making it in some mysterious way an emanation of the people.[32]

In 1796, four years after a great Belfast Harpers Festival, Edward Bunting published his first volume of sixty-six tunes. But it was 1802 that was Bunting's *annus mirabilis* as a collector, for it was in that year that he made a tour of Connacht and part of Munster to collect folk tunes, employing Patrick Lynch to go ahead of him and take down the Irish words of the tunes, for although he himself had no Irish he appreciated, indeed, he was probably the first in Ireland to appreciate that the words to the tunes are no less important than the tunes themselves. Bunting's second volume appeared in 1809, but his third and final volume was not published until 1840, some three years before he died.

Bunting's work of collecting folk tunes was continued by others such as Henry Hudson, George Petrie (the associate of O'Donovan and O'Curry on the Irish Ordnance Survey), William Forde, John Edward Pigot (the close friend of Thomas Davis), James Goodman (Rector of Skibbereen and Canon of Ross and, for the last twelve years of his life, Professor of Irish at Trinity College), and Patrick Weston Joyce (the author of *Irish Music and Song* [Dublin, 1888] and *A Social History of Ancient Ireland*, I and II [London, 1903], among other works). Unfortunately, most of their collections are still in manuscripts which have never been catalogued or collated, and so the exact number of tunes they contain, excluding duplicates and variants, cannot be stated. But together with the collection made by the Irish Folklore Commission they must constitute a vast treasure house of song unsurpassed in abundance and diversity by that of any nation of comparable area and population. In quality, too, they have commanded the admiration of some of the most discerning critics. 'Of all the countries in the world,' wrote Sir Arnold Bax, 'Ireland possesses the most varied and beautiful folk music.'[33]

We do not know which song Rosa Dartle sang to her own accompaniment on the harp to produce in David Copperfield the reaction which Dickens so vividly describes, but it could be any one of scores of Irish love songs:

> I don't know what it was, in her touch or her voice, that made that song the most unearthly I have ever heard in my life, or can imagine. There was something fearful in the reality of it. It was as if it had never been written, or set to music, but sprung out of the passion within her; which found imperfect utterance in the sounds of her voice, and crouched again when all was still. . . (chap. xxix)

It could have been 'Domhnall Óg', perhaps one of the most popular folk songs of Connacht and of the Scottish Highlands.

Donal Ogue

Donal Ogue, when you cross the water,
Take me with you to be your partner,
And at fair and market you'll be well looked after,
And you can sleep with the Greek king's daughter.

You said you'd meet me, but you were lying,
Beside the sheepfold when the day was dying,
I whistled first, then I started hailing,
But all I heard was the young lambs' wailing.

You said you'd give me—an airy giver!—
A golden ship with masts of silver,

Twelve market towns to be my fortune
And a fine white mansion beside the ocean.

You said you'd give me—'tis you talk lightly!—
Fish-skin gloves that would fit me tightly,
Bird-skin shoes when I went out walking,
And a silken dress would set Ireland talking.

Ah, Donal Ogue, you'd not find me lazy,
Like many a high-born expensive lady;
I'd do your milking and I'd nurse your baby,
And if you were set on I'd back you bravely.

To Lonely Well I wander sighing,
'Tis there I do my fill of crying,
When I see the world but not my charmer
And all his looks the shade of amber.

I saw you first on a Sunday evening
Before the Easter, and I was kneeling.
'Twas about Christ's passion that I was reading,
But my eyes were on you and my own heart bleeding.

My mother said we should not be meeting,
That I should pass and not give you greeting;
'Twas a good time surely she chose for cheating
With the stable bare and the horse retreating.

You might as well let him have me, mother,
And every penny you have moreover;
Go beg your bread like any other
But him and me don't seek to bother.

Black as a sloe is the heart inside me,
Black as a coal with the griefs that drive me,
Black as a boot print on shining hallways,
And 'twas you that blackened it ever and always.

For you took what's before me and what's behind me,
You took east and west when you wouldn't mind me,
Sun and moon from my sky you've taken,
And God as well, or I'm much mistaken.[34]

More probably it was a folksong of the simpler, less sophisticated kind, which is well represented by the various versions of 'How well for the Birds':

How well for the birds that can rise in their flight
And settle together on the one bough at night,
It is not so with me and the boy of my heart,
Each morning the sun finds us rising apart.

How well for the flowers when my sweetheart goes
walking,
How well for the house when he sits in it talking,
How well for the woman with whom he'll be sleeping,
Her morning star and her star of evening.

As white as the sloebush in spring is my darling,
As bright as the seabirds from wave to wave swarming,
As the sun fills the ocean all day with its gleaming,
Rising and setting he fills all my dreaming.[35]

It is not without significance that after compiling *Love Songs of Connacht* (1893) Douglas Hyde went on to write *The Story of Early Gaelic Literature* (1895), and then *A Literary History of Ireland* (1899); for Hyde, the *Love Songs* were but a part of the Irish literary tradition. *A Literary History of Ireland* was a volume of inestimable value at the time of publication in that it introduced the public to the treasures of Irish literature for the first time; it is still well worth reading for its sympathetic handling of the subject.

It is also significant that the literary revival of which Hyde was a part not only drew inspiration and material from the Gaeltacht but also caused the Gaeltacht to produce literature of a new kind. Indeed, it is one of the welcome features of that revival that some of its classics have been produced by the people of the Gaeltacht itself, in particular: *An tOileánach* by Tomás Ó Criomhthain (*recte* 'Criomhthain from Mac/'ac Cromhthain*), *Fiche Blian ag Fás* (1933, 1976), by Muiris Ó Súileabháin, and *Peig .i. A Scéal Féin* (1935), by Peig Sayers.[36] To these, some would add *Séadna* by Peadar Ó Laoghaire (first published in *Irisleabhar na Gaedhilge*, 1894–1901, then in book form, Dublin, 1904 and again in 1988), but it is not strictly comparable to the other books mentioned and deserves to be treated separately. The strangeness of the life treated in these three biographies no doubt contributed in some measure to their popularity in the original as it certainly did in the subsequent translations. *An tOileánach* was translated into English by Robin Flower as *The Islandman* in 1937; *Fiche Blian ag Fás* was translated into English by Moya Llewelyn Davies and George Thompson as *Twenty Years A-Growing* (1933), into French by Raymond Queneau as *Vingt ans de Jeunesse* (1936), and into German by Elisabeth Aman under the title *Inselheimat* (1956); *Peig* was translated into English, under that title, by Bryan Mac Mahon in 1974.

In his Introduction to *Twenty Years A-Growing*, E. M. Forster commented,

... it is worth saying 'This book is unique', lest he [the reader] forget what a very odd document he has got hold of. He is about to read an account of neolithic civilisation from the inside. Synge and others have described it from the outside, and very sympathetically, but I know of no other instance where it has itself become vocal, and addressed modernity.[37]

Forster is no doubt exaggerating in order to drive home his point; after all, we have no idea of what life was like in the neolithic age, but we can guess that it did not bear much resemblance to life on the Great Blasket Island at the end of the nineteenth and the beginning of the twentieth century. However, at their best, *Fiche Blian ag Fás*, *Peig*, and *An tOileánach* give us the impression that we have the story and the thoughts of three persons who were in immediate and direct contact with their fellow men and with their environment, in a language which reflected not only the lively intelligence of its users but also the full adequacy to which it had been brought by a long process of development. Of the three books, *An tOileánach* stands up best to rereading, partly because it is less of a sociological document than the other two and depends less on the 'strangeness' of the life depicted, and partly because it is a better linguistic reflection of a more individual character and outlook. Whatever the ultimate reason, *An tOileánach* becomes on frequent perusal and rereading a book which one cherishes. One can understand why Máire Mhac an tSaoi has called it one of the solid achievements of Irish literature, and why David Greene proclaimed, 'Here, at last, is the speech of the people producing results far beyond the power of O'Leary, and it will live as long as the Irish language is read'.[38]

Books describing the various Gaeltachts (and one must remember that they included 'stories' such as those of Máire, [*v. infra*, p. 282], as well as autobiographies and reminiscences by people born and bred in the Irish-speaking districts) enjoyed such popularity that they produced a reaction and the inevitable parodies. The most celebrated parody is *An Béal Bocht* by Myles na gCopaleen, one of the many *noms de plume* of Brian O'Nolan (1912–66), published in 1941 and— in translation under the title *The Poor Mouth*—in 1973. In Anglo-Irish as in Irish, the phrase 'putting on the poor mouth' means making a pretence of being poor in order to gain some personal advantage from creditors or prospective creditors, continual grumbling at being poor, etc. People other than Irish speakers tend to do this, and indeed *An Béal Bocht* is full of sarcastic comment on aspects of Irish life both within and without the Gaeltachts. Myles's

caricature of the folklore collector in the Gaeltacht, down from
Dublin, is especially good:

> There was a gentleman from Dublin travelling through the country
> who was extremely interested in Gaelic. The gentleman understood
> that in Corkadoragha there were people alive who were unrivalled in
> any other region and also that their likes would never be there again.
> He had an instrument called a gramophone and this instrument was
> capable of memorising all it heard if anyone narrated stories or old lore
> to it; it could also spew out all it had heard whenever one desired it. It
> was a wonderful instrument and frightened many people in the area
> and struck others dumb; it is doubtful whether its like will ever be there
> again. Since folks thought that it was unlucky, the gentleman had a
> difficult task collecting the folklore tales from them.
>
> For that reason, he did not attempt to collect the folklore of our
> ancients and our ancestors except under cover of darkness when both
> he and the instrument were hidden in the end of a cabin and both of
> them listening intently. It was evident that he was a wealthy person
> because he spent much money on spirits every night to remove the
> shyness and disablement from the old people's tongues. He had that
> reputation throughout the countryside and whenever it became known
> that he was visiting in Jimmy's or Jimmy Tim Pat's house, every old
> fellow who lived within a radius of five miles hastened there to seek
> tongue-loosening from this fiery liquid medicine; it must be mentioned
> that many of the youths accompanied them.
>
> On the night of which we speak, the gentleman was in the house of
> Maximilian O'Penisa quietly resting in the darkness and with the
> hearing-machine by him. There were at least a hundred old fellows
> gathered in around him, sitting dumb and invisible, in the shadow of
> the walls and passing the gentleman's bottles of spirits from one to the
> other. Sometimes a little spell of weak whispering was audible but
> generally no sound except the roar of the water falling outside from the
> gloomy skies, much as if those on high were emptying buckets of that
> vile wetness on the world. If the spirits loosened the men's tongues, it
> did not result in talk but rather in rolling and tasting on their lips the
> bright drop of spirits. Time went by in that manner and it was rather
> late in the night. As a result of both the heavy silence inside and the
> hum of the rain outside, the gentleman was becoming a little
> disheartened. He had not collected one of the gems of our ancients that
> night and had lost spirits to the value of five pounds without result.
>
> Suddenly he noticed a commotion at the doorway. Then, by the
> weak light of the fire, he saw the door being pushed in (it was never
> equipped with a bolt) and in came a poor old man, drenched and wet,
> drunk to the full of his skin and creeping instead of walking upright
> because of the drunkenness. The creature was lost without delay in the

darkness of the house but wherever he lay on the floor, the gentleman's heart leaped when he heard a great flow of talk issuing from that place. It really was rapid, complicated, stern speech—one might have thought that the old fellow was swearing drunkenly—but the gentleman did not tarry to understand it. He leaped up and set the machine near the one who was spewing out Gaelic. It appeared that the gentleman thought the Gaelic extremely difficult and he was overjoyed that the machine was absorbing it; he understood that good Gaelic is difficult and that the best Gaelic of all is well-nigh unintelligible. After about an hour the stream of talk ceased. The gentleman was pleased with the night's business. As a token of his gratitude he put a white pipe, a jot of tobacco and a little bottle of spirits in the old fellow's pocket who was now in an inebriated slumber where he had fallen. Then the gentleman departed homewards in the rain with the machine, leaving them his blessing quietly but no one responded to it because drunkenness had come in a floodtide now through the skull of everyone of them who was present.

It was said later in the area that the gentleman was highly praised for the lore which he had stored away in the hearing-machine that night. He journeyed to Berlin, a city of Germany in Europe, and narrated all that the machine had heard in the presence of the most learned ones of the Continent. These learned ones said that they never heard any fragment of Gaelic which was so good, so poetic and so obscure as it and that [they] were sure there was no fear for Gaelic while the like was audible in Ireland. They bestowed fondly a fine academic degree on the gentleman and, something more interesting still, they appointed a small committee of their own members to make a detailed study of the language of the machine to determine whether any sense might be made of it.

I do not know whether it was Gaelic or English or a strange irregular dialect which was in the old speech which the gentleman collected from among us here in Corkadoragha but it is certain that whatever word was uttered that night, came from our rambling pig.[39]

The Irish in *An Béal Bocht* parodies that of the native Irish speakers. For instance, in the above excerpt, the phrase 'the like(s) will never be there again' echoes the oft-repeated phrase in *An tOileánach* 'mar ná beidh ár leithéidí arís ann' ('for the likes of us will never be here again'). Another phrase in *An Béal Bocht*, translated 'a child among the ashes,' repeats Máire's oft repeated cliché about the child 'in a thachrán ar fud a' ghríosaigh'. It may well be, as Máirtín Ó Cadhain has suggested, that 'In satirizing the life and customs as described in Gaeltacht books, it [*An Béal Bocht*] finished off for ever the folklore man of the early part of the century.'[40]

Of course, it is inconceivable that any of the three Gaeltacht books mentioned should have been written and published were it not for the Irish literary revival. When the pioneers of that revival began to use Irish as a literary medium, they were picking up a language that had long since been restricted to the narrow confines and the stark life of the Gaeltacht, a language which was fast breaking up into three or four dialects because it had no recognized and accepted standard form, a language that could not express the more urban life of the Galltacht without straining its resources and adding to them.[41]

When the Gaelic League began its work, the people of the Gaeltacht, the people who lived their lives in and through the Irish language, were for the most part illiterate in the sense that they neither read nor wrote their language. The League faced the task of persuading them to become literate in their native tongue, and this meant the reversal of the process whereby they had been accustomed to think that the only way to climb out of their chronic poverty was to forget their own language and to embrace English.

On the other hand, the leaders of the Gaelic League had to ensure that the people of the Gaeltacht, and the people of other parts of Ireland who were now learning the language, had a literature worth reading and cultivating in their own day and age: they could not be expected to be content with the literature of a bygone age. But a modern Irish literature did not then exist, and it could be argued that the Irish literary tradition, glorious as it had been in the past, had now been reduced to almost nothing.

> A hundred years ago Irish literature, once the greatest in Western Europe, had declined to a collection of folksongs and traditional stories. There was little new writing, the language had lost its standards, and the dialects (which presumably had always existed) were now its only living form. Although modern Irish writing is historically related to the writing of previous centuries, the immediate succession is through a peasant society and a folk literature.[42]

The implications of this fact are many, but let us spell out one, perhaps the most important one as far as Irish prose is concerned. When Irish culture and civilization were flourishing, Irish prose was used in the service of the history, the law, the medicine, and the politics of the country; in other words Irish was the official language. But it was replaced by English once the country had lost its independence, and in this way the natural development of the language was halted; henceforth, Irish became the linguistic medium of a people whose *Lebensraum* was gradually being eroded and whose interests were becoming increasingly more limited.

All this is reflected in the first attempts of the men of the revival to create a modern Irish literature. The native speakers among them can be seen to be groping for a literary style and literary models. Others for whom Irish was a second, an acquired language, were desperately rummaging in old or fairly old manuscripts in search of words and idioms: there was no such thing as a satisfactory dictionary of the language. It is no wonder that their Irish often smacks of the antiquarian. Some tried to imitate the classical prose of the seventeenth century while others favoured the long-winded style of eighteenth-century writers. A strong reaction to all this was inevitable: indeed, the absence of such a reaction would have meant that any attempt at a literary revival was doomed to failure.

One reaction is illustrated in the life and work of Father Peadar Ó Laoghaire (1839–1920).[43] Born in Co. Cork in a Gaeltacht which was at that time showing very few signs of the disintegration which was soon to overtake it, he was educated for the priesthood in Maynooth where Archbishop MacHale apparently inspired him to take an interest in his native tongue. He then returned as a parish priest to the Cork Gaeltacht. It is significant that he was fifty-five years old before any composition of his was published and that he had written some forty books or booklets before he died. His literary career was almost wholly due to the influence of the Gaelic League. Indeed, we are told that he abandoned the study of Irish altogether for some time after reading O'Curry's statement that it was the duty of a scholar to collect as much as possible of the ancient learning of Ireland before the death of the language made such collecting impossible. And the fact that his writings reflect the influence of the Gaeltacht with which he was connected as both child and adult is hardly surprising. For him, Irish was the language of the Gaeltacht, and one can almost say that his world was the world of the Gaeltacht.

His best known work, *Séadna*, first published as a serial and then in book form (1904), is based on a folk-tale motif, the man who sold his soul to the devil; and although there have been attempts to dissociate the literary work from the folk-tale and to claim considerable literary merit for it, it has the basic folk-tale attitude toward narrative, plot and character. This should not occasion any surprise, because as one who was writing to a people with whom he was wholly familiar, he tried to assimilate his story to the kind of narrative that they knew and expected. Indeed, it is obvious that he is exploiting his wealth of childhood memories, clothed, as they were, in the language of his youth. It is of singular interest that *Séadna*, for that very reason, has more appeal than his autobiography, *Mo Sgéal Féin* (1915), which is no more than a record of the events in which he took part, and which lacks all sophistication and psychological complexity.

That does not mean that *Séadna* and *Mo Sgéal Féin* were not popular with the public for which they were written. Ó Laoghaire has himself described the welcome which *Séadna* received:

> I have had on several occasions a peculiar experience regarding the story of *Séadna*. I have read it for native Irish speakers, for old people whose minds are still absolutely free from the paralysing influences of our Anglo-Irish speech. I have been astonished at the manner in which the story penetrated their whole being, roused a host of sleeping memories, brought back to them with vividness the people and the surroundings, the scenes, the joys, the sorrows, the thoughts and the conversation of their early youth. The old people everywhere recognise at once in this story a true picture of the social surroundings of their own early youth, and their hearts are intensely moved at the recognition. If there be, therefore, people who find that they cannot see 'anything' in it, the fault must be in their own mental vision. A story without 'anything' in it could never produce the effect which I have seen this story produce upon Irish-speaking old people.[44]

It is easy to understand why Ó Laoghaire's *Séadna* had such a warm welcome from the people of his own Gaeltacht. Here, instead of stilted, bookish Irish, instead of a ponderous style based on seventeenth- and eighteenth-century models, they could now read the language which they themselves spoke and in a style with which they were familiar from their own oral, folk tradition. Unfortunately, there were other Gaeltachts, and to their inhabitants the Irish of *Séadna* was not so immediately intelligible. Still, it was an improvement on most of the material previously offered to them. And all were convinced that what was needed in language textbooks as well as in literature was *caint na ndaoine* 'the language of the people'. No wonder that Ó Laoghaire wrote in 1900:

> In order to preserve Irish as a *spoken* language, we must preserve our *spoken* Irish. That is to say we must write and print exactly what the people speak . . . I am determined to write down most carefully every provincialism I can get hold of. Then I shall be sure to have the people's language.[45]

And no wonder that he proceeded to modernize some of the Old Irish sagas, to translate such well-known works as the Four Gospels, the

Acts of the Apostles, Thomas à Kempis's *De Imitatione Christi*, as well as to write another 'novel' (*Niamh*), plays and textbooks.

It so happened that the people's language which Ó Laoghaire used was both vigorous and dignified. What Robin Flower had to say about Peig Sayers' language applies to some extent to Ó Laoghaire's:

> She has so clean and finished a style of speech that you can follow all the nicest articulations of the language on her lips without any effort; she is a natural orator, with so keen a sense of the turn of phrase and the lifting rhythm appropriate to Irish that her words could be written down as they leave her lips, and they would have the effect of literature with no savour of the artificiality of composition.[46]

Ó Laoghaire's language was studied extensively, not least by professors of Irish such as Cormac Ó Cadhlaigh, whose two books *Ceart na Gaedhilge* (n.d.) and *Gnás na Gaedhilge* (1940) depended extensively on it for examples, T. F. O'Rahilly, who edited some of Ó Laoghaire's works on Irish idiom, and Osborn Bergin, who, with Shán Ó Cuív, produced *Séadna* in the modernized orthography they were sponsoring.[47]

Aodh de Blácam, writing in 1929, claimed in effect that Ó Laoghaire's style became the standard of modern Irish writing and that he made a modern Irish literature possible.[48] There is pardonable exaggeration of an underlying truth in his statement. Ó Laoghaire was trying to establish a standard form for the Irish language and he almost succeeded in getting Munster Irish accepted as such. Unfortunately, that dialect was not the most widely spoken in Ireland, even at that time, and it was dwindling at a faster rate than the others. It might be fairer to say with an earlier critic of Ó Laoghaire's work that

> an tAthair Peadar set himself to write not a well-planned piece of art but a well-written piece of Irish: his thought was of the tricks of idiom, and not of the ways of literature.[49]

But well-written Irish was so scarce that it is no wonder that *Séadna* was accepted as literature, and that no less a critic than Patrick Pearse greeted it with the words, 'Here, at last, is literature'.[50]

Appointed editor in 1903 of *An Claidheamh Soluis*, one of the periodicals to come into existence under the aegis of The Gaelic League, Patrick Henry Pearse (1879–1916)—or as he was known in Irish, Pádraic Mac Piarais—soon found that the task of re-establishing Irish as a literary medium was as difficult if not more difficult than restoring it as a spoken language.[51] In common with editors of other Irish papers and periodicals, he found that his would-be contributors believed that anything written in tolerable Irish should be accepted for publication, and that the one great source of material was the rich oral traditions of the different Gaeltachts. Indeed, it is surprising how many children (at that time often the only literate members of the typical Irish-speaking family) were employed to write down folk-tales or odd pieces of folklore collected from oral tradition. Consequently, one of Pearse's first tasks was to convince his readers and writers that a short story was altogether different from a folk-tale and that the technique of writing the former differed from that of reciting the latter. He tried to do this as much by example as by instruction. Thus in 1905, he wrote a short story, *Iosagán* ('Jesukin'), and four years later had this to say about it in his school magazine, *An Macaomh*:

> *Iosagán* has been described by an able but eccentric critic as a standard of revolt. It was meant as a standard of revolt, but my critics must pardon me if I say that the standard is not the standard of impressionism. It is the standard of definite art form as opposed to folk form. I may or may not be a good standard bearer, but at any rate the standard is raised and the writers of Irish are flocking to it.[52]

The 'able but eccentric critic' was the Revd Dr Richard Henebry (De Hindeberg) (1863–1916), who had been a student of Celtic under Thurneysen and Zimmer and had been appointed a professor of the subject in University College, Cork, after a period of teaching in the United States. In a piece of powerful invective he had to his own satisfaction convicted Pearse's story of 'impressionism', 'Hellenism' and 'Keltic Note', in addition to 'Béarlachas' (Anglicisms), bastard grammatical forms and slang, and had concluded:

> Considered as an emancipation from these [the educational influences exerted by Pearse], then if Irish literature is the talk of big, broadchested men, this is the frivolous petulancy of latter day English genre scribblers, and their utterance is the mincing of an under-assistant floor walker of a millinery shop.[53]

Three features in *Iosagán* attracted criticism, the attitude of the story-teller—'this ethereal, extracorporeal, omniscient intelligence', the abrupt opening of the story—'this now popular explosive opening', and the detailed descriptions of persons and of natural scenery which, it was claimed, were holding up the action. The yardstick of criticism, it is obvious, was the oral folk-tale, where the opening is usually the conventional 'Once upon a time, and a good time it was, there lived a man . . .,' where characters are observed merely as initiators of actions, and where all descriptions, either of persons or of scenes, are regarded as irrelevant and uninteresting.

Pearse was aware of the issues involved in his argument with Henebry and his followers. He was trying to drag Irish literature into the twentieth century:

> This is the twentieth century; and no literature can take root in the twentieth century which is not of the twentieth century . . . We hold the folktale to be a beautiful and gracious thing only in its own time . . . and its time and place are the winter fireside, or the spring sowing time, or the country road at anytime. Thus, we lay down the proposition that a living literature *cannot* (and if it could), should not be built up on the folktale.[54]

As editor of *An Claidheamh Soluis*, Pearse exercised considerable influence on the course of the literature which was gradually emerging in modern Irish. His literary judgements, although not very original, were sound and for the period very salutary, and his literary contributions, although not numerous (a handful of lyrics, two plays, and a few short stories)—and not masterpieces, were by no means negligible and served as useful models.

His short stories were collected and published in two volumes, *Iosagán agus Sgéalta Eile* (1907) and *An Mháthair agus Sgéalta Eile* (1916). Read today, the stories strike one as rather sentimental and somewhat unrealistic, but perhaps one should remember that Pearse was, among other things, an educator as well as a writer, and that some of his stories were meant for children rather than adults. There can be no doubt that he had a certain simplicity of vision of the kind that he found or thought that he found in children. It should be noted that his second volume of short stories has a quality of astringency lacking in his first and shows a greater mastery over the form of the short story. Granted, however, that his talent for the short story may have been modest, it had an altogether disproportionate influence on his time.

One of the first writers to respond to Patrick Pearse's call for short stories not modelled on the folk-tale and for a more modern literature was Pádraic Ó Conaire (1882–1928).[55] Though he was of Irish-speaking parents, Ó Conaire was brought up in Galway to speak English until he was about eleven years old—when his mother died. His father, faced with the collapse of his once flourishing business, had fled to America some years before. The young orphan was given a home by an uncle who kept a shop in Rosmuc in a thoroughly Irish-speaking locality, and he quickly learnt Irish. He was given a secondary school education and succeeded in passing a Civil Service examination which secured him a post in the Board of Education in London. There, apparently, he threw himself into the strongly nationalistic Irish community, undertaking to teach Irish to others in various night schools, and, to judge from his later work, reading fairly extensively in world literature. At that time, the demand to have the classics of other literatures translated into English was already making itself felt and gradually being met, and Ó Conaire would have had no difficulty in finding English translations of the works of the best known writers in French, German and Russian.

In 1904, the *Oireachtas* awarded him the first prize for a short story entitled 'Páidín Mháire'; two years later he won the same award for his short story, 'Nóra Mharcuis Bhig'. In 1908, he received the prize award for an essay on 'Sean-Litridheacht na Gaedhilge agus Nua-Litridheacht na hEorpa'.[56] This is a most interesting document in that it throws light on Ó Conaire's acquaintance with the Russian realists. He mentions, among others, Turgenev, Tolstoy, and Gorky, and shows that he knew that they had turned their backs on the folk-tales and folk-songs of their people in order to achieve literary realism. That is why he counsels Irish writers to follow in their footsteps. They should not concern themselves with the past nor with its literature (it is uncertain how much Ó Conaire knew about either), but rather with the present and with the frightening world which was emerging in it. The challenge to the writer was to describe this world, and such a challenge could not be met unless the writer was prepared to search his own heart and reveal its secrets to his fellowmen.

Obviously, Ó Conaire was interested in the theory as well as in the practice of literature, and in 1910 he completed what was to be his most ambitious work, the novel *Deoraidheacht*. In it he describes the life of a troupe of circus people in London. The description is vivid and obviously based on acute observation. There can be no doubt that he was consciously attempting to do in Irish what his literary heroes had done in English, French and Russian, and his attempt was to a certain degree a success, for *Deoraidheacht* is no mean achievement.[57] Perhaps it was too much of a *tour de force*, not for the author, but for his literary medium at that time. A writer, unless he is an outstanding genius, needs a tradition to support him in his chosen genre.

Ó Conaire returned to live in Ireland in 1914, apparently abandoning his common-law wife and children in London. (It is worth noting that women and orphans play a large part in Ó Conaire's writing, and that part needs to be studied carefully.) Whether or not he was prompted by the idea that in Ireland he could devote himself entirely to literature and thereby make a living is not certain. It is probable that one reason for his return was that, as a writer, he felt the need to know his readership as well as to renew acquaintance with the sources of his inspiration, with his childhood memories. Unfortunately, Ó Conaire soon found that an Irish author could not live on his writing even if he was prepared to do every kind of hack work. But he must have derived considerable satisfaction from having been in Ireland to witness the events of 1916, and it is significant that his one considerable achievement after returning was a collection of short stories depicting various reactions to the Insurrection, *Seacht mBuaidh an Éirghe Amach* (1918).

Before he died, a pauper with nothing to his name but a reputation as a writer, Ó Conaire had become a legend in Ireland with the result that it is extremely difficult to separate fact from fiction in the stories told about him. We cannot, however, escape the conclusion, borne out by his writings, that he was a much more complex character than the legend would lead us to believe, and that he had more than a little of that determination which in different circumstances would have helped him to develop into a writer of importance.[58]

He has been criticized on many counts: that his Irish is not grammatically correct, that it shows the influence of English in phrase and idiom, and that it is generally nerveless. In his own defence, he could have retorted that he was writing before the wealth of his dialect had been revealed, before any agreement had been reached as to the standard form of the language, that he did not set out to exploit the resources of any one dialect, and that in any case one could be a Peadar Ó Laoghaire in one's complete mastery of one dialect and still fail to produce great literature.

On behalf of Ó Conaire one could also claim that he was the first writer of modern Irish to study the techniques of the art in other modern literatures and to apply them successfully to his own practice. Furthermore, in his best work he brought to the writing of his short stories and his novel a maturity of outlook and experience unknown in Irish before his time. Although he is not a writer of the stature of Dostoevsky or even of de Maupassant, one hears echoes of these and other masters in his work and one feels that he tries to grapple with life at the same depths as they did. It is not surprising that Stephen Mac Kenna could say of him:

You have in P. O'C. absolutely the only writing you can imagine an European reading ... P. is often grammatically careless and inconsistent, sometimes confused ... but he belongs to the European kind.[59]

Professor T. de Bhaldraithe sums up his significance for modern Irish literature:

He performed a miracle for his own time. He succeeded in learning the craft of the short story; he succeeded in liberating himself from the chief faults which were ruining the attempts of the period—lack of structure, verbosity, over-addiction to outworn phrases, and restricted content. He succeeded in writing literature which was modern both in form and content in a language which had hitherto run wild for lack of cultivation.[60]

The prose we have discussed so far was by writers who, apart from Pearse, came from the Munster and Connacht Gaeltachts. It must not be assumed that the Donegal Gaeltacht did not produce prose writers, although the most prolific and genuinely talented of them were two brothers named Séamus Ó Grianna and Seosamh Mac Grianna (deriving their patronymic from two different forms of A'Grianna). They were born into a family steeped in Irish folklore and it is perhaps no wonder that both should have devoted themselves to Irish writing.

Séamus Ó Grianna (1891–1969), who wrote mostly under the pseudonym 'Máire', started his literary career by writing a few promising novels in the 1920s, including *Caisleáin Óir* 'Golden Castles' (1924), but he did not develop into a novelist of significance and chose rather to write scores of stories which tend to be short tales rather than short stories, and seem to be variations on a few basic themes or motifs. Indeed, it has been suggested (rather maliciously) that they could be grouped according to the motifs in Stith Thompson's classification system,[61] but a more benevolent critic has praised them because together they present a picture of life in the Donegal Gaeltacht.[62] One does not need to be benevolent to praise their language, for Máire's Irish Gaelic has the same vigour and suppleness as that in the aforementioned Blasket Island autobiographies—*An tOileánach*, *Peig*, and *Fiche Blian ag Fás*—and, in addition, a greater measure of literary intention. Among his best collections of tales is *Cioth agus Dealán*, which contains the notable 'Maghnus Ó Súileachán', 'An Aisling Bhréige', 'Grást' ó Dhia ar Mhicí', and 'Faoi na Fóide 's Mé Sínte'.

One should remember that the role of every writer in a minority language is a particularly hard one and that the rewards are so small that to retain some sort of artistic integrity in the face of such widespread indifference requires extraordinary determination and involves not a little suffering. This is well illustrated in Seosamh Mac Grianna's literary career (1900–69).[63] Mac Grianna first intended to pursue a literary career in English, but on reading Ó Conaire's *An Chéad Chloch*, he resolved to devote himself to his mother tongue. His first compositions appeared under the pseudonym 'Iolann Fionn' and attracted very favourable comment. There can be no doubt that he had a genuine gift as a writer and that, had he had the kind of patronage which another Greene, Graham Greene, had in England, he could have developed into a writer of significance.

A staunch individualist (even as a schoolboy he did not take kindly to discipline), he fled the restrictions of a secure career as a qualified teacher and of family life. (It is not certain whether he was married to the woman who lived with him for a while and bore him a child.) Instead, he endeavoured unsuccessfully to live on his writing, trying to make up on translation work what he could not make on his art. Unfortunately, An Gúm, the government's publishing agency,[64] failed to recognize his talent, and in addition to delaying the publication of his original work, added insult to injury by giving him the works of third and fourth rate English writers to translate into Irish.

One of the novels whose publication seems to have been unnecessarily delayed by An Gúm was *An Druma Mór* ('The Big Drum') (1972). It opens with a description of the Gaeltacht and of a village in it, Ros Cuain, and goes on to explore the significance of the village band and its drum in the life of the village. The hero (or anti-hero) is Proinsias Ó Dúgáin, whose life is described in some detail, including his attempt to turn his back on Ireland and the Irish language and his personal failures through lack of education. On his return to his native village, he tries to secure a leading role for himself. He organizes 'The Sons of Patrick' in opposition to 'The Hibernians', and successfully plans a raid to capture the village band's big drum for his own organization. Events in Ros Cuain, however, are overtaken by national affairs—the organization of the Volunteers, the 1916 Insurrection; in the end, Proinsias Ó Dúgáin finds himself sentenced to a week's imprisonment on an island, under the surveillance of former members of 'The Sons of Patrick'.

The author's attitude toward the protagonist is ambivalent: he sees him now as a pathetic figure, now as a human being seeking self-validation. He sees—and sees through—the lives of the villagers, and he describes them with sympathy, wit, humour and irony. However, he does not distance himself from the characters and the events he describes, and in the end the whole account becomes somewhat incredible.

An Grá agus an Ghruaim (1929) is a volume of well-written short stories that show to advantage the poetic nature of Mac Grianna's prose, his intelligence, and his lively imagination; but in the last analysis they do not measure up to the demands of the short story as a genre. The best of the lot, perhaps, is the last in the collection, 'Creach Choinn Uí Dhomhnaill, AD 1495' ('Conn O'Donnell's Plunder Raid').

Mo Bhealach Féin 'My Own Way' (1940), probably Mac Grianna's best composition, is a fragment of autobiography.[65] As the title ('My Own Way') suggests, it bears testimony to the sturdy individualism of the author as he trudges down his chosen path and reveals his preoccupation with what have come to be regarded as the main problems of existentialism: time, place, identity and homelessness. Mac Grianna was a literary *homo viator*.

Liam O'Flaherty (1897–1984) is well known to the English-speaking world as a novelist and short story writer. In fact, he was born on Inishmore, one of the Aran Islands, and was brought up an Irish speaker; he wrote some twenty Irish short stories, most of them published in the collection entitled *Dúil* (1953). There were two distinct periods in his life when he seems to have devoted considerable time to writing in Irish, namely, 1924–5 and 1946–52. All his stories seem to have been published in English, but some of them were originally composed in Irish, e.g., 'Teangabháil', 'An Beo', and 'An Chulaith Nua'. In turn, some of the stories composed in English were translated into Irish, e.g., 'Bás na Bó' and 'Daoine Bochta'. It is said that he wrote a hitherto unpublished novel in Irish.

O'Flaherty was primarily a short story writer. Indeed, Frank O'Connor has said that, 'If one wanted to write a thesis to show how the novel was not an Irish form, but that the short-story was, one could do worse than take O'Flaherty for text.'[66] It should be noted, too, that O'Connor believed that

> the Irish short story is a distinct art form: that is, by shedding the limitations of its popular origin it has become susceptible to development in the same way as German song, and in its attitudes it can be distinguished from Russian and American stories which have

developed in the same way. The English novel, for instance is very
obviously an art form while the English short story is not.[67]

O'Connor was, of course, referring to the short story written by
Irishmen in English, but what he says is true to some extent of the
short story written in Irish. It is certain that a very good anthology of
Irish short stories could be made, a not unworthy companion to the
anthologies made of Anglo-Irish short stories.[68]

Although he was born and bred in the Gaeltacht, O'Flaherty was
not compulsively attached to it, and although he gave some
memorable evocations of Aran, for instance in 'Skerrett' (1932), he
did not restrict himself to describing life there. His primary interest
was that of an acute observer of men, whatever their nationality and
background, and his main concern was to describe them and their
doings precisely with no commendatory or condemnatory comment.
He once said to Sean O'Faolain, 'If you can describe a hen crossing a
road, you are a real writer'.

Professor Tomás de Bhaldraithe once compared the Irish and
English versions of O'Flaherty's bilingual short stories.[69] The
comparison is instructive because although O'Flaherty's command
of Irish was at least potentially as complete as his command of
English, he did not succumb in his Irish writing to the temptation
which seems to inhere in it, especially in the hands of a craftsman, to
be verbose and rhetorical.[70] It is obvious that he used the scissors, a
practice which he recommended, so it is said, to Máirtín Ó Cadhain.
Dúil, O'Flaherty's volume of short stories in Irish, is 'perhaps the
most remarkable collection of short-stories' in the language,[71] and
one of them, 'An Teangabháil' ('The Touch'), it has been claimed,
must be 'among the very greatest short stories, by any yardstick'.[72]
One would like to think that O'Connor's description of the English
short story writer is also true of the Irish:

> O'Flaherty is one of the most exciting of story-tellers. He flings himself
> on a theme with the abandonment of a child, completely unaware of
> any reflections that might be made on it. 'The Fairy Goose' is an
> amazing example of his skill. In its miraculous avoidance of any of the
> crudities that reflection would demand—satire, irony, farce—it stands
> with 'Home Sickness' as one of my two favourite stories.'[73]

Máirtín Ó Cadhain (1907–70) came from Co. Galway, whose
people are closely linked in dialect as in their way of life with those on
the Aran Islands, and so shared the same general background as Liam
O'Flaherty. Although there are some significant differences between

the people of Connemara and those of Aran, they are far from enough to explain the tremendous contrast between these two writers: the one a staunch defender of his Gaeltacht and passionately involved in its survival, the other to all appearances indifferent to its fate and no more concerned with it than with any other part of the globe. And yet both are consummate artists of the short story.[74]

Ó Cadhain has told us that he could have written in English as Patrick McGill or Liam O'Flaherty did.

> I had a choice at some point. But I feel a satisfaction in handling my native language, the speech handled by generations of my ancestors. I feel that I can add something to that speech, make it a little better than it was when I got it. In dealing with Irish I feel I am as old as New Grange, the old Hag of Beare, the great Elk. In my eyes, in my ears, in my dreams, I carry around two thousand years of that dirty old sow which is Ireland.[75]

These lines are worth quoting not only because they express Ó Cadhain's full commitment to Irish but also because they reveal why writers of no mean literary ability are prepared to stake their future on the future of the Irish language even though, as he himself has remarked, there are times when they are afraid that the death of the language will precede their own. If, as many believe, Ó Cadhain is the best prose-writer produced by his generation in Ireland, it is ironic that a language which has so few speakers and readers can boast of such a fine writer.

Máirtín Ó Cadhain came from a district renowned for its wealth of Irish, of folktales and of folk-lore, and significantly some of his first 'literary' efforts were in the recording of folk-tales and folklore. It is probable that he would have developed a profound interest in the Irish language had he not had a day's schooling—indeed, many a shanachie developed such an interest. Yet it is altogether fitting that he should have ended his days as Professor of Irish in Trinity College, for although he was not a trained philologist in the manner of Osborn Bergin, his interest in the language as a literary artist, combined with his interest in its linguistic features in the tradition of the best shanachies, made his knowledge of it so thorough as to be unrivalled in his day. All readers of his prose can understand why a distinguished critic once said (rather paradoxically) that, whereas no one can read the Irish of other modern writers without some knowledge of English, one cannot hope to read Ó Cadhain's Irish without a real knowledge of the Irish language—in all its dialects past and present, and in its literature of today, yesterday, and in the beginning. It is not altogether surprising that some of his books have been published with pages and pages of glossary.

The Gaeltacht probably inspired him with the ambition to be a teller of tales; later there came the ambition to be a writer of short stories and a novelist. His formal education influenced him to a certain extent, for he was trained as a primary school teacher. But his informal education as an omnivorous reader during a period of unemployment and of incarceration was probably a more decisive influence; he was first dismissed from his teaching post for his IRA views (ultimately through the intervention of the bishop), and then during the Second World War he was imprisoned along with other members of the IRA by the Irish Government. During this time he learned Scottish Gaelic, Welsh and Breton, as well as some French and German. Apparently he learned some Russian also, but it was soon forgotten. He learned these languages in order to appreciate their literatures at first hand, and he published translations of a number of short stories.

Ó Cadhain's first published short story was 'Scóllántacht na Gaoithe' (1926), and his second 'Maide an Tailliúra' (1929). His first volume of short stories, published with a glossary, appeared in 1941, under the title *Idir Shúgradh agus Dáirire agus Scéalta Eile*. This was followed by four volumes of short-stories of which the last, *An tSraith Dhá Tógáil*, appeared in 1970, a few weeks before his death.[76] Only one of his novels appeared during his lifetime, namely *Cré na Cille* (1949), but chapters of two others appeared in periodicals: 'Athnuachan' (*Feasta*, Samhain, 1951), and 'An Féas agus an Fhéasóg', a fragment of a novel *Barbed Wire*, in *Dóchas*, 1964. Though *Cré na Cille* is Ó Cadhain's masterpiece and deserves to be discussed independently of his short stories, it throws a great deal of light on his short stories, and a study of both is necessary to a proper understanding of his work.

With respect to Ó Cadhain's language, two influences are seen to be at work: tradition and education. He began with a shanachie's wealth of spoken Irish and his conscious pride in his use of it. In the course of the years, he developed a tighter and firmer control of this treasure while adding to it from his study of Irish literature. Both developments proved beneficial and both were seen as necessary by Ó Cadhain.

> Every writer now feels that to speak of a modern urban society which Ireland is more and more becoming, no one dialect nor even all the dialects are adequate. If you are a native speaker, your basic dialect will be your diction. A great deal of Irish has become available since

the beginning of the present century and everyone of us knows a great deal more about the language we are endeavouring to write. Some of us—not all writers I am sorry to say—are acquainted with Irish literature since the Old Irish period. We try to borrow words and phrases, judiciously I hope, from this literature. For instance I have myself taken the phrase *báire baoise, Eoghan ar a bháire baoise*, which means something like 'sowing his wild oats' in the old text *Cath Muighe Léna*, the Battle of Moylena. The phrase would immediately mean something to an Irish speaker as both words are well known separately, though not joined together, in present day Irish. Those of us who can read Scottish Gaelic would be immediately attracted by a phrase such as *teine bhial na hoidhche* 'the fire of the brink of the night', which would be immediately recognized in Irish, though not known I think.[77]

Parallel with this linguistic development there was a literary development. In his early short stories Ó Cadhain seemed to be reluctant to abandon completely the mould of the folk-tale, and as a result there was a certain lack of compression and some diffuseness of style; there was an inclination to remind the reader, to nudge him to awareness that he was being served with a story—and, it would be fair to say, a story about people in a strange community, for there are anthropological overtones in that early work. Greater familiarity with the short story as a genre used by such masters as de Maupassant and Chekhov and with the achievements of other prose genres produced in Ó Cadhain a clearer vision of the effects at which he was to aim, and a greater confidence in his ability to use the necessary techniques.

But in the case of a writer like Ó Cadhain to speak of command of language and technical competence is not enough. His vision as a writer is a vision of a people who seem to have been waiting for some artist to come along to see and hear them, for some artist to express them in such a way they could never hope to express themselves, to capture their lives in the hiatus between thought and speech. These are the people of Cois Fharraige, and as long as there are readers of Ó Cadhain's work, they will continue to live.

Cré na Cille, we have suggested, is a necessary counterpart to Ó Cadhain's short stories. As the title implies, the setting is in the church cemetery, where the dead are visualized as living and re-living the days they walked the earth. The setting reminds one of Sartre's *Huis Clos* (to be imprisoned is, in a way, to be dead); the action is limited and attention is perforce concentrated on thoughts and their expression, on fears and hopes, hatreds and loves, frustrated intentions and vain resolves. Máire Mhac an tSaoi's words are worth quoting:

> It is not altogether surprising . . . that *Cré na Cille*, our one outstanding contemporary prose work, should treat of a typical mythopoeic theme: the entire narrative is recounted through the conversations of a community of corpses buried under the church-yard clay. Typically, Irish country people conceive of death at three levels: one orthodox Christian, one rational, and one primaeval; in this last the dead are present, resentful and vindictive beneath the actual sod. All three co-exist without conflict in the folk mind and this is the stuff of our one entirely mature contemporary piece of prose.[78]

The Gaeltachts are found in countrysides which afford the most splendid scenes of natural beauty in Ireland, if not in Europe. The stranger tends to see the people of these idyllic outposts in a glow of romantic sentiment, and indeed there is much to admire in them—in their struggle to scrape a meagre living in a land devoid of all but the barest natural resources. But poverty is not always ennobling, and although life seems to be made up of simple pieties and time-hallowed conventions, as in the Middle Ages in retrospect, it is other than it seems. To step into the world of *Cré na Cille* from the world of *Séadna*, the world of *Iosagán*, and even the world of *Páidín Mháire* is to step from the world of shadows into a world of stark realities; there is no need to apologize for these realities, no need to assume, as at least one critic has done, that here we have a world left untouched by either Jansenism or Puritanism. Few will find fault with Máire Mhac an tSaoi's well-considered judgement on *Cré na Cille*:

> Overweighted, overburdened, too heavy for the thread of story though it is, *Cré na Cille* is the only thing in Irish, apart from *An tOileánach*, that has a weight and importance out of the ordinary. In the presence of a creative talent so undeniable as that of Máirtín Ó Cadhain, the critic has no choice but humility; he can analyse, but he recognises a value which is independent of him. Ó Cadhain's work lives with a life which owes nothing to literary artifice. As Mauriac has Les Landes, so Ó Cadhain has Cois Fharraige. It does not matter whether the picture is realistic. It has its own life. This is no easy writing, or pleasing writing. the place we see is a remote countryside, inhabited by a gloomy, solitary people, but the whole vibrates with a strange force, the like of which is not to be found in any other Irish writer today.[79]

§3

One can imagine that the writers whose primary interest was poetry rather than prose were faced with the same dilemma as that which confronted Pearse when he had to decide against the oral folk-tale in favour of the art form of the short story. But it seems that for them the traditional forms of poetry did not hold the same appeal as the traditional forms of prose did for their colleagues, and thus they were more susceptible to the temptation to imitate the poetic forms which were popular in Anglo-Irish and in English.[80]

Here we should distinguish between two traditional forms: on the one hand, that of the folk poets, and on the other, that of the professional bards of the literary tradition from the days of its glorious past down to the days of its inglorious end. To appreciate the folk poets one needed understanding of their function and sympathy with their aims; both Robin Flower and Patrick Pearse had such an appreciation. Thus Robin Flower writes of Seán Ó Duínnlé:

> His poetry is the poetry of the country-side, full of traditional idiom and the lively turns of speech born of the sharpening of wit upon wit in the banter of every day. Its subjects are the tragedies and humours and triumphs of the simple village life. A sudden storm overwhelms a boat in Ventry Bay, a woman of the Island weaves herself a quilt, the poet's ass dies, an Island boat wins a race, a cartful of people coming home well primed from market is overset by the roadside, a farmer is evicted in the Land War, an old man marries a young wife—these and a dozen other happenings become the talk of the country-side, and the poet is on hand with his verses, which are passed delightedly from mouth to mouth, every stroke going home among a people nursed in such poetry, and electrically alive to each turn of phrase, each trait of character, each subtility of allusion to events known to everybody. Taken out of its language and environment, such poetry is like the sea anemone, which lies dead and exhausted on the rocks at the ebb of tide, but flowers into strange and lively colour when the water of its own element flows over it once more. It can hardly be understood out of its own countryside. Translated and imprisoned in a book the virtue goes out of it, and it becomes a curiosity and a riddle.[81]

And these are Pearse's views of Colm Wallace (Colm de Bhailís):

> One must beware of approaching a singer like Colm Wallace in a severely critical spirit . . . This is no professional poet; indeed scarcely a poet at all. Here is a naive, sprightly, good-humouredly satirical personality, a peasant living among peasants, who sings like the lark

from the very joyousness and tunefulness of soul . . . He has no
'Philosophy of life'—not he; he warbles to while away a Summer's day,
to 'shorten the road' on a tramp across the bogland, to repay the
hospitality of a bean tí who has given him a night's cheer. The ordinary
prosaic events of his daily life, the sights and encounters he makes on
his way to a fair—such are the inspirations of his verse . . . Much of
Colum's poetry lacks real inspiration, much of it, from the technical
standpoint, limps hopelessly. Yet good qualities it does possess—
indeed, must possess, to have achieved its undoubted popularity
throughout a whole country—a certain energy and vivacity, a tuneful
swing, a whimsical playfulness of fancy . . .[82]

Perhaps it would be true to say that folk poets such as Seán Ó Duínnlé
and Colm Wallace could never capture the attention of the new body
of Irish readers which was being formed by the Gaelic League
Movement, and there was no reason why the new writers would have
sought to imitate them. Rather it was the *traditional* poets who had
claim on the new writers and gradually their works were becoming
better known. In the course of the nineteenth century, a number of
volumes appeared presenting the poetry of the preceding century.
John O'Daly (1800–78) published among other books *Reliques of
Irish Jacobite Poetry* (1844), the work of *Tadhg Gaedhealach Ó
Súilleabháin* (1858), *The Poets and Poetry of Munster*, which went
through several editions from 1849 to 1866, and *The Irish Language
Miscellany* (1876). There were examples of folk-songs in some of
these books and more examples became available with the
publication of Bunting's books and those of his successors. One
should also remember that translations of Irish poetry were becoming
available through the labours of Edward Walsh (1805–50), James
Clarence Mangan (1803–49), and Samuel Ferguson (1810–86).

The most popular poet in Ireland during the nineteenth century
was Thomas Moore (1779–1852), and that, no doubt, was what
induced Archbishop Mac Hale (1791–1881), a native Irish speaker
from Co. Mayo, to translate some of his poems into Irish, and why
Tomás Ó Néill Ruiséal published *A Selection of the Most National
and Popular of Moore's Melodies with Translations in Irish by the late
Most Rev. J. Mac Hale* in 1899. Mac Hale was himself very popular in
Ireland as a champion of the Irish people and a defender of the Irish
language.[83] When he died on 7 November 1881, the *Gaelic Journal*
referred to him as 'the great defender of and supporter of the Irish
language', and added, 'It requires no words of ours to keep the great
prelate's memory green . . . the poet who gave us Homer's heroic

page and Moore's sweet lyric in our country's language for the first time'.

Mac Hale's translations of Moore's lyrics enjoyed great popularity, but as literature they were disastrous. They are an attempt to transplant English metres into Irish and are in a diction which is a mixture of the ordinary speech of the people and archaic forms; there is some reason for saying that some of the versions, e.g., that of 'Remember the Glories of Brian the Brave', are neither poetry nor translations nor Irish. A volume not unlike Mac Hale's translations is Niall Mac Giolla Bhrighde's *Blátha Fraoich: Songs in Irish and English* (1905).

Gradually, however, most of the works of the seventeenth- and eighteenth-century poets, in particular those of Munster, were collected and published, including those of Keating, Piaras Feiritéir, Séafra Ó Donnchadha, Aodhagán Ó Rathaille, Seán Clárach Mac Domhnaill, Eoghan Ruadh Ó Súilleabháin, Seán Ó Neachtain, Piaras Mac Gearailt, Tadhg Gaedhealach Ó Súilleabháin, Filí na Maighe, Donnchadh Ruadh Mac Conmara. By 1910, only a few of the poets of the period from 1600 on were not represented in print. The editing was not very scholarly, and in some cases it required unorthodox methods—for instance, when some poems had to be retrieved from oral tradition. But the editions usually included a vocabulary, biography and metrical notes, and they succeeded in revealing the nature of the Irish poetic traditon since the beginning of the seventeenth century. At the same time, the works of some of the classical poets of the period 1200–1600 were being edited and annotated, and Douglas Hyde's history of Irish literature, represented by his two volumes, *The Story of Early Gaelic Literature* (1895) and *A Literary History of Ireland* (1899), was uncovering the greatness and the splendour of the literary tradition in Ireland.

Hyde himself was opposed to the fashion of imitating English literary models, and as one would have expected, there was a reaction against the translations of the type produced by Mac Hale. In the *Gaelic Journal* for June 1892, we find Dr Richard Henebry (De Hindeberg; 1863–1916) attacking these translations and the compositions based on their style.

> All the requirements of Irish verse-building are ignored, and instead, the whole scheme of English prosody, such as full rhyming endings, poetic license and the like is regarded as essential. This vitiated taste derives its origin from the example set by Dr. Mac Hale's translation of Moore's Irish melodies.

It was natural that these views should be noted by the promoters of the *Oireachtas* and of its poetry competitions, and gradually there emerged a group of poets whose attitude to their art was different from their immediate predecessors and whose equipment included a superior knowledge of traditional Irish prosody, of its embellishments and its diction. These are the real founders of modern Irish poetry.

Their manifesto was the two volumes *Saothar Suadha* I (1908) and II (1911); in these a return to the traditional moulds is espoused. Thus Father Dinneen (an tAthair Pádraig Ó Duinnín) shows that there had been no advance in Irish poetry until the works of Keating and O'Rahilly had been published, and Piaras Béaslaí argues the case for adopting the traditional metres. Tórna (Tadhg Ua Donnchadha) advocates translating poems from Old and Middle Irish and poems from languages other than English (he himself translated from Welsh and German). Incidentally, he bemoans the lack of an adequate Irish critical terminology, and with his colleagues shows that he is interested in the form as well as the content of literature, i.e., with metre, rhythm, etc.

But it was not as easy as some of its advocates had thought to shed all traces of English influence. Thus Douglas Hyde (under the pseudonym 'An Craoibhín Aoibhinn') published a slim volume of poetry entitled *Ubhla de'n Chraoibh* (?1900) which shows the influence of Thomas Davis and Thomas Moore as well as of the folk-songs which he had been collecting. Reviewing Tórna's *Leoithe Andeas* (1905) in *An Claidheamh Soluis* (29 July 1905), Pearse praised the volume for its lyrical pieces but censured it for its adherence to old conventions. It was time, he said, to abandon the *spéir-bhean*. Tórna was at his best, according to Pearse, when he was simple and natural and when he was describing nature, which he understood and loved.

The following year Pearse discussed the dilemma which Irish poets faced and the choice which was theirs: either to resuscitate the poetic conventions of the eighteenth century or to accept the new poetic conventions.[84] Whichever course they followed, their duty was to reveal the thoughts in their hearts. Piaras Béaslaí, Tórna, and Osborn Bergin (Ó hAimheirgin; 1872–1950) were in favour of returning to the native poetic conventions, although they differed to some extent as to how far they should go in rehabilitating those conventions. In February 1912, Bergin wrote a modern poem in *deibhi* metre,[85] and in the same year Pearse wrote his lyric 'Fornocht do chonnac thú' ('Naked I saw Thee').

The poems which Pearse published in 1913 in *Suantraidhe and Goltraidhe* illustrate and exemplify his poetic theory.[86] He preferred the contemporary lyric form to the old poetic conventions and he was determined that his poems should reveal his innermost thoughts; to that extent they have an immediacy and an authenticity lacking in most poems of that period. Sincerity serves to commend simplicity and to compensate for subtlety. Here is a translation by Thomas MacDonagh of 'Fornocht do chonnac thú':

> Naked I saw thee,
> O beauty of beauty!
> And I blinded my eyes
> For fear I should flinch.
> > I heard thy music,
> > O sweetness of sweetness
> > And I shut my ears
> > For fear I should fail.
>
> I kissed thy lips,
> O sweetness of sweetness!
> And I hardened my heart
> For fear of my ruin.
> > I blinded my eyes
> > And my ears I shut,
> > I hardened my heart
> > And my love I quenched.
>
> I turned my back
> On the dream I had shaped
> And to this road before me
> My face I turned.
> > I set my face
> > To the road here before me,
> > To the work that I see,
> > To the death that I shall meet.[87]

Try as we will, we cannot dissociate Pearse the poet from Pearse the patriot, for this poem and others like it have a nuance which they would not have, had Pearse not been one of the heroes of the 1916 Insurrection. As W. B. Yeats wrote in his eulogy of 25 September 1916, 'Easter 1916':

> I write it out in verse—
> Mac Donagh and MacBride
> And Connolly and Pearse
> Now and in time to be,

> Wherever green is worn,
> Are changed, changed utterly:
> A terrible beauty is born.[88]

A volume which enjoyed great popularity at the time of its appearance and which can be taken as representative of the poetry produced by the old native school was Bergin's *Maidean i mBéarra agus Dánta Eile* (1918). A scholar unrivalled in his knowledge of Irish at that time, Bergin was also something of an artist, and he added the artist's interest in the use of language to the philologist's knowledge of its resources. This is shown to full advantage in the best poems of that collection: they are lyrics, well executed, musical, pleasing in both form and content, yet they strike one as a scholar's exercises in verse rather than as utterances of a poet who has no choice but to speak through poetry.

To this school belonged also Piaras Béaslaí (1881–1965), Liam Gógan (1891–1979) and Séamas Ó hAodha (1886–1967), and although Irish was a second language for most of them, the poetry they produced is far superior to that of the few native Irish speakers who published about the same time, poets such as Father Pádraig Ó Duinnín (1860–1934), Donnchadh Ó Liatháin, Roibéard Bheldon, Pádraig Ó Miléadha, and Áine Ní Fhoghladha (the last three from Munster).[89] Thus, while on one side there is a number of native Irish speakers who did not produce many poets, on the other there is a group for whom Irish is a second language but from whom has sprung a greater number of poets.

The poets who have learned Irish must confront the issue of writing in a language that is not their mother tongue. They are also painfully aware that the public they are addressing consists less of native speakers than of learners, and that the same public is being addressed at the same time not only by English poets but also by Anglo-Irish poets who themselves have a long tradition behind them. Although this latter tradition does not stretch back as far as that of poets writing in Irish, each has something to say to their modern descendants. Under these circumstances, perhaps it is understandable that it has taken time for modern Irish poets to find their *métier*. Perhaps they did not find it until the Second World War, when Ireland was isolated and forced back on its own resources—culturally as well as economically, and when the Irish-language movement seemed to revive and showed its vitality in the re-establishment of the *Oireachtas*, and the publication of new periodicals (e.g., *Comhar*) and an increasing number of books.

Whatever the reason, after 1939 there appeared a new generation of Irish poets for whom poetry was of the first importance. From that time on, the number of genuine poets and the quality of their verse seemed suddenly to increase significantly. Poets like Séamas Ó Céilleachair, Caoimhín Ó Conghaile, Máirtín Ó Direáin, Seán Ó hÉigeartaigh, Seán Mac Fheorais, Micheál Mac Liammóir, Art Ó Maolfabhail, Réamonn Ó Muireadhaigh, Séamas Ó Néill, Máire Mhac an tSaoi, Seán Ó Ríordáin, Seán Ó Tuama, Eoghan Ó Tuairisc, and Tomás Tóibín spring to mind—even the work of poets such as Liam S. Gógan and Monsignor de Brún, who chronologically belonged to an earlier generation—seems to reflect this greater artistic achievement.[90] And the poets themselves came to feel that they were being read, discussed and criticized. This is shown in one way by the number of volumes of poetry published. In 1964, Seán Ó Ríordáin, Eoghan Ó Tuairisc, Réamonn Ó Muireadhaigh, Micheál Mac Liammóir, Caoimhín Ó Conghaile, Seán Ó hÉigeartaigh, and Art Ó Maolfabhail all published books of poetry. This does not mean, of course, that all these were poets of genius nor that most of their poems were masterpieces, but it does indicate that there was a general level of poetic competence and ability. It suggests too that some fine poems were being produced, comparable to some of the finest produced in other languages.

We may mention three poets in particular (although this does less than justice to the others) who have attracted the attention of the critics, namely, Máire Mhac an tSaoi, Máirtín Ó Direáin (1910–88), and Seán Ó Ríordáin (1917–77).[91] Of these, Ó Direáin is the only native speaker in the strict sense; indeed, as such he is exceptional among poets of his generation. Among other things, his development as a poet was marked by a progressive mastery of the craft and by an ever increasing awareness of himself and of his society.[92]

Referring to the view that 1939 was a turning point in the history of Irish poetry, Ó Direáin agreed that there was a change in the form and the subject matter but questioned whether the change was as great as it was made out to be. At the same time, he agreed that there was a need for change, for one of the difficulties facing him and others who were trying to write poetry at that time was the lack of models.

> In matters of form and style we were greatly handicapped by having no proper models of the kind we needed badly, that is, some authoritative poet atempting to deal with contemporary style. If our poetry had been at full flood, rather than at an ebb, from , say, 1900 onwards, such a poet would have existed and the change would not have appeared so

strange when it came; but it did not appear from the work of the poets of that period that they felt either pain or passion. It must be said too, and I am not blaming them for it, that their work did not indicate that they were exploiting the language to its full extent, whatever the reason may have been. We had two choices when we began, to go on using the traditional style which had been squeezed dry long before we were born, or to use the natural power of the language as we knew it. We took the second choice. As Eliot says: *since our concern was speech, and speech impelled us to purify the dialect of the tribe.* So it was with us.[93]

He goes on to say that he and his fellow poets had been accused of imitating English poets, e.g., that Seán Ó Ríordáin had modelled his poetry on that of Eliot although most of it had been written before he had read any of Eliot, and that he himself had been accused of imitating the work of English poets. That would have been difficult for him for he knew hardly any of their work. He had no basis to work on other than what he had heard: 'the dialect of the tribe':

> I had to base the rhythm of my poetry on the natural rhythm of the language itself as I had heard it and had heard nothing else during my seventeen years of living.[94]

This does not mean that all that a poet needs is the speech he has heard during his youth to express every thought that casts a shadow on his mind; that is the necessary basis, to be sure, but he must have more than that. It is the poet's duty to set words dancing in front of our minds. There are words aplenty on which rust and dust have gathered and one 'might as well put them to serve as torches of delight before us' (*Níor mhiste a gcur ionas go mba lóchrann aitis inár bhfianaise iad*).

One is impressed by the unpretentious nature of Ó Direáin's devotion to his craft. In one poem, 'Clochadóir' ('Mason') (*Dánta 1939–1979*), he describes how he saw a mason on a scaffolding, working on a house, how he saw him measuring, weighing and judging the stones and noticed how many stones and spalls he handed down to his helper when they did not fit precisely into the new edging, and concluded:

> Mise a bhéarfadh cuid mhór
> ar a bheith chomh deas chuig mo ghnó.
>
> And I for my part would give a great deal to
> be as fine at my own work.

One can assume that the mason Ó Direáin had in mind was one he had seen at work near his island home, for he found there an essential honesty which he missed in mainland Ireland—especially in the cities. In his poem 'Ionracas' ('Honesty') he tells us,

> Dúirt file mór tráth,
> Go mba oileán is grá mná
> Abhar is fáth mo dháin;
> Is fíor a chan mo bhráthair.
>
> Coinneod féin an t-oileán
> Seal eile i mo dhán,
> Toisc a ionraice atá
> Cloch, carraig is trá.[95]

A great poet once said, the subject and the impetus of my poetry is an island and a woman's love. What my brother sang is true.

But I myself will keep the island a while longer in my poetry because of the honesty of stone, rock and strand.'

Unfortunately, the islanders are no longer safe:

> Tá cleacht mo dhaoine ag meath,
> Ní cabhair feasta an tonn mar fhalla.[96]
>
> My people's way of life is decaying,
> The sea's swell no longer serves as wall.

Dishonesty is reflected in the way words are used. In his poem 'Ualach' ('Burden'), he speaks of the poet's burden and pride, and of his humility, which is not really humility but danger's disguise (folach priacail):

> Is freastal an dá thrá
> A chuireann a mheabhair ar fán,
> Is a fhágann ina lár
> Geit den aiteas riamh di.
>
> Ní chuirfí poll ar a onóir
> Dá mairfeadh cion ar an mbriathar,
> Ach chuaigh an briathar ó chion
> Is minic ise ina criathar.[97]
>
> And coping with two strands
> Sets his mind astray,
> And leaves in his heart
> A tension that never springs from delight.

> There would be no chink in his honour
> If words were still regarded with love,
> But since the love of words has gone
> His honour has often been turned into a sieve.

W. H. Auden has said somewhere that every man's world is made up of the sacred and the profane—that is, that which is sacred and profane to him. Applying this to Ó Direáin, one could say that the sacred to him is the life which he lived on Inishmore during his youth and all that it embraced, in physical environment and in spiritual community. Although he turned his back on the island in the sense that he eventually chose not to live there, he did not cease to identify himself with it and its people; indeed, it became for him a symbol for all of Ireland, the Ireland which is gradually losing its hold on the past and losing its soul in the process. One of Ó Direáin's permanent achievements is that he made Inishmore a part of the consciousness of every reader of Irish; he brought it to life, as it were, so that no literate Irish speaker could ever again think of Ireland without thinking of Aran, nor of Aran without thinking of Ireland.

Ó Direáin left Aran before he could appreciate it, before he could see, hear, smell and feel it fully, and he felt guilty over having left it (see his poems 'Olc Liom' 'I Regret' and 'Stoite' 'Uprooted'). In the beginning, his longing for the island was somewhat sentimental, and this is reflected in his poetry. There is too much idealization of the place in it, and while the poetry calls for sympathetic reading, the reader finds it difficult to extend all the sympathy that is required, for the vision is too simple, too unsophisticated. But in his later poetry, Aran is less the direct, more the indirect subject, and the longing for the lost island has been deepened to a longing shared by all men for a paradise lost. Yet both the longing and the loss are viewed ironically, for there is in Ó Direáin's mature work a transparent integrity: he looks critically at himself as well as at his world (see 'An Dá Phortráid', 'The Two Portraits').

One of Ó Direáin's most illuminating poems is 'Cranna Foirtil' ('Hardy Trees')[98] where he invokes his birth into a world of security based on the support of simple belief and homely ritual, and where he bids farewell to those supports without relinquishing his belief in a world of permanence.

> Soul! stand your ground;
> Clutch at every rooted thing.
> Be not like a beardless youth
> When your friends have failed you.

You've often seen a red-shank
Solitary on a washed rock;
If he got no titbit from the sea
There was no reproach.

Your head came without a lucky caul
From your own obscure dominion,
But the wood of your cradle was confidently hung
With protective timbers.

The props they used for you were perished props:
Iron tongs above you,
Your father's garment beside you,
And a poker stuck in the fire.

Stand fast by your staunch moor-poles
That shore you up against all tides,
And maintain your vision's spark;
To let that go is death for you.[99]

There is a later poem, 'Fuaire' ('Coldness'), obviously related to
'Cranna Foirtil', in which he voices his scepticism about the validity
of his attitude to the 'Props', although he has no faith in the 'props'
offered to him by others.

Stand fast by my protective props!
Is there an alternative?
Since, in your regard
The horn of plenty is empty till death.
Yet I know in my heart—
Bitter and all as it is to say—
That these same props
Are as cold as the sky.[100]

Máire Mhac an tSaoi (Máire MacEntee) (1922–) has brought to
her poetry a highly cultivated mind and a rare intelligence. A
graduate of University College, Dublin, she started on a career in
Celtic scholarship, but presumably found it too constricting and
abandoned it for a career in the diplomatic service; the latter involved
foreign travel and gave her the opportunity to use and extend her
knowledge of other modern languages. She has a thorough
acquaintance with European literatures, and is well-grounded in the
culture of the Gaeltacht and the Irish literary tradition. Moreover,
she is an artist in her appreciation and use of the Irish language. This
is well illustrated in her slim volume of translations, *A Heartful of*

Thought (1959), which contains renderings of the popular 'Una Bhán' and some of the more sophisticated *dánta grá*. Indeed, 'a heart full of thought' would serve very well as a title for the collection of her own poems, which she published in three volumes, *Margadh na Saoire* (1956), *Codladh an Ghaiscigh agus Dánta Eile* (1973), and *An Galar Dubhach* (1980), for in them she combines a profound interest in the thoughts of the mind and the emotions of the heart. An edition of all her poems was published in 1986, *An Cion go dtí Seo*.

Although she was raised in Dublin, she spent a great deal of her childhood in the Gaeltacht, in Dunquin, where she learned the local dialect. But her knowledge of Irish goes far beyond knowledge of any dialect, for she has a thorough acquaintance with the literary tradition and a familiarity with the resources of the language won only by those who passionately cultivate it. Some of her utterances have the same stamp as the centuries-old proverbs which one hears (or used to hear) so often on the lips of the Gaeltacht folk, as in these examples from the poem 'Fógra' in *Margadh na Saoire*, p. 51:

Ach ní mór don taoide casadh, is sé dán na hoíche teacht.
Nuair a theipeann ar an dtaitneamh is tarcaisneach a bhlas.

The tide must return and it is the fate of the night to come.
When the liking ceases, its flavour is distasteful.

Indeed, her style is derived from both sources—*caint na ndaoine* ('folk speech') and the literary tradition. Perhaps it could be said that her knowledge of the literary tradition has enabled her to identify those qualities in *caint na ndaoine* which best exemplify the genius of the Irish language.

There is a quatrain in her first volume of poems, in which she incorporates a quotation from a *dán grá* which in turn catches the spirit of that genre:

Ar an mórshlua—

'Daoine sona an méid nach mair'—
File i ngrá gan gruaim á rá
Dó nach fearr is fios anois?
Fada fé bhrat talún atá.[101]

'Happy lovers who have died!'
The complacent poet said—
None knows better if he lied;
He is indeed a long time dead.[102]

Her poem 'A Fhir Dár Fhulaingeas . . .' shows the influence of the *deibhí* metre and echoes some of the characteristic insights of the *dánta grá*:

> Goin mo chroí, gad mo gháire,
> Cuimhnigh, a mhic mhínáire,
> An phian, an phláigh, a chráigh mé,
> Mo dhíol gan ádh gan áille . . .
>
> Cruaidh an cás mo bheith let ais,
> Measa arís bheith it éagmais;
> Margadh bocht ó thaobh ar bith
> Mo chaidreamh ort, a ógfhir.[103]

> Wound my heart, spancel my laugh,
> Remember, you shameless youth,
> The pain, the plague that torments me,
> And that my recompense is to be luckless and
> unlovely.
>
> Hard is my lot to be by your side,
> Worse still to be away from you,
> A wretched bargain on all counts
> My association with you, young man.

The word *caidreamh* in the last line recalls the poem 'Ceist':

> Domhsa ní sásamh intinn mo chéile:
> Domhsa ní dóchas suaimhneas ná codladh
> Ó mheisce na bhfocal,
> Ach formad folamh,
> Fuadar gan toradh.
>
> Glac peann is toit leis aghaidh an leathanaigh,
> Gach leamhlíne scaoilte tarraicthe,
> Allas is saothar—
> Ach ní bhfaighir blas orthu
>   Mire gach tosaigh nuair a bheidh traochta
>   Bhfuil caidreamh dá moltar nach bocht mar an
>   gcéanna?

> For me, there is no satisfaction in my husband's mind.
> For me, rest and sleep do not mean hope
> Because of the intoxication of words,
> Only an empty envy,
> Effort that bears no fruit.
>
> Take a pen and with it mar the page's face,
> Slack, long-winded, insipid, line after line

Sweat and labour—
But you won't savour them.
Ecstatic beginnings ebb away in wretchedness
Is there any bond that people praise that doesn't
suffer from the same defect?[104]

In the back of her mind, there is the constant thought that *caidreamh*, an intimate personal relationship, is difficult to establish and still more difficult to maintain. It could be said that the themes of her poems are love, unrequited love, love outside or against the conventions, love and marriage, motherhood, and so on, but that would be misleading, for the word *caidreamh* ('love; intimacy; intercourse;' etc.) is so ambiguous and wide ranging in its connotations that the theme needs to be re-examined and defined anew.

The poem 'Jack' illustrates well another aspect of her poetry.

Strapaire fionn sé troithe ar airde,
Mac feirmeora ó iarthar tíre,
Ná cuimhneoidh feasta go rabhas sa oíche
Ar urlár soimint aige ag rince,

Ach ní dhearúdfad a ghéaga im thimpeall,
A gháire ciúin ná a chaint shibhialta—
Ina léine bhán, is a ghruaig nuachíortha
Buí fén lampa ar bheagán íle . . .

Fágfaidh a athair talaimh ina dhiaidh aige,
Pósfaidh bean agus tógfaidh síolbhach,
Ach mar conacthas domhsa é arís ní cífear,
Beagbheann ar chách mar 'gheal lem chroí é.

Barr dá réir go raibh air choíche!
Rath is séan san áit ina mbíonn sé!
Mar atá tréitheach go dté crích air—
Dob é an samhradh so mo rogha 'pháirtí é.[105]

The fair strapping youth six feet tall, a farmer's son from the west, will not remember any longer that I was dancing one evening with him on a cement floor.

But I will not forget his arms around me, his gentle laugh and his 'civil' talk—he in his white shirt and his hair freshly combed, fair under the lamp with its meagre supply of oil . . .

His father will leave him land, he will marry a woman and rear offspring, but he will never be seen again as he was seen by me, regardless of every one, as he endeared himself to me.

May he have forever the best of everything, blessing and good fortune wherever he is, according to his deserts may he be fulfiled—that summer he was my choice partner.'

It is quite clear that the poet understood her experience completely, its one-sidedness, its transience, and that she savoured it to the full. Typical of her experiences generally seem to be her comprehension of 'Jack' and his incomprehension of her; her understanding extends to an appreciation of his background in the Gaeltacht and of his and the Gaeltacht's inability (i.e., of her fellow man's inability) to understand her. Hence her feeling of loneliness, of *uaigneas*.

A more ambitious poem, perhaps her most ambitious (and, according to some critics, her most successful) is 'Ceathrúintí Mháire Ní Ógáin'. There is a proverb, *Ná bí ag deanamh Máire Ní Ógáin díot féin*, i.e., 'don't be making a fool (a Máire Ní Ógáin) of yourself,' 'don't be silly.' The poem is an exploration by the proverbial girl herself, Máire Ní Ógáin, of her 'foolishness', or rather of her tender heart and her generous love.[106] One must be wary of attributing the feelings described in the poems to their author, but there is a directness and a freshness in her expression of love which suggests that the echoes of the *dánta grá* are deliberately made to suggest similar experiences. Here is a translation of 'Sean-Ghalar' ('The Old Disease'):

What was in your face that made me yield to your words:
All you did was look at me, and my good sense deserted.
The sidelong glance of the blue eyes, your light step;
They have tortured my heart, and I shall not soon recover.

And what a mean trick you played on me, my slender lad,
When you shyly took me by surprise, without me noticing!
Never until now has there seemed to be any bond between us,
Other than an exchange of greetings on the way to Mass.

The young women of this district have run after you,I suppose.
Perhaps they were taken in, in their foolishness, but little I
                                    cared for their plight!
But that's no use to me now, as I sit by the ditch,
Waiting in the hope that you'll pass me on the way to the shore.

And, my slender lad, this week is passing slowly,
And every bite I eat, it's a wonder it doesn't choke me.
Great God of Glory, it's not worth living the way I do!

What a contrary business this love is, once you get caught up
in it.
Like a fresh breeze from the sea in the dull heat of the day,
I can feel you coming close to me, and to me one look at you
Is brighter than the flower of the yellow flags as they spread
themselves in the sun.
And I'd be much better off if you stayed away from me forever!

And, my slender lad, it would suit me well to break free of you.
My people would make a match for me a long way away from
here.
The psalm-singing of the clergy, the sacrament of the Church,
They would bring me to my senses—If I could only forget you.[107]

It has been said that whereas *Margadh na Saoire* makes us question
the opinions and conventions of love, marriage, and personal
relationships, *Codladh an Ghaiscigh* gives us grounds for hoping that
there are answers to these questions. The young girl has become a wife
and a mother and is prepared to put her trust in the love she has
found. Perversely, perhaps, the young girl's explorations of her
emotions seem to make better poetry than the older woman's,
although the latter's are more original and at times poignantly
moving.

The inadequacy of prose translations to convey the magic of Máire
Mhac an tSaoi's personal music will be painfully apparent to readers
of the original Irish. Here are two English renderings from her own
pen.

No Compromise

'I do not understand the fear of death . . .'
And when she spoke I heard the bugles blow,
I saw the raging mob, blood in the streets,
And there were flames from torches and the wind
Filling the flags in that Frenchwoman's speech.

And I took fright, that she should be so strange,
Knowing how hard it is to lose the sun;
'Alas,' I said, 'long in the churchyard rests
The body and it's lonely in the clay.'
But she turned towards me her wide open eyes,
And, proud, uncomprehending, did not yield.[108]

Harvest of the Sea

We went off to the wake of the 'Whelpish youngster'
And in the door of the room his mother was waiting
'*O little son, age was not your portion,*

And it is the nature of youth to be wild and scapegrace—'
                                                    And Ochone!

Imprinted on my eyes the unpleasant features of her son
And the eerie stammer of his speech a pain in my ears—
We have drowned the ugly fledgling a second time—
Once in the tide-race and once submerged in flattery—
                                                    And Ochone!

Two black cinders light up at me from his countenance,
My swift slap left that mark of five fingers
That time I caught him with his fist in the crock—
It is to you I tell it, hole in the wall,
                                                    And Ochone!

Hark to the mother! '*How he behaved towards me!*
And after he left prison he returned to Confession—'
The sea-wife has spread her blue-green hair over Conaing—
Has abducted the Whitsuntide child from the shadow of the gallows!
                                                    And Ochone!

An abortion reborn from the burial-place of unbaptized infants
Constantly whimpering after lost humanity!
A changeling in non-being going down the wind
Pitiably castrated by this last insult!
                                                    And Ochone!

Do not rely on me, poor wretch!
In your own quality at least you existed, however sordidly—
But dead and living do not suit together—
Hook your own ground! I am not the bard to lament you.
                                                    And Ochone!—

Force his grip from the gunwale—let them have it their own way—
Set up the waxen image among the candles
The Phoenix arrayed after his corpse-washing—
And let the spent clout sink to the sea-bed
                                                    And Ochone!—

I'll tell you a tale of the wake of the whelpish youngster,
Never was seen before such a splendid funeral,
Clerics and laymen and black was made white there,
And the hare-lip was hidden below the coffin-lid!
                                                    And Ochone![109]

   The word 'modern' is an ambiguous term but it has a definite
connotation and there are occasions when its use is unavoidable.
Gabriel Josipovici has pointed out that, 'the great modern revolu-

tionaries did not say: "Don't look at the world the way people have been doing for the last four centuries, it's wrong"; but "Don't look at the world the way people have been doing for the last four centuries, it is lazy." Habit and laziness, not faulty vision, is what they were trying to fight . . .';[110] if that is so, then Séan Ó Ríordáin (1917–77) is *the* modern poet writing in Irish.[111] Ó Ríordáin calls upon his readers to look at the world not in the habitual way but in a wholly unconventional way. Indeed, it is a topsy-turvy world for him and he views it with a deep despair hidden by a defensive elfish humour. He has a discernible philosophy, but it seems to be merely a means of trying to keep his despair under control, and it is the despair rather than the philosophy which has given us some of the most powerful and most unconventional poems ever written in Irish. His poetry is far too complex to be described in a few paragraphs, but his attitude towards Irish and the tradition in which he has chosen to write is significant and deserves comment.

He was born in a Breac-Ghaeltacht area, in Ballyvourney, in 1917, when Irish was rapidly disappearing. This was reflected in his family. His mother had very little Irish and English was the language of the hearth. On the other hand, Irish was the language of most of the population of the area, especially among the middle-aged and the old; it was also the language of Ó Ríordáin's grandmother and of her house, which stood not far from his own home and which he frequented in his childhood. There and in other neighbouring houses he heard Irish stories, Irish anecdotes and Irish poetry, and there he found a secondary world of fantasy:

> Chonac saol mar scéal fiannaíochta
> Fadó, fadó, ar maidin,
> A mhúnlaigh an tslat draíochta
> A bhíonn 'na láimh ag leanbh.
>
> Bhí cailleach chríon sa chúinne,
> A dhá hordóig ag casadh
> Go tionscalach mar thuirne,
> Ag piseogaíocht go gasta.[112]
>
> I saw a world like a tale of the Fiana,
> Long, long ago, one morning,
> Created by a magic wand
> Held in a child's hand.

> There was an old woman in the corner,
> Her two thumbs turning
> Busily like a spinning-wheel
> Cleverly casting spells.

This world of fantasy proved decisive in his literary career, and it made him receptive to the influence of Daniel Corkery and to his exposition of the Irish literary tradition:

> Do dhein dá anam cluas le héisteacht,
> Is d'éist gan trua
> (Dó féin, ná d'éinne mhúnlaigh bhéarsa),
> Gur thit anuas
>
> Do phlimp ar urlár gallda an lae seo
> Eoghan béal binn,
> Aindrias mac Craith, Seán Clárach, Aodhgán,
> Cith filí.[113]
>
> He made of his soul [His soul was made into] a ear
> to listen
> And he listened mercilessly
> (For himself, or for any versifier)
> So that there descended
>
> Suddenly on today's Anglicized scene
> Eoghan sweet lips,
> Aindrias Mac Craith, Sean Clárach, Aodhgán,
> A shower of poets

It opened his ears to the call of Irish literature:

> Tá focail ann dá mb'eol dom iad
> Folaithe i gceo na haimsire,
> Is táim ag cur a dtuairisc riamh
> Ó chuir an ré an tsaint orm:
> Táid scaipithe i leabhraibh léinn,
> Is fós i gcuimhne seanóirí,
> Is ag siúl na sráide im chuimhne féin,
> Och, buailim leo is ní aithním iad.[114]
>
> There are words if they were known to me
> Hidden in the mist of time;
> And I am looking out for them
> Since the age has made me hungry for them:
> They are scattered abroad in learned books

And still in the memory of old men
And walking the street in my own mind.
Alas, I meet them and I do not recognize them.

Conscious of being one in a long line of poets stretching back to antiquity, he feels that the wealth of this tradition is his to carry and to reveal. At the same time he realizes that the long life of the language is spent unless it can be adapted to the needs of the new age which is dawning. This is strikingly expressed in 'Duan an Oireachtais' (1948), where the native literary tradition is personified as 'An Droimeann Donn Dílis', 'the true flower of the kine' etc., of the popular folk-song.

Yet Ó Ríordáin is conscious that the English heritage is threatening the texture of the Irish language and the existence of its culture; he knows that he himself is bilingual, and that his grasp of the language is weak compared with that of his ancestors:

A Ghaeilge im pheannsa,
Do shinsear ar chaillis?
An teanga bhocht thabhartha
Gan sloinne thú, a theanga?

Bhfuil aoinne inár dteannta
Ag triall ar an tobar?
Bhfuil aon fhocal seanda
Ag cur lenár gcogar?[115]

O Irish in my pen,
Have you lost your ancestry?
Are you a poor, bastard language,
O language?

Is there any one with us
Making for the well?
Is there any aged word
Aiding our whisper?

There are times when he feels that he is paralyzed, that he cannot take up the challenge which the Irish tongue presents him:

Tá m'aigne fé ghlas,
Níl agam cead isteach
Le go ríordánóinn an farasbarr neamhscríte,
Gach barra taoide ait
Dár chraol an mhuir isteach
O bhíos-sa féin go deireanach i m'intinn.[116]

My mind is locked,
I am not allowed in

To poetize after my fashion the unwritten surplus,
Every pleasant high tide
The sea has cast inside
Since I was last there.

In one poem he addresses the Irish language as 'A Theanga Seo Leath-Liom' ('O Language Half-mine'),[117] and yet he commits himself to it deliberately and consciously.

Who cause this our conjunction,
    O language but half-mine?
If you refuse to function
    Let's choose a selling line.

Another language twits me
    And wants to be my wife,
I'm schizophrenic, it splits me,
    I lead a double life.

O with you we must go and dwell
    To be absorbed and won
Or we will lose our citadel
    and you your garrison.

Half minds are unabrasive
    And won't grind rough or fine;
You're tough and you're evasive
    And are so far half-mine.[118]

For him, the Gaeltacht and, for a short while at least, the Blaskets were a source from which the old Irish tongue and culture could be heard. Thus in his poem, 'Na Blascaodaí', he says,

Níor chualamar riamh an macalla
Ach i bhfad uainn ó chnocaibh i gcéin,
Ach anseo tá an stáisiún forleatha
Óna gcraolann an macalla féin,
Tá imigéiniúlacht 'nár n-aice,
Is aisiompó eagair san aer.

Tá uaigneas na mara oraibh
Is uaigneas na mbád,
Tá uaigneas na leabhar oraibh
Is uaigneas na ndán,
Is fá thuairim ár seanaigne
Déanam ólachán.[119]

We have never heard the echo
Except afar from us from the hills far away,

But here there is the broadcasting station
Whence the echo itself is broadcast;
There is remoteness near us,
There is the reverse order in the air.

You have the loneliness of the seas
The loneliness of the boats,
You have the loneliness of the books
And the loneliness of songs,
And for our old nature
Let us make lamentation.

Important though the theme of language and culture is in Ó
Ríordáin's work, one is conscious of doing an injustice to the poet in
considering it apart from his other themes, and especially in
considering it without reference to his idiom and technique, since his
novelty and originality lie not so much in his views as in the way he
communicates with us on a deeper level than that of intellectual ideas.
Thus, as Seán Ó Tuama reminds us, we are conscious of a strange,
even foreign sophistication, hitherto unknown in Irish verse, as we
read the first verse of 'Adhlacadh Mó Mháthar':

Grian an Mheithimh in úllghort,
Is siosarnach i síoda an tráthnóna,
Beach mhallaithe ag portaireacht
Mar scread-stracadh ar an nóin-bhrat.[120]

A June sun in an apple orchard,
A rustle in the silk of afternoon,
The droning of a bad-tempered bee
Loudly ripping the film of evening.

Ó Tuama sees in the second line an image born in English
(cf. 'a rustling in the noonday silk') rather than in Irish, or at least
an image born in a different milieu from the Irish. In the same way,
Ó Tuama feels that the synaesthesia in the second half of the quatrain, especially in the compound *scread-stracadh*, bears the marks
of importation from a poetics already established on the Continent
and in England but strange and foreign to Irish literature. However, he goes on to say that as we read Ó Ríordáin's poetry, the
feeling of strangeness recedes and that the poet's images, his
compounds and his style become more natural, more native of the soil
of Ireland.

But even more Irish than that poem is what Ó Tuama calls the
'positive, sunny section' of the poem 'Cnoc Mellerí'. Be that as it may,

it certainly gives expression to the 'cartoonist side of his imagination';
the opening verse may be translated thus:

> The storm was snorting in Melleray last night
> And days of soft sin lying like a sickness on my mind,
> Days that were soft couches of the cosy down of life,
> And fleas of lust in thousands were hopping there inside.[121]

The reference to the 'fleas' reminds us of the poem 'Domhnach Cásca'
('Easter Sunday'), when his mind wandered at Mass and spiritual
contemplation gave way to corporal concerns:

> Tá moncaithe im thimpeall
> Go tionscalach
> Ag piocadh na míola
> Dá chéile anseo.[122]

> There are monkeys all round me
> Busily
> A-picking the fleas
> From each other here.

Rarely do we find in modern Irish poetry such a consciousness of the
war between flesh and spirit. The poem 'Reo' expresses poignantly
another aspect of the poet's experience of loss after his mother's
death, although the 'objective correlative' in this case is perhaps used
too obviously to serve its purpose.

> *Frozen*

> On a frosty morning I went out
> And a handkerchief faced me on a bush.
> I reached to put it in my pocket
> But it slid from me, for it was frozen.
> No living cloth jumped from my grasp
> But a thing that died last night on a bush,
> And I went searching in my mind
> Till I found its real equivalent:
> The day I kissed a woman of my kindred
> And she in the coffin, frozen, stretched.[123]

Ó Tuama concludes a thorough and acute examination of Ó
Ríordáin's poetry with the remark that in the end what makes it so
uncommon, so extraordinary is that it reveals fully and unashamedly
the personality of an individual in a way never previously done in
Irish. The examination, it should be noted perhaps, was undertaken
partly as a reply to O'Brien's treatment of Ó Ríordáin in *Filíocht
Gaeilge na Linne Seo* (1968).[124]

Throughout his adult life, Seán Ó Ríordáin had to fight against ill
health, and no one who reads his poems can fail to realize that he was
hammering out his poetry on the anvil of his own suffering as well as
that of the language in its struggle to survive. There is no doubt that
he was a *file faoi scáth an bháis* 'a poet under the shadow of death'.[125]
Here is a poem born in his experience of illness, 'Fiabhras' ('Fever'),
translated by Richard Ryan.

> The slow climb out of the bed
> From the wet heat of its valley
> To where its mountains step off into nothing . . .
> So far to the floor now
> Though perhaps, there is, somewhere,
> A long way off, a world that still works.
>
> We are in a region of sheets here—
> The thought of a chair in this place!
> So hard now to believe
> Sunlight back in the other world
> Where we stood once high as a window.
>
> The frame has dissolved and
> His image is rising out of the wall—-
> No quarter there anymore:
> Wraiths ring me now,
> I think the world is melting . . .
>
> A region is growing out of the sky,
> There is a neighbourhood resting on my finger-tip—
> So easy to pick off a steeple!
> There are cows on the road to the north,
> But the cows of eternity are still making noise.[126]

Another poem, 'Claustrophobia', sees life from the sick bed:

> Beside the wine
> There is a candle and terror,
> The image of my Lord
> Seems to have no power,
> The rest of the night
> Is like crowds without,
> Night reigns
> Outside the window;
> If my candle goes out
> In spite of me now
> Night will leap
> Right into my lung,

My mind will be overcome
And terror created for me,
I shall be turned into night,
To be a living darkness:
   But if my candle lives on
   For one night alone
   I shall be a republic of light
   Till daylight comes.[127]

His sense of terror in the face of such fragility is expressed
metaphysically in 'Na Leamhain' ('The Moths'):

Whirr of a fragile moth, a page turning,
A spoiling of tiny wings,
A night in Autumn in the bed-room,
Torment of a fragile thing.

Another night in a dream I saw
A pair of great moth-wings,
They were as wide as wings of angels
And as a woman fragile things.

was my care to lay a hand on them
Lest they go straying through the night;
To possess them in the best of sanctuaries
And bring them to the fulness of delight.

But I spilt all the blessed gold-dust
That on each wing was poured,
And I knew then that I was left without numbers,
The numbers of manliness for ever-more.

And the ten numbers strode out of the error,
Their authority still greater than ever before,
And a sound was heard of races dealing in numbers,
And all were heard save me alone.

Whirr of a fragile moth, a page turning,
The diaphanous in ruin,
A night in Autumn and the moths are flying,
Great my heed on their little bruit.[128]

§4

Whatever difficulties the new writers in Irish prose and verse had to
face, they were less than those that confronted writers who faced the

challenge of writing plays in Irish, for before 1882 there is no record of any play produced or written in the language.[129] The reasons for the absence of any plays in Irish are not far to seek. One can safely dismiss the reason advanced by Dr Henebry and Tomás Mac Donnchadha that the element of pretence or make-believe involved in drama made it unacceptable to the Irish mind. The real reasons are more tangible. In modern times the drama needs a theatre building and a theatre-going audience, both requisites which can be supplied only by reasonably well-populated areas such as towns and cities. Although there must have been a good deal of Irish spoken in Dublin, Belfast and Cork down to comparatively recent times, it was not spoken by the upper and middle classes—in other words, not by the theatre-going class. Even after the Irish language movement had started, it is safe to assume that the need for drama in Irish was felt not so much by the public but by those enthusiasts who believed that an Irish literature was necessary for the preservation of Irish and that Irish drama was an essential component of that literature.[130] This is why we find among the important figures in early Irish-language drama the same people as in the other fields of literature: Douglas Hyde, Father Peadar Ó Laoghaire, Patrick Pearse, Father Pádraig Ó Duinnín, etc. 'They suffered', said Micheál Mac Liammóir, 'even more than Yeats, from the illusion that the theatre was purely the business of the writer, and as far as one can gather from a study of the period, they produced no actor of note except, it seems, Dr Hyde himself, whose performance in a comedy of his own was praised by Lady Gregory, no poor judge of the actor's art'.[131]   The earliest plays in Irish were primarily written for publication and only incidentally produced—and by non-professional actors at that. Father Seán Ó Cearbhaill published an Irish play, *Amharca Cleasacha* in *The Gaelic Journal* in 1882. In 1895, Eoghan Ó Neachtain published in the *Galway Pilot* an Irish translation of a play, *An Cailín Bán*, and three years later, Micheál Mac Ruaidhrí translated and adapted an English play by John Cannon, *The Dentist*. The same year saw the production of *Gaelic Tableaux* in Letterkenny (Leitir Ceanainn) and Belfast.

The establishment of the Irish Literary Theatre by W. B. Yeats with the help of Lady Gregory and Edward Martyn in 1899 and the Anglo-Irish literary movement in general with its avowed intention of 'opening up this fountain of legend', provided an additional stimulus to the writers of Irish plays.[132] *The Countess Cathleen*, produced in the Molesworth Hall in Dublin, in 1899, showed what could be done.

However, the writers of Irish plays did not find it easy to turn their backs on the familiar Gaeltacht scene.

Father Ó Laoghaire's play *Tadhg Saor* was staged in Macroom (Maghchromtha) in 1900: it is regarded as the first play to be written and produced in Irish. Other plays by him were *Bás Dalláin* (1900), *Lá na nAmadán* (1901), *An Sprid* (1902). They all reflect the fact that Ó Laoghaire had no experience of the theatre.

A start was made on historical plays in Irish by Father Pádraig Ó Duinnín in *Creideamh agus Gorta* (1901), and by Pádraig Ó Seaghdha (Conán Maol; 1855–1928) in *Aodh Ó Néill* (1902), but due to the number of scenes in them and the lack of true dramatic interest, it is difficult not to regard them as historical pageants. Ó Duinnín's *An Tobar Draoitheachta* (1902) lent itself more easily to stage production than *Creideamh agus Gorta*.

Douglas Hyde's association with Yeats and Lady Gregory introduced him more directly to the theatre than either Ó Laoghaire or Ó Duinnín. His play *Casadh an tSúgáin*, was produced in the Gaiety Theatre, Dublin, in 1901 (21 October), in a programme which included also *Diarmuid and Grania*, written by George Moore and W. B. Yeats. It is said to be the first play written in Irish to appear on the professional stage and the first play to bring Irish folklore into the theatre. Other plays followed from Hyde's pen: *An Pósadh* (1902), *An Tinncéir agus an tSídheog* (1902), *Teach na mBocht* and *An Cleamhnas*, both in 1903. If the last two plays are compared with two Anglo-Irish plays produced the same year, Synge's *Riders to the Sea* and Padraic Colum's *Broken Soil*, it will be obvious that the Irish Drama movement compared with the Anglo-Irish movement was still in its infancy.

Patrick Pearse had been interested in playwriting and acting even in childhood and retained his interest in them throughout his life. When a number of the National Theatre Company's founding members broke away in 1906 and met to consider forming a new group, Pearse was one of the speakers invited to address them. One result of that meeting was the establishment of Cluithcheoirí na hÉireann (or Theatre of Ireland).

As editor of *An Claidheamh Soluis*, Pearse occasionally discussed both Anglo-Irish and Irish drama, and he was under no illusion as to the superiority of the former to the latter; indeed, as late as 1906, we find him saying that no one as yet had written a successful Irish play. But whereas Yeats urged Anglo-Irish writers to go to the people, to observe their ways and to listen to their talk, Pearse was at pains to show that the Irish playwright need not necessarily concern himself with the Gaeltacht nor with the Gaeltacht family. He complained that in almost every Irish play the same character types appear: the husband and wife, the father-in-law, the young farm-hand, and the girl from the neighbouring farm. They always seemed to gather in the same kitchen, to do the same dances, and to talk in the same way about the same topics.[133]

Pearse advocated both by precept and by example the need to represent the heroic deeds of the past on the stage, and it is perhaps significant that 1906 saw some notable attempts at writing historical plays: among them *Cormac na Coille* by Piaras Béaslaí and *An Bealach Buidhe* by Peadar Ó Laoghaire.

Between 1909 and 1916, Patrick Pearse wrote eight dramatic works, six in Irish and two in English. Written expressly for school production at St Enda's, they included two three-act outdoor pageants, a three-act passion play, one short sketch, and four one-act plays. Two of the latter, *The Master* and *The Singer*, show that their author had some talent as a dramatist, had he chosen to develop it, and although as plays they are weakened by his characteristic fault—stilted dialogue—they are of absorbing interest because they give us a unique insight into the mind of the man who was to lead the Insurrection in 1916.

That Pearse's dissatisfaction with Irish drama was shared by others is indicated by the fact that *An tOireachtas* in 1911 offered a prize for the best entry on the prerequisites for dramatic composition. The winner was Padraic Ó Conaire, who made his contribution to Irish dramatic literature by writing *Bairbre Ruadh* (1908) and *An Droighneán Donn* (1925).

Irish drama has drawn heavily on translations from other literatures—French, German and Italian as well as English, but perhaps we need mention here only Pádraig de Brún's translations from Greek into Irish of the Sophoclean plays: *Antigone, Oedipus Rex* and *Oedipus at Colon*.

Theatre depends not only on playwrights, of course, but also on actors and appropriate buildings, and so it needs more organization than other departments of literature. In 1913 *Na hAisteoirí* (The Actors) was established under the directorship of Piaras Béaslaí, a man who, with Liam Gógan, Leon Ó Broin, Micheál Mac Liammóir and Gearóid Ó Lochlainn, may be said to form the first generation of the Irish (Gaelic) theatre profession. In 1922, *An Comhar* (or *An Comhar Drámuíochta*) was set up under the directorship of Gearóid Ó

Lochlainn (1884–1970), himself a playwright as well as an accomplished actor and producer. He was succeeded by Micheál Mac Liammóir (1899–1978), who had spent four years in Galway supervising, with government support, *Taidhbhearc na Gaillimhe*, which he had inaugurated with a production of his own play *Diarmuid agus Gráinne* (1928).[134]

Since the twenties much has been accomplished in Irish drama, but unfortunately much more needs to be done. By now the number of Irish plays in script or in print must be considerable. It is said that even in 1904 there were 50 Irish plays in manuscript. By 1962, An Gúm had published 234 Irish plays of which some 100 were translations. Raidió Éireann broadcast more than 600 short plays between 1927 and 1974, but extremely few full-length plays (it appears that *Diarmuid agus Gráinne* by Mac Liammóir and *Na Connerys* by Liam Ó Murchú were the only two). Raidió na Gaeltachta promises some interesting developments. There was a complaint that during the early years of its existence Teilifís Éireann gave only a meagre two percent of its time to Irish and made no worthwhile contribution to Irish drama. Of the theatres in Ireland, the Damer and the Peacock in Dublin, the Taidhbhearc in Galway, the Everyman in Cork and Amharclann Ghaoth Dobhair in Donegal staged plays in the Irish language from time to time, but the Damer is now closed, and Amharclann Ghaoth Dobhair apparently has not presented an Irish play for some time.

The Society of Irish Playwrights had a membership of eight in 1974. Perhaps four should be added to this to give an idea of the actual number of Irish playwrights. The Abbey offers a bursary of £1,500 every year to provide an author with the leisure to write a play in Irish or English (*Rafteirí* by Críostóir Ó Floinn was produced on one of these bursaries[135]) and *An tOireachtas* offers annual prizes for plays in Irish. Yet it remains true that 'Playwriting [in the Irish language] has made very little progress'.[136]

On the other hand, as one might expect, the theatre holds as much fascination for the writer in Irish as for the writer in English, and it should come as no surprise that the more serious and ambitious Irish writers have not been able to resist the call to write plays. Diarmaid Ó Súilleabháin (1932–1985), whose novels earned him a considerable reputation before his comparatively early death, wrote several plays including *Bior* (1965), *Macalla* (1966), *Ontos* (1967), *Na Fir Aduain*, *An Deisceart Domhain*, and *Lens*.[137] Seán Ó Tuama, better known as a poet and literary critic, published three short plays in 1967 under the title *Moloney agus Drámaí Eile*.[138] Séamas Ó Néill (1910–81), the author of *Tonn Tuile* (1947) and other novels as well as short stories and poems, has written plays, the best known of which perhaps is *Iníon Rí Dhún Sobhairce*; it was produced in the Taidhbhearc in 1953 but remained unpublished until 1960. The writings of Eoghan Ó Tuairisc (Eugene Watters, 1919–82) also include poems, novels, and plays, and deserve attention because they manifest the originality of a most interesting mind.[139] Although Ó Tuairisc was initially more eager to win fame for his writings in English, it was his work in Irish that gained him recognition. His first success was with his historical novel *L'Attaque* (1962) (*Dé Luain*, 1966, did not fare so well), but his poems and plays, notably *Lá Fhéile Míchíl* (1966), *Aisling Mhic Artáin* (1978) and *Fornocht do Chonac* (1981), also won him respect.

Even writers better known for their contributions to English than to Irish literature have on occasion made obeisance at the altar of Irish language drama, e.g., Liam Ó Flaithearta (O'Flaherty), who wrote *Dorchadas* in 1926. Unlike Ó Flaithearta, Brendan Behan (Ó Beacháin; 1923–64) began his literary career with a commitment to Irish in full accord with his political commitment to the unification of Ireland.[140] He wrote articles and poems in Irish (some of the latter are included in *Nua-Bhéarsaíocht 1939–49*, Dublin, 1950), and the plays which won him an international reputation—*The Quare Fellow* and *The Hostage*—were first written in Irish under the titles *Casadh Súgáin Eile* ('The Twisting of Another Rope') and *An Giall*.[141] Apparently, while he was in prison, Behan translated his play *The Landlady* into Irish and submitted it to the Abbey Theatre, but without success.

The fact that Irish plays are studied as part of the syllabus for a degree in Irish and that careers in radio and television appeal as strongly to young people in the Irish Republic as elsewhere should ensure a more discriminating and more adult audience for Irish plays. And that will hopefully prevent such exhibitions of *naïveté* as occurred when Máiréad Ní Ghráda (1899–1971), who had already won an Abbey Theatre award for her play *Giolla an tSolais* in 1954, submitted her play *An Triail* in the *Irish Life* competition.[142] One of the adjudicators was so aghast at the brothel scene that he expressed the hope that it would never be performed. (It *was* performed in the original Irish in the Dublin Theatre Festival in 1964, and again in Dublin in English in 1965.)

The last word on Irish drama, as far as we are concerned, can safely be left to Micheál Mac Liammóir, whose contributions to Irish literature in plays, essays, poetry, and translations should not be forgotten among his great contributions to the English theatre both in Ireland and abroad:

> The existence of Gaelic drama is, at the moment of writing, still a dream. From every point of view it is a dream, with the added disadvantage of both nightmare and reality. If the drama in English has dragons to fight, the drama in Irish has a hundred more. Apart from the question of populace, of full time actors and of their maintenance, of the endless complications besetting the development of the professional theatre . . . the very material at the disposal of writers of Irish is limited.[143]

§5

In tracing the history of Modern Irish literature it has been found necessary to refer several times to contemporary literary criticism. The problems to which that criticism addressed itself were real enough, but at least some of them were not literary and those that were did not always have literary treatment.

The question of *caint na ndaoine*, the speech of ordinary people, as we have seen, was posed at an early stage in the revival. The best known advocate and the most successful writer of *caint na ndaoine* was Father Peadar Ó Laoghairc, and the success of his *Séadna* indicated that he did not lack popular support. The leading and most articulate spokesman of those who opposed *caint na ndaoine* was Dr Richard Henebry (De Hindeberg). In a series of articles in *The Leader*, beginning in November, 1908, and continuing into the following spring, he attacked the grammar, the syntax and the idioms of 'Revival Irish'. All modern writers of Irish, with the exception of Ó Laoghaire, were, according to him, writing Irish that was first conceived in English, i.e., translation Irish.

In an article 'Is Irish a Living Language?' Pearse retorted that Henebry, in refusing to recognize the changes in spelling, grammar, and syntax that had been accepted by the people who spoke and wrote it, was treating Irish as a dead language and divorcing literature from the spoken language so completely as to make literature impossible, for literature had to be based on living speech.[144]

In a review of *Séadna* in its book form (1904), Pearse praised Ó Laoghaire for using the language of the people to write in a form and style that were his own. He proceeded to make the following comment on future Irish prose:

> If *Séadna* may be taken as a foretaste then we may say that the Irish prose of tomorrow, whilst retaining much of the lyric swing and love of melody of later Irish prose, will be characterised by the terseness, the crispness, the plain straightforwardness, the muscular force of what is best in mediaeval Irish literature . . . It will be founded on the speech of the people, but it will not be the speech of the people; for the ordinary speech of the people is never literature, though it is the stuff of which literature is made.[145]

In the 30 January 1909 instalment of his series to *The Leader*, Dr Henebry began a three-week attack on Pearse's short story *Iosagán*, starting with its narrative form, which, he said, made it 'not the talk of a chronicler telling his tale of happenings, but rather the musings of a hypothetical, extra-corporeal intelligence that is omniscient.'[146] He also objected to the 'explosive' or abrupt beginning as a deviation from Irish practice and a betrayal of the Irish tradition. Most of all, he found fault with the detailed descriptions which are intercalated and interrupt the action of the story.

> . . . this ethereal intelligence is petulantly nice in insisting upon the inalienable rights of trifles, and perpetually strives to encompass the apotheosis of the utterly unimportant. And the more trifling an item, or, in other words, the less connection it has with the plot, the greater its importance.

Obviously, Dr Henebry's standard of comparison was, as we have seen, the folk-tale.

As his lecture to the New Ireland Literary Society in March, 1897, on 'Gaelic Prose Literature' shows, Pearse had acquired a good knowledge of Irish literature from the sixth to the sixteenth centuries; that he was prepared to continue learning is clear from his lecture to the Society in January, 1898, on 'The Folk Songs of Ireland', where he drew extensively on Hyde's *Love Songs of Connacht*. But his interests were literary rather than scholarly, and it is striking testimony to his intelligence and acumen that unlike Henebry he saw clearly what the needs of Irish literature were at the time: 'We have far too little imaginative writing in Irish. Our writers, so to speak, are afraid to let themselves go.'[147]

The writers and poets who succeeded him have either consciously or unconsciously followed his advice, for he urged them to free themselves from the forms and conventions of the folk-tale and the poetry of eighteeenth-century Munster and to take their subjects from the life within and without them. He also laid down the principle that while they should base their style on the living spoken language, they should familiarize themselves not only with the various modes of contemporary writing in other countries but also with all the modes of their own literature from its beginnings to the present day.[148] To help them to achieve the latter, Douglas Hyde had already provided writers as well as the general public with a useful guide in *The Story of Early Gaelic Literature* (1985), a work soon to be superseded by his *A Literary History of Ireland from Earliest Times to the Present Day* (1899).

One of the most interesting literary critics in Ireland in the period between the two world wars was Daniel Corkery (Dónall Ó Corcora, 1878–1964). Professor of English literature in University College, Cork, short story writer, novelist, dramatist and literary critic, Corkery, although he wrote mostly in English, was an enthusiastic supporter of the Gaelic League and did very useful work as a propagandist for its ideal that Ireland should be Irish-speaking as well as free.[149]

Corkery had the interests both of a scholar and writer in literature and as an avowed anti-Romantic in the tradition of Matthew Arnold, he was concerned to show that Irish literature was classical through and through, and that the new generation of Irish writers should be aware of this and should align themselves with that tradition rather than seek models in English and continental literatures which, since the Renaissance, were mainly romantic and anti-classical—or, in his terms, barbaric. In his book *The Hidden Ireland* (1925, 1927, 1941), he wrote with deep sympathy and imaginative insight of the Munster poets of the eighteenth century, who, in spite of appalling economic and social conditions remained true to the Irish literary tradition and succeeded in their own way in adding to it. It has been shown since that he was writing with insufficient research and with unhistorical assumptions, but his bias was a salutary corrective at the time.[150] His book on *Synge and Anglo-Irish Literature* (1931) is based on the proposition that a literature to be worthy of the name must express the life of the nation for the nation itself and for none other. 'The writers in a normal country are one with what they write of. The life of every other people they gaze upon from without, but the life of their own people they cannot get outside of'.[151] His claim was that the Anglo-Irish writers for the most part compose not for the people of Ireland but for the English-speaking world to which Ireland is a closed book, and they try to look at Ireland with the eyes of foreigners. It is not difficult to imagine the hostile reaction it produced in people whose literary hero was James Joyce.

In March 1930 the first number of *Humanitas*, a short-lived literary periodical, appeared with the intention of providing a window on European literature to Irishmen who, presumably, were in need of one; the premise was that only through familiarity with European literature could genuine Irish literature be produced. The writer of the main article in that inaugural issue was Monsignor de Brún (1889–1960)[152], a scholar as well known for his general erudition as for his contributions as poet and translator to Irish literature. He complained of the 'poverty' of Irish writing compared with the writing of other nations, a poverty which was due to the fact that, unlike writers of other nations, Irish writers did not read the works of the great European authors and in particular the great authors of antiquity. Ireland, as de Brún explained elsewhere, had not experienced the Renaissance and this had left it in a backwater.

Corkery, recognizing the challenge to his own views, replied to de Brún, and this led to a lively and intellectually stimulating exchange of views.[153] Corkery's main argument was that to be classical a literature need not draw on the classical literatures of Greece and Rome, and that Irish literature is classical by virtue of the same qualities which made those literatures of antiquity classical.[154]

To be an outstanding literary critic one needs to produce a corpus of critical writing dealing not only with one author or with one period but with a wide variety of authors and periods. Perhaps Corkery did not qualify under those conditions but he did produce a body of critical writing which was remarkable for its consistency, its integrity, and its literary quality, and seems to have influenced writers as unlike each other as Frank O'Connor or Sean O'Faolain and Seán Ó Ríordáin.[155]

Beside him, his immediate contemporaries fade into insignificance. Seosamh Mac Grianna's essay on Pádraig Ó Conaire, *Pádraic Ó Conaire agus Aistí Eile* (1936), is vigorous and occasionally perceptive. Liam Ó Rinn's *Peann agus Pár* (1940) assessed objectively the weak condition of Irish literature and preached the virtues of honest literary craftsmanship and hard work. His book, *Mo Chara Stiofán* (1939, 1957) is interesting not only as indirectly another plea for the practice of the craft of letters but also because it is an exercise in literary biography unique in Irish at the time of its publication.

Frank O'Brien's *Filíocht Ghaeilge na Linne Seo* introduced the methods of the American 'new criticism' to the study of the modern Irish poetry with interesting but not always valid results. The book was reviewed extensively—and most competently by Seán Ó Tuama, whose essay on Seán Ó Ríordáin's poetry in *Studia Hibernica* is the best of its kind in Irish, and whose book, *An Grá in Amhráin na nDaoine*, is an outstanding contribution to literary scholarship and a clear demonstration that Irish is fully developed as a language of scholarship.[156]

Another perceptive critic who deserves to be mentioned even in such a brief survey as this is Tomás Ó Floinn. He has translated Old Irish poems and stories into Modern Irish, including *Athbeo* (Dublin, 1955), *Scéalaíocht na Ríthe* (—with Proinsias Mac Cana, Dublin, 1956), *Ath-Dhánta* (Dublin, 1970), *Aisling Mhic Conglinne* (Dublin, 1980), *Toghail na Téibe* (Dublin, 1983) and has written, mostly in *Comhar*, some fine essays which have enlarged the public's understanding of the innovating work done by Máirtín Ó Cadhain, Seán Ó Riordáin and others.

The early seventies saw increased activity in the field of literary criticism. *Irisleabhar Mhá Nuad* has tended to concentrate more than it used to on literary criticism,[157] and the monthly periodicals *Feasta* and *Comhar* have given more space to it. *Léachtaí Cholm Cille*, produced more or less annually, serves both literary criticism and literary scholarship. Breandán Ó Doibhlin (1931–), Professor of Modern Languages at Maynooth, has written very perceptively on some aspects of modern Irish literature and his *Litríocht agus Léitheoireacht* (Cork and Dublin, 1974) and *Aistí Critice agus Cultúir* (Dublin, 1975) deserve to be mentioned. But the most notable contributions to Irish literary criticism have been in *Scríobh* (1974–), edited by Seán Ó Mórdha, of which several volumes have appeared to date.

Several important works of scholarship in the Irish language have been written that may be placed alongside Ó Tuama's *An Grá in Amhráin na nDaoine*,[158] although some of the most outstanding achievements have been in the field of biography, and more especially political biography; Leon Ó Broin's *Parnell* (1937) and Seán Ó Luing's *Art Ó Gríofa* (1953) are good examples of the latter genre. *An Duinníneach* by Proinsias Ó Conluain and Donncha Ó Céileachair and books like Seán Ó Coileáin's carefully researched *Seán Ó Ríordáin* will lighten the burden of future historians of Irish literature.

And the future of Irish literature?

Douglas Hyde expressed the optimism of his fellow language-enthusiasts in the words, *Tá an Samhradh le teacht fós le congnamh Dé,* 'The Summer is yet to come with God's help'. Perhaps this optimism was not justified, but that there has been a remarkable renaissance of Irish literature in the twentieth century is an incontrovertable fact, as indisputable as the fact that some of the best work ever written in Irish has been produced by the leading figures in that renaissance.

And they are not without promising successors. By 1970, the year which brings to an end the period surveyed in this book, young writers were appearing outside the Gaeltachts whose commitment to the Irish language was as absolute as that of their most committed predecessors who had been born and bred there. And their commitment to literature and to Irish literature in particular seems equally absolute.[159]

But the number of potential readers of Irish—some 400,000—is not increasing and the number of native speakers of Irish—perhaps some 40,000—is continually shrinking;[160] and even if a literature can be produced in a language not acquired with the first experiences of childhood, it is certain that it will not continue without the assurance that its voice is heard by an appreciative public. As Máirtín Ó Cadhain said, 'It is hard for a man to give of his best in a language which seems likely to die before himself, if he lives a few years more.'

Notes

1 *Civitas Dei*, lib. xix, cap. 7, 'At enim opera data est, ut imperiosa civitas non solum iugum, verum etiam linguam suam domitis gentibus per pacem societatis imponeret . . .'

2 *Spenser's Prose Works*, ed. R. Gottfried (Baltimore, 1949), pp. 118–19.

3 *S. P. Henry VIII*, ii, pt. iiiA, 310.

4 Kenney, *Sources*, I, 51–3. See also D. Hyde, 'Irish as a Spoken Language' in *A Literary History of Ireland*, pp. 608–37; the first chapter of B. Ó Cuív, *Irish Dialects and Irish-Speaking Districts* (Dublin, 1951); D. Piatt, *Stair na Gaedhilge* (Dublin, 1933); D. Corkery, *The Fortunes of the Irish Language* (Dublin, 1954), chapter XI especially.

5 It may be, as has been suggested, that there were more people speaking Irish Gaelic in 1831 than ever before; see Corkery, op. cit., p. 114.

6 D. Coffey, *Douglas Hyde* (Dublin, Cork, 1938), p. 32; Hyde, *A Literary History of Ireland*, p. 636. On Hyde as an original writer see G. W.

Dunleavy, *Douglas Hyde* (Irish Writers Series, Bucknell University Press, 1974).

7 Philip Barron appears to have been the only Irish Catholic during this period to perceive that people ought to have an Irish education. See D. Ryan, *The Sword of Light* (London, 1939), p. 111ff.; S. Barruadh, 'Aithbheochaint na Gaedhilge' (M.A. thesis), chapter 11. But a society was formed by Protestants in 1818, 'The Irish Society—for the Education of the Native Irish Through the Medium of Their Own tongue'; see T. Ó hAilín, 'Teagasg tré Ghaeilge san 19ú hAois', *Comhar*, Nollaig, 1949, 20–21. One should not, however, forget the use made of the Irish language by Irish Catholic priests in their preaching and catechizing; see Pádraig Ó Fiannachta, 'Litríocht an Lae, 1800–1850', *Feasta*, Aibreán, 1972, 3–8, *Éigse* 12, pt. i (1967–68), 1–28. It was to assist priests to preach in Irish that John O'Brien, Bishop of Cloyne, published his dictionary, *Focalóir Gaoidhilge-Sax-Bhéarla* in Paris in 1768. It seems that Irish was taught in the Irish College there as well as in some other continental seminaries in the eighteenth century.

8 Kenney, *Sources*, I, 51–2. Cf. Maureen Wall, 'The Decline of the Irish Language', in Brian Ó Cuív, ed., *A View of the Irish Language* (Dublin, 1969), p. 87: 'It has been estimated that one and a half million died during the Famine and between 1846 and 1851 a million emigrated'. Tadhg Ó Donnchadha expressed the opinion that there would be no more than some 50 people in all Ireland in 1882 who could both read and write Irish in the 'Gaelic' type. See E. M. Ní Chiarágain, Index to *Imleabhar na Gaedhilge 1882–1909* (Dublin 1935), vii.

9 Kenney, *Sources*, I, 54ff.; E. Cahill, 'Irish Scholarship in the Penal Age', *Irish Ecclesiastical Record*, v. Ser., 56, pp. 20–48; T. F. O'Rahilly, 'Irish Scholars in Dublin in the Early Eighteenth Century', *Gadelica*, 1 (1912), 156–62.

10 For the Irish background of Charlotte Brooke, see Philip O'Connell, *The Schools and Scholars of Breiffne* (Dublin, 1942), pp. 372ff. On her work and that of J. C. Walker, see R. A. Breatnach, 'Two Eighteenth-Century Irish Scholars', SH, 5 (1965), 88–97.

11 J. and J. B. Nicholls, *Illustrations of the Literary History of the Eighteenth Century* (London, 1817–58), VIII, 250.

12 See J. Warburton, J. Whitelaw, and R. Walsh, *History of the City of Dublin* (London, 1818), II, 930ff.; *B. M. Cat. Irish MSS*, III, 26ff. There were a number of enthusiasts working for the preservation of the Irish language in Belfast also: see S. Ó Casaide, *The Irish Language in Belfast and Co. Down AD 1601–1850* (Dublin, 1930) and Breandán Ó Buachalla, *I mBéal Feirste Cois Cuain* (1968).

13 'Six Hundred Gaelic Proverbs Collected in Ulster', *Ulster Journal of Archaeology*, 6 (1858), 172–83, 250–67; (1859), 278–87; 9 (1861), 223–36.

14 Kenney, *Sources*, I, 63ff; É de hÓir, *Seán Ó Donnabháin agus Eoghan Ó Comhraí* (Dublin, 1962).

15 'Irish Language Movement: Some Reminiscences', *Manchester Guardian Commercial*, European Reconstruction Series: Ireland (10 May 1923), pt. 2, p. 38. Cf. D. hÍde (Hyde), *Mise agus an Connradh* (Dublin, 1937), 14–15.

16 A good deal of information about the society can be found in J. J. Doyle, *A Pioneer of the Language Movement, David Comyn: 1854–1907* (Cork, 1927). See *Irisleabhar Muighe Nuadhat*, 1956, 89–92, for the history of a journal that was established to facilitate the study of the language as early as 1867.

17 The National Commissioners of Education decided 'That the Commissioners are prepared to grant Results' Fees for proficiency in the Irish Language on the same conditions as are applicable to Greek, Latin and French'; Doyle, op. cit., p. 19.

18 The original name was *The Gaelic Union Journal*. In 1891, five numbers of the *The Gaelic Journal* were published, with about 250 copies of each number. In the same year Father Eugene O'Growney was made editor. In no time at all a thousand readers were subscribing to the journal, and it reverted to monthly publication.

19 Kenney, *Sources*, I, 52.

20 See Hyde, *Mise agus an Connradh*, pp. 100–101. On the language teachers or *timthirí*, 'organizers' or 'agents' of the League as they were called, see 'Na Múinteoirí Taistil', *Feasta*, Márta, Aibreán, Bealtaine, 1965. On the Gaelic League, etc., see 'Founding of the Gaelic League,' chap. 2 in Michael Tierney, *Eoin Mac Neill: Scholar and Man of Action (1867–1945)*, ed. by F. X. Martin (Oxford, 1980); Pádraig Ó Fearaíl, *The Story of Conradh na Gaeilge* (Dublin, 1975); Seán Ó Tuama, ed., *The Gaelic League Idea* (Dublin, 1972); and on its precursors, M. Ní Mhuiríosa, *Réamh-chonraitheoirí* (Dublin, 1968).

21 See Donncha Ó Súilleabháin, *Scéal an Oireachtais 1897–1924* (Dublin, 1985).

22 P. Ó Conluain and D. Ó Céileachar, *An Duinnínach* (Dublin, 1958; rpt. 1976), pp. 133–4.

23 See P. Ó Tailliúir, 'Ceartliosta de Leabhair, Paimfléid, etc. Foilsithe in Éirinn ag Connradh na Gaeilge, 1893–1918', *Comhar*, Feabhra-Lúnasa, 1964, and D. Ó Súilleabháin, 'Foilseacháin agus Foilsitheoireacht Chonradh na Gaeilge', *Feasta*, Márta, 1971, 15ff., Aibreán-Bealtaine, 1971, 13ff.

24 Dr Mahaffy used this argument, saying that he had received it from an expert. Although he did not say who the expert was, it is generally believed that it was Atkinson. For the story, see Hyde, *Mise agus an Connradh*, pp. 77ff.

25 *The Irish Volunteer*, 7 February 1914.

26 In Ireland, as in the other Celtic countries of Great Britain, Scotland and Wales, it seems to be understood that a bilingual culture is the most that can be achieved in these days when even people with a well-established language of their own have to learn one or another of the languages which dominate international cosmopolitanism. It is not realized in Ireland, any more than it is in Scotland and Wales, that bilingualism is a feckless dream for a small country when a cosmopolitan culture underlies the one language and nothing but national pride the other.

27 For recent studies of Irish storytellers and their tales, see J. E. Caerwyn Williams, *Y Chwedleuwr Gwyddeleg a'i Chwedlau* (Cardiff, 1972), and Seán Ó Súilleabháin, *Storytelling in Irish Tradition: Scéalaíocht in Éirinn* (Cork, 1973).

28 There were several engaged in that work before him, e.g., Patrick Kennedy (1801–73), Sir William Wilde (1815–76), Jeremiah Curtin (1835–1906), Robert MacAdam (1808–95), William Larminie (1843–1900). *An Cumann le Béaloideas Éireann* (The Folklore of Ireland Society) was established in 1927 (its periodical is *Béaloideas*, 1927–), the *Institiúid* in 1930, and *Comisiún Béaloideasa Éireann* ('The Irish Folklore Commission') in 1935. This last has now merged with the Department of Irish Folklore at University College Dublin, and the initials IFC refer to the Irish Folklore Collection, the archives in the Department of Irish Folklore.

29 A translation into English has been made by Máire MacNeill and published under the title of *Seán Ó Conaill's Book* (Dublin, 1981). That Ó Conaill was not unique in his repertory has been shown by the publication of other books containing the lore of a single shanachie, notably, D. Ó Cróinín, ed., *Seán Ó Cróinín*, coll., *Scéalaíocht Amhlaoibh Í Luínse* (Dublin, 1971), a volume of 385 pages containing 56 international tales; D. Ó Cróinín, ed., *Seán Ó Cróinín*, coll., *Seanchas Amhlaoibh Í Luínse* (Dublin, 1980); D. Ó Cróinín, ed., *Seán Ó Cróinín*, coll., *Seanchas Phádraig Í Chrualaoi* (Dublin, 1982); Peadar Ó Ceannabháin, ed., Liam Coisdeala, coll., *Éamon a Búrc: Scéalta* (Dublin, 1983), and Kevin O'Nolan, ed. and tr., Liam Coisdeala, coll., Éamon a Búrc, *Eochair Mac Rí in Éirinn: Eochair, a King's Son in Ireland* (Dublin, 1982).

30 Some of these were collected in *Ubhla den Chraoibh* (Dublin, [1900]).

31 D. Corkery, *Synge and Anglo-Irish Literature* (Cork, 1931), p. 56.

32 According to A. H. Krappe, 'It is . . . clear that a considerable number of songs considered now old folk-songs have in all probability a literary origin . . . in periods of intense literary activity, literary products will sink, from the classes for which they were intended in the first place, to lower levels of the people. When the songs of the medieval troubadours had charmed the knights and ladies, and even after they have ceased to charm them, they still appealed to the peasants'; *The Science of Folklore* (London, 1930), pp. 154. On the question of the relation between literature and folklore, see Bo Almquist, *An Béaloideas agus an Litríocht* (Dublin, 1977), and more generally Max Lüthi, *Volksliteratur und Hochliteratur* (Bern and Munich, 1970).

33 Quoted by Donal O'Sullivan, *Irish Folk Music and Song* (Dublin, 1952). See also O'Sullivan's *Songs of the Irish* (Dublin, 1960); Breandán Breathnach, *Folk Music and Dance of Ireland* (Dublin and Cork, 1971).

34 Frank O'Connor, *Kings, Lords, and Commons* (Dublin, 1970), pp. 127–8.

35 Op. cit., p. 131.

36 One should not forget the part played by George Thompson in the composition of *Fiche Blian ag Fás*, by Máire Ní Chinéide in the production of *Peig*, and by Carl Marstrander, Robin Flower, Brian Ó Ceallaigh and An Seabhac (Pádraig Ó Siochfhradha) in the development of Tomás Ó Criomhthain, whose other book *Allagar na hInise* also deserves to be mentioned (there are two distinct editions: that of 1928, 186 pp., and the 2nd ed. in 1977, 355 pp.). See Breandán Ó

Conaire, 'Ómós do Thomás Ó Criomhthain', *Comhar*, 37, no. 3, 14–15; no. 4, 19–23; 'Tomás an Bhlascaeid', *Comhar*, 37, no. 9 (1977), 18–21; Seán Ó Coileáin, 'Tomás Ó Criomhthain, Brian Ó Ceallaigh agus An Seabhac', *Scríobh*, 4 (1979), 159–87. On Muiris Ó Súileabháin, see Nuala Ní Aimhirgin, *Muiris Ó Súileabháin* (Dublin, 1983).

37 Viking Press edition, 10th printing, 1963, p. v.
38 See Máire Mhac an tSaoi, 'Scríbhneoireacht sa Ghaeilge Inniu', *Studies*, 44 (1955), 86–91, esp. 86–8; David Greene, *Writing in Irish To-day* (Cork, 1972), 34; Máire Cruise O'Brien, 'An t-Oileánach', in John Jordan, ed., *The Pleasures of Gaelic Literature* (Cork, 1977), pp. 25–38. There are two editions of *An tOileánach*, one by An Seabhac, the other by Tomás's grandson, Pádraig Ua Maoileoin; basically, there is not much to choose between them.
39 *The Poor Mouth*, transl. P.C. Power (NY, 1974), pp. 42–5
40 J. E. Caerwyn Williams, ed., *Literature in Celtic Countries* (Cardiff, 1971), p. 147. On Brian O'Nolan, also called Flann O'Brien, see Anne Clismann, *Flann O'Brien: A Critical Introduction to his Writings* (Dublin, 1975); and Brendan Kennelly, 'An Béal Bocht', in John Jordan, ed., *The Pleasures of Gaelic Literature*, pp. 85–96. Of Myles na gCopaleen (Flann O'Brien, Brian Ó Nualláin/O'Nolan) it has been well said that he is both 'ultra-conservative' and 'ultra-modern'. His first three novels are based in part on medieval Irish tales but they are closely concerned with language and style and his world has affinities not only with that of James Joyce and Beckett but also with that of the *nouveau roman* and the Theatre of the Absurd. The Rabelaisian element in Irish literature comes to the surface in his work as it does in the writings of Joyce and Beckett, but he is too profligate with words to qualify as an artist of the first rank. (O'Nolan himself would no doubt take exception to the comparison with Rabelais, of whom he said, 'Rabelais is funny, but his stuff cloys. His stuff lacks tragedy'; 'A Bash in the Tunnel', *Flann O'Brien: Stories and Plays*, New York, 1976, p. 208.)
41 This does not, of course, mean that it was a language without outstanding virtues, for Irish has a wealth of vocabulary and of idiomatic and metaphorical expressions, and it is characterized by a liveliness and a flexibility which shows that it has not lost touch with life in all its concreteness as well as in its complexity. We cannot resist recalling O'Nolan's parody of the very richness of the language: 'While the average English speaker gets along with a mere 400 words, the Irish-speaking peasant uses 4,000 . . . there is scarcely a single word in the Irish (barring, possibly, *Sasanach*) that is simple and explicit. Apart from words with endless shades of cognate meaning, there are many with so complete a spectrum of graduated ambiguity that each of them can be made to express two directly contrary meanings, as well as a plethora of intermediate concepts that have no bearing on either . . . . The plight of the English speaker with his wretched box of 400 vocal beads may be imagined when I say that a really good Irish speaker would blurt out the whole 400 in one cosmic grunt. In Donegal there are native speakers who know so many million words that it is a matter of pride with them never to use the same word twice in a life-time'; 'The Gaelic',

in *The Best of Myles* (New York, 1968; Penguin rpt., 1984), pp. 278–9. On O'Nolan as an Irish writer see Breandán Ó Conaire, *Myles na Gaeilge* (Dublin, 1986).

In some ways, Gaelic is as flexible a language as English, but there are areas in which it cannot hope to compete without a great deal of development. Such a development will not occur unless its speakers and writers use it either from choice or by compulsion to express twentieth-century life in Ireland in all its aspects, urban as well as rural, industrial as well as agricultural. Some of the problems connected with this development remain unresolved; others have been more or less successfully solved. See Maureen Wall, 'The Decline of the Irish Language', in Brian Ó Cuív, *A View of the Irish Language* (Dublin, 1969), pp. 81–90.

42 D. Greene, 'The Background to Modern Writing in Irish', *International P.E.N., Bulletin of Selected Books*, 3 (1952–3), 37. It is becoming abundantly clear through recent research, however, that the Irish language was cultivated to a greater extent in the nineteenth century than was previously thought; see P. Ó Fiannachta, ed., *Litríocht an 19ú hAois*, *Léachtaí Cholm Cille*, 3 (1972). For the later period, see Muiris Ó Droighneáin, *Taighde i gcomhair Stair Litridheachta na Nua-Ghaedhilge ó 1882 anuas* (Dublin, 1936, 1937); M. Sjoestedt-Jonval, 'La littérature qui se fait en Irlande', EC, 2 (1937), 334–46; M. Mhac an tSaoi, 'Scríbhneoireacht sa Ghaeilge Inniu', *Studies*, 44 (1955), 86–91; Aodh de Blácam's *Gaelic Literature Surveyed* (Dublin, 1929, 1933), is valuable not only for the modern period but for the entire history of Irish literature. The 1973 ed. contains a chapter on 'The Twentieth Century: Prose and Verse', by Eoghan Ó Hanluain. See also Breandán Ó Doibhlin, 'Irish Literature in the Contemporary Situation', P. Ó Fiannachta, ed., *Litríocht na Gaeilge*, *Léachtaí Cholm Cille*, 1 (1970); Gearóid Mac Eoin, 'Twentieth Century Irish Literature', Brian Ó Cuív, ed., *A View of the Irish Language*, pp. 57–69.

43 See Osborn Bergin on Ó Laoghaire (O'Leary) in *Studies*, 16 (1927), 18–19, and cf. Douglas Hyde in the same journal, vol. 9 (1920), 299–300. A full study can be found in *An tAthair Peadar Ó Laoghaire agus a Shaothar*, by 'Maol Muire' (Dublin, n.d. [1939]). Cf. also Pádraig A. Breatnach, 'Séadna: Saothar Ealaíne', SH, 9 (1969), 109–24. Ó Laoghaire's *Mo Sgéal Féin* has been translated twice into English, by T. Ó Céirin, *My Story by Peter O'Leary* (Cork, 1970) and by Sheila Ó Sullivan, *My Own Story* (Dublin, 1973).

44 See P. Ó Laoghaire's inaugural address dealing with the revival of the Irish language, *Journal of the Ivernian Society*, 1 (1908), 65–8.

45 Peadar Ó Laoghaire, *Papers on Irish Idiom*, ed. T. F. O'Rahilly (Dublin, 1920), p. 138.

46 *The Western Island* (Oxford, 1944), p. 49, and quoted by W. R. Rodgers in his introduction to *Peig Sayers: An Old Woman's Reflections*, trans. Séamus Ennis (London, 1962), p. x. Gaeltacht people generally 'were very conscious of the niceties of language: a very common term of praise was to say that such a man or woman was a good talker, while to suggest the contrary about an individual was definitely derogatory'; Caoimhín Ó Danachair, 'The Gaeltacht', in Ó Cuív, ed., *A View of the Irish*

Language, p. 117. See also Gerard Murphy, *Glimpses of Gaelic Ireland* (Dublin, 1948), chapter I on 'Irish Folk-Poetry.'

47 *Shiána* (Dublin, 1914).

48 *Gaelic Literature Surveyed* (Dublin, 1929), pp. 378ff.

49 Ó Laoghaire's attitude towards the language was partly the same as that of the Irish scholars of his days and later. 'They were, and to a large extent still are, more concerned with the type of Irish and the idioms in a piece of writing than with its literary value'; so wrote Máirtín Ó Cadhain in 'Irish Prose in the Twentieth Century', J. E. Caerwyn Williams, ed., *Literature in Celtic Countries*, 142.

50 *An Claidheamh Soluis*, 24 Meán Fómhair, 1904), 1.

51 See Ruth Dudley Edwards, *Patrick Pearse: the Triumph of Failure* (London, 1977); Raymond J. Porter, *P. H. Pearse* (New York, 1973); Hedley McCay, *Patrick Pearse* (Cork, 1966). Pearse's literary essays have been collected and published: Séamus Ó Buachalla, ed., *Na Scríbhinní Liteartha le Pádraig Mac Piarais* (Cork, Dublin, 1979), and his short stories have also been re-published: Cathal Ó Hainle, ed., *Gearrscéalta an Phiarsaigh* (Helicon, 1979), with an interesting introduction. See also the early study by Séamus Ó hAodha, *Pádraic Mac Piarais, Sgéalaidhe* (Dublin, n.d.).

52 For a survey of the Irish-language short story, see Aisling Ní Donnchadha, *An Gearrscéal sa Ghaeilgeh, 1898–1940* (Dublin, 1981).

53 'Revival Irish', *The Leader*, 30.1, 1909, pp. 564–5; 6.2, 1909, pp. 587–8. De Hindeberg's writings were collected and edited by Seán Ó Cuirrín, *Sgríbhne Ristéird de Hindeberg* (Dublin, 1924).

54 *An Claidheamh Soluis*, 26, Bealtaine, 1906, p. 6.

55 For a full study of Ó Conaire's work, see A. Ní Chnáimhín, *Pádraic Ó Conaire* (Dublin, 1947), and the less ambitious but illuminating study by Seosamh Mac Grianna, *Pádraic Ó Conaire agus Aistí Eile*, (Dublin, 1936, 1939, 1969). Cf. Seán Ó Tuama, 'Pádraic Ó Conaire,' *Comhar*, Feabhra, 1953, 7–10, 23. Ó Conaire's birthday centenary was commemorated in the Márta, 1982, issue of *Feasta*, with several essays on his work, notably, Críostóir Mac Aonghusa, 'Pádraic Ó Conaire— Scríobhnóir', pp. 22–36. continued in Aibreán, pp. 6–18. See also Tomás de Bhaldraithe, ed., *Pádraic Ó Conaire: Cloch ar a Charn* (Dublin, 1982); Gearóid Denvir, ed., *Pádraic Ó Conaire, Léachtaí Cuimhneacháin* (Cló Chonamara/Ráidio na Gaeltachta, 1983). *Pádraic Ó Conaire* (Swords, 1982) is a translation into English of 15 of his best-known stories.

56 See Donncha Ó Súilleabháin, *Scéal an Oireachtais 1897–1924* (Dublin, 1984), p. 161. Pádraic Ó Conaire's essays have been published by Gearóid Denvir, ed., *Aistí Phádraic Uí Chonaire* (Indreabhán: Cló Chois Fharraige, 1978).

57 A new edition of the work, under the title *Deoraíocht* was published in 1974 with an introduction by Mícheál Mac Liammóir. See the chapter on the book in J. Jordan, *The Pleasures of Gaelic Literature* (Cork, Dublin, 1977), pp. 13–24, and Tomás Ó Broin, *Saoirse Anama Uí Chonaire: Compánach d'úrscéal fiontrach Deoraíacht* (Galway, 1984).

58 According to Máirtín Ó Cadhain, Seosamh Mac Grianna, Pádraic Ó Conaire, and Pearse were the only real writers who had appeared by the

mid-twentieth century. See 'Tuige nach bhfuil Litríocht na Gaeilge ag
Fás', *Feasta*, 2, 8 (1949), 8–11, 20–22; esp. p. 9. For surveys of more
recent prose, see *Comhar*, Nollaig, 1987, and especially Tadhg Ó
Dushláine, 'An Coimpléasc Priompallánach', ibid., 4–11. For the
impact of events in the Six Counties on the Irish novel, see Pádraig Ó
Siadhail, 'Na Sé Chontae, An Saorstát agus an tUrsgéal Gaeilge',
Comhar, Meitheamh, 1987, 28–33, Iúil, 1987, 21–27.

59 E. R. Dobbs, ed., *Journals and Letters of Stephen MacKenna* (London,
1936), pp. 218–19.

60 Quoted by David Greene, *Writing in Irish To-day* (Cork, 1972). The
original Irish is in Tomás de Bhaldraithe, *Scoth Scéalta le Pádraic Ó
Conaire* (Dublin, 1956), p. 7.

61 Máirtín Ó Cadhain, 'Irish Prose in the Twentieth Century' in J. E.
Caerwyn Williams, ed., *Literature in Celtic Countries*, p. 146. Seán Ó
Siadhail, 'Caidé a d'imigh ar fhear na haislinge?' *Irisleabhar Mhá Nuad*
1986, pp. 134–59, analyses Séamus Ó Grianna's development as an
author. N. Mac Congáil, 'An Bheirt Ghrianach', *Irisleabhar Mhá Nuad*
(1983), 20–30, discusses the works of Máire and his brother Seosamh, and
has elaborated that discussion in *Scríbhneoirí Thír Chonaill* (Dublin, 1983).

62 See also Cathal Ó Háinle, 'Seanchas "Mháire",' *Scríobh*, 5 (1981), 248–
57; Tomás Ó Fíaich, 'Saothar Mháire mar Fhoinse don Stair
Shóiséalta', *Léachtaí Cholm Cille*, V (1974), 5–30; Nollaig Mac Congáil,
Léargus ar 'Cioth is Dealán "Mháire" ' (Dublin, 1983).

63 See Proinsias Mac an Bheatha, *Seosamh Mac Grianna agus Cúrsaí Eile*
(Dublin, 1970) For the flavour of Mac Grianna's personality see his
essays, *Filí agus Felons*, ed. Nollaig Mac Congail (Dublin, 1988).

64 Roinn an Oideachais, 'An Gúm—Foilsitheoir Stáit', *Comhar*, 38 (1980),
18–19; Mícheál O Séaghdha, 'The *Gúm* and Translations', *The Leader*,
86 (1973), 69–72.

65 Declan Kiberd, 'Mo Bhealach Féin: Idir Dhá Thraidisiún', *Scríobh*, 5
(1981), 224–39; Liam Ó Dochartaigh, 'Mo Bhealach Féin: Saor
Nualitríochta', *Scríobh*, 5 (1981), 240–47; Séamus Deane, 'Mo Bhealach
Féin', John Jordan, ed., *The Pleasures of Gaelic Literature*, pp. 52–61.

66 *The Lonely Voice* (London, 1963), p. 38.

67 Frank O'Connor (sel. and intro.), *Modern Irish Short Stories* (The
World's Classics; OUP, London, 1957), ix.

68 See, e.g., Tomás de Bhaldraithe, ed., *Nuascéalaíocht: 1940–1950*
(Dublin, 1952).

69 'Ó Flaithearta—Aistritheoir', *Comhar*, Bealtaine, 1967, 35–37; 'Liam
O'Flaherty—Translator', *Éire-Ireland*, 3 (1968), 149–53. It has been
remarked that O'Flaherty's English is 'often subconsciously affected by
Gaelic speech patterns, and by the patterns of storytelling he heard as a
child when groups used to gather round the O'Flaherty hearth'; see
Robert Hogan et al., edd., *The Macmillan Dictionary of Irish Literature*
(1979), p. 525. On O'Flaherty's Irish and English, see also Seán
O'Faolain, 'Dúil', in J. Jordan, *The Pleasures of Gaelic Literature*, pp.
111–19.

70 Fiachra Ó Dubhthaigh, *Léargus ar 'Dúil' Liam Uí Flaithearta* (Dublin,
1982).

71 J. E. Caerwyn Williams, ed., *Literature in Celtic Countries*, p. 146.
72 Loc. cit.
73 *Modern Irish Short Stories*, p. xii.
74 For a comprehensive survey of the short story in Irish before Ó Cadhain, see Aisling Ní Dhonnchadha, *An Gearscéal sa Ghaeilge 1898–1940*.
75 J. E. Caerwyn Williams, ed., *Literature in Celtic Countries*, p. 151.
76 Ó Cadhain has studied the short story as a genre very intently. See Máirtín Ó Cadhain, 'An Gearrscéal sa Ghaeilge', *Scríobh*, 5 (1981), 100–5. See also Nollaig Mac Congail, 'Ó Cadhain agus an Gearrscéal', *Scríobh*, 5 (1981), 106–14; Máire Ní Annracháin, 'An Bheirt Mhicil. An Coimhthíos Sóisialta i nGearrscéalta Mháirtín Uí Chadhain', *Scríobh*, 4 (1979); Máire Ní Annracháin, 'Gnéithe den Chríostaíocht i nGearrscéalta Mháirtín Uí Chadhain', *Le Fiche Bliain, Léachtaí Cholm Cille*, X (1979). Needless to say, Máirtín Ó Cadhain's writings have become a fruitful field of research and it is impossible to keep track of them all. Of fundamental importance is Alan Titley's *Máirtín Ó Cadhain, Clár Saothair* (Dublin, 1975). The most ambitious study of his work to date is Gearóid Denvir, *Cadhan Aonair: Saothar Liteartha Mháirtín Uí Chadhain* (Dublin, 1987). Ó Cadhain's *As an nGéibheann* (Dublin, 1973; letters to Tomás Bairéad from internment) and his *Páipéir Bhána agus Páipéir Bhreaca* (Dublin, 1969) should be read for the light they throw on him and his opinions. Sister Bosco Costigan's book, *De Ghlaschloich an Oileáin: Beatha agus Saothar Mháirtín Uí Chadhain* (Conamara, 1987) is a useful interim biography. An Ó Cadhain lecture has been established. Gearóid Denvir's lecture in the series, 'Ó Chill go Cré—Léamh ar shaothar Mháirtín Ó Chadhain', published in *Comhar*, Eanáir (January), 1987, stresses the difference between Ó Cadhain's earlier and later work.
77 Williams, ed., *Literature in Celtic Countries*, pp. 143–4.
78 Robert O'Driscoll, ed., *The Celtic Consciousness* (1981), p. 253.
79 Máire Mhac an tSaoi, 'Scríbhneoireacht sa Ghaeilge Inniu', p. 90; quoted in translation by David Greene, *Writing in Irish To-day*, pp. 43–44. Cf. Breandán Ó hEithir, 'Cré na Cille', in J. Jordan, ed., *The Pleasures of Gaelic Literature*, pp. 72–84.
80 See Cathal Ó Háinle, 'Athbheochan na Filíochta 1882–1916', *Litríocht an 19ú hAois. Léachtaí Cholm Cille* III (1972).
81 *The Western Island*, pp. 99–100.
82 P. H. Pearse, 'Some Aspects of Irish Literature', *Studies* 11 (1913), 810–22.
83 See Aine Ní Cheanainn, *Seán Mac Héil—Aistí* (Dublin, 1983).
84 See Séamus Ó Buachalla, ed., *Na Scríbhinní Liteartha le Pádraig Mac Piarais* (Dublin, Cork, 1979).
85 For the poem, see Crádh Cridhe Eigeas (pen name), *Maidean i mBéarra agus Dánta Eile* (Dublin, 1918).
86 See Ciarán Ó Coigligh, *Filíocht Ghaeilge Phádraig Mhic Phiarais* (Dublin, 1981).
87 In Padraic Colum, ed., *An Anthology of Irish Verse* (New York, 1948), p. 325.
88 *The Collected Poems of W. B. Yeats* (London, 1961), pp. 202–5.

89 See such anthologies as Shán Ó Cuiv's *An Dórd Féinne agus Dánta Eile* (Dublin, 1927) and *Fiche Duan: A Selection of Gaelic Poems from the Best Modern Authors* (Dublin, 1919).

90 The anthologies mentioned in the previous note should be compared with the two edited by Séamas Ó Céilleachair, *Nua-Fhilí (1942–52)* (Dublin, 1956), *Nua-Fhilí (1953–1963)* (Dublin, 1968) to appreciate the difference in technique and outlook. See also Seán Ó Tuama, 'Donncha Ó Ceileachair: Scríbhneoir idir Dhá Thraidisiún', *Scríobh*, 1 (1974), 31–9.

91 That there were other poets of more than ordinary talents should not need emphasizing. Sean O'Faolain, 'Fifty Years of Irish Writing', *Studies*, 51 (1962), 93–105, pays tribute to the poetry of Tomás Tóibín, and Seán Ó Tuama's excellence as a critic of poetry should not blind us to his own poetic achievements. See his *Faoileán na Beatha* (1962) and *Saol fó Thoinn* (1978). The youngest generation of poets are best represented on the pages of *Innti* (1970–). For them and their work, see Eoghan Ó hAnluan, 'Cor Nua san Fhilíocht', *Scríobh*, 1 (1974), 67–74, Ciarán Ó Coigligh, ed., *An Fhilíocht Chomhaimseartha: 1975–85* (Dublin, 1987), Gréagóir Ó Dúill, ed., *Filíocht Uladh 1960–85* (Dublin, 1987), Pádraig Ó Fiannachta, ed., *An Nuafhilíocht* (Maynooth, 1987).

92 His publications include *Coinnle Geala* ('Bright Candles,' 1942); *Dánta Aniar* ('Poems from the West', 1943); *Rogha Dánta* ('A Choice of Songs,' 1949); *Ó Mórna agus Dánta Eile* ('Ó Mórna and Other Poems',1957; *Ár Ré Dhéaróil* ('Our Wretched Era', 1962); *Cloch Choirnéil* ('Corner Stone', 1967); *Crann is Cairde* ('Trees and Friends,' 1970); *Ceacht an Éin* ('The Bird's Lesson', 1979); *Béasa an Túir* ('The Customs of the Tower', 1984). Two anthologies of his works have been published recently: *Dánta 1939–1979* (1980) and *Selected Poems: Tacar Dánta*—in Irish and English (1984). A volume of his prose, entitled *Feamainn Bhealtaine* ('May Day's Wrack') appeared in 1961. See Liam Prút, *Máirtín Ó Direáin: File Tréadúil* (Maynooth, 1982); M. Mac Craith, 'Filíocht Dhéanach Mháirtín Uí Dhireáin', *Comhar*, 41, no. 10, 22–25, no. 11, 27–43; Micheál Ó Luanacháin, 'Máirtín Ó Direáin', in Seán Mac Réamoinn, *The Pleasures of Gaelic Poetry*, pp. 145–6. Máire Mhac an tSaoi, Eoghan Ó Anluain and others wrote appreciations of Ó Direáin's achievements as a poet for *Comhar*, Aibreán 1988, Bealtaine 1988.

93 See Ó Direáin's introduction to *Ó Mórna agus Dánta Eile*: 'Mise agus an Fhilíocht', also printed in *Dánta 1939–79*, pp. 215–6.

94 Ibid.

95 *Dánta 1939–1979*, p. 69.

96 Ibid., p. 55.

97 *Dánta 1939–1979*, p. 152.

98 The title has been translated as both 'Stout Oars' and 'Props'; *Dánta 1939–1979*, p. 65.

99 Transl. by Gearóid Ó Crualaoich, *International Poetry Review* (Celtic issue), Spring, 1979, p. 91.

100 Transl. as 'Chill', by Gearóid Ó Crualaoich, op. cit., p. 87.

101 *Margadh na Saoire*, p. 27.

102 *A Heart Full of Thoughts*, p. 12.

103 *Margadh na Saoire*, p. 50.

104 Translation is by Richard Skerrett.
105 *Margadh na Saoire*, p. 22.
106 Ibid., pp. 61–5.
107 Translation by Richard Skerrett.
108 *Irish Writing*, ed., S. J. White: Special Issue, 'Gaelic Writers', guest editor, Séamus Ó Néill, 33 (Dublin, 1955), p. 56. For the original see *Margadh na Saoire*, p. 28.
109 Carol Cosman, Joan Keefe, Kathleen Weaver, edd., *The Penguin Book of Women Poets* (1980), pp. 377–9. For the original see *An Galar Dubhach*, pp. 15–6.
110 *The World and the Book* (London, 1971), p. xvi.
111 His published poems are found in *Eireaball Spideoige* (1952; 2nd ed. 1970), *Brosna* (1964), *Línte Liombó* (1971), *Tar Éis Mo Bháis agus Dánta Eile*, ed., Seán Ó Coileáin (1978), *Scáthán Véarsaí* (1980), *Rogha Dánta* (1980). He also published with Seán S. Ó Conghail, *Rí na nUile* (1964, 1967). His contributions to the press, more especially the *Irish Times*, should also be noted: see Seán Ó Coileáin, 'Seán Ó Ríordáin, Iriseoir', *Feasta*, Deireadh Fómhair, 1983, 15–21.
112 *Eireaball Spideoige*, p. 70–71.
113 Ibid., p. 51.
114 Ibid., p. 36.
115 *Brosna*, p. 9.
116 Ibid., p. 28.
117 Ibid., p. 25.
118 Trans. by Seán Ó Tuama, in Seán Mac Réamoinn, ed., *The Pleasures of Gaelic Poetry*, p. 252.
119 *Eireaball Spideoige*, p. 94.
120 Ibid., p. 56.
121 Ibid., pp. 64–67.
122 Ibid., p. 74.
123 Trans. V. Iremonger, *International Poetry Review*, Celtic issue, Spring, 1979, p. 83.
124 Seán Ó Ríordáin's poetry has received considerable attention from the critics. See Breandán Ó Doibhlin, *Aistí Critice agus Cultúir* (FNT 1970); Seán Ó Tuama, 'Seán Ó Ríordáin agus an Nuafhilíocht', SH, 13 (1973), 100–67; idem, *Filí Faoi Scéimhle* (Dublin, 1978); idem, *Seán Ó Ríordáin: Saothar an Fhile* (Cló Mercier, 1975); Eoghan Ó hAnluain, *An Duine is Dual* (Dublin, 1980), a collection of essays on Ó Ríordáin, the man and his work, with a poem by Máirtín Ó Direáin; and especially Seán Ó Coileáin, *Seán Ó Ríordáin, Beatha agus Saothar* (Dublin, 1982; 2nd ed. 1985), reviewed by Ristéard Ó Glaisne in *Feasta* (Deireadh Fómhair), 1983, and Eibhlín Nic Ghearailt, *Seán Ó Ríordáin agus an Striapach Allúrach* (Dublin, 1989). The Bealtaine, 1977, issue of *Comhar* is dedicated to the memory of Ó Ríordáin, and on the tenth anniversary of his death an exhibition was held in Dublin and an accompanying booklet, *Mise: Seán Ó Ríordáin*, was published.
125 See Darach Ó Scolaí, 'File faoi Scáth an Bháis', *Feasta*, Aibreán, 1985, 16–9.
126 *International Poetry Review*, Celtic issue, Spring, 1979, p. 85.

127 Transl. by J. Gleasure, *International Poetry Review*, Celtic issue, Spring, 1979, p. 81.
128 Transl. by E. Ní Loinn, op. cit., p. 79.
129 On the remains of folk drama in Ireland, see Alan Gailey, *Folk Drama* (Cork, 1969).
130 See Pádraig Ó Giollagáin, 'Forbairt ar Amharclainn na Gaeilge', *Irisleabhar Mhá Nuad* (1974), 73–84; M. Ó Droighneáin, *Taighde i gComhair Stair Litridheachta na Nua-Ghaeilge*, chapter VIII, 'Drámaidheacht na Gaedhilge'; D. Ó Súilleabháin, 'Tús agus Fás na Drámaíochta i nGaeilge', *Ardán*, Eagrán an Earraigh, 1972, pp. 16ff.; Lorcán Ó Riain, 'Drámaíocht na Gaeilge', *Comhar*, Deireadh Fómhair, 1983, 27–8.
131 Michéal Mac Liammóir, *Theatre in Ireland* (Dublin, 1950). See also Una Ellis-Fermor, *The Irish Dramatic Movement* (2nd ed., London, 1954) and books on the history of the Abbey Theatre.
132 In 1908, Corkery and other Gaelic Leaguers founded 'The Cork Dramatic Society'--admittedly in imitation of The Abbey, but with the aim of staging Irish language as well as (if not rather than) English language plays; see G. B. Saul, *Daniel Corkery* (New Jersey, 1973), p. 23. A new dramatic society based in Cork was formed in the early fifties by Seán Ó Tuama and others.
133 *An Claidheamh Soluis*, 6 June 1906, p. 6.
134 Mac Liammóir, *Theatre in Ireland*, p. 36.
135 On Críostóir Ó Floinn's *Is é a Dúirt Polonius* and Ibsen's *A Doll House*, see Antonia Ní Murchú in *Irisleabhar Mhá Nuad*, 1986, pp. 43–84; see also D. Ó Muirí, 'Drámaí Chríostóra Uí Fhloinn', in P. O Fiannachta, ed., *Léachtaí Cholm Cille*, 10 (Maynooth, 1979), 92–130.
136 Máirtín Ó Cadhain in J. E. Caerwyn Williams, ed., *Literature in Celtic Countries*, p. 150. But cf. the statistics given above on plays broadcasted over Irish radio.
137 *Comhar*, Nollaig, December, 1986, contains several critical appraisals of Diarmaid Ó Súilleabháin's writings including an appraisal of him as a dramatist by Pádraig Ó Siadhail. Ó Siadhail refers to the seven plays mentioned, none of which has been published. Ó Súilleabháin also published several novels: *Muintir, Dianmhuilte Dé, Caoin Tú Féin, Trá agus Tuileadh, Ciontach, Aistear*.
138 On the plays of Seán Ó Tuama, see Pádraig Ó Siadhail, 'Drámaí Sheáin Uí Thuama', *Irisleabhar Mhá Nuad*, 1986, pp. 7–42.
139 Martin Nugent, *Drámaí Eoghain Uí Thuairisc* (An Sagart, Maynooth, 1984); Oilibhéar Ó Croiligh, '*Mistéir na Réabhlóide*: Tuairisc Téama', *Irisleabhar Mhá Nuad*, 1968, pp. 13–24. Máirín Nic Eoin has edited Ó Tuairisc's essays in *Religio Poetae agus Aistí Eile* (Dublin, 1987). For a lengthy study of Ó Tuairisc's work see Máirín Nic Eoin, *Eoghan Ó Tuairisc: Beatha agus Saothar* (Dublin, 1988).
140 Many of Behan's writings are autobiographical and much has been written in English on his life and work. Among Irish writings on the subject, see Donald Foley, 'Breandán Ó Beacháin', *Scríobh*, 2 (1975), 51–8; Alan Titley, 'Filíocht Breandáin Uí Bheacháin', *Feasta*, Deireadh Fómhair, 1972, 6–8; Samhain, 1972, 4–5.

141 It is true that there are conflicting reports concerning which of these was written first, and it must be admitted that the English version of the play differs somewhat from the Irish.

142 See Éamon Ó Ciosáin, 'Máiréad Ní Ghráda', I, *Feasta*, Márta, 1976, 13–6; II, Aibreán, 1976, 19–21.

143 Mac Liammóir, *The Theatre in Ireland* (Dublin, 1964), p. 64.

144 *An Claidheamh Soluis*, 21 February 1908, p. 9. Séamus Ó Buachalla has edited Pearse's critical writings in *Na Scríbhinní Liteartha le Pádraig Mac Piarais* (Cork, Dublin, 1979).

145 *An Claidheamh Soluis*, 10 September 1904, p. 8.

146 See *The Leader*, 1909, 30 January, 6 and 13 February; also Aisling Ní Dhonnchadha, *An Gearrscéal sa Ghaeilge*, pp. 59–60.

147 *An Claidheamh Soluis*, 28 March 1903, p. 3.

148 In this connection, Pádraic Ó Conaire's essay on 'Sean-Litridheacht na Gaedhilge agus Nua-Litridheacht na hEorpa', which won him an *Oireachtas* prize in 1908, is significant. It shows that Ó Conaire himself had read Turgenev, Gorky and Tolstoy, and that he was convinced that the only way forward for Irish writers was to turn their backs on what he called *sean-aimsireacht* ('old-fashionedness'); see above, pp. 280ff.

149 *What's this about the Gaelic League?* (Dublin, 1942), *The Philosophy of the Gaelic League* (Dublin, 1948), *The Fortunes of the Irish Language* (Dublin, 1954.)

150 L. M. Cullen, 'The Hidden Ireland: Re-assessment of a Concept', SH, 9 (1969), 7–47; G. B. Saul, *Daniel Corkery*, pp. 42–5.

151 Corkery, *Synge and Anglo-Irish Literature* (Cork, 1931).

152 'Ars Scribendi', *Humanitas*, March, 1930, 2–5.

153 Corkery (Ó Corcora), 'Na hEorpaigh Seo Againne?' *Humanitas*, June, 1930, 2–6.

154 See Corkery's 'Smaointe Fánacha ar an bhFilíocht', in *Feasta*, Eanáir–Deireadh Fómhair, 1954, and cf. his introduction to *Éigse na Máighe*, ed. R. Ó Foghludha, (1952), pp. 7–29.

155 Recently it has been fashionable to criticize Corkery, but he has not lacked defenders. See L. M. Cullen's art. cit. *supra*, n. 150; Seán Ó Tuama, 'Dónall Ó Corcora agus Filíocht na Gaeilge', SH, 5 (1965), 29–41; idem, 'Dónall Ó Corcora', *Scríobh*, 4 (1979), 94–108; Gearóid Ó Tuathaigh, 'Is do chuala Croí Cine Soiléir', ibid., 75–83; Declan Kiberd, 'Dónall Ó Corcora agus Litríocht Bhéarla na hÉireann', ibid., 84–93; Breandán Ó Buachalla, 'Ó Corcora agus an Hidden Ireland', ibid., 109–37; Colbert Kearney, 'Dónall Ó Corcora agus an Litríocht Angla-Éireannach', ibid., 138–51; Sean O'Faolain, 'Daniel Corkery', *The Dublin Magazine*, April–June, 1936, 49–61; G. B. Saul, *Daniel Corkery*. G. Denvir, 'Litríocht agus Pobal: Nua Litríocht na Gaeilge agus an Traidisiún', *Scríobh*, 6 (1984), 11–47 argues that before the work of Ó Conaire and Mac Piarais, the community (*pobal*), not the people, had been the central concern of Irish literature.

156 'Clár Léirmheastóireachta na Nua-Ghaeilge, 1940–65', *Irisleabhar Mhá Nuad*, 1966, 94–99, gives a very useful index to critical essays in English as well as in Irish periodicals.

157 See Antain Mag Shamhráin, *Litríocht, Léitheoireacht, Critic: Príomhghnéithe Crítice in Irisleabhar Mhá Nuad* (Dublin, 1986).
158 See especially Dáithí Ó hÓgáin, *An File. Staidéar ar Osnádúrthacht na Filíochta sa Traidisiún Gaelach* (Dublin, 1982).
159 David Greene, 'Fifty Years of Writing in Irish', *Studies*, 55 (1966), 51–59, was undoubtedly right when he wrote (p. 59), 'The existence of this Irish Literature is a miracle which the Irish people have not discovered: it remains to be seen whether it will accept or reject it'. See also Frank O'Brien, 'Another Revolution—Modern Poetry in Irish', *Éire-Ireland*, I (1966). M. Ó Murchú, 'An Ghaeltacht: Pobal i mBaol a Leáite', *Scríobh*, 6 (1984), 63–69, produces evidence for the increased use of the Irish language in all parts of the Republic during the period 1930–70 and gives the State credit for it, whereas A. Titley, 'An Scríbhneoireacht agus an Stát 1922–82', *Scríobh*, 6 (1984), 72–104, is highly critical of the State's contribution to the advancement of literature in the Irish language.
160 These figures probably err on the optimistic side. In 1956 Professor Brian Ó Cuív assessed the number of people who used Irish as their ordinary speech medium as 'no more than 35,000', and the number of people ignorant of English as 'no more than 3,000'. For a judicious and fair discussion of the achievements and the failures of successive Irish Governments in the promotion of the restoration of the Irish language see Tony Gray, *The Irish Answer* (London, 1966), especially pp. 222–3. For an up-to-date survey of the position of the Irish language in Ireland, see *The Irish Language in the Republic of Ireland 1983: Preliminary Report of a National Survey*, by Pádraig Ó Ríagáin and Mícheál Ó Gleasáin (Dublin, 1984); it updates the 1973 survey. Cf. *Report of the Committee on Irish Language Attitudes Research; Prejudice and Tolerance in Ireland*, by Mícheál Mac Gréil (Dublin, 1977). Donncha Ó Súilleabháin, *Cath na Gaeilge sa Choras Oideachais 1893–1911* (Dublin, 1988), re-cxamines the struggle to establish Irish as a fully accepted subject in the Irish educational system and the part played in it by such figures as Patrick Pearse, Douglas Hyde, and others. Liam Mathúna, *Pobal na Gaeilge: Oidhrí agus Ceannródaithe* (Dublin, 1987) has more to say on the current state of the language. Bord na Gaeilge, which as its name implies, is a body set up to look after the interests of the Irish language, published in 1988, *The Irish Language in a Changing World*. For a very recent discussion see Reg Hindley, *The Death of the Irish Language* (London, 1990)

INDEX

Fortibras (Fierabras) 136, 143
Fosterage of the House of Two Milk
    Vessels 136-7
Four Gospels 276
Four Masters, Annals of 37, 89, 138,
    167, 173, 176, 209
Four Stories of Mongán 28
Fragments of Ancient Poetry,
    Macpherson's 257
Francis, St of Assisi 122, 125
Frenzy of Conn the Hundred-Fighter 96
'Fuaire' 300
Furnivall, Lord (Lord Justice Talbot)
    176

Gaedel 95
*Gaelic Journal (Irisleabhar na
    Gaedhilge)* 259, 261, 270, 291, 292,
    315
'Gaelic Story-Teller' 265
Gaelic Tableaux 315
Galar Dubhach, An 301
Galway Pilot 315
*Gaodhal, An, The Keltic Journal and
    Educator* 259
Garrigan, Father John 203
'Gé shaoileas dá saoirse bheith seasgair
    sodhail' 214
Gearnon, Brother Antoin (Anthony
    Gearnon) 206
Gearóid Iarla (Earl Gerald), third Earl
    of Desmond 182
Geasa agus Buadha Riogh nÉireann 33
Gemmán 25
Genealogies of the Families of Ireland
    199
Gerald, Earl (Gearóid Iarla) 182
Gerald, Earl of Kildare 177
Giall, An 319
'Gile na Gile' (The Brightness of Bright)
    219
Gilla-na-naomh mac AEgan 167
Giolla an tSolais 319
Giolla Deacair, An 134
Giraldus Cambrensis 17, 68
Glór, An 264
Glossary, Cormac's 30, 31
Gnás na Gaedhilge, Ó Cadhlaigh's 277
Gógan, Liam 295, 296, 317
Golden Castles 282
Gonda, Jan 45
Goodman, James 268
Gorky, Maxim 280
Gougaud, Louis 68

Grá agus an Ghruaim, An 284
Grá in Amhráin na nDaoine, An 324
Gráinne 131, 132, 133, 136
Grammatica Celtica 259
Grammatica Latino-Hibernica 207
'Grást' ó Dhia ar Mhicí' 282
Gray, Thomas 257
Great Book of Genealogies 123, 199
Great Book of Lecan 123
Great Visitation to Guaire 26
Green, Alice 8
Greene, David 86, 169, 271
Greene, Graham 283
Gregory of Tours 72
Gregory, Lady Augusta 315, 316
Grey Parson (*An Pearsún Riabhach*)
    169
Grimm, brothers Jacob and Wilhelm
    265
Guaire 26, 85, 86, 89
Gualterus de dosibus 144
Guido 143
Guillaume de Palerne 138, 139
Guy (of Warwick) 139
Guy ocus Bevis 140, 142
Gwalchmai (Balbuaid, etc.) 137, 138

Haicéad, Pádraigín 194, 210, 215
Haliday, W. 258
Hall of the Mountain Ash 130
'Hardy Trees' 299
Harley 546 (B.M.) 144
Harley 6358 (B.M.) 136
Harrington, Sir Henry 176
Harrington, Sir John 138
'Harvest of the Sea' 305
Heartful of Thought, A 300
Hector 12
Hedderman, Denis 223
Hellmann, A. D. 46
Henebry (De Hindeberg), Richard 278,
    279, 292, 315, 320, 321
Henry VIII, King of England 255
Hercules 45, 165
Hermes 44
Hidden Ireland 322
Hippocrates, physician of antiquity 144
Hisperica Famina 67
Historia Ecclesiastica, Bede's 142
Historical Memoirs of the Irish Bards
    257
History of Ireland 6, 47, 209. *See also*
    under *Foras Feasa ar Éirinn* and
    Keating, Geoffrey